Psychology

From Research to Practice

150

CI

ED

Psychology
From Research to Practice

Edited by

Herbert L. Pick, Jr.
University of Minnesota
Minneapolis, Minnesota

Herschel W. Leibowitz
Pennsylvania State University
University Park, Pennsylvania

Jerome E. Singer
Uniformed Services
University of the Health Sciences
Bethesda, Maryland

Alfred Steinschneider
University of Maryland
Baltimore, Maryland

Harold W. Stevenson
University of Michigan
Ann Arbor, Michigan

PLENUM PRESS · NEW YORK AND LONDON

Library of Congress Cataloging in Publication Data

Main entry under title:
Psychology: from research to practice.
  "This book grew out of discussions at the meetings of the Board of Scientific Affairs of the American Psychological Association during the years 1972 through 1975."
  Includes bibliographies and index.
  1. Psychological research. 2. Psychology. I. Pick, Herbert L. [DNLM: 1. Psychology
– Collected works. 2. Research – Collected works. BF76.5 P978]
BF76.5.P79   150   78-16932
ISBN 0-306-31132-1

© 1978 Plenum Press, New York
A Division of Plenum Publishing Corporation
227 West 17th Street, New York, N.Y. 10011

Printed in the United States of America

Contributors

LAUREN C. ABBE • *Department of Psychology, University of Rochester, Rochester, New York*

RICHARD N. ASLIN • *Department of Psychology, Indiana University, Bloomington, Indiana*

MARTIN S. BANKS • *Department of Psychology, University of Texas, Austin, Texas*

GUNNAR BORG • *Institute of Applied Psychology, University of Stockholm, Stockholm, Sweden*

PATRICIA A. BROEN • *Department of Communication Disorders, University of Minnesota, Minneapolis, Minnesota*

ANN L. BROWN • *Center for the Study of Reading, University of Illinois, Urbana, Illinois*

JOSEPH C. CAMPIONE • *Center for the Study of Reading, University of Illinois, Urbana, Illinois*

CATHERINE R. FITZGERALD • *Department of Psychology, State University of New York, Buffalo, New York*

DAVID M. GREEN • *Laboratory of Psychophysics, Harvard University, Cambridge, Massachusetts*

RON HASKINS • *Department of Psychology, University of North Carolina, Chapel Hill, North Carolina*

ALETHA HUSTON-STEIN • *Department of Human Development, University of Kansas, Lawrence, Kansas*

IRVING JANIS • *Department of Psychology, Yale University, New Haven, Connecticut*

SARAH M. JONS • *Department of Communication Disorders, University of Minnesota, Minneapolis, Minnesota*

EDWARD S. KATKIN • *Department of Psychology, State University of New York, Buffalo, New York*

CONRAD L. KRAFT • *Crew Systems, Boeing Aerospace Company, Seattle, Washington*

LEWIS P. LIPSITT • *Department of Psychology, Brown University, Providence, Rhode Island*

DAVID T. LYKKEN • *Psychiatry Research Unit, College of Medical Sciences, University of Minnesota, Minneapolis, Minnesota*

LEON MANN • *Department of Psychology, Flinders University, Bedford Park, South Australia*

HARRIET L. RHEINGOLD • *Department of Psychology, University of North Carolina, Chapel Hill, North Carolina*

ARNOLD J. SAMEROFF • *Department of Psychology, University of Rochester, Rochester, New York*

S. JAY SAMUELS • *Center for Research in Human Learning, University of Minnesota, Minneapolis, Minnesota*

DAVID SHAPIRO • *Department of Psychiatry, University of California, Los Angeles, California*

JOHN A. SWETS • *Bolt Beranek and Newman, Inc., Cambridge, Massachusetts*

JACOBO A. VARELA • *University of Uruguay, Montevideo, Uruguay. Current affiliation: Visiting Professor 1977–1979, Department of Management, Wayne State University, Detroit, Michigan*

WILLEM A. WAGENAAR • *Institute for Perception TNO, Soesterberg, The Netherlands*

Preface

This book grew out of discussion at the meetings of the Board of Scientific Affairs of the American Psychological Association during the years 1972 through 1975. Members of the board felt that there was general misunderstanding by the public about the role of basic research in science. The problem was thought to be particularly severe in the case of the behavioral sciences but it appeared to be a reflection of a more general anti-intellectual attitude in the United States. At the same time basic researchers had been admittedly underconcerned with the practical application of their results. Yet many thoughtful scientists realize there is a very fruitful interplay between basic research and application. The proposal was made to prepare a book of case studies that demonstrate the application of basic research in psychology.

The book was organized to sample applications from a range of topics in psychology. The editorial board divided up responsibilities for these topics. Herschel W. Leibowitz focused on applications from experimental and engineering psychology and Jerome E. Singer organized the section on applications to social problems. Alfred Steinschneider took responsibility for the section on clinical applications of basic research in psychology and Harold W. Stevenson organized the section on applications of basic research to developmental and educational problems.

This book is not concerned with specifically applied areas of psychology, such as clinical psychology, industrial psychology, testing and measurement, applied experimental analysis of behavior, human factors, etc. These specialties are established vital endeavors. They are not now so directly dependent on basic research, although new knowledge is continuously incorporated into their practice. It is hoped that the chapters in this book illustrate how basic research contributes to some of the problems addressed by these specialties.

The editors are indebted to the secretarial staff of the Center for Research in Human Learning for great logistical support in organizing this book and in final preparation of the manuscript. The editorial assistance of William H. Warren is also gratefully acknowledged.

Contents

SECTION II
PSYCHOLOGICAL PRACTICE AND SOCIAL PROBLEMS

SECTION III
CLINICAL APPLICATIONS OF BASIC RESEARCH

SECTION IV
APPLICATION OF PSYCHOPHYSICS AND HUMAN
PERFORMANCE INFORMATION

Introduction

Basic scientific research is often justified in terms of its ultimate practical application as well as on the basis of the importance of knowledge for knowledge's sake. Both rationalizations are valid. Surely everyone can be excited by the basic research on radioactivity and its eventual application to the treatment of cancer. However, we also can be dismayed by the application of that same basic research in the development of atomic bombs. The sheer beauty and power of the theory of relativity excites those who master it. The elegance of the structure of the DNA model is impressive, as are the tremendous savings in life and human suffering brought about by antibiotics.

But when we turn to the behavioral sciences, we see no general theories of relativity—nor even special ones. We see no radiation treatments derived from years of fundamental research on radioactivity. Indeed the basic research in the behavioral sciences has been severely criticized for its irrelevance to the practical problems of the world and the pressing needs of society. It is the purpose of this book to demonstrate, by example, that basic research in psychology does have important useful outcomes. At the same time we should recognize that psychology hasn't yet discovered its transistor or constructed its theory of evolution. At present, from basic research in psychology we cannot produce a cure for schizophrenia, develop a curriculum for getting a retarded child through college, suggest a design for an automobile that will have no accidents, or teach parents how to raise their children so there will be no aggression in the society.

1

However, there are contributions to the solution of specific problems that basic research in the behavioral sciences can make. It is possible to identify the causes of some aircraft accidents and to improve safety devices and procedures to reduce the number of such accidents (see chapter by Kraft). It is possible to use new knowledge about cognition to aid mentally retarded children to learn more easily and effectively (see chapter by Brown and Campione) and to aid all of us in making crisis decisions in our lives (see chapter by Janis and Mann). It is possible to use recently discovered facts about speech perception to aid in the diagnosis of children with speech pathology (see chapter by Broen and Jons). It is possible to apply techniques developed in the laboratory for studying infant learning and perception to the diagnosis and treatment of pathology in infants (see chapter by Lipsitt). The contribution of basic research in psychology not only is in direct application of knowledge or procedures but is also in the development of methodologies to obtain certain kinds of information. Thus modern psychophysics in the form of signal detection theory has found wide application (see chapter by Swets and Green). Examples of these kinds of possibilities will form a major portion of this book.

In addition to such specific problems, basic research in psychology can provide a general knowledge base for helping to make intelligent judgments about rather broad issues. Nowhere is this more important today than in public policy. Thus basic research in social development has dealt with questions of how social attachments are formed with both significant adults and peers. This research has become directly relevant to formulation of policy concerned with child care. It is also vitally relevant to both public policy and individual concerns about the effects on children of unusual family configurations (see chapter by Rheingold and Haskins). Similarly basic research on observational learning in children has provided a general knowledge base about the effects of television. This knowledge is relevant for formulating public policy about television and should be helpful in developing television programs as well (see chapter by Huston-Stein).

How do applications of basic psychological research come about? One possibility is that many years of basic research with no practical aim serendipitously leads to knowledge immediately applicable to solution of a psychological problem. Such occurrences are extremely rare. What is more typical is that information that has long been available becomes relevant in the light of some new discovery. Thus, for example, information about a peculiar kind of perceptual aftereffect discovered in the 1930s was used in conjunction with recent research results about the perceptual development of animals to identify possible critical periods in human visual development (see chapter by Aslin and Banks).

Even when an almost obviously relevant new fact is discovered or idea conceived, much work is ordinarily required before the fact or idea can be applied. When Samuels and LaBerge (see chapter by Samuels) identified through their basic research an important stage in reading, it still remained to develop techniques and apparatus to determine how best to help children achieve that stage.

Initial applications of psychological knowledge to problem solution are often limited. But the very limitations are an impetus to further basic research. That is an exciting aspect of the scientific enterprise. The inadequacies of applications may suggest new basic information that is needed and new directions for the research to acquire that information. One example of this is in the application of basic research in linguistics and psycholinguistics. The phonology of language is conceived of in terms of distinctive features, a small set of distinctions that can characterize all the important phonetic distinctions of a language. Several alternative feature systems have been proposed but no one is sure which is most psychologically relevant. Attempts have been made recently to use the feature concept to guide speech therapy. The hypothesis is that feature distinctions trained in one speech context may generalize to other contexts and hence be an efficient method of therapy. Such generalization has occurred but the exact pattern would not be predicted by any current feature model. That fact has instigated further basic research into the psychological reality of feature systems.

In the behavioral sciences, perhaps even more than in the physical sciences, there are often ethical issues involved in the application of basic research. This is because the products developed typically directly affect people. They are often techniques, procedures, and methods. Their efficacy is typically not defined in certain success but in percent improvement or increased probability of success. But for any individual success or improvement is not guaranteed. A variety of ethical questions arise: At what point in the development of new techniques should they be applied? When do they cease to be experimental? To whom should new techniques be applied? Are there side effects of the applications? How can misuse be guarded against? Lykken outlines in his chapter on lie detection some of the kinds of dangers that may occur. Katkin, Garvey, and Shapiro in their chapter on the use of biofeedback strongly caution against overenthusiasm for a new technique.

Basic researchers in psychology need to be concerned about the practical value of their work. Such concern should motivate all socially conscious persons. In addition, in recent years societal pressure for relevance has also been brought to bear on psychology. However, basic knowledge is a strong and vital underpinning of sound application. If a psychological process is thoroughly understood, intervention can be carried out in the most salutory way. If a psychological process is thoroughly understood, application can be made with the widest generality. In recent years basic research in cognition, developmental psychology, social psychology, perception, physiological psychology, and sensory process has reached a point where significant applications are possible. The contributions to this volume represent examples of how basic research has become practical.

SECTION I

DEVELOPMENTAL AND EDUCATIONAL PRACTICE

Introduction

HAROLD W. STEVENSON

This section of the book deals with developmental psychology, currently one of psychology's most lively and exciting areas. There has been an enormous increase in interest in this field during the past 20 years. Whereas there were only a few hundred psychologists actively engaged in research with children and adolescents a few decades ago, there are now thousands. The number of research articles published each year continues to grow, attendance at professional meetings increases, and students continue to enroll in large numbers in courses in developmental psychology. Why this rapid development has occurred is something later historians will discuss. One reason, however, appears to be that much of the research by developmental psychologists is relevant to the solution of practical problems. As we hope you will discover when you read the articles in this section, results obtained in what may appear to be abstract and artificial conditions in the laboratory often have led to useful changes in rearing, teaching, and care of children. Psychologists conducting research with children often are convinced that they are engaged in a significant undertaking. What could be more rewarding than understanding relationships and conditions that could potentially produce improvements in the lives of children?

The problem in planning this section was to characterize such an active area adequately in a few chapters. Topics were selected, therefore, from among those in which there was extensive research, the research was well conducted, and efforts had been made at application. We were fortunate in recruiting outstanding psychologists to write the chapters. Each author is active in research and has displayed a willingness to consider how this research may benefit society. Their discussions should help dispel the notion that researchers sit in their laboratories, unconcerned with what goes on in the everyday world. Indeed, as is pointed out in several chapters, researchers cannot afford to be isolated from practical application, for research and practice influence each other in critically important ways.

The following paragraphs give brief descriptions of what you will find when you read the chapters.

LEARNING AND PERCEPTION

One of the breakthroughs in psychology during the past few decades has been the introduction of powerful new methods for testing and modifying infant behavior. These methods have had both scientific and practical consequences. For the scientist, they make it possible to answer theoretical questions about the content and structure of early behavior that had been matters of conjecture for centuries. For the practitioner, they serve as the basis for sensitive and reliable clinical techniques. Dr. Lewis Lipsitt, a longtime investigator at Brown University, describes these methods and their application in his chapter on the assessment of sensory and behavior functions in infants. The range of application has been broad, and Dr. Lipsitt gives examples of how methods such as conditioning and habituation have been applied to problems as divergent as feeding disorders and the early diagnosis of deafness.

SOCIAL DEVELOPMENT

Dr. Harriet Rheingold is an excellent example of a busy and productive scientist who finds time to lead her peers in discussions of how research can be applied to social problems. For this book she and her collaborator, Dr. Ron Haskins, both of the University of North Carolina, have written about early social development: the influence of infants and young children on their caretakers, how they become attached to their mothers and fathers, what happens when the infant or child is separated from them, how early experiences influence later behavior, and children's need for human companionship. Ways in which this research has led to changes in many professional and parental practices are discussed. But, as Drs. Rheingold and Haskins point out, the changes have been slow. They conclude with an indication of how far we still must go to reach the goal of fostering optimal human development.

MEMORY

Ann Brown and Joseph Campione, psychologists at the University of Illinois, have become well known for their studies of the development of memory processes and how these processes differ in children who have problems in learning and remembering. Their research has followed three lines: studies of children's spontaneous use of strategies that aid learning and memory, of ways in which children may be trained to adopt appropriate strategies, and of children's understanding of their own memory processes. From these and other studies has come a new and important hypothesis. Retarded or slow learning children may do poorly not because they have insufficient general capacities for learning and memory but because of their ineffective use of these capacities. Drs. Brown and Campione describe ways in which they and others have sought to develop training procedures to enable slow-learning children to improve their learning and memory by employing strategies that other children produce spontaneously.

READING

Perhaps the recent surge of interest by research psychologists in the problems of reading will help educators and clinicians resolve some of the issues that have been the source of so much disagreement about how children learn to read. Professor Jay Samuels of the University of Minnesota discusses some of this research in his chapter on laboratory studies of reading. Professor Samuels's experiences differ from those of many psychologists. He was led to the laboratory from the schoolroom. Now, once again, he is back in the schoolroom asking whether the results of laboratory research can be used to improve children's early instruction in reading. The chapter discusses theory and research in information processing, ways in which this material has been applied to reading, and the automaticity model of reading which has been proposed by Professor Samuels and his colleague, Dr. David LaBerge.

TELEVISION

What do we know about the influence of television on children's behavior? And on the basis of what we know can recommendations be made for improving children's programs? Dr. Aletha Huston-Stein of the University of Kansas deals with these questions in her discussion of how children learn from observation. The focus of her attention is on social behavior, and she discusses her own research and the research of others dealing with how observing aggressive or prosocial television programs may have a later influence on children's performance. As Dr. Stein points out, there has been frequent interplay between research and practice in the development of certain television programs for children. Clearly, however, the research and theory discussed in this chapter have not yet had the major impact on children's programming that would seem to be merited.

We hope that some of the excitement of research in developmental psychology is conveyed in these chapters. The material is sometimes complex and requires careful reading. When you are through, however, you should have some new insights about human behavior and how these have been applied in everyday life.

Assessment of Sensory and Behavioral Functions in Infancy

LEWIS P. LIPSITT

Important advances have been made over the past two decades in the recording and understanding of sensory and learning processes of infants. These have enabled the earlier detection, and often the amelioration, of conditions hazardous to the further development of the child. Health care professionals and researchers with special interests in infant behavioral processes have come increasingly to realize that even newborns are remarkably responsive to stimulation in all sensory modalities. Moreover, the quality and character of the environment play a role in the behavior of the baby right from the start. This means that (1) behavior is to an extent determined and modified by the stimulation that is supplied to the child, either inadvertently or deliberately, and (2) the baby and its caretakers constitute a virtual control system in which each responds to the other and each serves as stimulant to the other.

The young infant is a reciprocating organism from the outset, and both the baby and its mother (or whoever is caring for and interacting with the baby) have the capacity to affect each other. Appreciating this goes a long way toward understanding the essence of infancy (and motherhood) and, incidentally, toward appreciating the importance of infancy as practice for the future. By the same token, this view of the infant, even the newborn, as a reciprocating social creature necessitates

LEWIS P. LIPSITT • Department of Psychology, Brown University, Providence, Rhode Island. Preparation of this chapter was supported in part by a grant from the W. T. Grant Foundation to the Brown University Child Study Center.

that we try to understand learning disabilities and other developmental problems in terms of their earliest origins. (These points are elaborated in the chapter by Rheingold and Haskins.)

Recent research indicates that normal human newborns arrive in the world with all of their sensory systems functioning, and even with some specific abilities to learn (Appleton, Clifton, and Goldberg, 1975; Emde and Robinson, 1976; Horowitz, 1969; Kessen, Haith, and Salapatek, 1970; Lipsitt, 1963). There is a small amount of controversy, of course, concerning "the particulars." There are perceptual and motoric limitations and newborns cannot learn everything. Nonetheless, there is no question that the human neonate is a more responsive and "advanced" creature than has generally been supposed, possibly throughout the history of mankind.

The infant's sensory awareness and ability to profit from environmental manipulations has been only recently discovered and emphasized by the professional community. While not long ago there were serious restrictions (see Klaus and Kennell, 1976; Rothschild, 1967) upon the amount of contact that both normal newborns and prematures were allowed to have with other humans (even their parents), this imposed isolation has been lifted noticeably in the past decade. Several studies have demonstrated the facilitative effects upon development of the infant, as well as on the pleasure of parents, of special planned regimens of handling and interaction (Hasselmeyer, 1965; Klaus and Kennell, 1976; Rice, 1977; Siqueland, 1969; Solkoff, Yaffe, Weintraub, and Blase, 1969).

Some of the procedures that have evolved in the infant behavior laboratories already have had practical import. With greater investments in them and in the elaboration of the most promising techniques, further advances can be made in the care, treatment, and even the education of the young child. Most of such advances, of course, relate either to the treatment or to the prevention of developmental anomalies. Note should be made, however, that in all avenues of science our best exemplars of socially useful accomplishment usually relate, in the early stages at least, to the avoidance of misfortune. Only later does it become apparent that what has been good for the disorder may have some value for the understanding, care, and welfare of essentially normal persons as well. This has been especially well demonstrated in the fields of abnormal psychology and normal personality development, for example.

New knowledge of special techniques for educating the blind or the cerebral palsied child has also had fallout benefits for the field of normal-child education. Similarly, prosthetic devices developed for the seriously disabled often are appropriated later for the use of minor ailments and athletic injuries. Training procedures designed for dyslexic children are now used routinely with children who have minor reading problems.

Some of the techniques recently found successful in their applications to infants who have endured some type of perinatal stress, or to young children with sensory and learning deficits, will probably be found useful with essentially normal children.

NEGATIVE CONTRAST BEHAVIOR IN THE NEONATE

In the course of our research on taste preferences in newborns, we conducted a study in which three groups of infants were compared in their sucking behavior under conditions of different taste experiences (Kobre and Lipsitt, 1972). One group of babies was automatically and instantly given a drop of sucrose for every suck. The drop was small, only .02 milliliters (about one-sixth of a drop from an eyedropper), so it was possible to study these infants for fairly long periods without over-loading their stomachs. In fact, over the 20-minute period, the infants received less than an ounce of fluid. That group was compared with a group that received just plain distilled water throughout the same 20-minute time. It was found that the babies sucked more consistently and persistently for sucrose than for water. The infants who received sucrose only sucked an average of about 55 times per minute for the 20-minute period. The water-only group sucked an average of 45 times per minute. That was not surprising.

A third group in this experiment was especially interesting. It was given alternating periods of sucrose and water, so that for five minutes they sucked for sucrose, then were switched to water for five minutes, then back to sucrose, then to water again. This group sucked about the same number of times per minute as the sucrose-only group when they were sucking for sucrose, but when they were switched to water they did not merely fall to the level of the water-only group. They shut down their water-sucking responses much more. This group's response level fell to a point significantly lower, about 28 sucks per minute, than it would have been had they been given water in the preceding 5-minute period rather than sucrose.

This result tells us what some nurses working with newborns knew already. Perhaps many more will know it now. If the baby is primed with sugar-water just before being offered for nursing to the mother, as is sometimes done, this works against the success of breastfeeding. To the extent that single unsuccessful feeding attempts tend to discourage the mother from further breast-feeding attempts, as we think sometimes occurs, there could be enduring effects. Infants may turn away from their mothers if they have just previously experienced a sweeter taste than that obtainable from the mother's milk.

This type of "negative contrast effect" in newborns could have implications that reach even farther. It is not uncommon, for example, for breast-feeding newborns to be fed during the first few days both from the mother and with supplementary commercial milks, especially until the mother's own lactation process is running smoothly. Until that time, some colostrum (the thin liquid preceding the onset of stable lactation) is available but is often presumed not to be sufficiently nutritious for the baby. Well-meaning infant caretakers therefore often alternate the two types of feeding. To the extent that the commercial preparations are sweeter and hence more palatable than the mother's supply, the infant may be inadvertently diverted from the mother.

There are reasons to believe that these early days of feeding inter-action between the newborn and the breast-feeding mother are critical (Klaus and Kennell, 1976). First, there is increasing evidence that the infant is especially sensitive to tastes and taste changes (Crook and Lipsitt, 1976; Lipsitt, 1976; Nowlis and Kessen, 1976), and that the structural and physiological apparatus for sucking in the newborn is exceedingly well developed (Bosma, 1976). These facts coupled with the high probability that the newborn can learn from experience (Horowitz, 1969; Hulsebus, 1973) suggest that any adverse taste and feeding experi-ences that the infant endures will have a high probability of altering the baby's behavior on the next feeding. Again, the tendency to provide newborns with supplementary feedings, possibly beyond their nutri-tional needs, may have secondary effects upon the feeding interaction itself. One of the principal factors involved in the mother's production of milk is the presence and activity of the baby (Pryor, 1963; Raphael, 1976). To the extent that the infant is separated from the mother for some feedings, the less will be the maternal milk supply and the slower to become activated. Some mothers have even noted that bringing their infants to them often yields an immediate flow of milk. Others have indicated that the cry of the infant is sufficient to produce the so-called letdown reflex. These are some of the arguments that have in fact been made to favor rooming-in of the newborn with the mother immediately after the birth. All the arguments, it will be noted, suggest that ev-erything possible should be done to enhance rather than diminish the infant's attraction to the mother and her milk supply, and thus to in-crease the "pleasures of sensation" (Pfaffmann, 1960) which both infant and mother derive from the feeding interaction. A cardinal principle would be to avoid inflicting "negative contrast" on either party.

RESPIRATORY OCCLUSION, ANGER IN THE NEWBORN, AND FEEDING PROBLEMS

As we have observed, some nurses who think they are doing the mother a good turn by priming the baby's sucking response just before a feeding may actually cause the infant to reject the mother's milk. It is not uncommon for aversive or avoidance behavior to be set up in the first few days of life. As we will see presently, a certain amount of aversive behavior on the part of the infant is likely to occur quite naturally in the arms of the caretakers anyway, and there does not seem to be any advantage in promoting an overabundance of that. At the same time, it is not unlikely that defensive and even "angry" responses of the baby have some adaptive significance, and thus the total evasion or suppression of such behaviors would not seem to be well-advised.

The English pediatrician, Mavis Gunther, pointed out a number of years ago (Gunther, 1955, 1961) that the "feeding couple" (as she called the mother and child pair) can affect one another in subtle ways that must be clearly understood to help both of them surmount the tensions of their earliest moments together. It is quite natural, she noted, for the newborn to become occasionally smothered for brief moments during the course of feeding. The nostrils come very close to the mother's breast and are sometimes stopped up while the baby has a tight latch on the nipple. This can cause momentary difficulty in breathing, which the infant in turn will object to, often strenuously. When this happens the baby turns its head to and fro and pulls back from the nipple; the arms flail, the face often reddens, and, rather as a last resort if the blockage continues, there is a burst of crying, which throws the nipple from the baby's mouth with a gusto that can offend the mother. Mothers may become quite exasperated after a few such occasions, feeling themselves to be failures in coping with the baby's needs and frustrations (Newton, 1955).

As Gunther has indicated on the basis of her extensive observations of neonates with their mothers, a few simple pointers given to the mother will usually help her to adjust herself posturally, or to insert the nipple in a more felicitous way, so as to prevent the occlusion from occurring. The seemingly angry response of the baby was, after all, a matter of awkward stimulation (Lipsitt, 1976). Even an infant that is bottle-fed can show the type of behavior described, as it is quite possible for the shield of the nipple to come against the baby's nostrils while feeding, especially with nipples that are short and stubby. Moreover, the baby's lips are in the beginning quite pliable and fatty, and the nostrils very close to the upper lip. All of this tends to promote respiratory blockage while feeding.

There is a well-known psychological phenomenon called approach–avoidance conflict. This is the situation in which there is something available that a person wants and is in reach of, but getting it entails endurance of some negative consequence of taking this action. When a baby is simultaneously deprived of its capacity to breathe while latched on at the mouth to the nipple with an airtight seal, this is an approach–avoidance conflict. Under these circumstances, newborns will usually go through the pattern of behavior previously described, culminating in releasing itself from the nipple, taking in air, and regaining its physical and behavioral stability. The response of uncoupling from the breast is reinforced, as psychologists are inclined to say, which means that the next time the baby is put to the breast he may find the position less desirable than previously. The aversive or negative consequences of being at the breast may have come out ahead of the positive features, which at the outset were very strong. To the extent that newborns can learn in such situations, and we think they can, the baby will adaptively decline the next opportunity to get smothered! Indeed we would worry about an infant that did not object to the situation. The phenomenon of passive acceptance of aversive stimulation does exist and will be discussed in a later section.

Simple instructions to the mother concerning the necessity of helping the infant to cope with keeping its air passages clear can often produce rapid changes—first, in the behavior of the mother and, second, in the objections of the infant (Gunther, 1961).

There have been too few studies conducted that might inform us better about the crucial early moments of interaction between mother and infant, and about the lingering effects of these critical experiences. The few studies that do exist (e.g., Korner, 1974; Korner and Thoman, 1970; Thoman, Leiderman, and Olson, 1972) suggest that mother behavior *and* baby behavior are powerfully important in setting the stage for later interactions and perhaps for the discovery of conditions related to developmental aberrations. It is necessary to keep in mind that the mother and infant are a twosome, and each affects the other (Bell, 1971, 1975). One-way theories of human behavior and development need not apply.

Similar observations may be made for interactions between fathers and infants as well. As little as we know about early mother–infant relations, we know much less about the behavioral impact of fathers on their babies, and vice versa. It is only a recent development of modern society that fathers are even permitted to be a part of the birthing process. That is quite strange, considering that before the advent of modern obstetrical techniques, when most infants were born at home, the father was very much a part of the scene. But fathers were disenfranchised for a period of 50 years or so, during which time practices relating to obstetrics were becoming increasingly complex, hospitals were especially wary of the threat of infectious diseases, and the mother-to-be came to be treated essentially as a sick person (Klaus and Kennell, 1976). Both the mother and father have suffered through a historical period in which the natural bonding that normally takes place (in less well-developed technological circumstances) among the mother, father,

and baby in the earliest moments of life has been unnaturally interrupted. Often the mother is so heavily anesthetized that she is poorly
aware of the events that are happening, while the father is left at home, at
work, or in the next room. The situation is changing again, however.
Mothers are opting for fewer drugs at birth, hospitals are permitting both
parents to be present during labor and in the delivery room, the mother
and father are permitted to handle the baby, and sometimes an infant is
even put to the breast right in the delivery room.

It is to be hoped that where such innovations are being made, there
will be a strong desire on the part of the responsible persons to study
their effects. Many of the strong arguments that were made in the past for
forbidding the father to be in the delivery room with the mother, as can
be seen from the apparent success of the practice currently, have been
unwarranted. There is some basis for believing that separation of the
infant from either or both parents may have some negative repercus-
sions. For example, premature babies who are ordinarily separated from
their mothers for special care immediately after birth do better developmentally if their mothers have access to and contact with them (Klaus and
Kennell, 1976). (See chapter by Sameroff and Abbe.)

EATING AVERSION IN AN INFANT

Occasionally a scientist doing basic research on some aspect of
human development and behavior is called upon to apply some bit of
laboratory expertise to an immediate practical problem even under conditions in which it is probably premature to suppose that the laboratory
knowledge is sufficient to handle the complexity of the situation. Such
situations often present themselves as "the last resort." If the scientist
does not try his best guess, there is not much left to try. Such is the case in
the present instance, in which a young child's pediatrician, cognizant of
the work carried out in the author's laboratory on infant sucking, swallowing, and feeding, asked that we see a 15-month-old patient to implement a regimen of training that might resolve a very unusual eating
problem.

This little girl would not eat food in the usual fashion and was being
fed through a tube that had been surgically inserted into her stomach.
The problem was described by the pediatrician and by the clinical
psychologist collaborator as "psychosomatic." It was psychosomatic in
the sense that although the child, Debbie, did have physical problems
that probably precipitated the feeding aversion, there seemed to be no
physical conditions at the time which perpetuated the condition. Thus, it
was thought, some type of psychological training might overcome the
handicap, severity of which is reflected in the description that follows.

During pregnancy, Debbie's mother was fatigued, uncomfortable, and frequently nauseated. Debbie was a full-term baby and of normal weight. Very rapid breathing was observed shortly after birth, there was excessive flushing of the face, and the baby's eyes seemed inflamed and overactive. Laboratory tests revealed that Debbie had a low sugar problem, whereupon she was treated with intravenous 50% glucose. Because of seizures occurring at this time, Debbie was kept in the hospital for 16 days after birth and was then discharged with observations of low blood sugar, increased red cells, decreased blood platelets, and central nervous system impairment.

Debbie was a poor feeder from birth, apparently. At 3 months of age, she was hospitalized for study. She had vision problems, and her electroencephalogram indicated brain abnormality, although at this age diagnosis of such problems is difficult and nonspecific. Debbie was put on a low-protein, high-carbohydrate diet with sugar supplement. At discharge she had amino-acid problems resulting from protein ingestion.

The brief medical history indicates clearly that at least in the beginning Debbie's behavioral problems had an organic basis. She was a sickly child from birth. Still, her major problem at 1 year of age was behavioral. Following discharge from the hospital, Debbie had a profound disinterest in food. In her desperate struggle to get Debbie to take food, her mother would slap her daughter's buttocks gently, and when Debbie opened her mouth, her mother would put the food in.

By 7 months of age, Debbie's feeding problem was her most important feature and she was grossly underweight. She was brought to the hospital and an operation on her abdomen was performed, so that Debbie could be fed directly through a tube into the stomach. By this point, Debbie was objecting to all oral intake of food. The direct line to her stomach provided the essential nourishment to protect her life. For about 7 months, Debbie got all her nourishment through the tube, from three feedings a day, with her mother filling the bottle, then a funnel, and allowing the contents to drain into her stomach. While Debbie was receiving a special diet earlier in her life, by 14 months of age she no longer required a diet different from that for any other child her age. She no longer needed medication, either. Thus it was thought that this was a reasonable time to try weaning Debbie from the tube.

At this time Debbie was seen by a pediatric neurologist, who said that there was no organic basis whatever for Debbie's refusal to feed orally. Her sucking, chewing, and swallowing capabilities were physiologically intact. He concurred in the judgment that operant conditioning might provide some relief for the parents. Actually, it was a last-ditch, desperate effort.

In a preliminary observation period, we found Debbie to be alert, observant, a "pretty little blonde girl with big brown eyes." To provide a baseline on her food-handling and eating behaviors, small bits of cereals and a baby bottle with a nipple were placed in front of her on the high chair tray. She played with everything but never brought anything to her mouth.

In the next step, we placed food on a spoon and moved it near her mouth. Similarly, we put milk in a cup and brought it close to her lips. In all such instances Debbie turned her head away vigorously, pushed the spoon or cup away, and sometimes wept bitterly over the attempts to encourage her taking the food in the usual way.

Next we observed Debbie's feeding via the tube. With Debbie lying on her back the connecting tube was attached to the implanted tube in Debbie's abdomen. Debbie's mother poured the prepared formula into a funnel connected with the tube, and the food drained into Debbie's abdomen. During this procedure, Debbie became obviously uncomfortable, she thrashed about, her face reddened, she squirmed and grunted, and then she cried. The feeding process was in this instance, as in others observed, a clearly traumatic incident. Her behavior would be characterized as a brief temper tantrum, terminating when the feeding ended. Of interest from a behavioral and reinforcement point of view was the fact that toward the end of the feeding, the mother indicated that Debbie would soon throw up. Debbie cried throughout the feeding, the feeding terminated in throwing up, and then the crying ceased. Debbie was experiencing taste, which is normally a pleasantly reinforcing event, only in the reverse direction, when food was being cast off!

Also interesting from a behavioral point of view was the fact that as soon as the crying, and then vomiting, ceased, the tube was extracted, and the episode was finished. Debbie became pleasant again and seemed to enjoy her associations with everyone in the room. She had a clearly affectionate relationship with her mother, which resumed as soon as the obviously painful feeding was over.

Debbie was brought into the laboratory at the Women and Infants Hospital of Rhode Island, where the sensory and learning research had been carried on which prompted the referral of Debbie. The laboratory was equipped with automatic feeding devices to enable polygraphic recordings of Debbie's sucking behavior in relation to the objects that would be presented to her. Our intent was to reinforce Debbie progressively for bringing a sucking device to her mouth, and eventually to reward her for mouthing this device. The automatic nipple was preset to deliver sweet fluid whenever she put it in her mouth. The prepared tube and nipple were placed in the tray in such a way that Debbie could pull it, move it around, put it to her mouth, and play with it in any way she chose. The procedure was intended to capitalize upon the fact that although she had a strong aversion to other people placing things in her mouth, Debbie occasionally placed her own fingers and other objects in her mouth. If she did this with the self-administered nipple, baseline recording of mouthing activity could be obtained, following which squirts of sucrose could be given through the nipple for any moves of the nipple toward the mouth, near her lips, and especially when the nipple was placed in the mouth. It was frankly hoped that Debbie would be thus encouraged to put the nipple in her mouth, would newly appreciate the infantile pleasure of sucking, and would be taught that when she put a feeding object in her mouth something rewarding would follow.

Unfortunately, Debbie was not inclined to put the nipple into her mouth. In this she was a deviant, as we should have expected. This had been precisely her problem.

We next recruited Debbie's mother as accomplice. Debbie's mother was a natural and effective operant conditioner. She had proved this by having put Debbie through this painful feeding process for 7 months without losing her affection. Debbie was in turn closely attached to her mother. They had good eye contact, they smiled at each other often, Debbie looked to her mother whenever she seemed distressed and in apparent need of reassurance, and there were many types of interaction in which they engaged that were obviously rewarding to Debbie.

We asked Debbie's mother to sit in a special seat with Debbie in her arms. We put a blank nipple into Debbie's hands. As Debbie played with the nipple, she occasionally raised her arms, almost accidentally bringing it to her mouth. When this happened, all personnel in the laboratory, usually four of us besides Debbie's mother, gave Debbie abundant social reinforcement, with many exclamations of "Good Debbie." At first we sought simply to overwhelm Debbie with our good cheer and happy voices, making sure not to frighten her with it. We tried to make our joyful reactions occur as close in time as possible to the behavior that we wanted to encourage. Each time Debbie moved her hands closer to her face, we gave her our happy response. The procedure is one of so-called operant shaping, in which each of the subject's successive approximations to the desired response is reinforced. The technique is similar to that by which one encourages an animal to jump higher and higher in the air to obtain food.

We discovered Debbie liked to look at herself in a mirror. We decided to weave that reinforcement into the fabric of our social conditioning process. Whenever Debbie put the nipple in or near her mouth, we moved the mirror near her so she could look at herself. While looking at herself in the mirror, Debbie was also cuddled by her mother, praised, and rocked. These were all conditions, also, in which Debbie took great pleasure. Rather rapidly, over four sessions, and with the close collaboration of her mother, who continued these techniques at home, Debbie came to put the feeding object in her mouth more and more. Because so much of the training was in fact going on ·at home, it was impossible to keep proper records. Each successive session in the laboratory revealed substantial progress, which was recorded photographically, and finally we placed a feeding cup in Debbie's hands. Whenever Debbie put the cup to her lips, her mother cuddled her, sang to her, rocked her, and smiled. Upon our discovery that Debbie liked to hear music, we arranged a music box that her mother could activate with her foot whenever Debbie put the cup to her lips.

After the response of putting the cup to her lips had been acquired, it was then possible to put milk in the cup. Debbie accommodated by putting the cup to her lips with milk in it. It was sometimes messy, but she got fluid to her mouth. A spoon was introduced again, for which Debbie was reinforced in putting it near her mouth. Bits of food were put on the food spoon, and she took the whole thing to her mouth. We were well on our way by then to disrupting Debbie's previously learned expectation that food in the mouth would be unpleasant.

Over a 2-week period, Debbie increased her oral intake, in the laboratory and at home, to 14 ounces per day. Debbie's mother reduced her tube feeding gradually until Debbie was getting only one feeding per day by the tube, at the end of the day, instead of the three tube feedings prior to the training procedures.

Shortly after, we suggested that Debbie continue with these procedures, including the "music box treatment," at home only. We agreed to see her whenever her mother wished. Occasionally, about once every 2 weeks, Debbie was brought in for observation. To our satisfaction, it appeared that Debbie could actually go without any supplemental tube feedings. However, the mother seemed hesitant to dispense with at least one tube feeding per day. This problem eventually passed. Debbie's mother called one day to say it was all over; she had had the tube removed.

Periodically the parents bring Debbie for follow-up visits. Her eating patterns are without problems. Debbie is still seen in a special home training program. She is neurologically impaired, due to early metabolic imbalances associated with blood sugar level.

Operant conditioning and behavior modification techniques can often help to ameliorate infant behavior problems and their associated family tensions, within a short period of time and at minimal cost.

TESTING THE HEARING OF A NEWBORN CHILD

Much research has been done to document the hearing and other sensory capacities of the newborn child (Eisenberg, 1965, 1969). It has become very clear that newborn infants are keenly sensitive to sounds. They will startle to loud noises, and they will tend to become quiet and attentive to soft, rhythmic sounds, and especially to the sound of the human voice. Indeed, recent evidence suggests that the female voice is especially an attention-grabber, and that the baby's heart rate will even slow down for a few beats at the onset of the mother's voice (Ashmead and Lipsitt, in preparation; Brazelton, 1973; Brazelton, Koslowski, and Main, 1974).

One father, who happened to be a psychologist (Wertheimer, 1961), was in the delivery room at the time of his child's birth and administered a preplanned test. A toy cricket was sounded first at one side of the baby's head, just moments after birth. The child moved his eyes in that direction. Then the toy was sounded at the other side, and the eyes moved in that direction. Repetitive tests convinced the happy psychologist-father that his child could hear. Perhaps even more important, the directional gaze obtained in response to sound on either side of the head indicated that the baby was, perhaps in some primitive sense, capable of spatial localization. The integration of two or more channels of sensory input, and the acquisition of such integrative capacities, are surely among the more important and fascinating aspects of development.

More observations and studies need to be done to fully understand the processes that might be involved in these early sensory and motor linkages. We have made some beginnings. We know, for example, that when the newborn's palms are pressed, the mouth often opens and the head moves to a midline position; this so-called Babkin reflex can even be learned to other stimuli (Kaye, 1970). Sometimes very young babies can be seen seemingly to swipe with their hands at objects passing before them, even before the age by which we expect grabbing and reaching responses to occur (Bower, 1975). And it has become apparent from recent research that if you stick your tongue out at a 6-week-old when he is attentive to your face, he may well stick his tongue right back at you (Maratos, 1973; Meltzoff and Moore, 1977).

There are several ways in which such findings with newborns can be used to facilitate the testing of an infant's hearing. Conditioning techniques have been used to help detect deafness, for example (Aldrich, 1928). A tone of a certain intensity is sounded just before the administration of an aversive stimulus such as an air puff to the cheek or a scratch on the sole of the foot. If the infant acquires a conditioned anticipatory response to the tone after a number of trials, this is a demonstration of the fact that the tone was heard. As most modern researchers with infants can report, however, and as the research of Eisenberg (1969) demonstrates, polygraphic techniques involving the use of respiratory and cardiac measures of response to sounds that vary in intensity probably provide the most sensitive indices of auditory acuity in the young, inarticulate child.

DETECTING DISABILITIES IN THE NEWBORN

Recent studies suggest strongly that some of the first manifestations of developmental disability may be found in the earliest days of life. It is now rather well accepted that there are certain events surrounding birth, such as maternal anemia, an oxygen deficit at birth, or jaundice, which can have life-lasting influences on the infant who endures them. So many of us know persons whose lives may have started out with difficulties of this sort who are perfectly well now that we are sometimes inclined to doubt the significance of those events, and indeed most studies indicate that multiple-risk signs must be present for there to be enduring problems. It is a statistical matter, however, that on average those infants who are born prematurely, who are small and require prolonged administration of oxygen at birth, whose muscles seem limp or floppy (or conversely, overly tense and tight) do fare less well during the first year of life and in later years than infants whose "signs" or "indicators" were not so severe (Drillien, 1964; Sameroff and Chandler, 1975).

In summarizing a vast amount of data on the relationship between early competencies of the infant and later development, Appleton *et al.* (1975) found reason to believe that the earliest manifestations of sensory competence do give rise in a causative way to later sensorimotor and intellectual proficiencies: ". . . the competence of the older child in manipulating and comprehending the environment is probably based on interactions with the environment which are dependent upon processing sensory information. Through development of perceptual and sensorimotor abilities the infant can learn about his or her surroundings and can develop a practical understanding of reality. Early learning of skills and expectations appears to contribute to further learning and development" (p. 104).

Habituation is one of the earliest manifestations of the influence of environment on behavior. In habituation, the repetitive presentation of a stimulus that is initially effective in producing some response will come to have less and less influence on that behavior. For example, the first time a loud noise is sounded, the infant may startle and show displeasure. With increasing presentations, however, the sound will have less effect until, provided the sound is not truly raucous, response may wane entirely. In most instances, this is a sign that the stimulus has been assimilated and that it is appreciated now as an essentially innocuous background noise in the environment. Whereas the baby pre-

viously jumped, it may have only a small residual heart rate increase each
time the sound occurs.

Weak habituation manifested during the neonatal period may be
suggestive of later developmental lag, and absence of habituation has
been seen as a concomitant of serious brain deficiency (Brackbill, 1971;
Bronshtein, Antonova, Kamenetskaya, Luppova, and Sytora, 1958;
Lewis, Goldberg, and Campbell, 1969).

CRIB DEATH AND ITS CORRELATES

The sudden infant death syndrome (SIDS) takes perhaps as many as
8,000 babies in America each year in the first year of life, excluding the
especially hazardous first few days of life. The fallout in grief and despair
of the thousands of close survivors compounds the tragedy immeasur-
ably. Such deaths are especially difficult to endure for parents because of
the absence of definitive answers regarding the basic mechanisms underlying SIDS. The historical neglect of research attention to the nature of
the disorder, and the rather frequent popular confusion of the sudden
infant death syndrome with child abuse, have only recently abated
somewhat.

We need to know more about the precursors of crib death, but some
progress is being made. The first line of defense against it is to define
those conditions that are often present, prior to the death, in those
infants that have succumbed. Even descriptions of such conditions, in
the absence of satisfactory explanations, would be useful at this stage of
our understanding. The casual and necessarily anecdotal report of psychophysiological attributes of infants who have been "near misses"
would—or might—provide us with a lead or two into the biological
processes that may be operating in infants that die (Steinschneider,
1972). Crib death is not, or should not be, as much of a mystery as it has
seemed, for there are pathological precursors that can be seen even
during the newborn period. Psychophysiological factors might well be
involved in the final pathway to the condition that ultimately causes the
death of the infant, usually between 2 and 4 months of age. The possibility must even be considered that experience, and the effects that
experiences have on the young child, may be implicated.

One study (Lipsitt, Sturner, and Burke, 1977) began with the extensive perinatal and pediatric records of 15 crib death cases, then composed two control groups, one of these the very next birth of the same
sex, and the other the very next birth of the same sex and race.

Because of space limitations, it is not possible to provide here all the
data comparing these groups. Enough information can be given to convey the essence of the findings. It became apparent that the deceased

group varied from the controls in several ways, all of them in a direction connoting greater perinatal stress and biological hazard in that group. (1) There were reliable differences in Apgar scoring in the first few minutes of life, the Apgar test being a quickly administered scale for assessing the baby's vital signs, such as adequacy of respiration, heart rate, pallor, and muscle tone. The deceased group did more poorly than either control. (2) Infants were identified as having respiratory abnormalities significantly more often in the deceased group than in the second control. (3) The deceased group had mothers with anemia significantly more often than in either control group. (4) More of the eventually deceased infants required intensive care than did the controls. (5) The deceased infants were hospitalized for about 11 days, the first control group for 6 days, and the second control for about 7 days. (6) The infants that ultimately died were still requiring resuscitative measures at 5 minutes of age significantly more frequently than either control group.

It seems clear that the infants who succumbed between 2 and 5 months of age were already showing, in general and on average, that they were beginning life with some fragility. We need to know more about that fragility, and about the developmental processes that apparently transform seemingly minor insufficiencies into a morbid crisis a few months later. I use the term *minor insufficiencies* advisedly, for the literature on crib death, both in professional journals and in the public documents distributed to parents and the helping professions, tends to emphasize the "normality" of infants who succumb to the sudden infant death syndrome. Better record-keeping, and more intensive retrospective documentation of the perinatal histories of crib death cases, might well reveal a higher incidence of developmental aberrations in these youngsters than has been thought existed.

The terms *crib death* and *sudden infant death syndrome* are in fact diagnoses of essential ignorance, which is to say that the labels are used when no discernible sign of pathology in the deceased infant is present. While the terms are useful as temporizing diagnoses, and would be even more useful if it was generally appreciated that the diagnosis really means that we do not yet know the cause of the death, sudden infant death syndrome has come to be thought of as "death without cause." This has a stifling effect upon research endeavors that would seek the causes. One promising line of research relating to the causes of crib death has to do with the possibility that a basic learning disability is implicated (Lipsitt, 1977). This suggestion is based upon the observation that crib deaths have a peak period of occurrence in the range between 2 and 4 months of age. This is a critical time during development when many of the basic reflexes with which the baby is born are in transition. While these responses, like the grasp reflex of the newborn, are very strong at birth, they begin to weaken soon after, and some of them are gone by 5 months. Many of these reflexes, such as turning the head to a touch near the mouth, or the grasp reflex, go through an observable change. They are executed more slowly and seemingly on a voluntary rather than an obligatory basis.

The thinking in relation to crib death is that if a baby does not go through the transition smoothly from being an essentially reflexive creature to becoming a more intentional and reflective organism, a hazardous condition might develop in which the infant will not be able to adequately defend himself when, for example, threats to respiration present themselves. Little is now known about the origins of an adequate repertoire of defensive behavior. It is not unlikely that after the first weeks of life, much of this class of behavior is importantly dependent upon learning. Research is currently underway to explore this suggestion.

Concluding Comment

We have seen that numerous avenues of basic research into psychological and developmental processes of infants have provided some indications of how the findings might be used to promote the health, education, and welfare of young persons. It does not seem too much to hope that in the future, prenatal and birth conditions will be better regulated to optimize the condition and potential of the fetus and neonate. Education will be seen increasingly to begin in the nursery. Special training or stimulation will be implemented to reduce the probability of lasting deficits, especially in the premature infant and others who have a hazardous beginning. Such procedures will be used to enhance the learning capabilities of the infant. It is not too much to hope, even, that further explorations into the antecedents of various types of developmental jeopardy, including crib death, will be so much better understood in the near future as to enable the prevention of such developmental tragedies as these. While prenatal and neonatal research has in the past emphasized pediatric disease entities, it will be useful in the future for psychological processes to become better appreciated. Recent data indicate that the isolation of the premature infant from its parents and other stimulation for protracted periods of time must be diminished, and even normal newborns must be afforded the opportunity to experience a wide variety of stimulation in their early environment. At present it appears that psychological and environmental factors may be exceedingly important in the determination of fetal damage (e.g., the ingestion of drugs, smoking, diet) and that the well-being of newborns is markedly affected by the milieu in which they survive and, it is hoped, thrive.

ACKNOWLEDGMENTS

The writer is indebted to Dr. John Farley and Prof. Anthony Davids for their collaboration in the work with Debbie.

REFERENCES

Aldrich, C. A new test for hearing in the newborn: The conditioned reflex. *American Journal of Diseases of Children*, 1928, *35*, 36–37.

Appleton, T., Clifton, R., and Goldberg, S. The development of behavioral competence in infancy. In F. D. Horowitz (Ed.), *Review of child development research*. Vol. 4. Chicago: University of Chicago Press, 1975. Pp. 101–186.

Ashmead, D. H., and Lipsitt, L. P. The effect of vocal and non-vocal stimuli on the newborn's heart rate. In preparation.

Bell, R. Q. Stimulus control of parent or caretaker behavior by offspring. *Developmental Psychology*, 1971, *4*, 63–72.

Bell, R. Q. A congenital contribution to emotional response in early infancy and the preschool period. *Parent–Infant Interaction*, Ciba Foundation Symposium 33. Amsterdam: Elsevier Excerpta Medica, 1975.

Bosma, J. Introduction to the symposium. In J. Bosma and J. Showacre (Eds.), *Development of upper respiratory anatomy and function: Implications for sudden infant death syndrome*. U.S. Government Printing Office, 1976. Pp. 5–49.

Bower, T. G. R. Infant perception of the third dimension and object concept development. In L. B. Cohen and P. Salapatek (Eds.), *Infant perception: From sensation to cognition.* Vol. 2, *Perception of space, speech, and sound*. New York: Academic Press, 1975. Pp. 33–50.

Brackbill, Y. The role of the cortex in orienting: Orienting reflex in an anencephalic human infant. *Developmental Psychology*, 1971, *5*, 195–201.

Brazelton, T. B. *Neonatal behavioral assessment scale*. London: William Heinemann Medical Books (Spastics International Medical Publications). Philadelphia: J. B. Lippincott, 1973.

Brazelton, T. B., Koslowski, B., and Main, M. The origins of reciprocity: The early mother–infant interaction. In M. Lewis and L. A. Rosenblum (Eds.), *The effects of the infant on its caregiver*. New York: Wiley, 1974. Pp. 49–76.

Bronshtein, A. I., Antonova, T. G., Kamenetskaya, A. G., Luppova, N. N., and Sytova, V. A. On the development of the functions of analyzers in infants and some animals at the early stage of ontogenesis. In *Problems of evolution of physiological functions.* Moscow Academy of Science, 1958. Israel Program for Scientific Translations, 1960. Pp. 106–116. (U.S. Department of Commerce OTS 60-51066)

Crook, C. K., and Lipsitt, L. P. Neonatal nutritive sucking: Effects of taste stimulation upon sucking rhythm and heart rate. *Child Development*, 1976, *47*, 518–522.

Drillien, C. M. *The growth and development of the prematurely born infant*. Baltimore: Williams and Wilkins, 1964.

Eisenberg, R. B. Auditory behavior in the human neonate: 1. Methodologic problems and the logical design of research procedures. *Journal of Auditory Research*, 1965, *5*, 159–177.

Eisenberg, R. B. Auditory behavior in the human neonate: Functional properties of sound and their ontogenetic implications. *International Audiology*, 1969, *7*, 34–45.

Emde, R. N., and Robinson, J. The first two months. Recent research in developmental psychobiology and the changing view of the newborn. In J. Noshpitz and J. Call (Eds.), *Basic handbook of child psychiatry*. New York: Basic Books, 1976.

Gunther, M. Instinct and the nursing couple. *Lancet*, 1955, *1*, 575.

Gunther, M. Infant behavior at the breast. In B. Foss (Ed.), *Determinants of infant behavior.* London: Methuen, 1961. Pp. 37–44.

Hasselmeyer, E. G. The premature neonate's response to handling. In *Expanding horizon in knowledge: Implications for nursing,* Kansas City, Mo.: American Nurses Association, 1964, *11,* 15–24.

Horowitz, F. D. Learning, developmental research, and individual differences. In L. P. Lipsitt and H. W. Reese (Eds.), *Advances in child development and behavior.* Vol. 4. New York: Academic Press, 1969.

Hulsebus, R. C. Operant conditioning of infant behavior. In H. W. Reese (Ed.), *Advances in child development and behavior.* Vol. 8. New York: Academic Press, 1973.

Kaye, H. Sensory processes. Chapter 2 in H. W. Reese and L. P. Lipsitt (Eds.), *Experimental child psychology.* New York: Academic Press, 1970.

Kessen, W., Haith, M. M., and Salapatek, P. H. Human infancy: A bibliography and guide. In P. H. Mussen (Ed.), *Carmichael's manual of child psychology.* New York: Wiley, 1970. Pp. 287–445.

Klaus, M., and Kennell, J. *Mother-infant bonding: The impact of early separation or loss on family development.* St. Louis: C. V. Mosby, 1976.

Kobre, K. R., and Lipsitt, L. P. A negative contrast effect in newborns. *Journal of Experimental Child Psychology,* 1972, *14,* 81–91.

Korner, A. The effect of the infant's state, level of arousal, sex, and ontogenetic stage on the caregiver. In M. Lewis and L. A. Rosenblum (Eds.), *The effect of the infant on its caregiver.* New York: Wiley, 1974. Pp. 105–122.

Korner, A. F., and Thoman, E. B. Visual alertness in neonates as evoked by maternal care. *Journal of Experimental Child Psychology,* 1970, *10,* 67–78.

Lewis, M., Goldberg, S., and Campbell, H. A developmental study of information processing within the first three years of life. Response decrement to a redundant signal. *Monographs of the Society for Research in Child Development,* 1969, *34* (Whole No. 133).

Lipsitt, L. P. Learning in the first year of life. In L. P. Lipsitt and C. C. Spiker (Eds.), *Advances in child development and behavior.* Vol. 1. New York: Academic Press, 1963. Pp. 147–195.

Lipsitt, L. P. Developmental psychobiology comes of age: A discussion. In L. P. Lipsitt (Ed.), *Developmental psychobiology: The significance of infancy.* Hillsdale, New Jersey: Lawrence Erlbaum Associates, 1976. Pp. 109–127.

Lipsitt, L. P. Perinatal indicators and psychophysiological precursors of crib death. In F. D. Horowitz (Ed.), *Early developmental hazards: Predictors and precautions.* American Association for the Advancement of Science, 1977.

Lipsitt, L. P., Sturner, W. O., and Burke, P. M. Perinatal correlates of crib death. In preparation. 1977.

Maratos, O. *The origin and development of imitation in the first six months of life.* Unpublished doctoral dissertation, University of Geneva, 1973.

Meltzoff, A. N., and Moore, M. K. Imitation of facial and manual gestures by 2-week-old infants. *Science,* 1977, *198,* 75–78.

Newton, N. *Maternal emotions.* Part B. New York: Hoeber, 1955.

Nowlis, G. H., and Kessen, W. Human newborns differentiate differing concentrations of sucrose and glucose. *Science,* 1976, *191,* 865–866.

Pfaffmann, C. The pleasures of sensation. *Psychological Review,* 1960, *67,* 253–268.

Pryor, K. W. *Nursing your baby.* New York: Harper & Row, 1963.

Raphael, D. *The tender gift: Breastfeeding.* New York: Schocken Books, 1976.

Rice, R. D. Neurophysiological development in premature infants following stimulation. *Developmental Psychology,* 1977, *13,* 69–76.

Rothschild, B. F. Incubator isolation as a possible contributing factor to the high incidence of emotional disturbance among prematurely born persons. *Journal of Genetic Psychology,* 1967, *110,* 298–304.

Sameroff, A. J., and Chandler, M. J. Reproductive risk and the continuum of caretaking casualty. In F. D. Horowitz, M. Hetherington, S. Scarr-Salapatek, and G. Siegel (Eds.), *Review of child development research*. Vol. 4. University of Chicago Press, 1975.

Siqueland, E. R. Further developments in infant learning. *Proceedings of the 19th International Congress of Psychology*, July 27–August 2, 1969, London, England.

Solkoff, N., Yaffe, S., Weintraub, D., and Blase, B. Effects of handling on the subsequent development of premature infants. *Developmental Psychology*, 1969, *1*, 765–768.

Steinschneider, A. Prolonged apnea and the sudden infant death syndrome: Clinical and laboratory observations. *Pediatrics*, 1972, *50*, 646–654.

Thoman, E. B., Leiderman, P. H., and Olson, J. P. Neonate-mother interaction during breast-feeding. *Developmental Psychology*, 1972, *6*, 110–118.

Wertheimer, M. Psychomotor coordination of auditory and visual space at birth. *Science*, 1961, *134*, 18–32.

Growing Up Social

HARRIET L. RHEINGOLD AND RON HASKINS

In this chapter we consider how the research findings on the development of social behavior have affected the behavior of parents and the practices of all those professions and agencies that have the child's best welfare at heart. The first parts of the chapter present a summary of what we now know about the development of the infant's and young child's social behavior. The latter parts tell how this knowledge has already been applied. Beyond this, we present suggestions for desirable changes in practices based on what we already know, and further changes that may be anticipated as a result of future research.

A major task facing any society is how to rear its children so that they grow up to be responsive and responsible persons. We ask then how has psychological research contributed to carrying out that task? A classic approach begins with the earliest manifestations of social behavior. Even though we may not yet have convincing evidence that early behavior determines later behavior, as we shall consider in some detail, still in time its effects may be more clearly shown.

The practices of rearing children change from generation to generation. In general, current practices can be characterized as more permissive than those of the 1930s. For example, today we do not hear mothers worrying about weaning or toilet training, both major concerns a gener-

HARRIET L. RHEINGOLD and RON HASKINS • Department of Psychology, University of North Carolina, Chapel Hill, North Carolina. Work on this chapter was supported by NIH research grant number HD23620 from the National Institute of Child Health and Human Development to Harriet L. Rheingold.

ation ago. These changes result from research findings, but only in part; changes also result from the social temper of the times and the upheavals produced by such social movements as wars, civil rights legislation, and so on. Here we shall not trace changes in such practices (see Stendler, 1950; Wolfenstein, 1953, for excellent accounts) but rather shall restrict ourselves to the research findings of the last 30 or so years and show how they have affected practices. We then cast a wider net to look beyond parental practices to those of the professions and social agencies responsible for the care and welfare of children, to the practices of doctors, lawyers, judges, teachers, and of social and governmental agencies both state and federal.

On the topic of interest we cannot expect to find a point-to-point application of research to practice. Many years intervene between the formulation of a scientific principle and its successful application. Technological inventions may take only a matter of a few years, and there one often can see a point-to-point application. The effects of research on the development of social behavior are, in contrast, broad and pervasive. The gap between findings in the laboratory and practices in the home is large, and probably rightfully so. In the first place, research efforts do not move in a steady direction. Moreover, each new finding must be tested by different investigators before its generality can be established.

Knowledge of the social behavior of infants, especially, accrues slowly because the data come from only "natural" studies. We cannot carry out the definitive studies because we cannot experiment with children. We depend then on naturally occurring events and thereby come to know the effects of, for example, institutionalization, day care, and father absence. Such studies, being biased and confounded in many ways, usually have methodological flaws. Nevertheless, social policy must sometimes move before all the data meet the scientists' standards.

It is not time alone that slows the application of knowledge in this area but the requirement that knowledge be as complete as possible before change is instituted. Here wisdom cautions the scientist to be conservative, often to the exasperation of policy makers.

For brevity, this account concentrates on social behavior, with full recognition of the extent to which social behavior cannot be divorced from physical, perceptual, cognitive, and other areas of the child's development. The account is further limited to social behavior during the first few years of life of the normal child, primarily in Western culture, especially in our own country.

The first three sections, The Social and Socializing Infant, The Meaning of Attachment, and The Consequences of Separation, review some of the main findings that have affected practice. The next two sections, The Effects of Early Experience on Later Behavior and The Needs of Young

Children for Optimum Social Development, examine the general concepts that underlie the findings. The next section tells in some detail how the main findings have already been applied, while the final section shows how beneficial to the future of mankind would be other changes in practice based in part on some newer findings.

The Social and Socializing Infant

With each passing year new sensitivities and competencies of infants are discovered (Kessen, Haith, and Salapatek, 1970; Lipsitt, this volume). These leave no doubt that human infants are sensitive to the stimuli presented by the people in their environment. They are not only responsive to social stimuli but they are capable also of actively initiating and bidding for social contacts (Collis and Schaffer, 1975). From the earliest days of life their responses to people are modified by how people respond to them. Similarly, they are capable of modifying the behavior of others toward them (Rheingold, 1966). In these respects they are not very different from other social animals, but it is generally not recognized how early these competencies appear in even the human newborn.

These characteristics of human infants show that they are indeed social creatures from birth. They participate fully in interacting with the people in their environment, so much so that they have been ascribed an important role in affecting the behavior of their caretakers (Bell, 1968; Rheingold, 1969). Not at all are they passive creatures to be molded by their parents. Instead the evidence shows, and every thoughtful parent knows, that infants teach parents what they need to have done for them. Parents themselves, however, are no more passive than their infants. As infants modify the behavior of their caretakers, so caretakers modify the behavior of their infants. The rearing of a child, then, is a mutually interactive process (Brazelton, 1969, 1974); the role of children in their own rearing constitutes a new emphasis in our understanding of how children grow up.

As a consequence of the mutually interactive nature of rearing, the characteristics of the individual participants merit discussion. As parents differ in countless ways, so do infants from the moment of birth. Each infant is a unique individual, unique from the moment of conception, and at birth already a product of the interaction between genetic potential and the prenatal environment. Infants differ, for example, in activity level, perceptual sensitivities, temperament, and adaptability (Thomas, Chess, Birch, Hertzig, and Korn, 1963). As is true of the course of any endeavor in life, the course of rearing seldom runs smoothly, but smoother rearing results from parental sensitivity to the special characteristics of their own infant.

To infants' early social capabilities we add their sharing with other people what they see and find of interest in their environment. Everyday observation and laboratory studies (Leung and Rheingold, 1977; Rheingold, Hay, and West, 1976) reveal that by the end of the first year of life infants are already drawing other people's attention by pointing to objects. They also spontaneously offer both familiar and unfamiliar persons bits of food, their toys, and other things. That children so young share contradicts the egocentricity so often ascribed to them and reveals them instead as already able contributors to social life.

The Meaning of Attachment

These social infants, interested in and responsive to all the people in their environment, nevertheless after only a few months of experience begin to distinguish among them. To the approach of familiar persons they smile and coo sooner and longer (Laroche and Desbiolles, 1976); even though the evidence measured only the contrast between the mother and an unfamiliar person, we can safely extrapolate the finding to other familiar persons in the infant's life.

As the months pass, signs of the infants' ability to distinguish among people become sharper, keeping pace with the development of their cognitive and motor skills. Now infants begin to show special preferences for some, at first usually their mothers. This special class of responses has been labeled "attachment." To Ainsworth (1973) and Bowlby (1958, 1969) we owe the classic statement of attachment. Together with a fuller and more discriminating social responsiveness to their mothers goes not only the infants' seeking to maintain contact with them but their distress at separation. Attachments are affectional, discriminating, specific, and enduring, in infancy and childhood as well as in adulthood; but until the research was done, we did not know how early they developed.

Whence comes the affection? Familiarity, custom, and habit, though necessary, do not constitute sufficient explanations. Nor do satisfaction and pleasure by themselves. Nevertheless, the near universality of the attachment of infants to their mothers should not blind us to what qualifies as a remarkable achievement of infancy.

We would be doing both infants and the other members of their families a disservice, however, if we failed to add that infants form attachments not only to their mothers but to their fathers, siblings, and others with whom they regularly interact. Even as infants first give signs of being attached to their mothers, almost in the next day they extend these signs to their fathers, brothers or sisters, and grandparents (Schaffer and Emerson, 1964).

The role of fathers deserves a special note. We may assume that from the beginning of history fathers have been interested in their infants. Only lately, however, have psychologists realized that they have concentrated too long on the mother–child relationship to an exclusion of the father–child relationship or the mother–father–child relationship. Considering the increasing employment outside the home of mothers of infants and young children, and additional prods from the women's liberation movement, it is past time to study the behavior of fathers with their infants. Nevertheless, at least 30 years ago Gesell and Ilg (1946) wrote that a new age was dawning for fathers as participants in the rearing of children. Current observations in the hospital, for example, reveal the active interest and caretaking activities of fathers with their newborn infants (Parke and O'Leary, 1976). Other recent studies show that infants are as attached to their fathers as to their mothers (Lamb, 1975). We can surmise that even when mothers carry out most of the caretaking operations, fathers may be accorded quite special responses just because their contacts are more intermittent and more playful (Rheingold, 1966).

Mothers and fathers do not exhaust the categories of persons of consequence for the infants' social behavior. Siblings and peers too offer rich social stimulation (Eckerman, Whatley, and Kutz, 1975; Samuels, 1977).

The bonds to the people of importance in the infants' life do not limit their interest in other people. Although they generally respond in a more friendly fashion to other infants and children than to other adults (Lewis, Young, Brooks, and Michalson, 1975), they do not typically fear unfamiliar persons (Rheingold and Eckerman, 1973). The so-called fear of the stranger is the rarer rather than the commoner event, characteristic of some infants only briefly and of a very few for longer. It is true that laboratory studies can make infants uneasy by having the unfamiliar person behave in a stereotyped and intrusive fashion or by having the mother leave the infant alone in the unfamiliar environment with an unfamiliar person—and close the door. In real life infants do subject unfamiliar persons to careful scrutiny, but they often then smile and vocalize to them, friendly responses being more the rule than the exception.

Seldom considered but very real are the many advantages conferred on infants by their attachment to people. In the vicinity of their parents they are protected from danger and harm (Bowlby, 1969). The activities of people, children and adult, more competent than the infant provide models that stimulate and instruct, whether the activities involve things or people. Thus infants learn to speak the tongue of their familiars and to manipulate the objects of their environment. They also learn the roles that different people play and the role their culture assigns to them as young children. By interacting with people they come to define a concept of themselves—how like other adults and children they are in some respects and how different in other respects.

At the same time the infants' attachments to people confer great powers on those people. Because people are important for the infants' physical welfare and psychological development, infants must pay attention to their wishes and demands. And parents out of their concern and love for their infants—their own attachment—are able to discipline and train.

THE CONSEQUENCES OF SEPARATION

To separate a child from its mother frequently distresses both child and mother. There are many kinds of separation, however, and all do not occasion distress, while for those that do, the distress may be slight and temporary. Here we consider the many kinds, beginning with the milder and proceeding to the more severe.

In the course of a day—even in the most benign of environments, the homes of devoted parents—mothers in our Western culture leave their infants many times as they go about their homemaking activities or put their infants in cribs for naps and sleep. Infants typically accept such separations; they may evoke protest but seldom distress. Furthermore, as soon as infants are capable of locomoting, even by crawling, they themselves leave their mothers. As they leave, they do not cry; nor, having reached a certain distance, do they crawl back crying (Rheingold and Eckerman, 1970). Nor do they always follow their mothers; they often tarry to explore the environment and sometimes even run ahead (Corter, Rheingold, and Eckerman, 1972; Hay, 1977)!

Some other kinds of separation are also everyday occurrences in the lives of infants. Parents leave them for short periods with baby-sitters, relatives, and siblings, in or out of the home. Today even 12-month-old infants join neighborhood play groups for a morning or two a week. The protests, fussing, and even distress at these separations appear not to be severe. When they do occur, the usual story tells of the infant's recovery as soon as the parent departs.

Another kind of everyday separation occurs in the lives of infants and young children whose mothers work outside the home. According to recent figures (U.S. Bureau of the Census, 1976), a third of the women with a child under 6 years old are in the labor force. Whether the children are cared for in their own homes by others, in the homes of these other persons, or in day-care centers, a daily and relatively long separation occurs. Assessing the effect of maternal employment on the behavior of children turns out to be a very complex problem indeed. The immediate responses of the infants and children to such separation must vary considerably. What contributes to the children's responses are the nature of the parent–child relation and the substitute caretaker–child relation, as well as the setting the child is left in or taken to (Hoffman, 1974; Stolz, 1960).

Several ameliorating conditions should be kept in mind. The daily reunions at the end of the working day not only reassure the children but can be happy occasions, as occur with the daily return of fathers. Parents may well offer a rich and heightened interaction with their children in the shorter time they do have together. In addition, children who are cared for by more than one caretaker may profit by the more varied social stimulation. Throughout history, up to the present, the care of infants has been shared by fathers, grandparents, aunts, siblings, nursemaids, and governesses. Would humankind have fared better under the exclusive care of the biological mother?

The use of day-care centers for the all-day care of infants and children under school age is of current concern, a topic to which we shall return under Current Applications of Knowledge. Here it is only necessary to say that the studies so far available do not show a decline in the children's ability to distinguish their mothers from other caretakers and to accord them a preferred status (e.g., Farran and Ramey, 1977). Much research is sorely needed before we can properly evaluate the effect of day care on children's present and subsequent social behavior, not only with their parents but also with their siblings and peers.

There are, however, other kinds of separation that result in genuine distress for the infant and child. One of these needs little attention: the procedures in laboratories designed to measure responses to a contrived situation where the child is left alone with an unfamiliar person after what must be a bewildering series of comings and goings of mothers and persons. These artificial maneuvers often occasion distress to the child but fortunately only for brief periods of time and are followed, one trusts, by complete recovery.

Much more serious separations and distressing reactions occur when parents and children must be separated for longer periods by the child's entry into a hospital for illness, or the illness or forced absence of the mother, or other catastrophe occurring in the family (Bowlby, 1973). Illness, removal to an unfamiliar environment, care at the hands of unfamiliar persons, and painful medical procedures, the events attendant on the separation, exacerbate the response.

The absence of the father from the home also qualifies as a kind of separation, although its effects on the young child's social development have generally received less attention than the effects of mother–infant separation. Father absence, like maternal employment, has proved to be too comprehensive a factor to yield to definitive statements. Not only do the kinds of absences differ—because of military service, divorce, or desertion—but the evidence now available shows that its "behavioral and psychological effects are probably much less uniform and much less uniformly handicapping than is widely assumed" (Herzog and Sudia, 1973, p. 214).

The most encompassing of all separations occurs when the child is moved from one home to another as in adoption. Although distressing effects are commoner among older children, adoptions do usually result in happy outcomes for children and parents (Mech, 1973).

Separations, then, are of many kinds. Events leading to and following separation, and not separation itself, determine the effects on social development. Short-range effects differ from long-range effects. And long-range effects seem to reveal stronger relationships with contemporaneous than with previous conditions.

THE EFFECTS OF EARLY EXPERIENCE ON LATER BEHAVIOR

Do early experiences have a lasting effect? Do early social experiences have a lasting effect on social behavior? Do early experiences have greater effects than later experiences? These are the questions behavioral scientists are still asking, although as they proceed they have learned to ask the questions more precisely. Thus, one day we may be able to state which specific experiences, occurring when and for how long, have this or that effect on this or that specific behavior.

Even at this stage of our knowledge we can discuss, if not state, what is likely to be supported by eventual research. Any experience a child has probably has an effect on subsequent behavior. The questions we then ask are: Is that effect lasting? Are there critical periods of development during which experiences have a markedly greater effect on subsequent behavior? Are events during the first years of life crucial? Crucial for what?

Although an affirmative answer to each of these questions seems reasonable, the evidence to date does not support such an answer (Clarke and Clarke, 1976). We must look at the data, not our intuitions. We can even entertain the possibility that later experiences have greater effects, once children are old enough to understand the meaning of an event. To be sure, the cause of any present behavior can be found when we search for it in past events, so great are the inventive and imaginative powers of our minds. Such success is a daily experience among clinicians faced by the task of explaining problem behavior. But to predict from any current event or experience or even general assessment of behavior, developmental stage, or personality to later behavior often meets with a measure of failure.

In the first place, every event or experience is modified in some way by the next event or experience. Then, we cannot predict the events that life itself will bring, even if environments do not change markedly. Thus, in any attempt to predict the later social behavior of children from early experiences, we are likely to fail unless we take these facts into account. Children do not live in a vacuum after the early experience. Events occur in their lives that cannot be predicted—a new baby is born, the family moves, the mother and father acquire new friends, the child encounters a nurturant teacher—and all these events can have an effect. Their behavior is remarkably malleable and their capacity to recover from traumatic events heartening indeed (Clarke and Clarke, 1976).

All experiences, in summary, have an effect, but the resulting behavior is always being affected by subsequent experiences. Every experience has an effect and so is of consequence, but as yet we have no evidence that the effect is crucial. Similarly, we have no evidence of a period critical for normal social development (Caldwell, 1962). These conclusions notwithstanding, it behooves us not only to avoid any possibly deleterious experience but above all to provide the best possible experience for every infant and child.

THE NEEDS OF YOUNG CHILDREN FOR OPTIMUM SOCIAL DEVELOPMENT

All investigators of child development do accept the importance of a close parent–child relationship, such as occurs in families however constituted, for the child's social development. The state of knowledge in this area, however, is not such that psychologists can now state categorically how children should be reared. But given the pluralistic nature of our democratic society, categorical statements may not even be desirable. Still, enough is known to set forth some general statements on how optimal social behavior can be fostered within the family.

The most encompassing is the need for human companionship. Given their motor inabilities, infants cannot survive except at human hands, and fortunately human hands bring human companionship. Infants and young children can by themselves in the absence of human companionship find much to amuse and interest them, but another human being provides more interesting and more responsive stimulation. Still, one cannot then conclude that the more stimulation the better, because beyond some minimum the nature of the stimulation has greater consequence than the amount.

By their very presence human companions evoke responses in children; even infants do not wait on others to initiate a social interchange. Additionally, people provide stimulation by their responses. A special kind of stimulation occurs when the response of the other person follows directly on the behavior of the child. Sometimes it is claimed that children thrive best when such contingent responses occur consistently, an unfortunate misreading of human events; people are not automatons, and besides, a body of firm evidence supports the special effectiveness of an intermittent "schedule" of responding (Skinner, 1953).

What does social stimulation provide young children beyond just relief from boredom? From social stimulation they learn that their own behavior—their cries, smiles, and vocalizations—produces a response in others. Even the infant, by evoking a response from another person, acquires a sense of control over the environment and over the behavior of others. From this interaction stems knowledge of how people behave reciprocally; the "dialogue" (Schaffer, Collis, and Parsons, 1977; Stern, 1974), basic to all human social behavior, begins. From these dialogues infants come to understand other persons' facial expressions, gestures, voices and their tones, and eventually the meaning of their words. From social stimulation verbal dialogues arise, beginning with a word or two and continuing by 2 or 3 years of age with the reporting of events, the expressing of feelings and wishes, and the asking of questions.

For optimum social development even very young children profit by experiences with persons other than the mother, and even the father. Salutary indeed are interactions with different people, people of different ages and sexes, people who play different roles in their lives, some who carry out routine caretaking, others who engage them in "conversations" or initiate playful overtures. Such interactions stimulate, satisfy, and teach. From them children discern the differences among people. From these varied interactions children also learn what to expect from others and what is expected of them. Thus they acquire the customs of their culture and in the process the concept of themselves as individuals.

All these needs can be stated at once more generally and more precisely. For optimum social development children require a benign environment in which their caretakers and other people pay attention to them and appreciate their positive achievements.

CURRENT APPLICATIONS OF KNOWLEDGE

Research findings on the development of the social behavior of young children have affected the practices not only of parents but of a wide range of people in social services and government. We shall begin with parental practices, continue with the practices of the medical, social work, legal, and teaching professions, and conclude with the effects of knowledge on social and governmental agencies and legislators.

As knowledge grows about the contribution children make to their own rearing, parents have come to recognize and appreciate the special individual characteristics of each of their children. As they learn more about the psychologists' findings that even at birth the human infant is not a passive organism waiting to be socialized by them, they adjust their caretaking to the role of a participant in an interactive process rather than to that of lawgiver, of a teacher and guide rather than a commander and dictator. The research findings of the last 30 or so years have served also to relieve the mother of sole responsibility for the child's behavior (Chess, 1964). Not only is the behavior of an infant, as of any other person, always a product of genetic endowment, experience, and present setting, but in almost every child's life there are more persons than just the mother. It is no longer accepted that only a mutually satisfying one-to-one relationship between mother and infant ensures mental health, or, as has often been proposed, that the mother–infant interaction determines all later social interactions.

Such findings, and the change in advice to mothers, serve also to relieve the guilt of mothers who work outside the home. Women work for many reasons, not the least of which is economic necessity. But many mothers also on occasion freely leave the care of their young children to others as they continue their education or enrich their lives with other personal pursuits. These mothers justify such arrangements by the benefits to both themselves and their children. An army of baby-sitters perform parental duties, and cooperative and professional nursery schools care for little children part time as well as full time.

Practices of the medical profession have been altered in many ways to maintain contact between children and their parents, and thus to support and not disrupt the development of children's social behavior. For some 40 years hospitals have permitted parents to stay with their sick children by day and night. Furthermore, the desirability of fostering early acquaintance and adjustment between parents and their newborn infants finds expression in rooming-in practices. Thus, the newborn infant, at the choice of the parents, may spend part or all of the day in the mother's room instead of in the newborn nursery. Parental contacts are also permitted, and even encouraged, with premature infants in their special nursery.

Similar concerns for early interaction between child and parent may be seen in the increasing practice of "natural" childbirth and a renewed interest in home deliveries. Here fathers participate in the mothers' training, and both have the opportunity to come to know their infant from the moment of birth. Indeed it has been proposed that such early acquaintance has a salutary effect on the parents' subsequent behavior (Kennell, Jerauld, Wolfe, Chesler, Kreger, McAlpine, Steffa, and Klaus, 1974). Even though studies of lasting beneficial effects need further replication, early contact qualifies in any case as satisfying to the parents.

Pediatricians are also assuming a greater role as counselors of parents, now that they have relaxed their previous concern with formulas and feeding, and as their armamentarium of cures for the common childhood disorders increases. Their textbooks include chapters on normal social development and the psychological needs of children and parents (e.g., Vaughan and McKay, 1975), and in their daily practice they advise on the everyday concerns of parents as they meet the problems of their growing children.

The practices of caseworkers, lawyers, and judges have also been affected by advances in knowledge about the social development of children. The most obvious of these is the practice, begun in the 1940s and 1950s, of removing young children without families from institutions and placing them in foster families. Although the studies that led to this move (e.g., Goldfarb, 1945; Spitz, 1945, 1946) were "natural" studies without impeccable controls, nevertheless makers of social policy felt the possibility of damage was too great to await definitive studies.

For much the same reasons adoptable infants are now placed in adoptive homes as early as possible. Formerly, infants and children were reared in institutions and boarding homes until they gave clear evidence of normal physical and psychological development. Facts were accumulating, however, that most of these environments were not conducive to maximum development. We learned too of the limited ability of infant psychological tests to predict later intelligence (Bayley, 1949). Among social workers there also arose the sentiment that adoptive parents should be willing to assume the same risks of later normality that parents do in bearing a child. The younger the child at adoption, the less stress is imposed by a change in parental figures (Yarrow and Goodwin, 1973), and the greater is the opportunity for parents to participate in all stages of the child's development.

Social workers, lawyers, and the courts also strive to keep families intact. Custody in the case of separation and divorce is awarded those who can best meet the child's needs. Even when children are neglected or abused, removing them from their families is viewed as the last alternative, the first being the effort by courts and social agencies to provide psychological services to the parents. The family, however constituted, is socially and legally recognized as the single best environment to ensure the child's healthy social development.

The policies of federal and state governments have also made provisions for meeting the needs of children. The number of agencies, programs, and laws designed to promote the social development of children is so large as to defy enumeration. Outstanding among recently created agencies is the Office of Child Development with its Head Start and Parent–Child Centers programs. The National Institute of Child Health and Human Development, one of the National Institutes of Health, supports both intramural and extramural research on the social development of children. Congress has before it bills to establish a federal program of day care to ensure meeting the social (among other) needs of children while their parents work.

In this connection, we must herald the belated arrival of a new conception of the occupational requirements for caring for young children outside their homes. The Child Development Associate Consortium awards credentials to persons who demonstrate competence in working with young children in a child-development center. The first CDA credentials were awarded in 1975. Thus we now officially recognize that child care requires more trained skills than just baby-sitting.

Research findings about the development of social behavior have found their way into every level of teaching from high school to the university. Programs in the high schools of every state support courses in child care and parenting. During the 1976–1977 school year in North Carolina, for example, 80 counties offered advanced child development courses and 50 high schools maintained day-care centers under the Occupational Child Care Services Program. The social development of the young child is taught in colleges and schools of education. Seminars are conducted on the topic in universities. The research findings thus have provided a body of knowledge both interesting and instructive. The far-reaching effects on the future practices of the students as parents and professional workers must by any calculation be enormous.

Directives for the Future

We live under the comforting belief that our society cares deeply for its children and that we strive to the utmost to provide our children with the best in material, medical, educational, and psychological services. Yet the belief may be no more than an illusion, and current surveys are shattering the belief. In 1975 more than one in every six children under 18 was living in a single-parent, mostly female-headed home, a percentage almost double that in 1950. In 1974, 15.5% of American children were living in families whose ability to rear them was severely crippled by incomes below the government-defined poverty line. Of the 3.2 million children in families with incomes of less than $5,000, 60% lived in single-parent families. In 1974, there were 970,000 divorces or reported annulments involving 1.2 million children (*Toward a National Policy*, 1976).

Even though some of these figures may result in part from improved recording, we cannot accept them with any degree of complacency. We must believe that as a nation parents and social agencies are trying to do their best but that changes in the social and economic fabric of our lives demand an even greater commitment (Pifer, 1976). These changes include, among others, the increasing numbers of women working outside the home, the dissolution of families by divorce and their reconstitution by remarriage, the sheer numbers of people in our population, the dislocations caused by an altered economy, and the large number of families below the poverty level, to name only a few.

The family, old-fashioned as it may seem, constitutes the keystone to that renewed commitment. In every modern society, not only in the United States, the family survives as the single best environment for the rearing of children. This is true even in societies that also provide alternative group care for the children of working mothers (e.g., Sidel, 1972). Whatever measures support the family support the welfare of children, their health, intellectual progress, and social development.

With respect to the social behavior of the young child, the topic of this chapter, what directives to behavioral scientists and society in general can we suggest?

It is easy and routine for scientists to say we need more research, just as it is easy and routine for all social planners to say we need greater financial appropriations. Still, investment in research is an absolute necessity for any society and not a discretionary luxury (Kaplan, 1964). The first need is for basic research. Although the differences between basic and applied research break down on close examination, the claim for research divorced from practical application must be honored. Some scientists in any society in any period of time must be left free to pursue their own questions. The history of science has shown that the discovery of even apparently esoteric principles has so often resulted in the most encompassing advantages to man that basic research must be supported. On our topic, much much more needs to be learned about the genesis and course of social development. At the present time only 3.5% of all government-funded research in fiscal year 1975 had the "socioemotional" development of children as the primary focus, and only 3.0% focused on the family (Hertz and Mann, 1975). Are these areas of less importance than, for example, special education, which received more than twice as much support? More likely, the miniscule expenditures suggest the absence of guiding principles for conducting such research. Today, we still do not have scales for measuring desirable or even normal social behavior, a gap in knowledge that only basic research can supply.

The funding of research on more obvious problems, such as the causes and treatment of child abuse, the effects of long-term foster care, the rights of parents and children (Wald, 1976), needs no special plea. The discipline of child development in this country was founded to improve the health, rearing, and education of children (Sears, 1975); the need for research on social problems is as great today. To bridge the gap between the laboratory and the needs of children, graduate education, besides training students to contribute to knowledge, could well include seminars on the implications of research for policy, as well as encourage internships in relevant state and federal agencies. Developmental psychologists need also to find spokesmen among themselves who can accurately translate the research findings of their colleagues to the public.

Still more encompassing directives may be proposed for ensuring the optimum social development of children. Rearing a child should be accorded the status it deserves. Although no thoughtful developmentalist would now make categorical statements about how a child should be reared, surely every person will grant that no more important an activity exists. To bear a child does not automatically convey the knowledge, wisdom, and skill to rear that child. If children are our greatest natural resource, surely the rearers of those children must be recognized as the instruments of their greatness. Here we require no new legislation, no new research findings, only a change in society's awareness.

Similarly, society must change its cultural stereotypes of the roles of fathers. Research has shown how effective fathers can be as caretakers and has suggested their value for a child's social development. As a society we can begin to acknowledge that the care of infants and young children is not only natural and appropriate but also desirable masculine behavior. This directive can stand by itself and should not be viewed as just a response to the greater freedom of women (Pifer, 1976; Young and Willmott, 1973).

How shall men and women be helped to behave as effective rearers? We need some clearer statement of our goals and these depend on our values (Rheingold, 1973). Would courses in rearing be effective? More valuable may be the services of persons trained to assist parents, not so much by courses and general advice but by working intimately with each family to foster the infant's and young child's social development (Ainsworth, 1973).

A new profession, that of child-care specialist, would serve to elevate the status of rearing. The new specialization of Child Development Associate for day-care workers marks a step in that direction. Similarly we ought to eliminate the fairly recently coined term of *baby-sitter* from our vocabulary, together with its implication. Surely, infants and young children deserve more than baby-sitters. A proper commitment to the rearing of children would require that all who participate in the care of the young acquire training in how to ensure their optimal development.

Farther in the future, the portents for the optimal social development of children the world over are also favorable. Parents will have fewer children and their births will be spaced for the benefit of the children themselves. An appreciation of their precocious responsiveness to people, of their freely given trust and affection, will then force a more optimistic view of human nature.

REFERENCES

Ainsworth, M. D. S. The development of infant–mother attachment. In ⌐ M. Caldwell and H. N. Ricciuti (Eds.), *Review of child development research*. Vol. 3. *Child development and social policy*. Chicago: University of Chicago Press, 1973.

Bayley, N. Consistency and variability in the growth of intelligence from birth to eighteen years. *Journal of Genetic Psychology*, 1949, 75, 165–196.

Bell, R. Q. A reinterpretation of the direction of effects in studies of socialization. *Psychological Review*, 1968, 75, 81–95.

Bowlby, J. The nature of the child's tie to his mother. *International Journal of I ycho-Analysis*, 1958, 39, 350–373.

Bowlby, J. *Attachment and loss*. Vol. 1, *Attachment*. London: Hogarth Press, 1969.

Bowlby, J. *Attachment and loss*. Vol. 2, *Separation anxiety and anger*. New York: Basic Books, 1973.

Brazelton, T. B. *Infants and mothers: Differences in development*. New York: Delacorte Press, 1969.

Brazelton, T. B. *Toddlers and parents: A declaration of independence*. New York: Delacorte Press, 1974.

Caldwell, B. M. The usefulness of the critical period hypothesis in the study of filiative behavior. *Merrill-Palmer Quarterly*, 1962, 8, 229–242.

Chess, S. Editorial: Mal de mère. *American Journal of Orthopsychiatry*, 1964, 34, 613–614.

Clarke, A. M., and Clarke, A. D. B. (Eds.). *Early experience: Myth and evidence*. London: Open Books, 1976.

Collis, G. M., and Schaffer, H. R. Synchronization of visual attention in mother–infant pairs. *Journal of Child Psychology and Psychiatry*, 1975, 16, 315–320.

Corter, C. M., Rheingold, H. L., and Eckerman, C. O. Toys delay the infant's following of his mother. *Developmental Psychology*, 1972, 6, 138–145.

Eckerman, C. O., Whatley, J. L., and Kutz, S. L. Growth of social play with peers during the second year of life. *Developmental Psychology*, 1975, 11, 42–49.

Farran, D. C., and Ramey, C. T. Infant daycare and attachment behaviors toward mothers and teachers. *Child Development*, 1977, 48, 1112–1116.

Gesell, A., and Ilg, F. L. *The child from five to ten*. New York: Harper, 1946.

Goldfarb, W. Psychological privation in infancy and subsequent adjustment. *American Journal of Orthopsychiatry*, 1945, 15, 247–255.

Hay, D. F. Following their companions as a form of exploration for human infants. *Child Development*, 1977, 48, 1624–1632.

Hertz, T. W., and Mann, A. J. *Toward interagency coordination: FY '75 federal research and development activities pertaining to early childhood* (5th annual rep.). Washington, D.C.: Social Research Group, George Washington University, 1975.

Herzog, E., and Sudia, C. E. Children in fatherless families. In B. M. Caldwell and H. N. Ricciuti (Eds.), *Review of child development research*. Vol. 3. *Child development and social policy*. Chicago: University of Chicago Press, 1973.

Hoffman, L. W. Effects of maternal employment on the child—a review of the research. *Developmental Psychology*, 1974, *10*, 204–228.

Kaplan, A. *The conduct of inquiry: Methodology for behavioral science.* Scranton, Pennsylvania: Chandler, 1964.

Kennell, J. H., Jerauld, R., Wolfe, H., Chesler, D., Kreger, N. C., McAlpine, W., Steffa, M., and Klaus, M. H. Maternal behavior one year after early and extended post-partum contact. *Developmental Medicine and Child Neurology*, 1974, *16*, 172–179.

Kessen, W., Haith, M. M., and Salapatek, P. H. Human infancy: A bibliography and guide. In P. H. Mussen (Ed.), *Carmichael's manual of child psychology* (3rd ed.). Vol. 1. New York: Wiley, 1970.

Lamb, M. E. Fathers: Forgotten contributors to child development. *Human Development*, 1975, *18*, 245–266.

Laroche, J.-L., and Desbiolles, M. Stabilité de la différenciation mère-étranger chez le jeune enfant. *Enfance*, 1976, *29*, 63–75.

Leung, E. H. L., and Rheingold, H. L. *The development of pointing as social communication.* Paper presented at the biennial meeting of the Society for Research in Child Development, New Orleans, March 1977.

Lewis, M., Young, G., Brooks, J., and Michalson, L. The beginning of friendship. In M. Lewis and L. A. Rosenblum (Eds.), *The origins of behavior.* Vol. 4. *Friendship and peer relations.* New York: Wiley, 1975.

Mech, E. V. Adoption: A policy perspective. In B. M. Caldwell and H. N. Ricciuti (Eds.), *Review of child development research.* Vol. 3. *Child development and social policy.* Chicago: University of Chicago Press, 1973.

Parke, R. D., and O'Leary, S. E. Family interaction in the newborn period: Some findings, some observations, and some unresolved issues. In K. F. Riegel and J. A. Meacham (Eds.), *The developing individual in a changing world.* Vol. 2. *Social and environmental issues.* The Hague: Mouton, 1976.

Pifer, A. Women working: Toward a new society. Carnegie Corporation of New York Annual Report, 1976.

Rheingold, H. L. The development of social behavior in the human infant. In H. W. Stevenson (Ed.), Concept of development. *Monographs of the Society for Research in Child Development*, 1966, *31*(5, Serial No. 107).

Rheingold, H. L. The social and socializing infant. In D. A. Goslin (Ed.), *Handbook of socialization theory and research.* Chicago: Rand McNally, 1969.

Rheingold, H. L. To rear a child. *American Psychologist*, 1973, *28*, 42–46.

Rheingold, H. L., and Eckerman, C. O. The infant separates himself from his mother. *Science*, 1970, *168*, 78–83.

Rheingold, H. L., and Eckerman, C. O. Fear of the stranger: A critical examination. In H. W. Reese (Ed.), *Advances in child development and behavior.* Vol. 8. New York: Academic Press, 1973.

Rheingold, H. L., Hay, D. F., and West, M. J. Sharing in the second year of life. *Child Development*, 1976, *47*, 1148–1158.

Samuels, H. R. *The role of the older sibling in the infant's social environment.* Paper presented at the biennial meeting of the Society for Research in Child Development, New Orleans, March 1977.

Schaffer, H. R., and Emerson, P. E. The development of social attachments in infancy. *Monographs of the Society for Research in Child Development*, 1964, *29*(3, Serial No. 94).

Schaffer, H. R., Collis, G. M., and Parsons, G. Vocal interchange and visual regard in verbal and pre-verbal children. In H. R. Schaffer (Ed.), *Studies in mother–infant interaction.* London: Academic Press, 1977.

Sears, R. R. Your ancients revisited: A history of child development. In E. M. Hetherington (Ed.), *Review of child development research.* Vol. 5. Chicago: University of Chicago Press, 1975.

Sidel, R. *Women and child care in China.* New York: Hill & Wang, 1972.

Skinner, B. F. *Science and human behavior.* New York: Macmillan, 1953.

Spitz, R. A. Hospitalism: An inquiry into the genesis of psychiatric conditions in early childhood. *Psychoanalytic Study of the Child,* 1945, *1,* 53–74.

Spitz, R. A. Anaclitic depression: An inquiry into the genesis of psychiatric conditions in early childhood. *Psychoanalytic Study of the Child,* 1946, *2,* 313–342.

Stendler, C. B. Sixty years of child training practices. *Journal of Pediatrics,* 1950, *36,* 122–134.

Stern, D. N. Mother and infant at play: The dyadic interaction involving facial, vocal, and gaze behaviors. In M. Lewis and L. A. Rosenblum (Eds.), *The origins of behavior.* Vol. 1, *The effect of the infant on its caregiver.* New York: Wiley, 1974.

Stolz, L. M. Effects of maternal employment on children: Evidence from research. *Child Development,* 1960, *31,* 749–782.

Thomas, A., Chess, S., Birch, H. G., Hertzig, M. E., and Korn, S. *Behavioral individuality in early childhood.* New York: New York University Press, 1963.

Toward a national policy for children and families. Washington, D.C.: National Academy of Sciences, 1976.

U.S. Bureau of the Census. Daytime care of children: October 1974 and February 1975. In *Current population reports* (Series P-20, No. 298). Washington, D.C.: U.S. Government Printing Office, 1976.

Vaughan, V. C., III, and McKay, R. J. (Eds.). *Nelson textbook of pediatrics* (10th ed.). Philadelphia: Saunders, 1975.

Wald, M. S. Legal policies affecting children: A lawyer's request for aid. *Child Development,* 1976, *47,* 1–5.

Wolfenstein, M. Trends in infant care. *American Journal of Orthopsychiatry,* 1953, *23,* 120–130.

Yarrow, L. J., and Goodwin, M. S. The immediate impact of separation: Reactions of infants to a change in mother figures. In L. J. Stone, H. T. Smith, and L. B. Murphy (Eds.), *The competent infant.* New York: Basic Books, 1973.

Young, M., and Willmott, P. *The symmetrical family.* New York: Pantheon Books, 1973.

Memory Strategies in Learning: Training Children to Study Strategically

ANN L. BROWN AND JOSEPH C. CAMPIONE

INTRODUCTION

The aim in this volume is to present a series of case studies to illustrate how the accumulation of basic knowledge in psychology has led to information of applied value; the particular charge of this chapter is to consider developmental memory research in this light. Traditionally there has been a division between basic and applied developmental research, and the majority of research reviewed and described in this chapter would be regarded as basic since it is laboratory inspired and conducted. The problem of practical application is more difficult for the basic researcher as his studies are rarely initiated to answer specific applied questions. Nonetheless, while the possibility of practical application is of more central interest for the applied researcher, the topic cannot and should not be avoided by those concerned with basic research.

The task is made somewhat easier in the case of the development of memory strategies as several of the leading proponents in the field have been continually motivated by the combined purposes of addressing theoretical problems and, at the same time, applying information of practical significance directly in the form of training techniques to en-

ANN L. BROWN and JOSEPH C. CAMPIONE • Center for the Study of Reading, University of Illinois, Urbana, Illinois. The preparation of this chapter was supported by grants HD06864 and HD05951 and by a Research Career Development Award HD00111 from the National Institutes of Child Health and Human Development.

hance performance. Classroom applications have been discussed and attempts to design curricula that embody the successful features of basic training studies are already under way in several laboratories (e.g., Ross and Ross, 1972). Thus, the ties between the laboratory of the basic researcher and the practical needs of the classroom teacher are less nebulous than has traditionally been the link between developmental psychology as a science and education practice as a problem of cognitive engineering.

In this chapter, we will attempt to illustrate how basic research can inform educational practice and vice versa. To do this we will progress chronologically, giving first a brief encapsulation of the history of basic research in the area of memory development. So that the complexities of such procedures can be appreciated, we will next examine in more detail a series of case studies that illustrate the progress and problems of a few prototypical research programs. This will be followed by a description of the progress, problems, and practical significance of attempts to devise effective training techniques aimed at overcoming the inadequacies of the immature learner. Finally, we will attempt to describe some practical steps for training in the laboratory and in the classroom, given the current state of our basic knowledge concerning the young child as a memorizer.

We have limited our attention to a certain class of situations, those that deal with deliberate attempts to learn or remember, although we realize that much of what one knows is not the result of deliberate attempts to retain information. The child's knowledge of the world around him, of the people, places, and things that occupy his everyday world, is the more or less automatic product of this continuous interaction with a meaningful environment. This will not be a concern in this chapter. Here we will concentrate exclusively on the development of deliberate actions to facilitate the retention of information, actions, or skills we must master if we are to survive in schools. The natural development, susceptibility to training, and potential application of these skills to study situations will be the central concern.

We should stress that we make no distinction between learning and memory. Obviously, we measure what is learned by how much is remembered. Additionally, we do not believe that the knowledge we have is limited to a strict domain labeled "how to remember." Deliberate remembering is just one example of intelligent planning, and many of the difficulties that underlie the young child's problems with remembering are also behind his general deficiencies as an active problem solver on school-related tasks. Memory skills are specialized problem-solving activities tailored to the purpose of reconstructing past events; they are not different in kind from problem-solving skills in general.

We will concentrate our attention on experimental work with slow-learning children. Children with marginal academic skills, which render them at risk for special education, are found to experience particular problems in two main areas: strategic planning in school problem-solving tasks (including deliberate remembering) and reading effectively. Our interest in developing training routines to overcome some of these deficiencies stems from our belief that remediation aimed at children with marginal skills can be the most fruitful in terms of obtaining worthwhile educational improvements. It also reflects our belief that average children acquire many of the skills we will consider without explicit training; repeated contact with a variety of tasks in school, all requiring the same basic strategies, is probably sufficient to inculcate at least the very simple strategies we will describe. Slow-learning children, however, need direct and explicit training before they will acquire the skills; without intervention they may never acquire them (Brown, 1978; Campione and Brown, 1977).

HISTORY OF BASIC DEVELOPMENTAL RESEARCH IN MEMORY

Since the inception of experimental child psychology as a scientific discipline with some degree of external recognition and internal cohesion, a great deal of research effort has been directed to the problem of learning and memory in children. Thus, any history of that research must be only a very superficial guide to progress in the field. Secondary sources are available to elaborate on this brief overview and the reader is referred to a series of recent chapters by Flavell (1970), Brown (1975, 1978), and Hagen, Jongeward, and Kail (1975). Here we will give only an indication of the major trends, the motivations behind each trend, and the current state of the art.

CAPACITY DIFFERENCES. Although children's memory was a topic of interest even for the very early experimentalists (Binet and Henri, 1894; Binet, 1904; Galton, 1887; Hunter, 1917), concentrated attention on this topic did not become part of the mainstream of psychological research until the late 1950s and early 1960s. The majority of these early studies on the development of memory can be crudely categorized as demonstration studies of "capacity" differences, i.e., the older we get, the greater memory capacity we have. It was readily shown that on a variety of tasks, older children remembered more than younger children, and slow learners had more difficulty remembering than did those of average ability, hardly a surprising result. The predominant explanation was simply that immature learners have a limited memory capacity and as they mature this capacity increases, allowing them to retain more. The underlying metaphor is clearly a container metaphor; little people have little storage boxes or jars in the head but bigger people have more room. Any demonstration of inferior performance on the part of either young or retarded children, and such demonstrations were readily obtainable, "proved" this point.

Needless to say, the problem turned out to be somewhat more complex, and it did not take long for researchers to realize that certain reservations must be added. For example, the nature of the material that would be placed in the memory container was important. If the material was interesting to the child, or reinforced his preexisting beliefs, it was retained much better. Even very young children have excellent memories for certain categories of information—for example, real-world environments, location of objects, games like concentration, nursery rhymes, familiar songs, and Sesame Street chants (Brown, 1975). The anecdotal accounts of parents concerning the longevity of toddlers' memory for familiar people, places, and things appear to be factual (Huttenlocher, 1974). In addition, memory differences across levels of maturity could not simply be accounted for by differences in the size of the memory container, for if all that is required is recognition of past events or familiar objects, young children's memory is extremely efficient, possibly not less efficient than that of adults (Brown, 1975). Even young babies show excellent recognition of pictures (Cohen and Gelber, 1975). Further, if recourse to "capacity" differences were no longer suitable, the theoretical game would become one of trying to account for why developmental differences were obtained when they were. Given our interest here in application of basic research, the rejection of a capacity notion represents an important step; for if age- and intelligence-related differences are due to differing amounts of storage space available, it is not at all clear how one can attempt to remediate that difference.

So much for a simple capacity notion, and therefore the utility of simple demonstration studies. We knew that children remembered less well than adults, except when they remembered as much or more. The question became, when and under what conditions do children perform poorly, rather than, do they perform in general less well than adults.

MNEMONIC STRATEGIES. The mainstream of research during the 1960s and early 1970s was dominated by attempts to classify the common features of situations where the developmentally young routinely performed very poorly compared to adults. Situations meeting these criteria required that the child actively instigate a deliberate attempt to memorize, and usually demanded verbatim recall of impersonal material, often lists of items out of context. In order to perform efficiently on such tasks the memorizer must introduce a mnemonic strategy of some kind; for example, he might say the items over and over (rehearse them); he might elaborate the material so that it fits into a meaningful context (e.g., make up a story to help associate the items); or he might look for redundancies, repeated elements, or categories of information to reduce the memory load. Remembering there were four animals in a list of words will help retrieve the names of the animals; noting the repetition in the sequence 3 4 9 3 4 9 will reduce the load by half; noting that 1 4 9 2 1 7 7 6 1 9 4 1 is not simply a list of 12 arbitrarily chosen numbers but rather three very well-known historical dates will make the list easily retainable. All these strategies help the deliberate memorizer make more efficient use of a limited ability for verbatim recall.

During the late 1960s and early 1970s, developmental psychologists focused on the development of strategies of deliberate remembering. The simplest statement summarizing our state of knowledge was one made by Flavell (1970), that if a mnemonic strategy is required for efficient performance on a task, developmental differences will be obtained. Brown (1975) added the corollary that when the need for such strategies is minimal, the task will be relatively insensitive to developmental trends. Reviews of the literature have amply documented that the deliberate control of what to remember and what to forget, together with the strategic use of various tactics to aid these processes, is inadequate in the developmentally young. There seems a general consensus that the degree to which some deliberate mnemonic strategy is required will determine the extent to which developmentally related differences in performance will occur. As the child matures, he gradually acquires a basic repertoire of these skills, which emerge first as isolated task-dependent actions but gradually evolve into flexible, generalizable skills (Brown, 1975, 1978; Meacham, 1977; Smirnov and Zinchenko, 1969). With extensive use, strategic intervention may take on many of the characteristics of automatic and unconscious processing and only intensive introspective questioning can reveal the operations of the strategic device even to the operator. The use of strategies becomes second nature to the efficient problem solver.

Under instructions to remember, the mature memorizer employs a variety of strategies that are not available to the developmentally less mature individual. These strategies form a hierarchy from simple processes like labeling (naming each item once) and rote rehearsal (repeating items over and over) to elaborate attempts to extract or impose meaning and organization on the to-be-remembered material. For example, if the experimental task is to associate the words *fish* and *telephone*, i.e., be able to say "telephone" when the experimenter says "fish," older and brighter subjects may try to make up a sentence linking the two words, e.g., "The *fish* is talking on the *telephone*." Alternatively, the memorizer may form a mental image of a fish talking on a telephone. Both of these techniques have been shown to result in dramatic increases in subsequent memory for the associated pairs. Even in learning pairs of nonsense syllables, which were designed to allow the study of memory uncontaminated by meaning, subjects try to impose meaning. For example, in learning the pair "ril" and "tov," the subject might transform the syllables into words and then form a sentence such as "That's a ril (real) tov (tough) pair." When presented with "ril," he recalls the sentence, changes "tough" back to "tov," and responds. Again, such techniques are exceedingly effective aids to memory. Such techniques are commonly reported by students attempting to learn a foreign language vocabulary list. While many more examples could be given, the point is that the outstanding feature of a mature memorizer is the amazing array of complex strategies and transformations (for another example—change the 12 digits 1 4 9 2 1 7 7 6 1 9 4 1 into the three dates 1492, 1776, 1941) he will bring to even the simplest laboratory task (Reitman, 1970). As young children are not particularly adept at employing these operations, the extent or magnitude of developmental differences seems to be determined by the degree to which increasingly complex strategic skills can be applied.

TRAINING STUDIES. The next major interest to influence the field was a focus on training studies. This interest was generated for both basic and applied reasons but originally the impetus came from the importance of the outcome of such studies for developmental theory. Stated simply, the distinction was between what children "do do" when left to their own devices and what they "can do" when given appropriate instructions. If training children to use a mnemonic strategy results in enhanced performance, we can conclude that a part of the difference between their original (prior to training) level of performance and that of adults is due not to simple capacity differences but rather to children's failure to employ the strategy spontaneously. Such an outcome is of considerable theoretical significance and of even more importance to those interested in application. If effective memory depends in part upon the use of some simple strategies, and if young children can be taught to use them, the implications for instruction are obvious.

Although immature learners display a strategic deficit in a wide variety of memorization situations, the early training studies show that these deficiencies readily respond to training. The problem appears to be due to certain characteristic deficiencies in what the child does spontaneously rather than to what he can do if prompted. With even quite limited training programs immature learners can be induced to attempt a variety of deliberate strategies. As it seems that most of the simple strategies are easily inculcated, the educational potential is demonstrated. Thus, while the early research and theorizing centered on the role of capacity limitation, more recent work has emphasized the role of strategic processes. Further, while it is not clear how capacity limitations are to be remediated (stretch the memory boxes in the child's head?), it is readily apparent how to overcome failures to employ strategies—tell the children what to do. We can only be encouraged by the success of these initial attempts and regard them as the first step in the construction of training programs. At this time, we would like to discuss the evaluation of training programs in general to provide a context for the rest of the chapter.

To determine the degree of success of any training program, it must be evaluated against three basic criteria of effectiveness: (1) performance must improve as the result of training, both in terms of accuracy and in terms of the activities (strategies) used to effect this accuracy; (2) the effects of this training must be durable; it is obviously desirable to show that what has been trained can be detected after a reasonable time period has elapsed; (3) training must result in generalization to a class of similar situations where the trained activity would be appropriate, for without evidence of breadth of transfer, the practical utility of any training is doubtful. (*re om ued*)

Many of the early studies were successful in demonstrating that training effectively improved performance; however, considerably more difficulty was experienced when criteria 2 and 3 were used to evaluate the success of intervention. Although relatively brief instruction would lead to temporarily improved performance, the less experienced memorizer showed a marked tendency to abandon a trained strategy when not explicitly instructed to continue in its use. Several recent studies have shown that more extended training can result in durability of a trained behavior over a period of months and even years. But the tendency to maintain a trained behavior does appear to be related to developmental level. Very young or retarded individuals are more likely to abandon the strategy than are slightly more sophisticated trainees (Brown, 1978).

The criterion of success that presents the most problems is generalization, or transfer to appropriate new situations. Although there is some controversy over what constitutes a suitable transfer task (Belmont and Butterfield, 1977; Brown, 1978) there is general agreement that evidence for flexible generalization to new situations has been sadly lacking. This inflexibility in the use of trained skills in new situations is particularly problematic when the trainee is a retarded child. Both American and Soviet psychologists, not to mention parents and teachers, have repeatedly observed the difficulty mildly retarded children experience with generalization. Indeed it has been suggested that one of the major problems with slow-learning children is that they tend to use new information only in the specific situation in which it was acquired.

Successfully training the child to use a simple skill in one specified situation seems to be well within our competence as instructors; getting the child to use the information appropriately in other settings appears to be the major hurdle.

To encapsulate the results to date of training studies aimed at inculcating rudimentary mnemonic strategies, it would seem fair to say that young, inefficient, and slow-learning children do not tend to use a variety of simple memory strategies spontaneously. However, they can be instructed to use strategies quite easily, and their performance improves. This improvement can be relatively durable on the specific task used for training. Flexible use of the skills in new situations is rarely found. Given these findings, the next question concerned why the immature did not use the skills in the first place, or failed to use them intelligently once shown how. This led to an interest in the child's knowledge and control of himself as a memorizer, the currently popular area of metamemory research.

KNOWLEDGE ABOUT MEMORY STRATEGIES: METAMEMORY. Metamemory refers to the knowledge and beliefs one has concerning the activities of remembering and oneself as a memorizer. While the adult appears to know a considerable amount about his ability to study and acquire new information, the young child, in contrast, seems remarkably uninformed about his own strengths and weaknesses as a learner. In order to concoct a realistic plan for remembering, the memorizer must be capable of estimating his own limitations and of realizing the need for some deliberate plan in those situations where his memory capacity will be exceeded. The immature learner has difficulty with such requirements for he is generally not aware of his limitations in deliberate memorization tasks. Over and above the obvious problem of not knowing how to memorize efficiently, the young child does not seem to realize that he needs to memorize. He appears oblivious to the limitations of his memory and unaware that he can make more efficient use of this limited capacity by strategic intervention (Brown, 1978; Flavell and Wellman, 1977). A simple concrete example of this state of ignorance is that children in the early grade school years have difficulty estimating how many items they will be able to recall from a long list. They typically overestimate and predict that they can remember all of the presented items, even when they can only actually recall 30% of the items. Examples of underestimation are extremely rare and the incidence of realistic estimation increases dramatically between kindergarten and fifth grade. If the young child is not aware of his own limitations it is scarcely surprising that he fails to initiate a plan to remedy his shortcomings. Flavell and Wellman (1977) have shown that the young child is not aware of many aspects of himself as a memorizer and fails to appreciate the utility of strategies to help make remembering an easier task.

Such a state of ignorance concerning strategy usage should not seem surprising given the usual experiences of the preschool child. Prior to the school years, the child has existed without a pressing need to employ deliberate strategies of remembering, and seldom, if ever, is required to reproduce exact information or to rote learn or study. He has managed to acquire a language; he can comprehend an impressive set of conceptual relations; he can recognize familiar places and people and reconstruct the essential gist of meaningful events without the need to employ strategies. It is only when he encounters material that is not inherently meaningful or must be reproduced exactly that deliberate memorial skills become absolutely necessary. It takes time for him to recognize that these, in some sense artificial, situations exist and demand that he respond with something more than has been required in the past. He must, in fact, recognize that because of the nature of the material and the need for exact reproduction, he must apply a deliberate strategy or he will fail to retain the material. When repeatedly faced with these situations, as he is in school, the child gradually comes to know more and more about how to remember and thereby achieves insight into himself as a memorizer.

SUMMARY. In the previous section we have given a brief history of the way developmental psychologists have set about studying memory strategies. We know a considerable amount about the development of rudimentary memorization skills. Young and slow-learning children tend not to use them spontaneously or even to be fully aware that deliberate intervention on their part is a prerequisite for efficient performance. Training studies have shown that specific strategies can be inculcated quite readily but it is unlikely that the child will think to use a trained skill in appropriate new situations. As with the original passive behavior, which necessitated training in the first place, this transfer failure is thought to stem from a lack of knowledge concerning oneself as a memorizer. Before proceeding to an examination of the question of what to train we will give two detailed examples of training programs, which illustrate the general points made in this overview. In the first case study we will consider rehearsal as a strategy of rote recall; in the second we will consider the problems inherent in attempts to inculcate metamemorial awareness or general skills.

REHEARSAL: A CASE STUDY OF A MNEMONIC SKILL

In its most general sense, rehearsal refers to a side set of activities that can be used to keep information "alive" for a period of time. The most frequent form of rehearsal involves continued repetition (usually silently) of the material to be remembered. This activity is useful in at least two ways. First, if the amount of information to be remembered is relatively small, it can simply be kept "alive" from its initial presentation until it is needed. The classic example of this use of rehearsal is the constant repetition of a telephone number from the time it is first located in a telephone book until it is actually dialed. Alternatively, if the amount of information is too great to allow the memorizer to keep it all alive simultaneously, rehearsing portions of the material together can facilitate the formation of associations between items, thus enhancing immediate or delayed recall. For example, in attempting to remember a set of 16 items, rehearsing sets of, say, 4 items together results in much better recall than not rehearsing, even though not all of the items can be kept alive until the time when recall is required. Repeating the main points of a lesson prior to proceeding to the next section involves similar principles.

We have chosen rehearsal as one of our examples for a number of reasons. The main one is that rehearsal has been subjected to extremely close empirical and theoretical scrutiny. As a result, we know a great deal about the development of rehearsal strategies. We have also learned that this apparently simple skill turns out to be much more complex, and its usages more varied and sophisticated, than originally anticipated. As a result, a consideration of rehearsal research highlights the amount of analysis and ingenuity needed to devise an effective training program. Finally, the major findings involving rehearsal are also applicable to other mnemonic skills (Campione and Brown, 1977), and the statements made in this section can be assumed to be generalizable.

Training programs generally begin with a theoretical analysis of some specified task or set of tasks. The aim of this *task analysis* is to specify what the memorizer should do to maximize his or her performance. In the examples chosen here, one of the requirements identified as essential for effective retention is the use of a rehearsal strategy. Thus, if the target group, in our case slow-learning children, perform poorly on the task, it is at least possible that their recall level is low because they fail to rehearse properly, if at all. At this point in the research program, two questions must be asked. One is whether the task analysis seems accurate, i.e., whether rehearsal is necessary for efficient performance and whether mature memorizers actually do employ rehearsal strategies in the task. Assuming that the answer is positive, the second question concerns whether the target group does in fact fail to employ rehearsal. Assuming another affirmative answer, it then makes sense to embark upon a rehearsal training program.

The investigation of these questions requires the development of measures of rehearsal usage. While a number of measures have been employed, each of them has a number of associated problems. For example, observation of lip movements has been used to infer rehearsal activity; however, with older children and adults, rehearsal processes need not be accompanied by lip movements (one can rehearse silently), thereby precluding the usefulness of observing lip movements in developmental or comparative research. Another common measure of rehearsal has been the presence of a so-called primacy effect in a number of recall tasks. Consider a general case in which a number of to-be-remembered items are presented sequentially, and recall begins immediately after the presentation of the last item (i.e., there is no appreciable delay between the subject's seeing or hearing the items and his being asked to recall them). The typical finding with adults is that recall is best for the items from the beginning of the list (primacy items) and the items at the end of the list (recency items), and poorest for items in the middle. The recency effect is attributed simply to the fact that the delay between presentation of these items and their recall is sufficiently short that these items have not yet faded from the memory of even the most passive observer. In contrast, the primacy, or initial, items will have faded from memory unless some activity designed to maintain them has been carried out by the subject. A favorite theoretical candidate for this activity is rehearsal, and the appearance of a primacy effect has thus been taken as evidence for the presence of rehearsal processes. The problem here is that there are alternative theoretical accounts of the primacy effect which do not make recourse to rehearsal processes. Thus, primacy need not necessarily indicate rehearsal. This list of potential rehearsal indicators and their attendant problems could be continued, but we hope the point is clear.

In our view, the best solution to this problem is to resort to the use of converging operations, i.e., arrange an experimental situation in which there are a number of different potential indicators of rehearsal processes. Even if none of the measures is perfect, if all the indicators agree, we can be much more confident about any inferences drawn from the data. As an example, in some research from our own laboratory, as many as four indicators have been used and found to agree within one experiment (Brown, Campione, Bray, and Wilcox, 1973).

At this point, we will describe one research program that has emphasized the development of a training program. The task employed consists of having the subject see a series of items (consonants, digits, etc.) presented in succession in a series of windows, one item per window. After the last item has been displayed, a "probe item" is presented; this is simply a duplicate of one of the items the subject has just seen. His task is then to indicate the window in which that item had appeared. For example, if the series had been 6 1 2 4 5 3, and if the probe item were a 2, the subject should point to the third window from the left. In a number of experiments, Belmont and Butterfield (1969, 1971) have modified the task in one important way: They allow the subject to determine the rate at which the items are presented. Thus, the subject presses a button exposing the first item (which remains visible for 0.5 second) and can then wait as long as he or she wants before proceeding to the second item, etc. The pattern of pauses or delays following each item is then used as an additional index of rehearsal usage. For example, consider a six-item list. A likely pattern for a college student might be to proceed quickly until the fourth item had been exposed, then delay for a much longer time. Following items 5 and 6, only brief pauses would be observed, with the probe item being called for immediately. Such a pattern would be taken to indicate that the subject rehearsed the first four items together (i.e., 6124—6124—6124 over and over until well learned) and then very quickly viewed the last two calling immediately for the probe before forgetting the list. This strategy, termed a *cumulative rehearsal–fast finish* strategy, takes cognizance of the fact that the initial items must undergo rehearsal to be remembered, whereas the last items will still be alive in memory even if they are simply viewed without any accompanying activity, as long as the probe item is exposed quickly.

In this situation, the pause patterns shown by the subjects provide one source of evidence relevant to the possible use of rehearsal. Using this analytic procedure, Belmont and Butterfield (1969, 1971) have shown that college students invariably employ rehearsal strategies in this task, whereas retarded adolescents do not. The pause patterns of the retarded subjects are relatively flat and pauses after each item tend to be brief, indicating the lack of the type of active learning described for college students. The retarded subjects also perform more poorly than college students, and their performance is poorest on the primacy, or initially presented, items that they failed to overlearn. Thus, the overall pattern of their recall is nicely consistent with a rehearsal deficiency notion.

When retarded subjects are trained to rehearse, their pause patterns begin to look like those of college students, their overall recall accuracy increases, and the increase is most pronounced with the primacy items (Belmont and Butterfield, 1971). In the initial experiment in this series, the retarded subjects' accuracy increased considerably, showing the beneficial effects of training, but was still well below that of college students, leading to a further series of experiments (Butterfield, Wambold, and Belmont, 1973) aimed at refining the training techniques.

To modify the training procedure, a more detailed task analysis served as the starting point. We will go into considerable (possibly excruciating) detail here in order to make an important point: The development of an effective training or instructional routine requires attention to many details and can be much more complex than it may appear at first glance. The specific task involved a six-item series, and the strategy to be employed consisted of rehearsing the first three items as a set, and then quickly viewing the last three. The detailed task analysis is shown in Figure 1. Briefly, the subject first views each of the three initial items, then pauses and rehearses the set of items a number of times to prepare for future recall (steps 1 and 2). The second set of three items is then viewed (step 3), followed immediately by exposure of the probe item (step 4). This completes the study strategy. Once the probe is exposed, a retrieval plan must also be adopted, and the plan must conform to the study strategy. As indicated in step 5, the subject should first attempt to determine if the probe was contained in the second set of items, those which were viewed but not rehearsed. If it was, the subject responds (step 6); if it was not, the search continues to the set of rehearsed items to determine where the probe item occurred (step 7) before responding (step 8). What is crucial in the retrieval plan is the order of search. If the initial, rehearsed set of items is considered first, and if the probe item is not found there, the subject will be in trouble, as the second set of items (which were never rehearsed) will have faded from memory. The use of a passive viewing of the last three items is based on the assumption that the contents of memory will not have time to fade if the probe comes quickly enough. If, however, the subject himself imposes a long interval between seeing and being tested because he searches through the initial trio of items first, the main rationale for having used such a study strategy is violated.

In the first experiment reported by Butterfield *et al.* (1973), retarded adolescents were taught the "3–3" study strategy, and the result was a clear improvement in accuracy, from 36% correct to 65% correct. Even with this large increment, two points were of interest. First, performance was still well below that obtained with college students, and second, the relation between strategy use, as measured by pause patterns, and level of recall was not as strong as it might have been, suggesting the operation of some other factors. A likely candidate here appeared to be retrieval mechanisms. Training in the first experiment consisted of leading the subjects through steps 1–4 depicted in Figure 1. The implicit assumption was that steps 5–8 would be adopted spontaneously.

In the next experiments, steps 5–8 were trained explicitly, along with steps 1–4. As an example of the more detailed training, we take the following procedure used in their third experiment. In the first phase, the first step of the study strategy was taught. Each subject was trained to label each of three items and then to stop and repeat the set three times. They were then required to count to 10 before exposing the probe item and making their response. After six consecutively correct responses, they proceeded to the next phase. Here the second half of the study plan was taught, as subjects exposed three items quickly, called for the probe

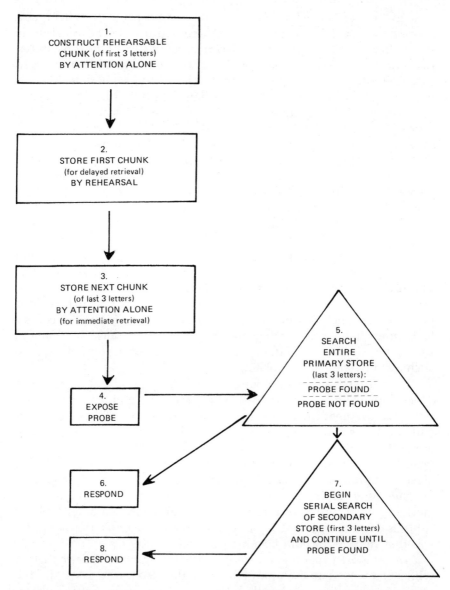

Figure 1. A task analysis of the six-item probed recall procedure (from Butterfield *et al.*, 1973).

item, and responded. Thus, the two study phases were trained separately. Following this, a series of six-item lists was presented in which the subjects were informed that the probe item would always be drawn from the second trio of items. After making their response, they were further required to repeat the rehearsed items in order. The point of this part of training was to explicitly teach the subjects to search the non-rehearsed set first. Finally, they were given a series of trials where the probe could come from any position, but the instructions to search the second set of items first were repeated. Following this training and one additional refinement, accuracy increased to over 80% correct. In summary, the "final performance of these subjects was 114 percent of that obtained from nonretarded adolescents on uninstructed 6-item lists, and 97 percent of that from nonretarded adolescents given active–passive learning instruction with 6-item lists" (Butterfield et al., 1973, p. 667).

The results of this program indicate clearly that dramatic improvements in memory performance can be brought about through detailed instruction. Elation over this success is tempered somewhat by a number of considerations. First, it is not clear how long-lasting the effects of training might be. At the longest retention interval tested, 1 week, performance was significantly lower than immediately following training, although it still remained above untrained levels. This is probably not a problem as long-lasting effects of rehearsal training have been obtained by Brown, Campione, and Murphy (1974). The trained subjects from an earlier experiment by Brown et al. (1973) were retested 6 months after the original training, and 80% of them continued to rehearse. The training afforded subjects in the original experiment was extensive, stretching over 12 days, and durable effects of training apparently can be expected if the amount of training is sufficiently great.

Somewhat more problematic, however, are questions concerning the generalized effects of training. That is, can any effects of training be detected on anything other than the specific task on which training occurred? Unless the answer is affirmative, the effects are sufficiently limited that they may not be of any instructional interest. While there has not been much relevant research to date, the indications are not promising. For example, the subjects in the Brown et al. research were given a generalization test after the 6-month retention test. The training and generalization tasks, while different, are similar in a number of ways. In the training task, the subjects were shown a series of four items, each from a different category, and were then cued with a category name and asked to recall the item from that category. They were specifically taught to rehearse the first three items together and then just to view the fourth one. The generalization task was the same as the task employed in the Belmont–Butterfield research just described. On this task, we could discern no effects due to training. No signs of rehearsal were obtained, and the trained subjects performed at exactly the same level as a control group given no training at all originally. Thus, while the subjects continued to rehearse 6 months after training as long as the task remained the same, the introduction of a different task eliminated the benefits of training.

In one important sense, the lack of convincing evidence for generalization is not too important, as the instructional routines were not designed to lead to such effects. Rather, the intent was to determine whether moderately retarded children could be trained to rehearse effectively at all. The answer to that question is clearly yes, and the potential viability of such programs clearly indicated.

Training Metamemory

As discussed in the previous section, careful training of memory strategies can result in dramatic improvements, and instructed retarded children can be trained to perform on a par with uninstructed college students. With practice, the effects of training are long-lasting. There is, however, little evidence for generalization, and two reasons for this unwelcome result can be proffered. First, as already suggested, the experiments and instructional routines were not designed to elicit generalization, and it remains an open question whether more effective training can be designed, a question that is currently being asked by a number of investigators.

A second possibility, and one that we personally favor, is that the kinds of strategies (such as rehearsal) that have been trained are too specific to particular tasks to be of general utility. We decided to direct some training efforts at more general determinants of performance (such as metamemory) rather than at specific skills or strategies. Instead of training only specific routines such as rehearsal, it seemed more profitable to direct training attempts at the development of knowledge about strategies in general. Procedurally, it is difficult to conceive of a method of teaching knowledge about strategy use to individuals who lack even the rudimentary strategies that form the basis of this knowledge. Yet, if we are interested in improving the child's general performance on a variety of similar tasks, we must consider both the specific gains from training (trained strategy use) and the general benefits (improved knowledge concerning memory tasks, leading to flexible strategy use).

To investigate the feasibility of this alternate approach, a series of training studies concerned with metamemorial knowledge were conducted with educable retarded children. These programs of research have been described in some detail elsewhere (Brown, 1978; Brown and Campione, 1977), and here we will describe one series that has resulted in some evidence showing generalized effects of training. In this work (Brown and Barclay, 1976; Barclay and Brown, 1976), we focused on a very simple general strategy, which could reasonably be supposed to have a wide range of applicability. Basically, we attempted to train a "stop-check-and-study" routine. The specific task used, one of assessing readiness to recall, was adapted from a prior study with nonretarded children conducted by Flavell, Friedrichs, and Hoyt (1970). We first determined each individual child's "memory span," here defined as the maximum number of items he could consistently recall without error when given as much study time as he wished. On each of a series of subsequent trials, he was given a list of pictures equal to 1½ times that span. He was then instructed to continue studying the items as long as desired until he was sure he could remember all of them perfectly, and then to signal the experimenter that he was ready.

Immature children performed very poorly on the initial pretesting phase of the study. When first exposed to the longer lists (1½ times their span), only 4% of an MA 6 sample and 12% of an MA 8 sample gave even one perfect recall, poor performance considering the fact that the children were allowed as much study time as they wanted. One reason why the developmentally young perform so poorly on this task could be that they do not tend to introduce strategies of deliberate memorization, such as rehearsal and anticipation, involving self-testing elements, which would alert them to their readiness for a test. If children do not use such self-testing devices, they can hardly be expected to monitor their own stage of learning.

For this reason we trained groups of children in the use of three strategies of remembering: anticipation and rehearsal, both of which involve self-testing elements; and labeling, which does not. The labeling condition essentially served as a control treatment. All were required to go through each list once, naming each picture. This labeling trial was followed by a series of three more trials on which the procedures differed between the groups. Those in the anticipation group were trained to anticipate the next picture by saying its name before looking at it. The rehearsal subjects were trained to rehearse the items in sets of three (cat, shoe, cup, cat, shoe, cup, etc.). Finally, the label group was told to go through the list three more times, naming each item. All groups were further encouraged to continue with the instructed activity until they were sure they could recall all items. Training was continued for 2 days.

Following training, four posttests were given, a prompted posttest (one day after training) on which individuals were instructed to continue the trained strategy, and three unprompted posttests given 1 day, approximately 2 weeks, and approximately 1 year later. The main results are shown in Figure 2, which gives the percent of correct recall averaged across many trials. The break in the curve between posttests 3 and 4 indicates that not all individuals were retested on the final posttest; however, 78% of the MA 6 and 90% of the MA 8 children were available

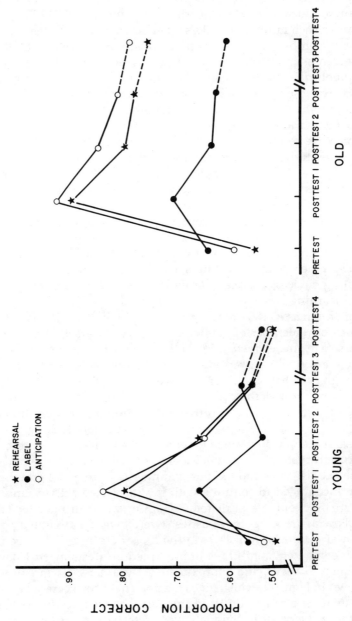

Figure 2. The proportion of items recalled as a function of mental age, training condition, and test phase (from Campione and Brown, 1977).

for retesting 1 year after the start of the study. As can be seen, both the younger and the older children in the anticipation and rehearsal groups perform significantly better on the prompted posttest (posttest 1) than on the pretest. Additionally, if we consider the anticipation and rehearsal groups, 72% of younger subjects recalled perfectly on at least one trial, compared with none on the pretest; the corresponding figures for the older subjects are 92% on posttest 1 compared with 8% on the pretest. Thus, training the useful self-testing strategies results in both enhanced performance (percent recall data) and improving monitoring (data on number of perfect recalls), compared with the control labeling group.

The MA 6 and MA 8 groups differed considerably on the last three (unprompted) posttests. For the younger group, performance on posttests 2, 3, and 4 was not significantly different from the pretraining level, whereas for the older group, performance on all posttests differed significantly from the pretraining level. Thus, as in previous studies concerned with direct training of a strategy, training facilitates performance, with the effect being somewhat durable for the older children but transitory for the younger ones.

The younger child's dependency on continual prompting was particularly well illustrated on the 1-year follow-up tests, which consisted of 4 days of testing. On the 2 initial days, the children were given unprompted posttests identical to the previous unprompted tests, and it is these data that are included in Figure 2. On the third day, the experimenter reverted to the prompting procedure, demonstrating and reminding the child of his trained strategy and urging its continued use. The fourth day of the 1-year follow-up was a further unprompted posttest. These data are included in Table 1. Note that both the younger and the older children benefit from the prompting, although the effect is less dramatic

Table 1. Proportion Correct on Recall-Readiness Posttests[a]

| | | Posttests | | | | | | |
| | | Original data | | | 1-year follow-up | | | |
Group	Condition	Prompt	No prompt	No prompt	No prompt	No prompt	Prompt	No prompt
	Anticipation	.82	.62	.52	.50	.48	.81	.57
MA 6	Rehearsal	.77	.61	.49	.46	.50	.90	.63
	Label	.60	.56	.55	.46	.58	.78	.54
	Anticipation	.92	.84	.81	.80	.72	.95	.85
MA 8	Rehearsal	.89	.82	.81	.74	.73	.84	.83
	Label	.74	.65	.63	.60	.61	.67	.63

[a]From Brown (1978).

for the older children who were performing quite adequately without the prompts. Of main interest is the failure of the younger children to maintain their enhanced performance on the final nonprompted test. Without continual prompting, the younger children show little evidence of the effects of intensive training.

Given the poor performance of the younger group, we made no attempt to test these children for evidence of generalization. The older children looked more promising, however, so we decided to see whether they would show the benefits of the recall readiness training on quite a different task. Systematically studying material until it is judged to be well enough known to risk a test, is, of course, a very general strategy, as any student could attest. Therefore, we were hoping that even with very different materials, the children who had received extensive training would show some generalized benefits.

The transfer task selected was one that we believed to be more representative of the type of study activity required in the classroom. Most studying requires the student to extract the main ideas of prose passages and repeat the gist of the ideas in his own words. Our question was: Would training recall readiness on the simple rote-list learning task help children on the more typical school study activity? We reasoned that if we could find transfer under these conditions our training would really have practical utility; if we did not, we could always revert to less ambitious transfer tasks, those more like the training vehicle.

There were four groups of subjects, the older children who had been trained in three groups—anticipation, rehearsal, and labeling—and a new group of children matched for IQ, MA, and reading scores with the trained subjects and, in fact, selected from the same special education classrooms as the previously trained students. All students were reading at second to fourth grade level. The two successfully trained groups, anticipation and rehearsal, who had shown evidence of correctly estimating their readiness to recall were the groups from which we hoped to obtain transfer. The new students formed a control group that would enable us to compare our trained children to others who shared important characteristics (age, IQ, class placement, reading scores) with the experimental groups but had not received training. The fourth group, labeling, also served an important control function. They had been in as many sessions as our experimental groups and had interacted with the tester just as much, but they had not been trained in successful recall readiness and had not improved notably above pretraining levels.

All students received 6 days of testing. On each day they were given two short stories, which were of second grade reading difficulty. On each trial the students read a story through with the experimenter and received help with any words they did not know. They were then told to

Table 2. Recall-Readiness Generalization Test

Groups	Anticipation	Rehearsal	Label	New
Mean study time (sec)	103.7	105.6	57.6	62.4
Mean proportion of idea units recalled	.50	.49	.35	.37
Proportion showing some overt study activity	.67	.64	.40	.29

continue studying the story until they were sure that they could retell all the main events in their own words. During their study time the tester recorded any overt activity and the amount of time taken before the child indicated he was ready to test his memory. The major data of interest are given in Table 2. Both the amount of time spent studying and the number of idea units recalled were significantly greater in the two trained groups than in the two control groups. Those children who successfully maintained their trained ability to judge their recall readiness for a list of unrelated items appeared to show the benefits of this training on a prose learning task, nice evidence of successful generalization.

Because of the importance of these data we are currently replicating the main features of the experiment. One additional indication of successful transfer which we will consider more fully is our first crude classification of the observed external study behaviors. The proportions of children showing any evidence (even once on 12 stories) of a few broad classes of activities relevant to studying are also shown in Table 2. Such activities included underlining, circling key words, writing notes, rereading, self-testing, lip movements, etc. Even though evidence for strategic study activities was generally scarce, the difference between the trained and untrained groups was again apparent, with two-thirds of the trained children showing some relevant activity compared with one-third of the untrained subjects.

PRACTICAL IMPLICATIONS OF TRAINING STUDIES

Although we have concentrated on a few research programs, the information obtained from them is fairly representative of our current knowledge. Now the question is what, if anything, can be learned from these basic research programs that could have any implications in terms of guiding educational practices?

First let us consider the successes achieved so far by training studies. We know a considerable amount about how to train basic memory strategies. Some improvement in performance tends to follow even quite cursory intervention. When detailed task analyses of the type introduced by Butterfield, Wambold, and Belmont are employed, one can effect dramatic improvement, such that retarded persons perform at least as well as untrained adults. These data are extremely important from both theoretical and practical perspectives. Theoretically, they demonstrate that one pervasive hypothesis of a developmental deficit, the smaller capacity mentioned earlier, cannot tell the full story. The performance of memorizers depends as much upon what they do as upon who they are. The practical effects are obvious. If, in some cases, training fails to bring about improvement, it is no longer sufficient to appeal to some fundamental capacity limitation of the child. Rather, attempts to refine the training technology would be indicated.

The same general task analysis approach has been applied effectively in other situations where the desired end product is improvement *on the training task*. Gold's (1972) work is an excellent case in point. Severely retarded institutionalized people can readily be trained to carry out complex assembly tasks if the job is broken into easily manageable subunits, an intelligent task decomposition achieved through detailed task analysis. In the area of vocational training, the chief goal of the training procedure is to achieve quick, errorless performance on the training task, for, armed with this skill, the hitherto unemployable individual is in a position to earn a living wage.

These results are more than just encouraging and indicate that well-worked-out instructional technologies can achieve dramatic results with retarded individuals (and young children). While we certainly do not want to argue that any individual can be taught to do anything, it is clear that retarded children can do much more than early theories, and indeed current opinion, would have us believe. To summarize, the results from a number of research programs indicate that if the aim of training is to inculcate the skills necessary to achieve excellent performance on any of a wide variety of tasks, the combination of a thorough task analysis and detailed training is quite likely to achieve the desired outcome.

While the point regarding task-specific training has been made, there is still one important factor that must be considered if we are interested in more academic skills. In educational settings, and particularly in special education programs, the aim is in some sense to effect changes in general intellectual functioning. Rather than regarding the goal of training as excellent performance on a specific isolated task, the desired end product is to effect a general improvement in understanding which would be reflected on a whole class of similar tasks—a much more demanding specification. This aim can again be defended theoretically and practically. Theoretically, one could argue that without evidence of broad transfer, training may have resulted in the mastery of a rote rule but may not have produced any real change or general advancement in the child's knowledge of the world (Kuhn, 1974). Demonstrating adult-like performance on a single task is sufficient evidence for those who are interested in proving that intellectual immaturity is not necessarily an impediment to efficiency on any one specific task. However, there are strong reasons to believe that there are limitations to the young thinker's ability to reason. If this is true, mere training on a rote response will not affect this ability until an appropriate level of cognitive maturity is reached. Intellectual growth may be accelerated, but training can achieve only a small increment (Inhelder, Sinclair, and Bovet, 1974). Within the memory-training field, advocates of this more conservative position look for generalization as the index of successful training. As we have seen, while the evidence for generalization following training of specific mnemonic strategies, such as rehearsal, is less than impressive, there is some positive evidence when more general skills are the subject of training.

To summarize somewhat, we would regard the general findings obtained to date as conducive of at least mild optimism. Both the efficacy of specific training and the possibility of obtaining generalized results have been demonstrated. While the evidence for generalization remains weak, it is also the case that little in the way of concerted effort has been expended in this area. The initial work was necessarily addressed to showing that training on a task could itself be effective. Better designed training procedures could lead to enhanced generalization, even of rote learning and memory strategies. Further, the results of our recall read-iness work seems to indicate that the likelihood of obtaining gener-alization may be increased if we more carefully select the skills that are the subject of our training attempts.

Following up on this latter point, we would like to argue that in order to justify future detailed task analyses, efficiency in the skill that is the subject of training should ideally be an end result in itself. There are two situations where this would be the case. The first is where mastery on the trained task is itself of great practical use, even in the absence of any generalization. An example of such a program would be Gold's assembly task training for severely retarded individuals. A second case where it would be worth the detailed task analysis approach is if the skill trained is by definition applicable to a great range of situations, for example, reading. Few would deny the practical utility of searching for a workable training program for reading, based on thoughtful and de-tailed task analyses. Reading is by definition a generalizable skill, a perfectly desirable end product of an intensive training program.

While it should be clear that we find real cause for optimism in the data from current training studies, we would like to conclude this chapter by indicating some of our biases about the directions future research in this area should take. We believe that it is time to rethink the types of skills we have attempted to train. How often does the mature memorizer rehearse? Probably not often. If children do not generalize a rehearsal strategy because they fail to see its utility, this could be a realistic appraisal of the enterprise. After all, they all tell us that they write down telephone numbers (Brown, 1978); one of the authors writes down telephone numbers.

An alternative strategy would be to train general, metamemory skills, which could have great generality across a variety of problem-solving situations, skills such as checking, planning, asking questions, self-testing, and monitoring. These skills are transsituational, i.e., they apply to many forms of problem-solving activity rather than being restricted to a certain limited task domain. Indeed, if one is interested in the ecological validity of the processes we select for study, the skills subsumed under the heading of metacognition (Brown, 1978) do appear to have recognizable counterparts in "real-world, everyday life" situations. Checking the results of an operation against certain criteria of effectiveness, economy, and common-sense reality is a metacognitive skill applicable whether the task under consideration is solving a math problem, memorizing a prose passage, following a recipe, or assembling a piece of furniture. Self-interrogation concerning the current state of one's own knowledge during problem solving is an essential skill in a wide variety of situations, those of the laboratory, the school, or everyday life.

Thus, the types of cognitive activities that we believe to be suitable for intensive intervention should have certain properties: (a) they should have transsituational applicability, (b) they should readily be seen by the child to be reasonable activities that work, (c) they should have some counterpart in real-life experiences, and (d) their component processes should be well understood so that effective training techniques can be devised. Our bias directs us to a subset of general metacognitive activities that we feel admirably fit the prescription—checking, monitoring, and reality testing, etc. This is, of course, still too ambitious and we would advocate the selection of a few basic skills for intensive study. The ones we have chosen can be subsumed under the general heading *self-interrogation*.

The eventual aim is to train the child to think dialectically, in the sense of the Socratic teaching method. In the Socratic method, the teacher constantly questions the students' basic assumptions and premises, plays the devil's advocate, and probes weak areas, using such techniques as invidious generalizations and counterexample (Anderson, 1977; Brown, 1978; Collins, 1977). The desired end product is that the student will come to perform the teacher's functions for himself via self-interrogation. Although the sophisticated skills described by Collins are obviously not directly applicable to young slow-learning children, the basic principles underlying the approach are. We have begun at the very simple level of teaching the child to self-interrogate when faced with a certain class of problems (instructions, math problems, a laboratory task, etc.). The type of self-interrogation that we think might work is to provide the child with a routine set of questions to ask himself before proceeding, e.g.: (a) Stop and think! (b) Do I know what to do (i.e., understand the instructions, both explicit and implicit)? (c) Is there anything more I need to know before I can begin? (d) Is there anything I already know that will help me (i.e., is this problem in any way like one I have done before)?

We are currently attempting to train educable retarded children to follow instructions both verbal and written and to perform a variety of simple prose comprehension tasks, all in the context of a meaningful activity, like assembling a toy or following a recipe. In the course of these activities, they must deliberately and overtly pass through a self-interrogation routine like the one described above. We believe that devising simple systems for eliciting self-awareness and conscious control over one's own activities is an important form of training because the end product is desirable in its own right, it should have transsituational applicability, and it should improve both the child's cognitive and meta-cognitive skills and his feeling of personal competence and control.

Acknowledgments

The authors would like to extend their especial appreciation to Mrs. Wilma Noynaert, Assistant Director of Special Education for the Peoria Public Schools, who has continually provided support and encouragement and has made access to special education classes readily available. The authors would also like to thank Mrs. Carolyn Long for her patience and skill in testing the children and, of course, the children themselves for their willing and active participation.

References

Anderson, R. C. The notion of schemata and the educational enterprise. In R. C. Anderson, R. J. Spiro, and W. E. Montague (Eds.), *Schooling and the acquisition of knowledge.* Hillsdale, New Jersey: Lawrence Erlbaum Associates, 1977.

Barclay, C. R., and Brown, A. L. *Long-term maintainance of recall-readiness efficiency in educable retarded children.* Unpublished manuscript, University of Illinois, 1976.

Belmont, J. M., and Butterfield, E. C. The relation of short-term memory to development and intelligence. In L. P. Lipsitt and H. W. Reese (Eds.), *Advances in child development and behavior.* Vol. 4. New York: Academic Press, 1969. Pp. 30–83.

Belmont, J. M., and Butterfield, E. G. Learning strategies as determinants of memory deficiencies. *Cognitive Psychology*, 1971, *2*, 411–420.

Belmont, J. M., and Butterfield, E. C. The instructional approach to developmental cognitive research. In R. V. Kail, Jr., and J. W. Hagen (Eds.), *Perspectives on the development of memory and cognition*. Hillsdale, New Jersey: Lawrence Erlbaum Associates, 1977.

Binet, A. Les frontières anthropométriques des anormaux. *Bulletin de la Société Libre pour l'Etude Psychologique de l'Enfant*, 1904, 430–438.

Binet, A., and Henri, V. La mémoire des phrases (Mémoire des idées). *Année Psychologique*, 1894, *1*, 24–59.

Brown, A. L. The role of strategic behavior in retardate memory. In N. R. Ellis (Ed.), *International review of research in mental retardation*. Vol. 7. New York: Academic Press, 1974. Pp. 55–111.

Brown, A. L. The development of memory: Knowing, knowing about knowing, and knowing how to know. In H. W. Reese (Ed.), *Advances in child development and behavior*. Vol. 10. New York: Academic Press, 1975. Pp. 103–152.

Brown, A. L. Knowing when, where, and how to remember: A problem of metacognition. In R. Glaser (Ed.), *Advances in instructional psychology*. Vol. 1. Hillsdale, New Jersey: Lawrence Erlbaum Associates, 1978.

Brown, A. L., and Barclay, C. R. The effects of training specific mnemonics on the metamnemonic efficiency of retarded children. *Child Development*, 1976, *47*, 70–80.

Brown, A. L., and Campione, J. C. Training strategic study time apportionment in educable retarded children. *Intelligence*, 1977, *1*, 94–107.

Brown, A. L., and Smiley, S. S. Rating the importance of structural units of prose passages: A problem of metacognitive development. *Child Development*, 1977, *48*, 1–8.

Brown, A. L., Campione, J. C., Bray, N. W., and Wilcox, B. L. Keeping track of changing variables: Effects of rehearsal training and rehearsal prevention in normal and retarded adolescents. *Journal of Experimental Psychology*, 1973, *101*, 123–131.

Brown, A. L., Campione, J. C., and Murphy, M. D. Keeping track of changing variables: Long-term retention of a trained rehearsal strategy by retarded adolescents. *American Journal of Mental Deficiency*, 1974, *78*, 446–453.

Butterfield, E. C., and Belmont, J. M. Assessing and improving the cognitive functions of mentally retarded people. In I. Bailer and M. Steinlicht (Eds.), *Psychological issues in mental retardation*. Chicago: Aldine Press, 1977.

Butterfield, E. C., Wambold, C., and Belmont, J. M. On the theory and practice of improving short-term memory. *American Journal of Mental Deficiency*, 1973, *77*, 654–669.

Campione, J. C., and Brown, A. L. Memory and metamemory development in educable retarded children. In R. V. Kail, Jr., and J. W. Hagen (Eds.), *Perspectives on the development of memory and cognition*. Hillsdale, New Jersey: Lawrence Erlbaum Associates, 1977.

Cohen, L. B., and Gelber, E. R. Infant visual memory. In L. B. Cohen and P. Salapatek (Eds.), *Infant perception: From sensation to cognition*. Vol. 1. New York: Academic Press, 1975. Pp. 347–403.

Collins, A. Processes in acquiring and using knowledge. In R. C. Anderson, R. J. Spiro, and W. E. Montague (Eds.), *Schooling and the acquisition of knowledge*. Hillsdale, New Jersey: Lawrence Erlbaum Associates, 1977.

Flavell, J. H. Developmental studies of mediated memory. In H. W. Reese and L. P. Lipsitt (Eds.), *Advances in child development and behavior*. Vol. 5. New York: Academic Press, 1970. Pp. 181–211.

Flavell, J. H., and Wellman, H. M. Metamemory. In R. V. Kail, Jr., and J. W. Hagen (Eds.), *Perspectives on the development of memory and cognition*. Hillsdale, New Jersey: Lawrence Erlbaum Associates, 1977.

Flavell, J. H., Friedrichs, A. G., and Hoyt, J. D. Developmental changes in memorization processes. *Cognitive Psychology,* 1970, *1,* 324–340.

Galton, F. Supplementary notes on "prehension" in idiots. *Mind,* 1887, *12,* 79–82.

Gold, M. W. Stimulus factors in skill training of the retarded on a complex assembly task: Acquisition, transfer and retention. *American Journal of Mental Deficiency,* 1972, *76,* 517–526.

Hagen, J. W., Jongeward, R. H., Jr., and Kail, R. V., Jr. Cognitive perspectives on the development of memory. In H. W. Reese (Ed.), *Advances in child development and behavior.* Vol. 10. New York: Academic Press, 1975. Pp. 57–101.

Hunter, W. S. The delayed reaction in a child. *Psychological Review,* 1917, *24,* 74–87.

Huttenlocher, J. The origins of language comprehension. In R. L. Solso (Ed.), *Theories in cognitive psychology: The Loyola symposium.* Washington, D.C.: Winston, 1974. Pp. 331–368.

Inhelder, B., Sinclair, H., and Bovet, M. *Learning and the development of cognition.* Cambridge, Massachusetts: Harvard University Press, 1974.

Kuhn, D. Inducing development experimentally: Comments on a research paradigm. *Developmental Psychology,* 1974, *10,* 590–600.

Meacham, J. A. Soviet investigations of memory development. In R. V. Kail, Jr., and J. W. Hagen (Eds.), *Perspectives on the development of memory and cognition.* Hillsdale, New Jersey: Lawrence Erlbaum Associates, 1977.

Reitman, W. What does it take to remember? In D. A. Norman (Ed.), *Models of human memory.* New York: Academic Press, 1970. Pp. 470–509.

Ross, D. M., and Ross, S. A. *An intensive training curriculum for the education of young educable mentally retarded children.* Final report, Project Nos. 142106 and H932106A, DHEW, U.S. Office of Education, December 1972.

Shif, Z. I. Development of children in schools for the mentally retarded. In M. Cole and I. Maltzman (Eds.), *A handbook of contemporary Soviet psychology.* New York: Basic Books, 1969. Pp. 326–353.

Smirnov, A. A., and Zinchenko, P. I. Problems in the psychology of memory. In M. Cole and I. Maltzman (Eds.), *A handbook of contemporary Soviet psychology.* New York: Basic Books, 1969. Pp. 452–502.

Televised Aggression and Prosocial Behavior

ALETHA HUSTON-STEIN

Historical Development of Television in the United States

The advent of television is one of the most significant changes in people's lives in the 20th century. Television spread so quickly after its introduction in the post-World War II period that the majority of American homes had television sets by the mid-1950s. By the end of the 1960s, a higher percentage of American homes had television sets than refrigerators or indoor plumbing. At the present time, close to half of American homes have two or more televisions.

People of all ages spend a large amount of their time watching television. Though exact figures are difficult to obtain, all investigators agree that children and adolescents spend at least 2 or 3 hours a day watching television. These averages are misleading, however, because there are wide individual variations. For example, in one sample of children, the average amount of viewing on weekdays was approximately 3 hours, but over one-fourth of the children watched no television at all and over one-fourth watched more than 5½ hours (Lyle and Hoffman, 1972).

Almost as soon as television became a mass medium, social critics expressed concern about its possible harmful effects, particularly for children. Some were concerned about the passivity induced by having constant entertainment readily available in the home. Others were con-

ALETHA HUSTON-STEIN • Department of Human Development, University of Kansas, Lawrence, Kansas.

cerned that children would withdraw into fantasy or that families would stop talking to one another as they all sat hypnotized in front of the tube. But the most serious and persistent concern was about violence in the programs (Merriam, 1968; Wertham, 1968). Television was not the first mass medium to portray extensive violence, but it brought that violence into people's homes in unprecedented quantity and with greater vividness than had been the case for radio, movies, and comic books—other media that previously had been criticized. In Senate hearings on juvenile delinquency in the 1950s, Senator Estes Kefauver wondered aloud about the possible contribution of television violence to young people's criminal behavior. Senate hearings were held again in 1961; in 1968, hearings were held by the National Commission on the Causes and Prevention of Violence. In both, the contribution of television to the increasing violence in American society was a major focus (Liebert, Neale, and Davidson, 1973). At the conclusion of the 1968 hearings, Congress appropriated $1 million to fund 23 new research projects and some 37 other review papers to provide more definitive information on the issue. We now turn to an examination of some of the psychological theory and research that formed the basis for many of these studies.

VIOLENCE AND AGGRESSION

IMITATION LEARNING. The predominant theory of children's personality development in the late 1950s was a combination of psychoanalytic and social learning concepts (Sears, Maccoby, and Levin, 1957; Sears, Rau, and Alpert, 1966). Identification with parents was proposed as a major process by which children incorporated or imitated many of their parents' characteristics. According to the theory, children would identify more strongly when parents were warm and affectionate than when they were relatively cool and nonnurturant. Some naturalistic studies of parents and young children had supported that hypothesis, but there were so many additional variables at work during studies of parent–child relations as they occurred in the complexity of "real life" that firm conclusions were difficult to draw.

Therefore, a number of child development researchers decided to simulate the process of identification in the laboratory by studying imitation. One of those researchers, Albert Bandura, carried out a study in which children were assigned to a warm, nurturant adult model who played with them or to a cool, nonnurturant model who was busy while the children played alone. The model and the child then played a game where each had to guess in which of two boxes a sticker was hidden. As the model chose a box, she said, "March, march, march," and marched to the box; then she knocked a small rubber doll off the top of the box quite aggressively. Children's imitation of these and other behaviors was scored.

The findings of the study supported identification theory—children who had experienced warm interaction with the model imitated her behavior more than those who had experienced nonnurturance. But there were no differences in imitation of the aggressive behavior— knocking over the doll—because *over 90% of the children imitated aggression*. A few children became so involved in hitting the doll that it flew 4 feet across the room to knock another doll off the other box (Bandura and Huston, 1961).

Bandura immediately saw the importance of this high rate of imitative aggression and designed several more studies to explore it systematically (see Bandura, 1969). In these studies, children watched an adult engaging in aggressive behavior—hitting a Bobo doll with a mallet, shooting dart guns, and the like. Then they were left alone in a play room with similar toys, and aggressive behavior was scored. The results were the same whether the child saw the model live, on film, or in a "cartoon" format on a television set (Bandura, Ross, and Ross, 1963a). Children imitated aggression both specifically (e.g., sitting on the Bobo doll and pounding it with a mallet) and generally (i.e., showing aggressive behavior that was not identical to the model's behavior).

Bandura (1969) developed a theory of imitation based partly on these studies, and he has conducted extensive research on factors that influence imitative behavior and learning. Some of this research will be discussed in later sections as it relates to mass media. Even on the basis of these early studies, however, he and others concluded that the most likely effect of television violence on children was to instigate aggressive behavior.

SOCIAL PSYCHOLOGY OF AGGRESSION. A second strand of basic research grew out of theoretical questions concerning the nature of aggression itself. Two important and conflicting positions were represented by Leonard Berkowitz and Seymour Feshbach, respectively. Berkowitz (1962) was initially concerned with exploring and modifying the frustration–aggression hypothesis, a proposition that had been published in the late 1930s by a group of learning theorists (Dollard, Doob, Miller, Mowrer, and Sears, 1939). That group had proposed that frustration always led to "the instigation to aggression"; conversely, aggressive behavior always implied that some frustration had preceded it.

In its most extreme form, the frustration–aggression hypothesis had been generally dismissed by psychologists, but Berkowitz's theory of aggression incorporated it in a more complex and precise form. He proposed that frustration produced anger, which in turn predisposed a person to behave aggressively, but a number of other factors determined whether aggression would actually be exhibited. Personality differences, such as one's tendency to feel anxious about aggression, and situational cues could each make aggression more or less likely. One situational cue was observing violent behavior by someone else.

Berkowitz and his collaborators (Berkowitz, 1964, 1970) conducted a series of studies with college men testing aspects of the theory. In a typical study, the subject waited a few minutes in a room with another student (who was a collaborator in the experiment). In the conditions designed to produce anger, the "stooge" made insulting remarks to the subject while they waited. Subjects were then shown a film, either a violent boxing scene or a neutral, nonviolent film. Finally, they had an opportunity to administer electric shocks to the collaborator or to rate the collaborator on a questionnaire. As predicted, men who were angry and saw a violent film were more aggressive than those who were not angry or who saw a nonviolent film. Unlike the studies of children, seeing the film did not increase aggressive behavior unless the subject was angry.

CATHARSIS. The work of both Bandura and Berkowitz led to similar conclusions: observation of violence, filmed or otherwise, instigates aggressive behavior. Both used similar theoretical foundations in building their own theories of imitation and aggression, respectively. A contrary view was derived from psychoanalytic theory by Seymour Feshbach (1964). According to that view, catharsis, or draining off of aggressive energies, may result from observing aggressive behavior by someone else, particularly if the person is angry. Feshbach tested this theory in relation to film violence in some studies that were very similar in design to those of Berkowitz. He obtained results that were consistent with his theory—men who were angered showed less aggression on a questionnaire after observing a violent film than they did after observing a nonviolent film. Because these results were directly opposite to those obtained by other researchers, considerably more research was stimulated. The weight of the evidence supports the findings of Berkowitz and Bandura (Feshbach, 1970).

APPLICATIONS TO MASS MEDIA EFFECTS. When social scientists attempted to generalize from the work of Bandura, Berkowitz, Feshbach, and other psychologists to the effects of the mass media, many questions were raised. Stein and Friederich have recently commented: "Aggression in television programs may be less clear or less salient than it is in a laboratory-made sequence. Children's attention may be less focused in a natural setting. The fact that a permissive adult has exposed the child to the model in the laboratory may be an important disinhibitor that is not present in 'real life.' Most behavioral observations are conducted immediately after exposure in situations very similar to the ones in which the models were observed. Therefore, these studies do not indicate how durable the behavioral changes are nor how much disinhibition would generalize to other situations. They also provide no information about generalization to other types of aggressive behavior, particularly behavior that is serious and potentially harmful" (1975, p. 192).

Quite often, generalizations cannot be drawn from basic research to applied questions without additional research to bridge the gap between the laboratory and the field. Basic research can provide information about the fundamental processes that is uncontaminated by the myriad of additional factors present in naturalistic situations, but additional research is required to determine under what natural conditions those processes operate.

The field experiment is one means of combining the virtues of laboratory experiments with the natural conditions of field settings. One field experiment conducted with preschool children was designed to test the effects of both violent and prosocial television on the natural behavior of preschool children (Friedrich and Stein, 1973; Stein and Friedrich, 1972). During a 9-week nursery school session, children were observed in the classroom during all activities. Their behavior was scored for aggression; prosocial interactions such as cooperation, helping, and verbalizing their feelings; and self-regulatory behavior such as task persistence, rule obedience, and tolerance for minor frustrations (delays in getting what they wanted). After a 3-week period that provided baseline information, children were randomly assigned to one of three television viewing conditions: violent, prosocial, or neutral television. The violent programs were "Superman" and "Batman" cartoons; the prosocial programs were "Mr. Rogers' Neighborhood"; the neutral programs were miscellaneous children's films without aggressive or prosocial content. Children saw a television program each day for 4 weeks; the last 2 weeks served as a postviewing follow-up period.

Violent programs affected two areas of behavior: tolerance for minor frustration and interpersonal aggression. Children who saw violent programs decreased in tolerance for frustration. Interpersonal aggression (hitting, calling names, teasing, and the like) was higher after violent programs than after the other programs, but only for children who were initially above average in aggression. This finding was consistent with other studies suggesting that violence has more effect on aggressive behavior for people who are already aggressive than for those who are not. Note, though, that this does not mean that those people would be just as aggressive without television. It means that violent television adds significantly to aggression displayed by those who are already prone to behave that way. In this study, violence was related to serious interpersonal aggression, not to playful or fantasy aggression. Thus, the critics who questioned whether the playful aggression shown in laboratory studies would generalize to more serious behavior appear to have been answered.

Three field experiments were also conducted with adolescent boys in residential schools and institutions. The theories of Feshbach and Berkowitz, respectively, guided these studies. In the first (Feshbach and Singer, 1971), boys from 8 to 18 living in residential settings were randomly assigned violent or nonviolent television "diets" for 6 weeks. Stein and Friedrich summarize their findings: "Counselors and adult supervisors rated the amount of aggression demonstrated by the boys they worked with daily. In three upper-middle-class schools, there were no differences between viewing groups. In four lower-class institutions, aggression of the group with the nonviolent diet increased slightly over the six weeks while that of the group with the violent diet decreased" (1975, p. 202).

This result appears at first glance to support a catharsis hypothesis. Even Feshbach and Singer, however, were reluctant to conclude that catharsis had occurred, primarily because the nonviolent television diet was less attractive and therefore possibly frustrating to the boys in that group. In a replication of this study using better controls, Wells (1973) found that boys liked the violent diet better than the nonviolent diet and that it approximated their usual viewing more closely than did the nonviolent diet. He suggested that the violent diet ought to be called the control group and the nonviolent diet the experimental group. In the replication study, there were virtually no differences in aggressive behavior between the two groups (Wells, 1973).

Another series of field experiments, based on Berkowitz's previous work, was conducted in the United States and Belgium with adolescent males in penal institutions (Parke, Berkowitz, Leyens, West, and Sebastian, 1975). Boys saw feature-length movies that were either violent or nonviolent every night for a week. They watched no television during that week, but the loss was compensated by releasing them from required study hours. The violent and nonviolent movies were equally well liked. Aggressive behavior was observed before, during, and after the movie week. In the American sample, boys who saw violent movies increased in aggressive behavior more than those who saw the nonviolent movies; the same difference occurred in Belgium, but only in cottages where the boys were already fairly aggressive (note the similarity to the findings with preschoolers).

CONCLUSIONS. These studies, along with a variety of others, generally indicate that the results of the theory-based laboratory studies of Bandura and Berkowitz do apply to the naturalistic effects of television

violence on real aggressive behavior. Heightened aggression o[
children or adolescents watch violent television under many c[
such aggressive behavior can be suppressed by situational constraints, but often it is not. Other factors related to television viewing, particularly deprivation of programs that children like to watch, can also lead to aggressive behavior. Finally, aggression is especially likely to increase for children and adolescents who are already aggressive. The net result is that the people with the greatest potential for harm to other people are the ones most likely to be inspired to violence by television.

These conclusions are supported in correlational studies where children's natural viewing patterns have been examined in relation to their aggressive behavior (McLeod, Atkins, and Chaffee, 1972a, b). One particularly interesting investigation was a 10-year longitudinal study of children from ages 8 to 18. The entire third grade in a small town (about 800 children) was studied in depth in 1960. For the boys in the sample, aggressive behavior at school was correlated with the amount of violence they liked to watch on television at home (Eron, 1963). When these boys were studied 10 years later, those who had watched a lot of television violence at age 8 were still more aggressive than those who had not. In fact, television viewing in the third grade predicted later aggression better than any of the child-rearing practices or family characteristics that were studied (Eron, Lefkowitz, Huesmann, and Walder, 1972; Lefkowitz, Eron, Walder, and Huesmann, 1972). Although there were no correlations of television and aggression for girls in this study, other studies (McLeod et al., 1972a, b) have found relationships for both girls and boys.

Prosocial Television

Just as violence was deplored over the years, so the potential of television for benefiting children was lauded, but the few early programs designed for that purpose had miniscule audiences. Educational television was stereotyped as dull, didactic, and commercially disastrous. Then along came "Sesame Street." Much to the surprise of even the strongest proponents of the program, it gained a large viewing audience among its target group—preschool children—as well as among many adults and older children.

"Sesame Street." This program was designed from the beginning with close collaboration of developmental psychologists who were experts on children's cognitive development. They used their knowledge to recommend what skills at what level of difficulty should be taught. For example, "Which of these things is not like the others?" is designed to teach children to classify or to place objects in abstract categories, a skill studied extensively in developmental theory and literature (e.g., Elkind, 1961). In the first season of "Sesame Street" the producers designed single-classification problems in which the objects were grouped on the basis of one category (e.g., an orange, a banana, a pear, and a toy car). Available research indicated that preschool children would not be able to understand double classification or the fact that an object can belong to two different categories simultaneously (e.g., an orange could be grouped with other round things or with fruits in the following example: an orange, an apple, a ball, and a banana). After the evaluation of children's learning from the first year of "Sesame Street" (Ball and Bogatz, 1970), the producers decided to try double classification because children had learned the single-classification skills better than researchers had expected them to. Apparently, however, double classification was too difficult, because children studied during the second season of the program did not learn that skill (Bogatz and Ball, 1971). Principles of learning such as modeling, repetition, focusing narrowly on the material to be learned, presentation of the same material in different modes (pictures, words, etc.) were also drawn from many sources including basic research (Lesser, 1974).

In the early seasons of "Sesame Street," social relationships and emotional development were minor themes that served as background to the intellectual and academic instruction goals of the program. In more recent years, however, research on children's social development has been used to design segments that are focused on social relationships and self-concept. For example, consider the vignette in which Ernie and Bert are lying in their beds. Each time Bert almost gets to sleep, Ernie starts talking. Bert gets more and more annoyed and finally makes some remark about how Ernie does not understand how he (Bert) feels. Ernie then becomes quiet and a dream sequence occurs in which they have changed places. Bert is talking and Ernie is trying to sleep. The gist of the whole piece is learning to put yourself in someone else's place to understand that person's feelings.

This segment reflects research on the development of children's social understanding based on the theory of Jean Piaget (Shantz, 1975). Piaget noted that young children were "egocentric" in their social interactions. By this term, he did not mean they were merely self-centered; instead, he meant that they lacked the ability to understand that someone else had a different perspective from their own. Very young children assume that an object looks the same to someone standing on the other side of it as it looks to them. They also assume that other people know what they know, even when those people have had no opportunity to get the same information. For instance, they will talk to a strange adult about "Billy" without explaining who Billy is.

Egocentrism limits young children's ability to be empathic or to understand other people's feelings. They assume that other people have the same feelings that they have. Often that assumption is correct, but in cases where it is not, they may not perceive that another person feels differently. For example, when preschool children were shown a picture of a child sitting at a table with a birthday cake in front of him, they tended to think he was happy even when his face looked quite sad (Burns and Cavey, 1957). Or when they saw a videotape of an adult who frowned and looked annoyed when someone brought her a cup of coffee, they found it difficult to understand (Deutsch, 1974). In the segment described above, Ernie assumed that Bert was interested in talking because Ernie wanted to talk; he had difficulty understanding the clear cues from Bert that he was sleepy.

One of the ways children learn to be less egocentric is through taking the role of the other person. There is some evidence, for instance, that empathy and ability to understand others is higher when parents point out the consequences of a child's behavior, especially as it affects others (Hoffman, 1970). Statements like "It hurts baby brother when you hit him just like it hurts you when someone hits you" apparently do have some effect. Actually taking the place of the other person or sharing in the same experience is even more effective in teaching the child to understand that person's perspective (Aronfreed, 1968). This technique of role reversal was also used in the Bert and Ernie vignette.

"Sesame Street" is a good illustration of the powerful television programming that can be designed when solid research findings are integrated with skilled, creative production techniques. A critical step in making basic research useful is carried out by the social scientist who translates it from the theory and laboratory context and applies it to a particular social need. While one can identify particular features of "Sesame Street" that are fairly direct translations of basic research findings, the less direct contributions are equally important. In Lesser's description of the early planning of the program, he said, "Academics who contributed constructively used their professional knowledge as background music; the information was in the backs of their minds and they used it when it was relevant, but they drew on anything that might help" (1974, p. 58).

The success of "Sesame Street" in teaching children while drawing large audiences helped to bury the myth that educational television could not be commercially viable. It drew the attention of the public and of researchers to the few already existing programs that were designed to enhance children's development, and it stimulated the development of many more.

"MR. ROGERS' NEIGHBORHOOD." Another program for young children, "Mr. Rogers' Neighborhood," was designed primarily to enhance social and emotional development. Psychologists were involved in the planning of the program; in addition, Mr. Rogers, the creator of the series, was trained in child development as well as in music and theology. Both the content and the slow, gentle style of the program are guided in direct and indirect ways by theory and research on children's development, particularly the theory of Erik Erikson (1963).

"Mr. Rogers" programs often deal with common fears and conflicts of young children that are postulated in Erikson's theory. In one series, for example, Henrietta, a puppet cat, is afraid that she will be replaced by Collette, a glamorous, Parisian tiger puppet who is coming to visit her neighborhood. First, Henrietta dresses up in fancy clothes and makeup like Collette's, then she gets angry at Collette and knocks her picture to the ground. Finally, she wishes that a cake baked for Collette would fall and be ruined. Throughout these episodes, other characters attempt to understand and to help Henrietta. She is finally reassured when they insist that she attend a party for Collette because she is the only one who can introduce everyone. One theme of this series is the young child's fear of being replaced by a new baby—one of the common concerns identified in Erikson's theory. The angry actions and wishes along with the guilt and fear stimulated by them are also drawn from Erikson's theoretical propositions.

Many of the themes and behaviors shown on the program are also consistent with observational learning theory and research. Characters exemplify helping, cooperation, sharing, understanding others' feelings, verbalizing one's own feelings, tolerating frustration, persisting at difficult tasks, and the uniqueness and basic worth of each person. In the laboratory, it has been demonstrated that children imitate affectionate behavior, helping another child, altruism and sharing, setting high standards for oneself, delay of gratification, mature moral judgment, and overcoming fears (Bryan, 1975; Hoffman, 1970). This literature provides information about some of the kinds of prosocial television content that have potential to influence children.

Studies of prosocial television programs are less numerous than those focused on violence. So far, most have studied "Mr. Rogers' Neighborhood." In the field experiment with preschool children described earlier (Friedrich and Stein, 1973; Stein and Friedrich, 1972) the group who saw "Mr. Rogers" programs showed increased task persistence and spontaneous obedience of rules in the classroom. Those children from homes where the parents were less well educated also showed increased cooperation, helping, sharing, and verbalizing feelings after seeing "Mr. Rogers." In another field experiment, children who saw a series of "Mr. Rogers" programs shared more and were less aggressive than a control group, but they were not more helpful or cooperative (Shirley, 1974).

Observational learning theory also formed the basis for another approach to studying "Mr. Rogers" and "Sesame Street" (Coates and Pusser, 1975). These investigators analyzed how often televised characters gave one another positive reinforcement and punishment. Positive reinforcements included praise, sympathy, approval, friendly reactions, and the like; punishment included criticism, contradiction, verbal and physical aggression. Both programs had high frequencies of positive reinforcement, but "Sesame Street" also contained a fair amount of punishment. "Mr. Rogers" had very little of the latter. The second step in this research was to see whether children imitated the style of social interactions shown in the two programs. For that purpose they deliberately selected contrasting segments—"Sesame Street" programs with a relatively high amount of punishment and "Mr. Rogers" programs with high positive reinforcement. Children's classroom behavior was observed before, during, and after 1 week of viewing the programs. Children who saw "Mr. Rogers" gave more positive reinforcement to others in the nursery school after seeing the programs. In some groups, children who saw "Sesame Street" gave more positive reinforcement and more punishment to others (Coates, Pusser, and Goodman, 1976). This study illustrates the use of basic concepts in deciding what dimensions to use in content analysis of a television program and in observing children's behavior as it is influenced by that content.

COMMERCIAL PROGRAMS. Not just coincidentally, when our discussion moved from violent to prosocial television, it also shifted from commercial to public (i.e., nonprofit) programs. One group of social scientists, however, have reasoned that commercial programs are probably not all bad. Even though most do not deliberately attempt to teach prosocial behavior, many do show helping, cooperation, persistence in the face of difficulty, and the like. Therefore, children might learn some prosocial behavior as well as aggression from commercial programs.

These investigators (Rubinstein, Liebert, Neale, and Poulos, 1974) undertook a content analysis of some 400 commercial programs looking for prosocial themes such as helping, sharing, cooperation, self-control, and the like. Their expectations were correct—they found a considerable amount of prosocial content. Next they conducted a study in which one group of children saw a "Lassie" program where helping was a major part of the plot; a second group saw another "Lassie" program without an emphasis on helping; a third group saw a neutral program. The children who saw the program with the helping theme were more helpful in a later testing situation than those who had seen the other programs (Poulos, Rubinstein, and Liebert, 1975).

This group of investigators went one step farther than most psychologists who do television research. They made some television programs of their own using what they knew about modeling of prosocial behavior. The programs are 30-second "commercials" that advertise prosocial behavior. For example, one segment shows two children who rush to one swing where both attempt to get on. The action freezes, and a narrator points out the conflict and asks the viewer what can be done. Then the actors decide that they can take turns on the swing, and narrator points out what a cooperative solution that is. The 30-second format was chosen partly because commercial stations would broadcast them free as public service announcements.

Each of the 30-second announcements was evaluated to assess how attentive children were, how well they understood the message, and how much they imitated the behavior shown. For the segments released so far, including the one described above, all three forms of testing have been positive (Poulos, Liebert, and Schwartzberg, 1975).

INCREASING AND DECREASING THE IMITATION OF TELEVISION PROGRAMS

Clearly, children learn from and imitate a wide variety of television content. The next logical question is, what can be done to modify the effects of television? How can the effects of violence be reduced? How can prosocial content be made more effective? The answers to these questions are just beginning to emerge. They, too, grow out of basic knowledge about learning and behavior. In this section, we will examine a few of the many possible factors that can modify the effects of observing violent or prosocial television.

CONSEQUENCES FOR VIOLENCE. Let us begin with violence. Defenders and apologists for the commercial television networks often justify the portrayal of criminal and violent acts by pointing out that the villain is ultimately punished. The villain may be punished, but the hero, who is equally violent, is usually rewarded. In fact, violence is rewarded and punished about equally often (Gerbner, 1972). Nevertheless, television programs could be designed so that violent actions were punished. Would that make children less likely to imitate the violence? This is one case in which basic research suggests one answer, but application to television suggests another.

In the laboratory, observing someone else being punished for aggressive behavior makes children less likely to imitate that aggression. For example, in one study, children saw a film of a child being aggressive. There were three possible endings: the child was rewarded by being praised and getting to keep a lot of toys, the child was punished by being scolded and losing toys, or no consequences occurred. In a play session after the films, children who had seen the model punished were less aggressive than the other two groups. Their behavior was similar to a group that had not observed any film (Bandura, Ross, and Ross, 1963b).

But, Bandura (1965) asked a second question. The children who saw the model punished inhibited aggressive behavior; but they might have watched as closely and remembered the model's behavior just as carefully as the other children. If that were true, then those children might easily imitate the aggression at some other time or in some other place where there was little threat of punishment. To test this idea, he conducted another study that was similar to the first—children saw a film in which a child model was rewarded, punished, or received no consequences for aggression. Then the children were observed at play. The new feature of this study was a questioning period after they played in which they were offered prizes for recalling as much of the model's behavior as possible. This type of questioning was designed to find out how much they had learned rather than how much they spontaneously imitated or performed the model's behavior. The results supported the prediction: all three groups recalled similar amounts of behavior. Punishment reduced imitative performance, but it did not prevent the child from mentally learning the violent behavior.

MOTIVES OF THE MODEL. A second issue represents an elaboration of Berkowitz's proposal that the viewer's emotional reactions and perceptions as well as external situational factors influence aggressive reactions. Some people are made anxious by aggressive impulses and inhibit them as a result. This anxiety will be greater, he proposed, if they observe violence that is morally wrong or unjustified; that is, which is based on motives that are morally unacceptable. On the other hand, if the violence is portrayed as justified or morally right, then people will probably be less anxious and will be more likely to be aggressive.

In one study testing this hypothesis college men saw a violent film of a prize fight but were given two different introductory story lines. They were told either that the loser in the fight had previously been mean to his opponent (hence the opponent's aggression was justified) or that the loser was just an average guy who had done no one any harm (and hence the opponent's aggressiveness was unjustified). Men who were already angry when they saw the film in the justified condition were more aggressive later than those who saw the unjustified version (Berkowitz, 1970).

Consequences to the model and the motives portrayed for violence were studied in real television programs as a result of these laboratory findings (Collins, 1973; Leifer and Roberts, 1972). As might be expected, it was difficult to find real television programs where either the consequences or the motives were as clear-cut as they were in the laboratory studies. Most television programs portray both justified and unjustified aggression with both positive and negative consequences. The hero is justified and is rewarded; the villain is unjustified and is punished. Nevertheless, some programs were located that fell primarily at one end of the continuum or the other, and, in another study, programs were edited to make them relatively pure cases.

Following Bandura's findings, one might expect children to learn equally well from programs that show different motives and consequences for violence, but to behave more aggressively when violence was justified or rewarded. In these studies, children's understanding of the elements of the plot was measured as an index of learning. Their tendency to behave aggressively was measured as an index of performance or imitation. Children from 4 to 16 years old were studied to determine age differences in understanding and behavior.

The results of these studies were consistent. Neither motives for aggression nor portrayed consequences for behavior affected children's learning of television content or their aggressive behavior tendencies. *The only feature of the television programs that affected aggression was the amount of violence.* Unpleasant consequences or bad motives for violence performed by a television character did little to reduce children's reactions to that behavior.

Why do motives and consequences affect children's imitation in laboratory research but not in studies of real television programs? Maybe consequences to the model serve mainly as an indicator to the child of what might happen to a person in a similar situation. In effect, the message is, "You will be punished for behaving like the model in this setting." If so, children may imitate in other situations where they think punishment is unlikely. If that is true, then punishing the villain in a television program will probably have little effect because the people and settings in most television programs are quite different from those in a child viewer's environment. Unfortunately, the effects of violence do seem to generalize across that gap, and the plot context in which violence is presented does little to modify those effects.

AGE DIFFERENCES. As expected, older children understood and remembered more of the television programs than did younger children (Leifer and Roberts, 1972). Preschool and kindergarten children in particular understood little of the motives or consequences for violence. Children of this age have difficulty in making connections among elements in a plot, especially if they occur at different times in the program. If a program is interrupted by a commercial, young children seem to have difficulty connecting events that happened before with those that happened after the commercial (Collins, 1973). In many television programs, the criminal is caught or killed in the last 2 minutes after 50 minutes of successful adventure. That message may be lost on many children.

CONSEQUENCES FOR PROSOCIAL MODELS. Can we increase children's imitation of prosocial television by showing rewards for that behavior? One would expect the answer to be yes, but again it must be qualified. Even in the laboratory, some studies have failed to find increases in helping, sharing, and the like when the model was praised by an adult (Bryan, 1975). In one ingenious naturalistic study, however, children who were socially withdrawn in nursery school saw a film of a child getting involved in play and group activity. This "hero" met with friendly reactions by other children and had lots of fun. The children who watched the film became more involved in social activity afterward (O'Connor, 1972). Maybe the positive consequences shown in this film were more natural and more realistic than the somewhat artificial praise by an adult used earlier.

ROLE PLAYING AND VERBAL LABELING. If one could stimulate children to rehearse and act out the prosocial behavior they see on television, if should help them to incorporate that behavior more thoroughly. How does one stimulate such rehearsal? What kinds of rehearsal are useful? If we knew the answers to those questions, then teachers and parents might use television programs as a foundation for teaching certain kinds of behavior. These ideas were explored in a series of studies conducted by Lynette Friedrich and this author.

Two types of rehearsal were suggested by basic research findings: verbal labeling and role playing. Verbal labeling refers to naming prosocial behavior so that the child can put it in a category such as "helping" or "sharing." A few years before this research was done, investigators of children's cognitive development had identified a developmental shift in children's ability to use verbal labels at about age 6. This shift was demonstrated in a study of observational learning conducted with 4- and 7-year-old children. The children saw a series of film clips of a model performing different actions in pantomime, such as jumping up and down, rubbing hands together, and the like. For some children, the adult who watched the movie with them gave each action a name and asked the child to repeat the name. The control group was told to watch carefully. Then the children were asked to demonstrate as many of the model's actions as they could remember. The 4-year-olds remembered twice as many of the modeled behaviors in the verbal labeling condition as they did in the control treatment. They were obviously helped by the fact that the adult provided a name for the behavior, which aided them in rehearsing it. The 7-year-olds did equally well in the two conditions, probably because they could generate verbal labels themselves in the control condition (Coates and Hartup, 1969).

We have already described the rationale for using role playing to rehearse prosocial content in the previous discussion of "Sesame Street." Because young children tend to be egocentric, taking others' roles is especially useful in helping them to understand feelings and actions of others. In addition, children spontaneously try out all kinds of roles in play; the repetition and rehearsal involved should increase what they learn and understand.

In our research, role playing and verbal labeling were used to increase children's understanding and recall of the "Mr. Rogers" program. After each of four ½-hour programs, children spent 15–20 minutes in a small group session. In the verbal labeling rehearsal, the adult read them a short storybook that summarized some of the important themes of the program and labeled them. Children in the role-playing rehearsal acted out sequences from the program with puppets.

Both learning or recall of the program content themes and performance of helping behavior were studied in the few days following the last program. The two types of rehearsal had different effects. Verbal labeling increased children's learning and understanding of the program themes but had little effect on their helping behavior. By contrast, children who had experienced role playing were more helpful than those who had not but did not learn as well as those who received verbal labeling (Friedrich and Stein, 1975).

CONCLUSIONS. Obviously, much more needs to be learned about ways of enhancing the effects of prosocial television or minimizing the effects of violence. On the basis of the available information, we made the following suggestions for prosocial programming in an earlier paper:

> Prosocial behavior should be followed by positive consequences that are intrinsic to the behavior and that would be likely to occur for the child viewer who imitated. Care should be taken not to negate a sequence of cooperative or helpful behavior with a slapstick ending. Emphasis should be placed on the efficacy of prosocial behavior: it succeeds.
>
> A variety of models—both similar and dissimilar to child viewers—embodying warmth, power, and status should be employed in order to maximize appeal and generalization. For young children warm, supportive adults may be very potent models.
>
> Clear narration and verbal labeling of action appear to enhance learning for young children. For older children, explanation and persuasive reasoning about the behavior may add to the impact of the model, but the model's example is crucial. Models in any format should act out the behavior as well as labeling it.
>
> Rehearsal of content may be stimulated by the toys available to children [such as] Batman capes and Sesame Street puppets. (Stein and Friedrich, 1975, p. 236)

How Does Research Affect Television Programming?

We have reviewed some of the knowledge about television effects that has grown out of basic psychological research. Many questions remain, but a lot is already known. How much does this knowledge affect the kind of television programs broadcast for children or at hours when many children watch? Very little. Content analyses of violence in network television have been conducted every year since 1967. The amount of violence has changed very little during that time. In 1975, nearly 80% of all network programs contained some violence; there was an average of 7.4 incidents per hour. On Saturday morning children's programs, 93% contained violence with a rate of 18 incidents per hour (Gerbner and Gross, 1976). The children's programs are a little less violent than they were in the late 1960s, but the average American child still witnesses murders, muggings, fistfights, bombings, and brutality of all kinds as everyday events in the living room.

The report of the Surgeon General's Advisory Committee on Television and Social Behavior (1972) concluded that there was a causal relationship between television violence and aggressive behavior in children. This conclusion is even more striking because 5 of the 12 members of the committee were network executives or consultants who were resistant to drawing this conclusion until the evidence became overwhelming. Why, then, haven't television programs changed?

The simple answer to this question is money. Commercial television makes profits through attracting an audience that can be sold to advertisers. The principal goal of all commercial programs is to obtain as large an audience as possible regardless of how it is done. And television executives and producers believe that violence (or "action" as they sometimes call it) is the surest way to get an audience. So long as the primary goal of television is to sell products rather than to promote the development and welfare of the viewers, commercial considerations will remain paramount (Melody, 1973). If other ways of obtaining large audiences were developed through research, network television might change more than it has in the past 5 years.

Prosocial content has been increased to some degree in commercial programs, at least partly as a result of research findings. Nevertheless, changes have been minimal, and a great deal more could be done. The most creative and conscious use of new ideas from research appears in programs made for public television. The contrast with commercial programs is striking. Public television can be concerned with viewer welfare as a primary rather than a secondary goal. Through government and foundation funding, many new programs for children have been developed focusing on everything from math skills (e.g., "Infinity Factory") to feelings (e.g., "Inside Out"). Psychologists and specialists in all aspects of children's development are closely involved in planning and evaluating many of these programs. Though they deliberately use many of the techniques (other than violence) devised by commercial producers to maximize audience appeal, they employ those techniques to convey content that is stimulating, educational, and varied. In most nations of the world, children's television is not dependent on advertising revenue and its content resembles our public television programs. Melody (1973) is an economist who has developed a plan for gradually removing all children's television in this country from commercial financing. The changes in programming that could result would greatly benefit future generations of children, and, ultimately, our whole society.

REFERENCES

Aronfreed, J. *Conduct and conscience: The socialization of internalized control over behavior.* New York: Academic Press, 1968.

Ball, S., and Bogatz, G. A. *The first year of Sesame Street: An evaluation.* Princeton: Educational Testing Service, 1970.

Bandura, A. Influence of models' reinforcement contingencies on the acquisition of imitative responses. *Journal of Personality and Social Psychology,* 1965, *1,* 589–595.

Bandura, A. Social-learning theory of identificatory processes. In D. A. Goslin (Ed.), *Handbook of socialization theory and research.* Chicago: Rand McNally, 1969. Pp. 213–262.

Bandura, A., and Huston, A. C. Identification as a process of incidental learning. *Journal of Abnormal and Social Psychology,* 1961, *63,* 311–318.

Bandura, A., Ross D., and Ross, S. A. Imitation of film-mediated aggressive models. *Journal of Abnormal and Social Psychology,* 1963a, *66,* 3–11.

Bandura, A., Ross, D., and Ross, A. Vicarious reinforcement and imitative learning. *Journal of Abnormal and Social Psychology,* 1963b, *67,* 601–607.

Berkowitz, L. *Aggression: A social psychological analysis.* New York: McGraw-Hill, 1962.

Berkowitz, L. The effects of observing violence. *Scientific American,* 1964, *210,* 2–8.

Berkowitz, L. The contagion of violence: An S-R mediational analysis of some effects of observed aggression. In W. J. Arnold and M. M. Page (Eds.), *Nebraska symposium on motivation.* Vol. 18. Lincoln: University of Nebraska Press, 1970. Pp. 95–136.

Bogatz, G. A., and Ball, S. *The second year of Sesame Street: A continuing evaluation.* Vols. 1 and 2. Princeton: Educational Testing Service, 1971.

Bryan, J. H. Children's cooperation and helping behaviors. In E. M. Hetherington (Ed.), *Review of child development research.* Vol. 5. Chicago: University of Chicago Press, 1975. Pp. 127–182.

Burns, N., and Cavey, L. Age differences in empathic ability among children. *Canadian Journal of Psychology,* 1957, *11,* 227–230.

Coates, B., and Hartup, W. W. Age and verbalization in observational learning. *Developmental Psychology,* 1969, *1,* 556–562.

Coates, B., and Pusser, H. E. Positive reinforcement and punishment in "Sesame Street" and "Mister Rogers' Neighborhood." *Journal of Broadcasting,* 1975, *19,* 143–151.

Coates, B., Pusser, E. H., and Goodman, I. The influence of "Sesame Street" and "Mister Rogers' Neighborhood" on children's social behavior in the preschool. *Child Development,* 1976, *47,* 138–144.

Collins, W. A. Effect of temporal separation between motivation, aggression, and consequences: A developmental study. *Developmental Psychology,* 1973, *8,* 215–221.

Deutsch, F. Female preschoolers' perceptions of affective responses and interpersonal behavior in videotaped episodes. *Developmental Psychology,* 1974, *10,* 733–740.

Dollard, J., Doob, L., Miller, N., Mowrer, O., and Sears, R. *Frustration and aggression.* New Haven: Yale, 1939.

Elkind, D. The development of the additive composition of classes in the child: Piaget replication study III. *Journal of Genetic Psychology*, 1961, *99*, 51–57.

Erikson, E. H. *Childhood and society* (2nd ed.). New York: Norton, 1963.

Eron, L. D. Relationship of TV viewing habits and aggressive behavior in children. *Journal of Abnormal and Social Psychology*, 1963, *67*, 193–196.

Eron, L. D., Lefkowitz, M. M., Huesmann, L. R., and Walder, L. O. Does television violence cause aggression? *American Psychologist*, 1972, *27*, 253–263.

Feshbach, S. The function of aggression and the regulation of aggressive drive. *Psychological Review*, 1964, *71*, 257–272.

Feshbach, S. Aggression. In P. H. Mussen (Ed.), *Carmichael's manual of child psychology* (3rd ed.). Vol. 2. New York: Wiley, 1970. Pp. 159–260.

Feshbach, S., and Singer, R. *Television and aggression*. San Francisco: Jossey-Bass, 1971.

Friedrich, L. K., and Stein, A. H. Aggressive and prosocial television programs and the natural behavior of preschool children. *Monographs of the Society for Research in Child Development*, 1973, *38* (4, Serial No. 151).

Friedrich, L. K., and Stein, A. H. Prosocial television and young children: The effects of verbal labeling and role playing on learning and behavior. *Child Development*, 1975, *46*, 27–38.

Gerbner, G. Violence in television drama: Trends and symbolic functions. In G. A. Comstock and E. A. Rubinstein (Eds.), *Television and social behavior*. Vol. 1, *Media content and control*. Washington, D.C.: U.S. Government Printing Office, 1972. Pp. 28–187.

Gerbner, G., and Gross, L. P. Living with television: The violence profile. *Journal of Communication*, 1976, *26*, 172–199.

Hoffman, M. L. Moral development. In P. H. Mussen (Ed.), *Carmichael's manual of child psychology* (3rd ed.). Vol. 2. New York: Wiley, 1970. Pp. 261–360.

Lefkowitz, M. M., Eron, L. D., Walder, L. O., and Huesmann, L. R. Television violence and child aggression: A followup study. In G. A. Comstock and E. A. Rubinstein (Eds.), *Television and social behavior*. Vol. 3, *Television and adolescent aggressiveness*. Washington, D.C.: U.S. Government Printing Office, 1972. Pp. 35–135.

Leifer, A. D., and Roberts, D. F. Children's responses to television violence. In J. P. Murray, E. A. Rubinstein, and G. A. Comstock (Eds.), *Television and social behavior*. Vol. 2, *Television and social learning*. Washington, D.C.: U.S. Government Printing Office, 1972. Pp. 43–180.

Lesser, G. S. *Children and television. Lessons from Sesame Street*. New York: Random House, 1974.

Liebert, R. M., Neale, J. M., and Davidson, E. S. *The early window: Effects of television on children and youth*. New York: Pergamon, 1973.

Lyle, J., and Hoffman, H. Children's use of television and other media. In E. A. Rubinstein, G. A. Comstock, and J. P. Murray (Eds.), *Television and social behavior*. Vol. 4, *Television in day-to-day life: Patterns of use*. Washington, D.C.: U.S. Government Printing Office, 1972. Pp. 129–256.

McLeod, J. M., Atkin, C. K., and Chaffee, S. H. Adolescents, parents, and television use: Adolescent self-report measures from Maryland and Wisconsin sample. In G. A. Comstock and E. A. Rubinstein (Eds.), *Television and social behavior*. Vol. 3, *Television and adolescent aggressiveness*. Washington, D.C.: U.S. Government Printing Office, 1972a. Pp. 173–238.

McLeod, J. M., Atkin, C. K., and Chaffee, S. H. Adolescents, parents, and television use: Self-report and other-report measures from the Wisconsin sample. In G. A. Comstock and E. A. Rubinstein (Eds.), *Television and social behavior*. Vol. 3, *Television and adolescent aggressiveness*. Washington, D.C.: U.S. Government Printing Office, 1972b. Pp. 239–313.

Melody, W. *Children's television: The economics of exploitation*. New Haven: Yale University Press, 1973.

Merriam, E. We're teaching our children that violence is fun. In O. N. Larsen (Ed.), *Violence and the mass media*. New York: Harper & Row, 1968. Pp. 40–47.

O'Connor, R. C. Modification of social withdrawal through symbolic modeling. In K. D. O'Leary and S. G. O'Leary (Eds.), *Classroom management*. New York: Pergamon Press, 1972.

Parke, R. D., Berkowitz, L., Leyens, J. P., West, S., and Sebastian, R. J. Film violence and aggression: A field experimental analysis. In L. Berkowitz (Ed.), *Advances in experimental social psychology*. Vol. 10. New York: Academic Press, 1975.

Poulos, R. W., Liebert, R. M., and Schwartzberg, N. *Television's prosocial influence: Designing "commercials" for cooperative behavior*. Paper presented at the Annual Meeting of the American Psychological Association, Chicago, 1975.

Poulos, R. W., Rubinstein, E. A., and Liebert, R. M. Positive social learning. *Journal of Communication*, 1975, 25, 90–97.

Rubinstein, E. A., Liebert, R. M., Neale, J. M., and Poulos, R. W. Assessing television's influence on children's prosocial behavior. Stony Brook, New York: Brookdale International Institute, 1974.

Sears, R. R., Maccoby, E. E., and Levin, H. *Patterns of child rearing*. Evanston, Illinois: Row, Peterson, 1957.

Sears, R. R., Rau, L. R., and Alpert, R. *Identification and child rearing*. Stanford: Stanford University Press, 1966.

Shantz, C. U. The development of social cognition. In E. M. Hetherington (Ed.), *Review of child development research*. Vol. 5. Chicago: University of Chicago Press, 1975. Pp. 257–324.

Shirley, K. W. *The prosocial effects of publicly broadcast children's television*. Unpublished doctoral dissertation, University of Kansas, 1974.

Stein, A. H., and Friedrich, L. K. Television content and young children's behavior. In J. P. Murray, E. A. Rubinstein, and G. A. Comstock (Eds.), *Television and social behavior*. Vol. 2, *Television and social learning*. Washington, D. C.: U. S. Government Printing Office, 1972. Pp. 202–317.

Stein, A. H., and Friedrich, L. K. The impact of television on children and youth. In E. M. Hetherington (Ed.), *Review of child development research*. Vol. 5. Chicago: University of Chicago Press, 1975. Pp. 183–256.

Surgeon General's Scientific Advisory Committee on Television and Social Behavior. *Television and growing up: The impact of televised violence*. Washington, D.C.: U.S. Government Printing Office, 1972.

Wells, W. D. *Television and aggression: Replication of an experimental field study*. Unpublished manuscript, University of Chicago, 1973.

Wertham, F. School for violence. In O. N. Larsen (Ed.), *Violence and the mass media*. New York: Harper & Row, 1968. Pp. 36–39.

Application of Basic Research in Reading

S. JAY SAMUELS

> To the great Greek scientist Archimedes, the study of mathematics and physics
> meant far more than pure scholarship. Imaginative application of laws he formu-
> lated led to eminently practical inventions–from contrivances employing the level
> to an ingenious steam powered cannon.
>
> (*Time*, November 26, 1973, p. 58)

This chapter explores the relationship between basic and applied research in reading. In pursuit of this goal a brief description of the nature
and characteristics of basic and applied research is presented followed by
several illustrative examples of how basic research has contributed to the
field of reading.

CHARACTERISTICS OF BASIC AND APPLIED RESEARCH

Basic research may be thought of as that which originates with an
attempt to explain, describe, or increase our understanding of a naturally
occurring process or phenomenon. While applied research is directed at
issues of social relevance, basic research need not be. This is not to say
that the potential for social relevance may not be found in basic research,
but social relevance is not its immediate mission. Examples of basic
research with potential relevance for the reading process is typified by
work on selective attention, eye movements, pattern recognition, and
the structure of memory in comprehension.

Applied research, on the other hand, may be thought of as that

S. JAY SAMUELS • Center for Research in Human Learning, University of Minnesota,
Minneapolis, Minnesota.

which originates with a utilitarian aim in mind and represents an attempt to solve a specific, concrete problem in the shortest possible time. While research of an applied nature may draw heavily upon basic research findings when they are available, it is not essential that it do so. The immediacy of a social problem may be so compelling that attempts to solve the problem may begin in the absence of contributions from basic research. Furthermore, applied research need not follow on the heels of basic research and may precede and literally give birth to what will become an important class of basic research problems. Examples of applied research in reading include the development of methods and materials for teaching the deaf to read and the attempt to find effective techniques for teaching children to blend sounds to form words when using phonics.

Perhaps the difficulty one has in conceptualizing the functional roles of basic and applied research stems from faulty notions. Glaser (1973) has stated that "the sequence from basic research, to applied research, to development, to practice and application on which most of us were weaned is no longer applicable if, in fact, it ever was." A similar view has been expressed by David (1972): "It is essential that the impact of science on society be viewed not as a linear progression from discovery of knowledge to . . . products . . . but as a complex set of mutually dependent matters." These views suggest that basic and applied research and the problems of society should not be seen as separate entities in which information is fed along in a linear fashion. Rather, they exist in an interactive mode of operation.

An illustration of an interactive mode of operation pertinent to reading originated with a practical problem concerning airplane safety. During World War II, when badly damaged planes returned from missions, their pilots would radio to airport control towers requesting immediate permission to land. The practical problem had to do with the ability of the aircraft controllers to sort out the many competing messages coming in at the same time from the pilots and to respond appropriately to each of them. Research on selective attention, which dealt with questions such as how many things could the mind attend to simultaneously, actually had begun in the late 19th century and continued until the rise of behaviorism. However, because of the impact of behaviorism, with its emphasis on observables, the study of selective attention was virtually abandoned. The practical problem of airplane safety initiated basic research on selective attention, which led, in turn, to the development of theoretical models of attention. These models have been most useful in helping us to understand how the reader deploys attention when reading.

Before we leave this section on the role of basic and applied research, a final point should be made about one questionable use of basic research in the field of reading. In a facetious mood Wilson (1975) was moved to say, "Research is something we do to find out if we should have done what we did." This comment describes rather accurately one way in which research has been used by reading educators. The sequence of events may be drawn up as follows: first, there exists a widely used method that to some users, at least, has proven to be unsatisfactory. A new method, which supposedly overcomes the shortcomings of the older method, is developed and is used by a growing number of teachers. Before long, the high priests of each of the two methods oppose each other by writing learned papers to other high priests and by giving lectures to the practitioners, followers, and users of each of the methods. Neither method, it should be pointed out, originated from a research base. How then does one justify a method and, ideally, show its desirability? What has happened in reading is that practitioners look to empirical research for support.

This scenario can be illustrated with a specific and nontrivial case. From Colonial times to about the 1850s the most commonly used method in reading instruction was the alphabetic method. The student spelled each word in a sentence before saying the word. Thus, the sentence "The cat eats" was rendered as T-H-E "the" C-A-T "cat" E-A-T-S "eats." Spelling each word prior to pronouncing it interfered with comprehension, said the critics. From 1850 to 1908 a new method gained in popularity. This method emphasized comprehension over decoding and had the student pronouncing whole words without the need to spell individual letters. To justify the method, an experiment by Cattell (1885/1947) was used. This famous Cattell study found that a skilled reader could recognize a briefly exposed word as rapidly as a single letter, implying that for a skilled reader the unit of perception could be a word. The fact that Cattell used skilled readers and that the target population for reading instruction represents unskilled readers was ignored. Is this a single isolated example? Not at all. The debate is unresolved to this day and continues between those who advocate a phonics emphasis for beginning reading and those who advocate a meaning emphasis in early reading instruction.

What we have described is a situation in which a method existed followed by a search for justification and support from the scientific literature. This illustrative case is not, it would seem, the best way to develop and justify a new reading method. In the next section, we will demonstrate how basic and applied research have been used in appropriate ways to improve the psychology and pedagogy of reading.

Automaticity Theory

While it is true that it is reasonably common in the field of reading to find research used to justify an already existing method, it would be incorrect to view this situation as the exclusive manner in which research has been used. Basic research has an important function in reading and in this section we will attempt to demonstrate its role in the development of reading theory, methods, and materials. When information from basic research is made available it is frequently difficult to anticipate its effects and to predict which applied areas will find the information useful. A case in point has to do with the basic research on selective attention mentioned earlier, which originated with a practical question having to do with the ability of aircraft controllers to sort out and monitor the simultaneous competing messages radioed in by pilots. This research provided powerful constructs that helped us to understand the reading process, and through this understanding to develop new methods of teaching reading.

For years, a number of practical problems have bothered those who taught reading. Perhaps the most common reading problem encountered by those who work with children and do clinical diagnosis and remediation has to do with the beginning reader who has achieved some degree of decoding skill but who has difficulty with comprehension. This reading behavior might be described as "barking at print." Why is it that these students usually have little difficulty with comprehension when information comes through the ear but considerable difficulty when that information comes through the eye?

Another reading problem that at first appears to be very different from the "barking at print" problem has to do with the highly skilled reader, often a college student, who reads all the words on a page with ease but who comes away comprehending and recalling little of what was read. What mechanism allows a fluent reader to process text with poor comprehension and with poor recall?

Textbooks describe the acquisition of reading as a developmental process, not from the viewpoint of physical maturation but from the viewpoint of the development of an intellectual skill. What cognitive aspects of reading change as one changes from a beginning to a fluent reader?

These seemingly disparate aspects of reading are explainable in terms of selective attention and automaticity theory. Before going on, however, the term *decoding* should be defined since it will be used throughout this discussion. While it is true that the goal of reading is to comprehend the material printed on the page, for most readers there is a prior condition, namely, that the printed words be converted to some speech representation. This conversion can be in several forms, such as a spoken word that one can hear or a form that is silent. It is important to point out that decoding is not the same as comprehension since it is possible to decode a foreign language without understanding it.

The role of automatic decoding and its effect on reading comprehension is just beginning to be understood. For years reading teachers have been satisfied if their students were accurate in decoding words. Standardized tests of reading achievement, which are commonly used to indicate level of skill attainment, are tests of accuracy and give no indication of the automaticity of the behavior. While it is true that accuracy in decoding is necessary in reading, it is not a sufficient condition. In order to have fluent reading with good comprehension, the student must be brought beyond accuracy to automaticity in decoding.

The need for "automatic habits" in reading is not an entirely new idea. Huey (1908/1968, p. 104) wrote: "Perceiving being an act, it is performed more easily with each repetition . . . to perceive an entirely new word . . . requires considerable time and close attention . . . repetition progressively frees the mind from attention to details, makes facile the total act, shortens the time and reduces the extent to which consciousness must concern itself with the process."

In Fries's (1963) book, *Linguistics and Reading,* we find statements about the importance of automatic habits, but the term *automaticity* is not defined, nor are there explanations about the development and measurement of these automatic habits.

Since the present discussion places heavy emphasis upon the role of attention and automaticity, it is essential to review how these concepts have been used by researchers in the recent past.

Attention has two dimensions. The first dimension has to do with external observable components, usually associated with how one orients sensory receptors such as eyes and ears toward a stimulus. The other dimension of attention has to do with internal, nonobservable components.

The external, observable aspect of attention is important in reading acquisition. Lahaderne (1968) and Samuels and Turnure (1974) found that attentiveness to tasks assigned by the teacher was significantly related to reading achievement. In both of these studies a student was considered to be attentive if the student was following the teacher's instructions. Thus, if the instructions were to read from a particular book, the student was scored as being attentive if the student was engaged in that task and none other. An interesting finding from the Samuels and Turnure study suggests why in this country girls outperform boys in reading achievement. Direct classroom observation of children during reading indicated that girls were significantly more attentive during classroom reading instructions than were the boys. While some psychologists have offered a biological explanation having to do with earlier maturity as to why girls tend to outperform boys on verbal tasks, this latter finding would imply that cultural factors such as attention to task play an important role.

As important as external attention is to reading, the focus of this discussion, however, is on the internal components of attention that are not directly observable. Research on attention has moved in uneven waves. During the 19th century when the study of the effects of attention began, it was a favorite topic for introspective study. Interest then waned, but by the 1960s, as psychologists became interested in those processes that were not open to direct inspection, basic research on attention became an important area of study once again.

Research on attention has centered on three of its components: vigilance, selectivity, and capacity limitations. *Selectivity* refers to the ability to choose which among a variety of stimuli to focus upon, while *capacity limitations* refers to how many things the human mind can process at the same time. Of the three components—vigilance, selectivity, and capacity limitations—the latter two are most important for understanding the reading process.

While a number of competing models of attention exist (Kahneman, 1973), only the two that are the most relevant to reading will be summarized here. In Broadbent's (1958) investigations of how many things the human mind could attend to at once, a technique known as dichotic listening was used. With this technique a set of earphones was put on an experimental subject and one message was directed at one ear while a different message was directed at the other ear. Instructions to the subject might be to listen to the message in the left ear. The test, however, might be to find out how much information could be retained from each of the ears. A series of studies using the dichotic listening technique led Broadbent to conclude that humans could attend to and get meaning from only one thing at a time. When presented with two different messages, one to each ear, they selected one message at a time for processing. The inability of Broadbent's subjects to get meaning from two messages simultaneously led him to propose that there is a filter mechanism in the human brain which compels a person to attend selectively to one message and to ignore the others. In Broadbent's terms this filter has but one channel so that when tuned to a particular message, it permits that message to pass through for processing while blocking all other messages.

Subsequent to publication of Broadbent's (1958) filter model of attention, new experimental findings cast the model in doubt and suggested the need for revision. Moray (1959) found, for example, that people could notice that their names had been spoken even while they were listening to another message. It had also been found that if a person were listening to a message, changes in another message such as a shift from a male to a female voice could be detected.

The fact that information could be picked up from a message while attention was directed elsewhere was a serious blow to the Broadbent (1958) filter model. This finding led Triesman (1964) to suggest a revision. In Triesman's model, as in Broadbent's, an unfamiliar message can be processed if attention is drawn to it. An important difference between the two models is that Triesman's model accounts for the fact that well-learned messages can pass beyond the filter and be responded to appropriately even while at the same time an unfamiliar message is being processed with the aid of attention. Both the Broadbent and the Triesman models suggest that, when two unfamiliar messages are presented together, only the one upon which attention is directed will be processed for meaning.

If two simultaneous sources of information are presented, each requiring attention, the individual finds that both cannot be processed at the same time. What the individual may resort to then is the rapid switching of attention from one message to another. This is precisely what people do when they wish to take in several competing conversations and in psychological terms has been described as the "cocktail party problem," a situation encountered where a number of interesting conversations are going on simultaneously, each of which is competing for attention. Since the individual can only attend to one conversation at a time, several choices are available. The person can attend solely to one, ignoring the others, or may engage in attention switching. By switching attention back and forth, one may follow several conversations.

Broadbent's (1958) and Triesman's (1964) models of attention provide us with valuable insights as to how reading occurs. The fact that the brain can process only one unfamiliar message at a time has important implications for reading. As mentioned previously, the reading process may be broken into components consisting of decoding and comprehension. Before comprehension can occur decoding must take place. The beginning reader who has trouble with decoding is faced with a very difficult situation. Attention will be required for the decoding task. However, attention will also be required to derive meaning from the decoded material. Since attention can be on only one thing at a time, when it is on decoding, comprehension does not take place. Conversely, when attention is on the comprehension process, decoding cannot take place. However, by means of switching attention back and forth from decoding to comprehension, the beginning reader can manage to understand what is printed on the page.

Unfortunately, the strategy the beginning readers use of switching attention back and forth from decoding to comprehension is time-consuming and places severe strains on memory systems. Inadvertently, teachers have developed a widely used technique that gives the beginning reader the time required to access meaning. First, the students are told to read a short passage silently in order to get the answer to a question that the teacher has asked. Since the amount of time allowed for reading is reasonably generous, the students have time to work on the decoding task and then on the comprehension task. Usually, the teacher is unaware of the attention switching strategies just described which are used by the beginning reader to get the meaning. Many teachers are falsely under the impression that the students are reading just for meaning, when, in fact, they must first struggle with the decoding before getting to meaning.

The cognitive strategy used by the fluent reader in deriving meaning from the text is different from that used by the beginning reader in one important detail. Fluent readers are able to decode words automatically, that is, without attention. In stating that skilled readers can decode without attention, we are not referring to the observable aspects of attention such as looking at the words on the page. Rather, we are referring to the nonobservable aspects. Since the fluent reader is able to decode without attention, attention is available to be used for comprehension. Thus, fluent readers get two things done at the same time, decoding, which does not require attention, and comprehension, which does require it. The situation with the fluent reader who gets two things done at once is similar to the situation described by Moray (1959), who found that experimental subjects could process a conversation for meaning and at the same time could detect a well-learned signal such as their names. The only time the fluent reader would have to redirect attention back to the decoding task is when highly unusual words such as foreign names are encountered.

At this point a definition of *automaticity* is needed. Behavior is automatic if it can be performed without attention. Under ordinary circumstances, walking for an adult is automatic. When ice is on the ground attention may be required to prevent falling. A child may be able to recognize letters automatically, but attention may be required to recognize words. Thus, it is incorrect to consider that once the child has developed some automaticity in decoding, it will occur under all conditions. It is highly specific and related to conditions and tasks. Another way to think of automaticity is to consider two tasks that at unskilled stages could not be executed simultaneously (LaBerge, 1973). If both can be performed together after training, then at least one of them must have become automatic.

A further illustration of the concept of automaticity can be given. I recently asked a skilled typist to type a copy of an article I had given her. While she was typing I asked her questions about how her son was doing at school. She responded and this interplay between questions and answers went on while the typing continued. Two things were going on simultaneously, typing and answering questions. The typist was processing information coming in by eye and by ear. Since attention was required for processing the questions and answers it is assumed that the typing was automatic. Beginning typists cannot perform these two tasks simultaneously because their typing has not yet reached the automatic level.

Let us now move on to how this work on attention has been applied in reading. Somewhat more than two decades after the Broadbent model was published, David LaBerge, a colleague, and I began a year-long series of discussions on reading which culminated in the development of a reading model that we called an Automatic Information Processing Model. This model has been described in formal detail (LaBerge and Samuels, 1974) as well as for the practical needs of teachers (Samuels, 1976b).

The model of automatic information processing in reading attempts to do several things. First of all, it traces a variety of routes that information may take as it journeys from the page to its final destination as meaning. For example, it explains how printed words may be decoded into speech representations and finally processed into meaning. Or, parts of a word may be decoded. Then the separate sounds are blended together into a representation of a word from which meaning is derived. Still a third route might be direct from print to meaning. Whereas other models of reading tend to emphasize but one route, the automaticity model suggests that a variety of routes from print to meaning are possible depending upon the reader's skill, familiarity with the material, and purpose for reading.

Another important aspect of the model has to do with how attention is deployed during the reading process. The model differentiates between unskilled and skilled reading. In unskilled reading, the student must alternately switch attention back and forth between decoding and comprehension, a process that is highly inefficient since it tends to interfere with comprehension. On the other hand, in skilled reading, the student is able to decode automatically and focus attention on deriving meaning. The difference between how attention is deployed, whether it is switched back and forth between decoding and comprehension or whether it is focused primarily upon comprehension, is what differentiates the beginning reader from the fluent reader. In fact, it is through the deployment of attention that we can view reading as a developmental task. From a developmental view, beginning reading is characterized by decoding which requires attention, while fluent reading is characterized by decoding which is automatic.

The model of automatic information processing in reading is useful in explaining a number of phenomena observed in reading. One is the "barking at print" situation previously described. Some students seem to be reasonably accurate in decoding but have difficulty with comprehension. An explanation for this commonly observed classroom situation is that the student's attention is on decoding, which tends to impair the comprehension process. To help the students, greater fluency in decoding must be developed.

An effective method for improving reading fluency is through repetition and practice. One would imagine that this would be common knowledge for teachers. Unfortunately, many teachers attempt to cover a year's work in a year's time, so that many children are moved too rapidly through the pages of a book, never having had time enough to master what is on those pages. In addition, time spent on repetition is viewed by many teachers and supervisors as meaningless and purposeless "busy work," and to be avoided. The criterion performance level of work in reading is generally the accuracy level. When the child is at the accuracy level attention is still required. Consequently, we often find a situation in which students are moved too rapidly in reading, insufficient time for practice is allocated, and criterion levels of performance are set on mere accuracy. While accuracy is important, it is not sufficient, and if one wishes the student to reach the skilled developmental stage, the student must be given time to practice easy material so that automatic decoding skills may develop. While these pedagogical concepts are well known to athletic coaches and to music teachers, many teachers of reading have yet to accept and practice them.

Athletic coaches and music teachers are aware of the importance of repetition and practice for the development of mastery. Rather than try to develop too many skills in too little time, good coaches and music teachers want the student to work on a few skills until an established level of mastery has been reached. An example in point is the music teacher who gives the beginning student one or two short selections. The student is instructed to practice the pieces for a week. What the teacher hopes will happen is that after a week of practice the student will be able to play the selections with accuracy and fluency. Perhaps we should give serious consideration to the notion that we should transpose to the reading situation what the coaches and music teachers have learned. What they have learned is that for the development of certain kinds of skills there are only two things a good teacher can do. The first is to instruct the student how to be accurate at a skill. The second is to get the student to practice that skill to mastery. This practice may take place outside of school or in school. The old adage that "practice makes perfect" makes sense when applied to reading.

The second type of situation which the automaticity model helps us to understand has to do with the skilled reader who has difficulty remembering what was read. Since this type of reader can decode without the services of attention, attention is left free to direct at irrelevant factors, such as one's Saturday night date, which have nothing to do with the text. To help bring the student's wandering mind back to the task of comprehension, the technique of frequent self-testing while reading is often helpful. One type of self-testing involves the use of paraphrasing. Another type involves stating the key ideas. Both the paraphrasing and stating the key ideas can be done at the end of each page. Still a third technique for self-testing involves writing a test question for each page read. After reading several pages, the student stops and goes back to answer the questions before reading on. These self-testing techniques are designed to force the fluent reader to focus attention on comprehending the text.

Another applied aspect of the work on automaticity has to do with the "method of repeated reading." This method was designed to help beginning readers reach automatic levels of reading skill. The method is simple and can be used with only a minimum of training by parents and teacher-aids, for example. Rightfully speaking, it is an adjunct rather than a complete method of reading instruction. One way to use the method is to select a short, simple reading passage. The student reads the selection out loud and a record is kept of the number of word recognition errors and the time taken to read the short passage. Next, the student studies the passage and reads it aloud when ready, while a record is kept of errors and time. This process is repeated until a reading speed of 70 words a minute is reached. Then the student advances to another short selection and repeats the process. While a record of word recognition errors is kept, it is not necessary to have the error rate drop to zero. The reason is that there is a trade-off between accuracy and speed. When too much emphasis is placed on accuracy, the student becomes fearful of making mistakes and rate then tends to suffer.

Among the studies that have been completed is one in which the method of repeated reading was tested for a 2-year period with mentally retarded students. Important strides were made by these students in developing reading fluency. At first we thought the method might prove to be boring to the children, but when they asked for stop watches as presents for their birthdays so they could practice on their own, we realized our fears were unfounded. The children were pleased with the progress they made with each rereading of the passage. As many have observed, children enjoy repetition, asking to hear stories they have heard many times before. A more formal test of the method with children in regular classrooms indicated that children who used the method were superior to their controls in a variety of tests measuring word recognition and comprehension (Dahl and Samuels, in press). At Harvard, Chomsky (1977) has used a variation of this method with poor readers and has reported excellent results.

The final aspect of the applied work to be described here has to do with indicators of automaticity. At present our psychometric tests of reading skill primarily test accuracy. We now need tests of automaticity which are easy to administer, score, and interpret. Development of such tests is in its initial stages. For example, students are given instructions to read orally with the forewarning that they will be asked to answer comprehension questions. To ensure that a fixed reading rate is maintained, a reading rate pacer is used. Students who are not at the automatic decoding stages may be able to read orally but cannot answer comprehension questions because the fast rate of reading demanded by the task prevents them from switching attention from decoding to comprehension. Automatic decoders can comprehend while reading orally because their attention is on deriving meaning.

Still another promising indicator of automaticity consists of two sheets of paper, each containing 20 pictures of common objects. One sheet contains incongruent words printed across the picture. For example, there may be a picture of a dog with the word *tree* printed on it. The other sheet contains only the picture with no word. The task is to name only the picture and to ignore the word. When poor readers do this task, there is no difference in naming times for the two sheets. But when good readers perform the task, they are slower on the sheet containing the embedded incongruous words. These tests are in their infancy but show promise as practical tools for the teacher to use as indicators of automatic decoding processes (Ehri, 1976).

What we have done here is to trace how the findings from the basic research on selective attention were instrumental in the applied research represented by the development of a model of automatic information processing and the development of reading methods and tests. We go now to a second reading program whose origin can be traced to basic research.

THE WISCONSIN DESIGN

This program, called the Wisconsin Design for Reading Skill Development, has in a relatively short period of time made a significant impact upon how reading is taught. In 1967, it was merely an idea in Professor

Wayne Otto's head. Within the brief span of 10 years, it advanced to the point where currently the program is used in 4,000 schools by approximately 1,500,000 students, and the program has given birth to half a dozen commercial imitations.

A decade ago Otto noticed that teachers maintained poor quality control over their students' reading progress. While it is true that teachers were aware of the overall progress of their students, they were usually unaware of which reading subskills students failed to master. Consequently, he developed a series of diagnostic tests that are given at frequent intervals by the teacher in order to assess a student's skill level for each of the subskills deemed important in reading. If a student is found to be deficient in a subskill, there is a resource file keyed to hundreds of commercially available texts, which directs the student to appropriate reading activities. Progress tests indicate when a student has mastered each skill and can move on to the next reading level.

The effectiveness of the design has been substantiated through formal testing at three stages of development: pilot testing, small-scale field testing, and large-scale field testing. In the area of word attack (ability to pronounce words not previously encountered), with more than 1,000 schools using the materials, design users significantly outscored their control at each grade level. The comprehension phase is currently undergoing the evaluation-testing process so that judgments in this area cannot be made at the present time.

In terms of the role of basic research in the development of this project, a number of studies will be described. Since a complete survey of the many learning studies that are relevant to this topic would be inappropriate, the several that are described should be viewed as examples of the kinds of research that have been helpful. One of the more important studies that influenced the conceptualization of the design was done about three-quarters of a century ago by Bryan and Harter (1899) in their investigation of skill development in receiving Morse code. Their studies suggested that learning Morse code was a complex task requiring the simultaneous mastery of several components. When they studied the learning curve they noted periods of learning followed by plateau periods that seemed to indicate that no learning was occurring. However, they interpreted these plateaus as temporary periods devoted to the organization of component skills into larger units or as periods when the student was faced with having to master a particularly difficult component task. Thus, these plateau periods, rather than indicating the absence of learning, were important periods during which component subskills were integrated into higher-order units of behavior. When one studies the progress of beginning readers, one notes similar cycles of growth in skill acquisition followed by plateaus, further growth, and so on. These acquisition curves reflect processes similar to those described by Bryan and Harter.

Another important research study that influenced the design was done by Gagné (1962), who taught a group of students a mathematical problem-solving skill. He then gave a test of achievement, which indicated that success on the task was normally distributed. When Gagné broke his complex task into subskills and tested his students for mastery of subcomponents, he found that no student who failed a lower-order skill mastered a higher-order skill. He then systematically taught the students who had failed on the terminal behavior each of the necessary subcomponents of the task. When Gagné administered his achievement test a second time he found that all students had mastered the problem-solving skill. This study suggests that failure to master a complex task may be traced to an inability to handle a lower-order skill.

There are a number of implications from Bryan and Harter (1899) and Gagné (1962) studies which can be made with regard to reading. Reading is a complex skill requiring the mastery of subordinate skills, and, as in the reception of Morse code, it demands the integration of smaller units into larger units. What the Wisconsin Design set out to accomplish was essentially what Gagné did, to identify which reading subskills students were having difficulty with, and to teach students to master these skills. The assumption is that if students acquire the essential reading subskills and are given time to practice them in a meaningful way, the students will master the terminal goal of reading, just as Gagné's students mastered the mathematical problem-solving task.

One important decision made in the design was to test for subskill mastery at intervals frequent enough to be useful to the student. Unfortunately, much of the evaluation done in classrooms is done at the end of a large unit of work. This type of evaluation can do little to help the student who has had difficulty with the task. What is needed is the type of evaluation in which the student progress is monitored often so as to determine as soon as possible at which point there is a breakdown in the learning process. This type of frequent evaluation, which provides feedback for each individual, is the basis for quality control in the classroom. Just as industry needs quality control in order to maintain high standards, so too does education. Consequently, in the design a decision was made to diagnose reading problems on an individual basis, and remediation would consist of specific tasks to overcome the identified deficiencies.

Having made these decisions regarding general approach, the next task that the design group faced was formidable, indeed. How does one determine the decoding and comprehension subcomponents of a complex task such as reading? Despite the fact that learning hierarchies have a logical appeal, and that commercial reading series order the reading tasks as if we knew the nature of the hierarchy, the sad truth is that a validated hierarchy of reading skills in terms of order of learning and complexity does not exist.

Fortunately, there was some research available which could help in solving many of the applied problems. General guidelines regarding decoding subskills were provided by researchers such as Gibson (1965) and Venezky (1972). For specific guidance, curriculum manuals from public schools as well as suggestions from experienced teachers were used for the selection of decoding subskills. In the area of comprehension there were factor analytic studies available which indicated the components. For example, Davis (1944) discovered that the underlying components used in comprehension tests consisted of the following elements: literal and inferential comprehension, following the structure and sequence of a passage, recognizing the tone or mood of a passage, determining overall central thoughts, and vocabulary knowledge. Using the guidelines provided by the decoding and comprehension studies, the Wisconsin group was able to construct diagnostic tests to discover a student's mastery of the reading subskills.

Thus, with regard to the Wisconsin Design, we have seen how basic research on the nature of complex learning combined with research on the components of decoding and comprehension proved useful in the development of a program that helps teachers maintain quality control in reading.

READING FOR MEANING

The reading program called *Reading for Meaning* (Samuels, 1976a) evolved over a period of years, starting with a small-scale applied research study to determine how research on word recognition could be incorporated in a reading program. The information that was incorporated in the program was derived from several sources. One important source is rooted in concepts underlying cognitive psychology, which stipulate that seeing, hearing, and recognition are constructive processes. That is, sensory input into the human, storage of that information, and subsequent output are not identical because of the manner in which sensory information is transformed, reduced, elaborated, and used. What this suggests is that since recognition is a constructive process, output is frequently different from and greater than the sensory input. For example, given but a part of a picture, the mind is often able to construct the whole scene. What this implies for word recognition is that it is not necessary for the reader to identify all of the components of a word in order to recognize it. Accurate identification may occur when only a part of the word is apprehended.

Another source of information used in the reading program was derived from the experimental iterature on recognition. An early and important study on the role of context as a facilitator of recognition was done by Miller, Heise, and Tichten (1951). Under conditions of a noisy background, their subjects had to identify spoken words. They found that at a signal-to-noise ratio where it was almost impossible to identify a word in isolation, their subjects were able to recognize the same word when it was embedded in a meaningful sentence.

A similar study was done more than a decade later using visually presented words (Tulving and Gold, 1964). The subjects had to recognize a target word that was flashed. Each target word was preceded by a context that could be varied in length from 0 (no context) to 8 (the entire sentence), as in "Three people were killed in a terrible highway ____." Tulving and Gold found that with each increase in context, recognition became easier.

Other studies by O'Neil (1953) and Rouse and Vernis (1963) demonstrated that when words such as *table-chair* are exposed in succession, recognizing the first word aids in recognizing the second word. These studies, along with the studies by Tulving and Gold (1964) and Miller *et al.* (1951), suggest that context is a powerful facilitator of recognition. Furthermore, recognition did not have to be based on apprehension of all components in the target words. Thus, the program on word recognition that would be developed would train students to use context and partial cues from the target word. With this general approach in mind, Samuels (1970) developed a partial model of word recognition. The partial model of word recognition is not an entirely new idea. In many ways it is similar to the analysis-by-synthesis model of speech recognition.

According to the partial model of word recognition, four stages are involved in recognizing a target word presented in context. These stages are not steps in a teaching sequence but rather are steps in what may be thought of as a cognitive process. Assume that a person must recognize the target (underlined) in the context "Father cut the green <u>emerald.</u>" In stage one, the words preceding the target are read for meaning. In stage two, contextual information is used to generate one or more hypotheses as to the identity of the target word. Given the context "Father cut the green ____," words that can meaningfully fill that slot might be *emerald* and *grass.* In stage three, visual information from the target word, consisting of a letter or letters, is picked up and matched against the letters in the predicted word. In the final stage, if the first few letters picked up from the target word match the letters in the predicted word, the hypothesis is accepted. For example, one of the predicted words was *emerald.* Assume that the reader visually picks up just the letters *em.* Since these letters match the letters in one of the predicted words, the reader can accept the hypothesis. Speed of word recognition is determined partly by the amount of visual information from the target word necessary for verifying a prediction.

This partial model of word recognition served as the basis for the task analysis used in the Reading for Meaning program. In this program, students are taught how to use these four processing stages to recognize a word. In one of the stages, where the predicted word is matched against the letter cues from the target word, letter recognition is a prerequisite subskill. We found, however, that many youngsters had difficulty in letter recognition and naming; so we set out to design what we hoped would be an improved method for training letter naming.

Once again, basic research came to the rescue to aid in developing an improved program for letter-name learning. This basic research aid originated from two areas: research on associational learning and research on distinctive features.

Historically, paired-associate learning was considered to be a single-stage process. Continued research revealed, however, that contrary to earlier assumptions, associational learning is a complex, multistage phenomenon consisting of a stimulus learning stage, a response learning stage, and a hookup stage where stimulus response are joined (Keppel, 1968).

The other source of help for the development of this letter-name method came from research on the distinctive features. Jakobson and Halle (1956) had developed a theory explaining how the child acquired the phonemic aspects of language based upon noting contrasting features in how speech is produced. For example, the child would note the differences in the manner in which the following sounds are produced: /pa/ (labial), /ta/ dental, /ka/ (glottal). Impressed by the Jakobson–Halle notion of distinctive features in spoken language, Gibson, Osser, Schiff, and Smith (1963) investigated how letters are recognized. Their assumption was that distinctive features are used in visual discrimination. Using a confusion matrix and noting which uppercase letters are confused with each other, Gibson and her group concluded that letters are recognized by a feature-analytic process. Somewhat later, Pick (1965) discovered that if kindergarten children noticed the distinctive features of stimuli during training they made few discrimination errors on a transfer task.

The research studies on associational and distinctive feature learning provided the rationale for devising an improved method for teaching children to learn letter names. What we did was to separate the associational tasks into three stages, a stimulus learning, a response learning, and a hookup stage. During the stimulus learning stage we had the student learn the distinctive features of letters by having the student discriminate among letters that were visually similar. The visual discrimination phase has two parts to it. In the first part, the student is asked to do a simultaneous matching-to-sample task. For example, a group of four visually similar letters such as h, u, v, n would be shown. Then letter n is presented separately and the student is instructed to point to the one letter among the four that matches the n. The procedure is continued until all four letters are presented separately and matches can be done with accuracy and speed. The second part of visual discrimination training consists of a successive matching task. In the simultaneous matching-to-sample task just described the student is able to look back and forth from the letter presented separately to the alternatives in order to find the matching letter. In the successive task a match from memory is required. To accomplish this, once again letters h, u, v, n are shown and letter n is exposed and covered. The student is required to find its match from memory. This general procedure is repeated for other groups of visually similar letters such as $c, e, u, s; y, h, k, t; m, n, w, r; d, b,$ $p, q;$ and so on. By combining visually similar letters and requiring that the student locate specific letters within the grouping, the student is forced to notice the features of each letter in relationship to other letters that share similar features. When the student can perform the successive task with accuracy and speed, the next stages are introduced. The student is told the letter names and must then learn to hook up the appropriate names with the letters. When this method for teaching letter naming was compared with a traditional method, the experimental method proved to be a far more effective way to teach this skill (Samuels, 1973).

In this section we have explained how basic research was used to devise a curriculum for teaching word recognition strategies. The Reading for Meaning program that has been described now consists of a student workbook and a teacher's guide, which contains a brief rationale explaining the purpose underlying the program, detailed instructions on how to teach each unit, and materials for each unit. The program has gone through several empirical classroom tryouts and revisions, each of which has indicated that the experimental program is significantly superior to the control programs.

CONCLUSION

Before putting the final period to this chapter, let us summarize just two of the major points. First, contrary to the notion that the exclusive sequence of events is from basic to applied research and finally to utilization, there has emerged an alternative view known as the interactive mode of operation, in which an applied problem may provide the impetus for basic research. The final point is that basic research findings may be used in a field far removed in time and place from the original source. For example, research done on selective attention, to determine the ability of airport control operators to monitor messages, was used a quarter of a century later to devise a theory of information processing in reading.

REFERENCES

Broadbent, D. E. *Perception and communication*. London: Pergamon Press, 1958.

Bryan, W. L., and Harter, N. Studies in the telegraphic language, acquisition of a hierarchy of habits. *Psychological Review*, 1899, *6*, 346–376.

Cattell, J. On the time required for recognizing and naming letters, words, pictures, and colors. In *James McKeen Cattell, man of science*. Lancaster, Pennsylvania: Science Press, 1947. (Originally published by Piance, 1885.)

Chomsky, C. *When you still can't read in the third grade, after decoding: What?* Unpublished manuscript, Harvard University, 1977.

Dahl, P. R., and Samuels, S. J. Teaching high speed word recognition and comprehension skills. *The Journal of Educational Psychology*, in press.

David, E. E. The relation of science and technology. *Science*, 1972, *175*, 13.

Davis, F. B. Fundamental factors of comprehension in reading. *Psychometrics*, 1944, *9*, 185–197.

Ehri, L. C. *Do words really interfere in naming pictures*. Unpublished paper, University of California, Davis, 1976.

Fries, C. C. *Linguistics and reading*. New York: Holt, 1963.

Gagné, R. M. The acquisition of knowledge. *Psychological Review*, 1962, *69*, 355–365.

Gibson, E. J. Learning to read. *Science*, 1965, *148*, 1066–1072.

Gibson, E. J., Osser, H., Schiff, W., and Smith, J. An analysis of critical features of letters, tested by a confusion matrix. In *A basic research program on reading* (Cornell University and the United States Office of Education Cooperative Research Project No. 639). Ithaca, New York: Cornell University Press, 1963. Pp. 1–20.

Glaser, R. Educational psychology and education. *American Psychologist*, 1973, *28*, 557–566.

Huey, E. B. *The psychology and pedagogy of reading*. Cambridge: M.I.T. Press, 1968. (Originally published, 1908.)

Jakobson, R., and Halle, M. *Fundamentals of language*. The Hague: Mouton, 1956.

Kahneman, D. *Attention and effort*. Englewood Cliffs, New Jersey: Prentice-Hall, 1973.

Keppel, G. Verbal learning and memory. *Annual Review of Psychology*, 1968, *19*, 169–202.

LaBerge, D. Attention and the measurement of perceptual learning. *Memory and Cognition*, 1973, *1*, 268–276.

LaBerge, D., and Samuels, S. J. Toward a theory of automatic information processing reading. *Cognitive Psychology*, 1974, *6*, 293–323.

Lahaderne, H. M. Attitudinal and intellectual correlates of attention: A study of our sixth-grade classrooms. *Journal of Educational Psychology*, 1968, *59*, 320–324.

Miller, G. A., Heise, G. A., and Tichten, W. The intelligibility of speech as a function of the test materials. *Journal of Experimental Psychology*, 1951, *41*, 329–335.

Moray, N. Attention in dichotic listening: Affective cues and the influence of instructions. *Quarterly Journal of Experimental Psychology*, 1959, *11*, 56–60.

Muehl, S., and Kremenak, S. Ability to match information within and between auditory and visual sense modalities and subsequent reading achievement. *Journal of Educational Psychology*, 1966, *57*, 230–239.

O'Neil, W. M. The effect of verbal association on tachistoscopic recognition. *Australian Journal of Psychology*, 1953, *49*, 33–338.

Osgood, G. E. *Method and theory in experimental psychology*. New York: Oxford University Press, 1953.

Pick, A. D. Improvement of visual and factual form discrimination. *Journal of Experimental Psychology*, 1965, *69*, 331–339.

Rouse, R. O., and Vernis, J. S. The effect of associative connections on the recognition of flashed words. *Journal of Verbal Learning and Verbal Behavior*, 1963, *1*, 300–303.

Samuels, S. J. Recognition of flashed words by children. *Child Development*, 1970, *41*, 1089–1094.

Samuels, S. J. The effect of distinctive feature training on paired-associate learning. *Journal of Educational Psychology*, 1973, *54*, 164–170.

Samuels, S. J. *Reading for meaning*. Minneapolis: Research and Development Center for Handicapped Children, University of Minnesota, 1976a.

Samuels, S. J. Automatic decoding and reading comprehension. *Language Arts*, 1976b, *3*, 323–325.

Samuels, S. J., and Turnure, J. E. Attention and reading achievement in first grade boys and girls. *Journal of Educational Psychology*, 1974, *66*, 29–32.

Tichener, E. B. *Lectures on the elementary psychology of feeling and attention*. New York. Macmillan, 1908.

Triesman, A. Selective attention in man. *British Medical Bulletins*, 1964, *20*, 12–16.

Tulving, E., and Gold, C. Stimulus information and contextual information as determinants of tachistoscopic recognition of words. *Journal of Experimental Psychology*, 1964, *66*, 319–327.

Venezky, R. L. Language and recognition in reading. *Wisconsin Research and Development Center for Cognitive Learning, Technical Report*, 1972, 188.

Wilson, T. Universal Press Syndicate, 1975.

SECTION II
PSYCHOLOGICAL PRACTICE AND SOCIAL PROBLEMS

Introduction

JEROME E. SINGER

This section contains three illustrative examples of applications of social psychology. Social psychology itself is somewhat hard to define: it is an amorphous subdiscipline touching upon sociology, psychophysiology, clinical and experimental psychology. Basic research in the field covers a wide variety of topics. Depending upon the investigator and the mood of the times, studies in self-identity, attitude change, emotion, propaganda, group influence, personal value structures, architectural influence on behavior, prejudice and discrimination, public opinion, and an untold host of other areas have all been counted as social psychology.

All this variety should suggest that there are any number of applications of social psychology. And indeed there are. Historically, these applications have dealt with such topics as, for instance, attitude change in food preferences—a topic spurred by a World War II need for people to eat a variety of foods to prevent acute shortages of the most popular kinds. Also studied were the factors relating to racial tension and the easing of prejudices in public housing projects. Studies on the development of values of black and white children educated in segregated schools were used as important exhibits in the landmark *Brown* v. *Board of Education* Supreme Court case. A large part of the human potential movement—from leadership training to T groups and beyond—flows directly from the direct application of the theoretical work by Kurt Levin and his colleagues and students. There is a good portion of industrial psychology dealing with organizational development or motivation and morale which could also be considered applied social psychology.

Survey research techniques, voter preference studies, consumer market research—the list of such applications is a very long one and the applications themselves have touched all of us both directly and indirectly.

The three applications in this section are part of that applied tradition in social and personality psychology. They discuss ways in which the theoretical research from the psychologists' laboratories can be put to uses that can influence and shape our daily events.

THE POLYGRAPH AND LIE DETECTING

The chapter by David Lykken on the use of the polygraph for the detection of lies represents a case of science catching up with technology. The polygraph itself is a simple instrument: it records a number of physiological events—heart rate, respiration, skin resistance, and the like—from the surface of the body and displays these activities in the form of a graph over time. Two separate traditions have grown up in the use of the polygraph. One is an academic-research tradition in which psychologists use the device to study personality and the relation of behavior to peripheral physiology. The other tradition is the commercial adaptation of the machine to use in lie detecting.

Both traditions were founded on the same general set of assumptions. Behavior of various sorts, such as emotion or arousal, have physiological consequences. Lying is one particular behavior that produces arousal. Therefore, lying can be identified by scanning the polygraph record for physiological arousal. (This is, of course, oversimplified.) And while psychologists in the academic-research tradition were investigating the basic interrelationship of emotion, arousal, and physiological activation, almost independently the commercial users were developing lie-detection services. Although it would appear that the latter use would be an applied development of the former research, there was surprisingly little connection between the traditions. The application preceded much of the foundation research.

Lykken's chapter is a recounting of his experiences in applying basic polygraphic research to an evaluation of the use of the machine and associated techniques to lie detection. One strength of his application is the power of the basic techniques of evaluation and analysis when applied to the use of the polygraphs in lie detector tests. Since he began his studies, other psychophysiologists have joined Lykken in studying lie detection. Although some of them do not agree with all of Lykken's conclusions, they all share a common theme—the use of experimental evidence from basic psychological research to develop and comment on a practical application of a set of psychological principles.

IMPROVED DECISION MAKING

In a simpler day and age, when our culture was more homogeneous, our universe more ordered, and our choices more narrowly focused, decisions were probably simpler. But in our complicated present-day environment, each of us, in deciding on a job, a place to live, an education, a mate, is faced with decisions of enormous complexity. Irving Janis and Leon Mann discuss the basic psychological research: studies of how people make such decisions and of the quality of the decisions they make. Not surprisingly, they report that for many people the decision-making pattern or style is affected by the pressures and emotional issues raised by a pending decision and its alternatives. For example, if people must choose whether to undergo a particular surgical operation, all their options may be so anxiety producing that they may short-circuit an effective decision scheme in an effort to get the problem settled and out of mind.

The applied part of the Janis and Mann chapter lies in their depiction of the decision-counseling process. Here the collected research and evidence on the nature of the way in which effective decisions are made is applied to advising and focusing on the person who must decide. The emphasis is not on choosing for the person or questioning the values underlying the evaluation of alternatives but rather of rationalizing the process and helping the decider take advantage of all the relevant information available. And, of course, the question to be asked of such application is, does it work? Is decision counseling helpful in producing a set of more satisfactory decisions from those people counseled? Informally, Janis and Mann also look into the further question of the costs of decision counseling. Is it a major enterprise? Does it require procedures so cumbersome that its use is not justified by the decisions to be made? Does it only benefit a few or is it of general assistance?

The exploration of these matters is one of the strengths of the Janis and Mann article. For all too often, applications of basic findings are entered into with insufficient regard for their cost-effectiveness. Some procedures or applications are beneficial, but not worth the effort they entail. The Janis and Mann chapter, by attending to this issue, also serves as an illustration not only of a social psychological application but also of the process by which the application is operationalized.

TECHNIQUES OF MODIFYING ATTITUDES

The chapter by Jacobo Varela is a partial description of techniques by one whose primary business is applying social psychology. Strictly speaking, Varela is not a psychologist, that is, he does not do basic research or psychological theorizing. Rather, he is an engineer, whose interests lie in the conversion of scientific knowledge to practical technology. As consultants, engineers function by taking the principles of physical science and applying them in practical fashion to the problems at hand. Varela's unique contribution was to treat the findings of psychology in the same way.

Attitude change is an old topic in social psychology and a great deal of basic research has gone directly into its study of attitude formation, change, and organization. Indirectly, many theories from dissonance to reactance to the structure of intellect are also involved. The correct mix of theories or strategy of persuasion in any given case is not self-evident even to those who do some of the research and are aware of all the basic findings and principles. Consider an obvious example of attempted attitude change—a salesman attempting to sell a product. Although the salesman may have some general techniques in his repertoire, the optimal sales presentation at any given time will take the nature of the product, the client, the general market, and past interactions into account. Despite a large accumulation of information on attitude change, there are no general rules about how to tailor such a presentation. The chapter by Varela gives three case studies, demonstrations by his students, of how to engineer attitude change from general principles to a tailor-made persuasion.

There are many places in our society where attitude change occurs. A few instances are the act of selling, just mentioned above; election campaigning; group decision making, such as a jury reaching a verdict; and families or friends coming to agreement. It is from the last arena that Varela has drawn his examples. All of us at one time or another try to influence the people close to us—sometimes to get their support for our own actions, sometimes for what we regard as their own good, and sometimes for other reasons, whether worthwhile or frivolous. The question is not whether the attempted persuasion is adaptive or even well advised (the answer to that question would be yes at times and no at times) but whether the engineering application of social psychology makes the attempts more persuasive. The general design of such persuasions is not an endorsement of their worth any more than an engineer's design of a bridge is an endorsement of the worth or need for the superhighways that it connects. The cases described by Varela are examples of the types of manipulation we all engage in. The difference, and the point of the chapter, is that the persuasions are focused and effective.

In spite of the apparantly successful results, the ethical issues raised by the work in Varela's article are too big to be addressed in an introduction. People report on manipulating the behavior of friends and relatives and making some important changes in their lives:

Do they have any business practicing amateur psychotherapy?

Does any counseling have the right to be directive, imposing the persuader's values and beliefs on his targets?

Does the fact that the targets didn't know they were being persuaded make a difference?

What is Varela's responsibility having designed the method?

Would it have made any difference if he had lectured on effective selling and the students extrapolated to personal persuasions on their own?

This list is far from exhaustive. The Varela chapter raises an almost endless set of questions. Many of them lurk in the background not just of the applications described in this book but in the technological use of physical and biological research as well. Discussions of means and ends, justifications, costs and benefits, and social ethics are left to the reader. There are no easy answers.

Attitude Change

JACOBO A. VARELA

Few human activities are older and more widespread than trying to convince someone of something. There are, of course, the professionals of persuasion, a group that includes salesmen, teachers, politicians, clergymen, missionaries, lobbyists, etc. However, all the rest of us indulge in this in one way or another. Ever since Eve persuaded Adam to eat the apple, humans have tried to persuade others to go to a party, take a course, take up a sport, resign from a job, grant a pay raise, take a trip, vote for a given candidate. The persuasion methods used have not varied greatly over the centuries. Except in the hands of a few apparently gifted individuals, such attempts at changing the attitude of others have generally not been very successful. The failure is even more marked when the attempt is directed at getting two persons to stop their bitter quarrel. As Gilbert Chesterton has said, "The full potential of human fury cannot be reached until a friend of both parties tactfully intervenes."

The fact that most attempts at persuasion or changing attitudes end in failure does not deter most of us from trying to use the same method time and again. The method, in general, is universal with slight variations and is usually direct. All the arguments favoring a certain position are marshaled as strongly as possible, the dire consequences of not following that course of action also being presented. The target of our persuasion attempt usually proves to be very refractory, something that

JACOBO A. VARELA • University of Uruguay, Montevideo, Uruguay. Current Affiliation: Visting Professor 1977–1979, Department of Management, Wayne State University, Detroit, Michigan.

leaves us nonplussed. "How is it," we wonder, "that in spite of all these clearly logical reasons, our subject remains, if anything, more adamant in what is often a pigheaded position that is not only wrong, inconsistent, inconsiderate but often damaging to him as well?" We focus the problem on the subject, seldom doubting that perhaps what needed improvement was the procedure that we used. It is much easier to attribute the failure to some unaccountable failing in our target's ability to reason than to our own action.

There have been some well-intentioned attempts at improving this state of affairs, chiefly in courses and books that describe "successful sales and persuasive techniques." Most of these are the product of persons who have had considerable experience, have discovered some "tricks," and are willing to share these experiences with others. However, in our modern age of technology, such methods are reminiscent of the methods used by ancient builders. The Romans, for example, discovered that by placing stones in certain ways, it was possible to construct an arch that could not only support itself but also carry loads. They did not know why this was so, nor could they design different types of arches or more complicated structures. Their arches, of course, will stand as tribute to their good engineering, perhaps too good by modern standards. The expense of building structures that last 19 centuries is to be questioned on economic and other grounds. However, the introduction in the 19th century of modern stress analysis, with its subsequent developments and refinements, has allowed modern engineers to build not only arches similar to those of the Romans but also much longer and thinner arches, supersonic airplane wings, high-speed elevators, radio telescopes, skyscrapers, and many other things that the Romans could never have accomplished with their trial-and-error methods.

The modern structures mentioned have been possible because there has been much basic research in many areas based on constantly refined theory. This has been coupled to a sophisticated technology that consists in the ingenious ability to put together findings derived from such basic research in widely different areas in order to obtain a desired product.

The object of this chapter is to show that it has been possible to design a technology of attitude change also based on research done in many different areas of the social sciences. This new technology is as far removed from the "persuasion" methods described in books and courses on "salesmanship" as the modern airplane wing is from the Roman arches. It is also as superior to the older method as the Verrazano bridge is to Roman arches when it comes to solving such problems as spanning the entrance to New York harbor at The Narrows.

However, the reader is advised that the attitude change methods to be described here are merely a portion of a much wider discipline that solves problems of interrelations between humans and that I have labeled "social technology." This technology is used in group problem solving, conflict resolution, personnel selection and training, promotions, individual and marriage counseling, and many other areas. Attitude change design is just one branch and a rather late offshoot of this much wider field. The interested reader will find other examples of this social technology elsewhere (Varela, 1971, 1975, 1977, 1978). In this chapter, we will concentrate on the new methods for getting people to change their attitudes.

ATTITUDE CHANGE BY SUCCESSIVE APPROXIMATIONS

To begin with, we will assume that at heart the person we are dealing with really wants to change an attitude or behavior. This desire may be conscious or subconscious, but for some reason or other it is held in check. For example, a person may wish to stop smoking but finds himself or herself totally unable to do so. The person may wish to seek psychiatric help but does not dare take the first crucial step, rationalizing that this may be a blot on the family. Another may realize that medication is needed and wishes to submit to it for health reasons but keeps postponing due to a fear of recognizing he is ill or other such mental block. Still another may be embarked on a criminal career, wishing at bottom to be a law-abiding person but not knowing how to get out of the law-breaking rut. There are many cases. If I cite the above as possible, it is because exactly those cases as well as many others have been solved by the use of the techniques to be presented here. However, rather than give many different types of problems, I will concentrate here on different types of solutions.

It might be objected that going to all this trouble with people that at heart already want to change is not very far-reaching. After all, with a little bit of cajoling or direct persuasion, it should be easy to make them change. Two replies may be made to this. The first is that it is not easy for such persons to change. It is extremely difficult to stop smoking if you want to, as many people have found out. It is even harder to abandon a career of crime. Therefore, in each one of those cases the person needs outside help because very rarely are single-handed attempts at changing an undesirable attitude or behavior successful. The second reply to this objection asks if we know of anybody who lives a life entirely according to his or her principles or beliefs. In general, we recognize that this is not so. Therefore, there is a large field for this type of work.

Having made these preliminary statements, it is now possible to describe how results are obtained. It will be noted that, in the cases mentioned, there was a desire to change but an inability to do so. This inability is due to pressure keeping the person from doing the desired thing. For example, the criminal may not go straight because he has friends who pressure him to continue and not to abandon his "buddies." As mentioned, a lady may be desperately conscious of needing psychiatric help but will refrain from so doing because it is a shock to her, and she feels it will also be a shock to her family. The heavy smoker may feel very nervous about dropping his habit, and this very nervousness may lead to even more smoking.

This kind of situation, in which the person wants to do something for one reason but at the same time is kept from doing it for a different one, has been called by basic research psychologists the *approach–avoidance conflict*. The very name implies that the person is in conflict as he (I will drop the "he or she" from now on, it being understood that I refer to both sexes in so doing) wishes to do something and at the same time does not. It was found that, in general, when we are close to achieving a goal, the avoidance or rejection aspect overpowers the attraction and so we back away. The lady is about to call the psychiatrist but, as she begins to dial the number, she gets cold feet and hangs up. Of course, later, away from the act we ask ourselves, "Why did I refrain? It was so easy and there was nothing there to stop me." This is possible because, as has been found, when we are far from the desired action, the attractions are stronger than the rejections. We therefore feel impelled back toward the desired action. This kind of seesaw effect of going to and from the object, back and forth, even mentally, can be very frustrating and provokes a good deal of anxiety. This anxiety is disagreeable, and human beings have developed defense mechanisms for coping with it. For example, some people become very aggressive, even with others who have nothing to do with their problem. Others become apathetic, losing an interest in life. Still others accuse everyone else of having the very difficulty that they themselves have. This is called *defensive projection*, because the person tends to project onto everyone else the thing that is bothering him. Psychologists have conducted research on a variety of such defense mechanisms.

An important thing to keep in mind about defense mechanisms is that they are symptoms of a conflict that the person is not able to resolve. We will therefore gain nothing by trying to correct the symptoms. If, for example, the person is aggressive, we will only make things worse by telling him he is so and trying to soothe him. It makes things worse because we are clamping down on what, in effect, is a safety valve. In the same way, if a person is made ill by being in a difficult conflict, something that is very common in humans (and animals), then we gain nothing by giving medicine. If the result of the conflict is a bad headache, aspirin may temporarily relieve the pain, but it will not solve the underlying cause. If I stress this point, it is because very often in daily life we do just that. We treat the symptoms rather than try to analyze the causes. We think it stupid to do this in other areas. For example, if the engine in an automobile starts to make an unaccustomed loud knock, we would consider it ridiculous to treat this by covering the engine with sound-absorbing material instead of getting a mechanic to find out and correct the cause of the knock. Nevertheless, this is precisely the type of approach we undertake with respect to human behavior phenomena. The approach–avoidance conflict concept and others allow us to diagnose the causes of such behavior.

Another very important finding from the social sciences can often be seen in daily life. This is what happens when we buy a car and are not too sure that our purchase was the best buy. Having bought the car, we persuade ourselves that the undesirable aspects we thought it had were not so bad after all. Often, when we commit ourselves to a certain course of action and tell others about it, we convince ourselves that the course was the right way to go, even though we might have had a contrary opinion prior to that commitment. This type of attitude change was brilliantly researched by Festinger (1957) who confirmed experimentally that this is a common aspect of human behavior. He named it *cognitive dissonance,* because the spoken behavior is dissonant with the privately held belief. Festinger showed that in virtually every case in which a person experiences such dissonance, there will be a strong tendency to change one of the cognitions and so achieve consonance. There are many other forms of dissonance.

Still another important finding refers to our attitudes toward things in general. We do not simply like or dislike; there are degrees. Psychologists have tried to make up scales to measure these degrees. One such scale consists of statements about the object in question that go in graded steps from the lightly to the strongly rejected. Someone who feels very strongly about the subject matter will probably reject all the statements, whereas one with a more moderate stand will reject a smaller number of these.

Finally, we will use a finding by Brehm (1966) that most people recognize as being very common. Brehm found that when we believe some freedom of ours has been threatened, we have a strong tendency to restore the threatened freedom. When someone tries to force me to think in a certain way, I may strongly oppose this, even if by so doing I distort my actual private belief. In other words, we often emphasize freedom to express thoughts and are willing to violate beliefs that are not too strongly held to guard that freedom.

Now with all the preceding, which gives only the slightest impression of having something in common, we will construct a technological product that will be very powerful for helping someone to take an action he wishes to take but dares not. The first case to be described was diagnosed, designed, and executed by Roberto D'Aiello, a student at the School of Engineering, University of Uruguay.

Miss A. is a little over 30 years old. She arrived in Montevideo from her home in the interior 6 years ago and started to work as a manual worker in the plant where she is still employed. She used to travel regularly to the interior to visit her mother and sister, who are her only living relatives. Eventually, she got into serious trouble because of a sentimental attachment to an in-law, a matter that caused her to become estranged from her family. Her mother and sister were particularly incensed. She eventually got over the attachment and has not seen the man for a year. However, she has great feelings of guilt and shame even though it was she who finally separated from the man.

At present, Miss A. lives alone. She would very much like to see her mother and sister again, because she not only feels alone but also believes that they would want to see her. They had been very close prior to the incident mentioned. She feels approach toward this trip for the reasons stated, but at the same time she feels avoidance due to fear of how she will be received. There is also an element of laziness in having to undertake a trip she has not made in many years. She shows the symptoms of being in an approach–avoidance conflict situation since she is depressed, apathetic, and lacking energy in her work.

D'Aiello decided to help Miss A. by designing a persuasion procedure to help her change her attitude and take the much-desired trip. In order to do so, he used the method of successive approximations that I have devised. This puts together Sherif and Hovland's (1961) latitude of rejection scale, in which attitudes are measured by the number of statements rejected—statements that are placed in increasing order of rejection, as stated earlier.

In this scale, there is a statement that is most rejected. Therefore, I reason that there is one statement that is least rejected (see Table 1). If the person could somehow, without pressure, be induced to assert publicly the least rejected statement, the person would experience cognitive dissonance and, as Festinger and Mills (Brehm and Cohen, 1964) have shown, would tend to change the private belief to bring it in line with the spoken utterance. The latitude of rejection would be reduced by one, and the person, therefore, would not be as antagonistic as before. There would now again be another least rejected statement. If this is spoken by the subject, the latitude of rejection is further reduced. The process could be continued until the final conclusion is accepted. Of course, the problem is how to get the person to make the rejected statement in the first place. This can be done by use of Brehm's *psychological reactance,* mentioned above, which states that a person will tend to restore a freedom when that freedom is felt to be threatened. If a person's freedom is threatened on a point that is not too important, then the desire to reestablish that freedom will be greater than the desire to continue adhering to the lightly held belief. D'Aiello therefore prepared a list of statements going from a belief that Miss A. felt most positively to one felt most negatively, which in this case is, "I am traveling at once to see my mother." The list of statements is shown in Table 1. Each is preceded by a Likert-like scale value showing the initial degree of affect, in this case going from +6 to −6.

With this scale prepared, D'Aiello approached Miss A. and started a conversation which he eventually allowed to lead up to how lonely and empty she felt. Reaching that point he said, "You must not be sad. After all your mother never did love you." This reactance-provoking statement brought an immediate strong response: "What do you mean she did not love me!" To this outburst (which I give in very abbreviated form) he replied, "All right, all right. Maybe you are right there but one thing is certain: She would not want to see you again." This was, of course, a direct contradiction of Statement 2. Again reactance was provoked. Miss A. again replied strongly that her mother wanted to see her; that mothers are always mothers, etc. On doing so, she now accepted Statement 2 and therefore persuaded herself through dissonance reduction that the statement was not just slightly but very true, that is, that her mother did want to see her. At this he asked, "Even after what you did?" She was silent for a while so D'Aiello added that the matter was still a burning question in the family. This she immediately denied, saying that that kind of attitude could not go on forever. He then insisted by using questioning: "You therefore think that what you did was not so damnable after all?" To this she answered, "It was serious—but such a long time has passed." Seeing that so much had been accomplished, D'Aiello decided to change the

Table 1

Statement number	Degree of affect	Statement
1	+6	My mother has always loved me very much.
2	+2	My mother would like to see me.
3	−1	What I did was not that bad.
4	−2	My mother will be willing to forgive.
5	−3	I love her very much in spite of her neglect of me.
6	−4	I wish to see her very much.
7	−5	I can easily make it back.
8	−6	I am going to see mother next weekend.

strategy a little, making her retrace the earlier steps: "Then you mean that your mother has always loved you, wants to see you, and that what you did is not that important now?" To this she gave immediate assent. D'Aiello immediately followed up with: "But she is not the kind to ever forgive you," thereby provoking further reactance. Miss A. went into a long explanation of how she, being the youngest, had been pampered by her mother, how her mother had often forgiven all kinds of trespasses in the past, and how she would probably do the same thing now.

At this point in the attitude-change attempt, one major objection had been overcome: her fear that her mother would reject her. There still remained the problem of her wishing to overcome the laziness of having to make a long uncomfortable trip, which she had been in the habit of doing in the past but had not done for some time. D'Aiello got a reaction to this by saying, "Well, I agree that your mother will forgive and be very glad to see you, but I believe that it is you who do not want to go." Her reaction was violent. "Of course I want to go. She is my mother!" He admitted that perhaps she wanted to go but probably could not because she was working. She, of course, immediately objected, saying that her work had nothing to do with it, since she had visited her mother years before and had been working then. He replied, asking as if incredulous, "But when can you go?" To which she replied, "Some weekend." "Which one?" he asked, creating more reactance and getting more commitment. She replied that she could go the very next weekend. To this he said with a bit of irony, "Come on now, you're going to try to get me to believe that you can actually go into this mobilization act just to see your mother?" "Of course I can," she replied. A few days later, she returned from her visit to her mother with her problem solved. D'Aiello had achieved his goal. A break in family ties of long standing was suddenly healed. Perhaps, if left to herself, Miss A. would eventually have visited her mother. By his action, however, D'Aiello speeded up a reconciliation that all concerned wanted but could not manage on their own.

CASCADING I

The above example showed how, by successive approximations, a person was aided in taking a much desired decision. The case was rather simple. However, there are cases in which it is not as easy to achieve this. A technique called "cascading" has been introduced to deal with such cases. It consists in arriving independently by means of successive approximations to conclusions, each of which is again related to the others. The sequence of conclusions leads to the final one. An example will again show how cascading can be used.

It was undertaken by Ariel Joubanoba, a student at the School of Engineering, University of Uruguay. The case involved Jose, a 72-year-old man who had been in very good health most of his life but who had been told by the doctor that he now needed to take some disagreeable medicine. There is approach in that Jose wishes to maintain his good health, but there is avoidance for several reasons. One is that he does not like medication. An even stronger rejection is the fact that taking it means recognizing that he has a complicated illness, which for Jose is proof that his health is declining. He is not willing to admit this. All the direct attempts by his relatives to get him to take this medication have been fruitless. Here we also see the reactance phenomenon in operation. As the relatives increasingly insist, Jose increasingly feels that his freedom to take or not to take the medicine is threatened and the more he rejects doing so. Joubanoba correctly saw that Jose had different degrees of latitude of rejection toward different types of medication. He felt that designing an attitude change attempt by successive approximations in one sole step would tend to give the purpose away and thereby provoke further rejection. He decided to divide it into three stages. At each of the stages, a conclusion would be reached. The two initial conclusions would lead to the final one: "I am going to start taking my medicine immediately." The three conclusions were:

Conclusion 1.	The eye drops I took were very good for my eyesight.
Conclusion 2.	Medication is in general a good thing.
Conclusion 3.	I am going to take the medicine the doctor has prescribed.

Joubanoba knew that Jose liked to talk and that he was not too seriously ill. He therefore would not find it too difficult to enter into a conversation. His scales for the three conclusions were as follows:

Conclusion A	Statement
1	My appendectomy was good and I recovered fast.
2	My cataract operation was brief and successful.
3	The surgeon was good in the postoperatory period.
4	The eye medicine he gave me was very good.
5	Eye medication is a good thing.
Conclusion B	
1	The medicine they gave Mary was effective.
2	Diego was practically saved by penicillin.
3	Medication is in general effective.
Conclusion C	
1	Patients should not be left to themselves but should be taken care of.
2	I need to take care of myself.
3	I must take my medicine.

With these statements in mind, Joubanoba approached Jose at his bedside and held a long, amiable talk. I will merely quote the things he said during this conversation in order to get Jose to make the above statements.

Conclusion A

Statement 1. Your appendicitis operation was not that successful. It took you a long time to recuperate.

Statement 2. Was your cataract operation long and painful?

Statement 3. Your surgeon was not very good in the postoperatory period.

Statement 4. The eye medication was not very effective.

Conclusion B

Statement 1. The eye medication may have been OK but I don't think that the stuff they gave Maria did her any good.

Statement 2. But when Diego was given penicillin, he had a strong allergic reaction.

Statement 3. But medicine, in general, is very expensive and not too effective.

Conclusion C

Statement 1. I believe that patients should be left pretty much to themselves without too much attention so they can recover alone as they used to in olden times.

Statement 2. But you, for example, don't need to lie in bed or take any medicine.

Statement 3. But taking medicine won't do you any good.

By getting appropriate reactions to each of these, Joubanoba reached the goal. Jose immediately took his medicine and continued to do so as long as the doctor prescribed, thereby noticeably improving his condition.

Cascading II

A much more complex case was that attempted by Connie Bloch Small, then a student at the New School for Social Research. When she brought the subject matter to my attention, she tried to do it by simple successive approximations. However, much as she tried, she could not see it working. She asked me if she could do it in two steps. To this I replied that there was no limitation on the ingenuity one could use in an attempt at helping someone else. She eventually came up with a design in five steps. It was the first case to be done by what we afterward called "cascading." Therefore, she deserves recognition for having been the first to design this type of solution. I believe the best I can do is to transcribe her final report exactly as she presented it.

The General Situation

Mrs. B. has had a history of family difficulties. She was born in Germany and raised during both the great European Depression and the Nazi regime. During the Depression, her father went bankrupt and committed suicide. Mrs. B. was a witness to this and was, thereafter, greatly affected by it.

Mrs. B. became responsible for her mother and younger sister. She also had to deal with the Nazis in order to enable her family, who were Jewish, to leave Germany in 1939. This was an extremely traumatic experience for her. She left school and worked so that her family would have enough money to live.

After moving to the United States, Mrs. B. met and married Mr. B., who had been very generous to her and her family. However, Mr. and Mrs. B. had very little in common with one another, and the marriage was not a satisfactory one. Mrs. B.'s mother was also a problem. She was a very depressed person, who constantly complained to Mrs. B. about her lot in life. This would continue to make Mrs. B. feel guilty, anxious, and unhappy.

Mrs. B. began to develop physical and psychological symptoms about 5 years ago. These symptoms took the form of large skin rashes on her body every time she felt anxious. In addition, she experienced periods of dizziness and blackouts when she would fall on the floor. Mrs. B. also became very depressed at that time. She spent much of her time sleeping or complaining of fatigue. She had little appetite and showed no interest in people or things around her. This condition would recur regularly.

Mrs. B. has resisted seeking psychiatric help.

Design of a Persuasion

My goal is to help Mrs. B. by designing a persuasion which will shape her attitude to seek help willingly from a psychiatrist.

I am using a model which incorporates successive approximations. Each statement will be in direct opposition to what Mrs. B. believes to be the truth. This technique will allay any problems with cognitive dissonance. I shall incorporate some statements of agreement, however, to solidify the main point in each level. These statements of agreement will be masked so that reactance will not become a problem.

I shall present the first two levels of the persuasion on the first day during and after lunch. The introduction of food will have a positive effect. Then, I will wait for 2 days in order for the Abelson "Sleeper Effect" to take hold. The dissonance caused by changes in her attitude should also be reduced. During the 2 days, I suspect she will seek social support for the new opinions.

On the third day, I will introduce the next three levels of my persuasion. I shall also make sure that she commits herself to the decision to seek psychiatric help, by telling her husband about it and by calling her son, a psychiatrist, to ask for names of competent therapists.

Statement #   I

1. You know, I don't think Barbara has ever looked as poorly or as unhappy. I understand that she and Bob are not getting along well.
2. She seems so sad and depressed. I guess she was never able to work out things that were bothering her.
   (She will disagree here.)
   (Oh, OK, I guess you're right.)
3. Do you know anyone else that has been able to overcome so much? (Yes, Carole.)
4. Oh! that's right! She certainly has changed, too! She's very involved with her work now, and is dating and seems to be very happy with her life. She used to be so depressed. Just like Barbara.

Conclusion to I

In order to be able to work out one's problems, one must be able to understand them.

II

Persuasion by Analogy (Same Conversation, Same Day)

Statement #

1. I don't think it is *that* important for one to understand what is bothering him.
2. Well, few if any people are able to see what is bothering us as well as we can ourselves.

3. I don't think that either Barbara or Carole had to consult someone to help them, though.
4. Oh, I guess you're right there, too, I suppose. However, what type of person could one consult?

Conclusion to II

It is helpful to turn to someone who is trained to be objective and to have insight, in order to understand one's problems.

III

Statement #

1. I'll bet you've never been happier in your life.
2. Well, you don't really have any reason to feel sad, anxious, or depressed. Your life has been gratifying and somewhat uncomplicated.
3. Your marriage has been good and your childhood relatively uneventful.
4. Oh. Right! I guess I forgot about those awful things that happened to you. They aren't pleasant to think about.
5. You don't really have any pressing problems now, though, do you?

Conclusion

I have had a disturbing childhood and unsatisfying marriage. I feel depressed a good deal of the time.

IV

Statement #

1. Your health is good, isn't it? I mean, you're not as tired as you used to be.
2. Oh, well, are the dizziness and blackouts gone?
3. I see. Did the doctors ever find out why you are experiencing those symptoms?
4. Oh. Then I take it you have no idea of why you are getting the skin rashes, either.
5. Well, if there's nothing wrong with you physically, then you shouldn't be having symptoms like that, should you?

Conclusion

I get dizziness, blackouts, and skin rashes. There is no physical basis for these symptoms.

V

Statement #

1. There probably is no way you can get rid of your fatigue or physical symptoms.
2. They must not bother your husband or your mother, then.
3. Well, I don't understand. If your husband or mother were in the same situation. I mean, if they were feeling really depressed and developed skin irritations and the like, and if the doctors couldn't find anything wrong, would it bother you or affect you?
4. What would you suggest in that case?
5. I suppose that's a good idea but who would you go to?

Conclusion

If I go to a psychiatrist I will help myself and my family. Mrs. B. immediately went to the phone, called her son, and got the name of a psychiatrist whom she immediately called and made an appointment.

DIAGNOSIS

As can be seen from the above examples, they all succeeded because the person who tried the attitude-change design knew the other person well. However, there are many instances in which we do not know the other person so well, or we may believe we know him but the problem may be so serious that the real cause may not be apparent. It is therefore essential to make an accurate diagnosis. Without such diagnosis, it is impossible to design appropriate action. This is one of the reasons why these designs cannot be used as cookbook recipes. What worked to make Jose take his medicine is not a cure for all those who shun medication.

One of the best diagnoses I have seen, which led directly to appropriate and effective action, was performed by Charles Ortiz, then a student at Columbia University. He made the several consecutive diagnoses over a period of time and brought them in until we both were satisfied that the final one arrived at the root of a serious problem. The symptom was the increasing use of drugs. Knowing that alcohol and drugs are often symptoms of escape from an approach–avoidance conflict, Ortiz undertook to find out why a friend of his was showing that particular behavior. From his successive reports, which I reproduce below in full, one can get a very good idea of how questioning an inadequate initial diagnosis gradually leads to the real cause. After that, the design and implementation of the solution was a relatively easy matter.

First Diagnosis: 10/19/73

Subject: Jim Taylor

Problem: Increasing use of marijuana (several times weekly) and experimentation with other drugs, notably LSD and cocaine, over a 2-year period.

1. *Physical condition:* Has asthma, which has been severely exacerbated several times because of prolonged marijuana use (5 or 6 days in a row); otherwise in good condition.

2. *Mental abilities:* Low in cognition of behavioral implications; has suffered slight loss of memory capacity, apparently because of drug use.

3. *Personality:* Fits the unconventional type more than any other category:

— Looks to others (his mother, his friends) for organization

— Resents domination intensely

— Very sociable, enjoys the company of friends immensely

— Has a flair for the comic and loves to entertain others

— Feels very anxious, uncomfortable when he has to spend any long periods of time alone

— Has illusions of fame and fortune but never sets realistic goals for himself (as far as becoming a musician is concerned)

4. *Interests:* His central obsession is with music; anything else is of minor importance. Jim plays the guitar proficiently but does not practice in any organized manner so as to develop his talent.

5. *Background:* the one person who is singly important in providing Jim with organization is his mother, who raised him without a father. Jim has two brothers, who both got married recently in succession, leaving him and his mother to occupy the apartment. He is attending Island College as a freshman but comes home every weekend.

Additional comments: Reasons given me for his use of drugs:

A. Primary: "To pass the time away." He says he has plenty of time and nothing to do with it.

B. Secondary: Pleasure.

Present situation: Being that he is in a "foreign" situation, he is limiting his drug use to the weekends at present, when he can get together with friends. The danger is that he will soon or eventually develop friendships at school, which will allow him to expand his drug use.

Definition of the Problem

Problem: The inability to organize his behavior so as to achieve desired goal end-states.

Symptoms: Increasing use of drugs.

Second Diagnosis 11/6/73

1. *Diagnosis:* Jim suffers from the inability to organize his behavior in a manner that would help him achieve desired goals. This inability to organize would appear to manifest itself most strongly in his increasingly frequent use of marijuana and in his experimentation with other drugs.

A. *Objective:* In order to confirm or disprove our diagnosis of the problem, our objective must be to improve Jim's organizational abilities. If, with such improvement, the symptoms persist, then the problem lies elsewhere.

B. *Specific Task Areas:* Jim's lack of organization is apparent in several areas that involve desired goals:

(1a) Appearance, as exemplified by the disorderliness of his room.

(1b) Goal: Jim would like to know where his things are, particularly his records, which are in no order whatsoever.

(1c) Distance from goal: Only slight, because despite his disorderliness, the room is small and the amount of effort required to find an object is just a bit more than minimal.

(2a) Eating habits: Instead of eating the full meals which his mother offers to make for him, Jim eats less-than-nutritional foods on the run, because he has no set or approximate hours at which to eat.

(2b) Goal: Jim is very skinny and admires those with heavy builds, expressing the desire that he could be likewise.

(2c) Distance from goal: Small, because Jim himself feels that he could gain weight just by eating more, even if on the run (and tries, at times, giving it up as unimportant).

(3a) Study habits: Jim continuously allows his work to pile up on him.

(3b) Goal: Jim would very much like to major in music (although he feels it is not absolutely essential to his becoming a musician) and is even interested in taking up psychology as part of a double major.

(3c) Distance from goal: Moderate, because Jim does well (about a B average) in his studies due to cramming, but sometimes his work piles up beyond the point where cramming can do any good.

(4a) Social activity: Instead of making plans, Jim frequently expects his friends to get together with him at short if not immediate notice.

(4b)   Goal: Jim is a very socially oriented individual, constantly looking forward to being with his friends.

(4c)   Distance from goal: Great, as Jim is disappointed more often than not upon calling his friends, only to find out that they have already made plans for the day.

(5a)   Musical practice: Jim practices with his guitar quite irregularly, picking it up for 3 or 4 days in a row, then dropping it 2 or 3 weeks.

(5b)   Goal: Jim's central interest in life is music, and he hopes to be a musician as creative as those he admires, if not more so.

(5c)   Distance from goal: Extreme, as Jim himself indirectly recognizes when he acknowledges that a friend of his, who began playing the guitar at the same time that he did, is far ahead of him in technique.

Third Diagnosis 11/10/73: The preceding task areas in which Jim shows a lack of organizational abilities are listed in the order of their increasing importance to Jim, as indicated by the goals. Strikingly, this same order parallels an increase in the distance from the goal. The result appears to be an approach–avoidance pattern, where as the goals become more important, and thus more approachable, this increasing importance makes organizational abilities necessary for goal achievement more and more essential, thereby also rendering the more important goals avoidable, at greater cost. For example, because his studies are not as important to him as becoming a musician, the organizational ability needed for studying is perceived as less, making studying approachable enough (say, once or twice a week, for a few hours) to enable Jim to do relatively well (as compared to his guitar, which he picks up two or three times every few weeks). This pattern can be observed all the way down the line. Jim may place his objects anywhere within his room, but he places them somewhere. He may not eat three full meals daily, but he eats more than once, daily. Then when we hit a more important area such as his studies, organization becomes less, finally hitting rock bottom with his unmet need to plan social encounters and his unmet need to practice with his guitar regularly. This paradoxical ability to organize (as faulty as it may appear) when the goal is not too important, and the extreme lack of this ability when the goal is very important, would seem to indicate that Jim does not necessarily lack the ability to organize but rather that he is wary of organization for some reason(s). If we can help him to organize his goal-directed behavior in those areas of least importance to him, the painlessness and the efficiency of organization should decrease his avoidance of our efforts to aid him with those goals most important to him. And ultimately his increasing capacity to organize should reduce his use of drugs as a defense against the organizational implications of his goals.

Fourth Diagnosis 11/16/73: Jim apparently suffers from a mental block to his organizational capacities which prevents him from achieving desired goals, particularly as these goals become more important (thereby making organization increasingly essential). From this point of view his use of drugs is a defense of this mental block, as it allows him to avoid goal directed behavior and its organizational implications.

   A. Objective: In order to confirm or disprove our diagnosis of the problem, our objective must be to break down Jim's mental block toward organization. If, with success, the symptoms persist, then the correct diagnosis lies elsewhere.

   B. Specific Task Areas: If our diagnosis is correct, then the task is not to improve Jim's organizational ability in specific areas, as postulated previously (11/6/73). Such a move, while it might reduce his mental block, would not necessarily eliminate it completely. Organization in certain areas need not be transferred to others, and it could break down in time through conflict with the blocking factor. Our task then, is to devise a strategy which will attack the source of the problem, his fear of organization. In the meantime we can utilize one of the previously postulated task areas in order to determine the viability of our course of action: The greater the ease with which Jim shows organizational ability in putting his room in order, for example (with as little coordination on our part as possible), the stronger our position will be that Jim's problem is due to a mental block and not to the inability to organize.

Results of Diagnostic Proof 11/25/73: Jim's response to my organizing his records was a complex one. To begin with, according to his mother, Jim arrived home on the day before Thanksgiving with a friend from school and exhibited no reaction. However, as soon as his friend left, he asked his mother who had "fixed up" his record collection and seemed very pleased. Then he immediately proceeded to organize the rest of his room, to his mother's astonishment. Meanwhile, I knocked on his door to say hello, but he didn't open (which is very unusual for Jim). Instead, he called out to me that he would drop by my house later and (again, according to his mother) continued organizing his room. When he did drop by later on, Jim thanked me for organizing his records and said (seemingly half jokingly and half seriously), "Don't tell anyone else that we put my room in order—it would ruin my reputation." He also told me that I was a "strange person" for doing what I had done, especially if I knew what type of person (unconventional, as he is and prides himself on being) he is. Jim then (apparently defensively) changed the subject quickly, before I could give him any answer.

Diagnosis (continued): Taking into account the results of this proof (which uphold our revised diagnosis on 11/6/73), Jim's personality (10/29/73) and his close friendship with Bill Jones (whose own problem could in turn be defined as a "severe lack of goal-directed behavior"—with a corresponding lack of organization), it would appear that we can now outline the cause for Jim's mental block toward organization (using attribution theory and dissonance theory as our methods of analysis). First of all, Jim has been an intimate friend of Bill Jones since early childhood. Bill, as we observed, is extremely lacking in organizational capacities. Bill is also a person who has many friends, despite his unstable personality. It is quite conceivable that early in their friendship Jim grew to associate Bill's obvious lack of organization with the fact that he was liked by many people. If so, we can easily see how Jim, through a process of social comparison with Bill, came to attribute his own being liked by others to a lack of organization on his part instead of to his personality. Now, let us examine the support that we receive for this position from Jim's personality and from the results of our diagnostic proof. As we saw previously (11/6/73—Specific Task Areas, 4a, b, and c, and 10/29/73—Personality), Jim is a very socially oriented person and he loves his friends as much if not more than music. Yet he is afraid of showing organizational ability to these friends, to the point of being unable (unwilling) to make plans with them for social encounters. And as we saw in our proof, he avoided notice of organization in front of the friend he brought home with him. He was also very desirous of keeping others from knowing that he had fixed his room ("Don't tell anyone else—it would ruin my reputation"). Finally, he felt that organization conflicted with his image (presumably the image for which he is liked), in not understanding my action, an action coming from a person who "knows what type of person he is." All of these responses correspond to the idea (presumably held by Jim at some level of awareness) that the effect (his being liked) is attributed to that condition (lack of organization) which is present when the effect is present and which is absent when the effect is absent. The most logical strategy we can use in order to break Jim's mental block toward organization then is to dissolve the link (in Jim's mind) between lack of organization and approval by others. Since such a link presupposes that organization leads to disapproval (or at the very least, neutrality), we could dissolve the link by proving to Jim that organization does not necessarily lead to disapproval but could even lead to approval. Such a proof would amount to a dissonance-provoking strategy in which the unexpected cognition of approval in response to organizing behavior disturbs the equilibrium (organization = disapproval/neutrality) leading to a reevaluation of organizational capacities: the removal of the mental block.

B. *Specific Task Areas (continued)* 12/3/73: Our central task is to get Jim to organize in a situation directly affecting or involving his friends, especially Bill Jones, who told us a couple of weeks ago that he and his family are moving to Alabama a few days before Christmas. The idea involved is that of throwing a surprise party for Bill, a final get-together of all his friends before he leaves. Such a party would necessitate a certain obvious amount of organization, and the person who throws it would be held in high esteem by the others, particularly by Bill, for his thoughtfulness. The specific task is to persuade Jim to throw the party, soon, utilizing several statements:

1. Bill is a very close friend of Jim's. This statement would unquestioningly fit a value of +5 on a scale reflecting Jim's attitudes.

2. Jim has been neglecting their friendship during the past few months, first of all because he's in school (Island College) during the week and secondly because when he comes home on weekends, he's trying to catch up on his school work and other chores left unattended during the week. Jim's attitude toward this statement would rate −1, since he would undoubtedly hedge a little before admitting that he had neglected a friend (particularly Bill) in some manner.

3. Jim wouldn't buy Bill a present in order to (a) make up for his negligence or (b) show that he values their friendship, since a present wouldn't be adequate to achieve these goals. This statement would rate −2 on Jim's attitude scale, since if he did have to admit to neglecting a friendship, he would desire the route requiring the least organization (less than making plans to get together to go out) in order to make amends or show how much he cares about a friend.

4. The best present that Bill could receive from his friends would be some sort of get-together before he left. This statement would rate −3 on Jim's attitude scale, even if it didn't imply that he, as a friend, would be one of the people giving Bill the party, since he sees both Bill and himself as shunning organization and he couldn't see Bill appreciating the efforts to organize a party for him (the reasoning: If Bill likes me, its because I'm disorganized). Therefore Bill must not approve of organization. Paradoxically, Jim appreciates organization by others but he doesn't understand the implications (I can like others even if they are organized) of his appreciation because of his mental block, a block which is geared toward achieving his being liked by others.

5. Jim would do anything for one of his friends. This statement would rate −4 on Jim's attitude scale, since "doing anything" presumably includes acts of organization, acts which he feels at the very least would lose him some approval.

6. Jim, being Bill's close friend, should be the one to throw a surprise party for Bill before he leaves. The rating of this statement would of course be −5, since it specifically indicates that Jim should engage in an act of organization which might (in his eyes) even cost him the friendship of the person for whom he is doing it, let alone the approval of other friends.

Thus, through a reactance-provoking discussion we must get Jim to reduce his latitude of rejection for the preceding negatively rated statements from 5 to 0. And the order would be:

+5 Bill is a very close friend of mine.
−1 I've been neglecting Bill lately.
−2 A present wouldn't be enough to (a) make up for that negligence or (b) show how much I've valued our friendship.
−3 More than anything else, Bill would appreciate a get-together with all of his friends before he leaves.
−4 I would do anything for one of my friends.
−5 I should be the one to throw the surprise party for Bill.

B. *Specific Task Areas (continued) 12/8/73:* Results of persuasion—To the best of my recollection, once we got around to the subject of Bill's departure, the conversation went as follows:

MYSELF: "Guess what, I'm going to throw a surprise party for Bill."

JIM: "You are!?"

MYSELF: "Sure, why not? I've known him for several years now, and he's become a pretty good friend of mine."

JIM: "That's true, but if you've known Bill for years then I've known him for ages. We were hanging around together way before we met you. Still, don't you think that a party's a lot of trouble to go to?"

MYSELF: "No, I feel it's the least I can do. Who knows when I'll see him again, once he's in Alabama. I'm so busy that I barely have time to see him now when he's here."

JIM: "Yeah, I know what you mean. I used to see him all the time before I started school. Now I don't even know what he's up to."

MYSELF: "At first I was going to give him a present, but then I decided that it wouldn't be enough to make up for my negligence, or to show him that I care about our friendship. What do you think?"

JIM: "I'd look at it the same way in your place."

MYSELF: "That's not the only reason I decided to give Bill a party. I'm sure he would like to be with all of his friends just once before he leaves."

JIM: "Damn right. I know some people he hasn't seen, in a long time—like me for instance. Seriously though, I know some friends of his that you don't know, and if Bill saw them he'd have heart failure. It's a beautiful idea!"

MYSELF: "I might as well do it if nobody else is going to. And, as busy as I am right now, I'd do anything for one of my friends."

JIM: "Hey, you know what? I just got an idea. I understand how busy you are, what with all your exams and papers. But I'm not that busy. Would you mind if I asked you to let me throw the party instead? You could help me of course."

B. Specific Task Areas (continued) 12/15/73: After the success of the persuasion, we talked about the party itself. It was decided, since Bill would presumably be increasingly busy as the day came for him to leave (December 23), that the party should be given as soon as possible, or December 14 at the latest. Before Jim left for school on Sunday, December 9, he took care of (a) making plans with Bill's mother (e.g., finding out what time he would arrive home from work on the 14th) and (b) calling up all of Bill's friends he thought should come. I took care of buying the food and drink during the week. Then the night of the party came.

Results of Bill's Surprise Party

1. Jim was apparently flabbergasted at Bill's appreciation for what he had done. Several times during the night I heard Bill tell Jim, "Thanks a lot, Jim, I really appreciate this," or words to that effect, and each time Jim replied in a very embarrassed tone, "Don't thank me, it was nothing." And the very first time that Bill thanked him, Jim actually turned red, something I have never seen him do.

2. Jim also reacted with embarrassment when anyone else, particularly his closer friends, complimented him for having given the party or over how good the party was. At one point Willie, a very good friend of his, told him, "I didn't think you had it in you to do something like this." Jim smiled, apparently pleased, and replied, "I didn't think so either."

3. If Jim's embarrassment was any measure of his surprise at Bill's reaction of appreciation, he was doubly surprised when Bill asked him when he would come down to Alabama to visit him. His astonished reply was, "You really want me to visit you?" Apparently, Jim's expectation of a negative reaction on Bill's part toward his organization of the party was only shattered at this point. Perhaps in his own mind he had viewed Bill's initial exclamation of appreciation as a matter of formality.

4. Most telling of all was the fact that toward the end of the party, the aforementioned Willie asked Jim if he wanted to go outside with him for a moment to smoke marijuana. Jim's reply was, "No, I think I should stay here and take care of my guests." An astounded Willie then commented to Bill, "I've seen everything, but I never thought I'd see the day when Jim would refuse. . . ."

Analysis of Results: It would appear that persuading Jim to organize a surprise party for Bill has resulted in the achievement of our objective—the dissolution of his mental block toward organization. Jim's expectations of disapproval and/or neutrality from his friends (and Bill in particular) were nullified by their obvious approval (and especially by Bill's extension of friendship—his invitation to visit him). Such a nullification, inducing dissonance, could only result in Jim's revision of the position that organization had held in his life previously (a negative one, as it supposedly led to disapproval). Furthermore, Jim could no longer attribute his being liked by others to a lack of organization. Instead, he could only attribute his being liked to his own personality, with organization as a means to his goals (in this case the expression of his friendship for Bill). The most tangible evidence of his new perspective on the capacity to organize was the fact that he did not avoid the organization of the party in favor of a chance to smoke marijuana but even welcomed it because it involved the desired goal of entertaining his friends. Jim subsequently gave up drugs completely, has become organized, initiates social contacts, and continues on excellent terms with his friends.

Serious Emotional Problems and Relationships

The brilliant diagnosis and solution performed by Ortiz show us how it is possible for us to help others to get out of situations into which they have somehow fallen and from which they are unable to extricate themselves. But the question might arise: Is it possible to do this when there is considerable emotionality involved and when there is more than one person involved, each creating problems for the other? (Such very unsound and mutually distressing relationships exist only too frequently.) I will give an excellent example of how this was done by Virginia Irving, a student in my course on social technology at New York University. I reproduce her final report exactly as written.

Guilt and Misery

Background

For the last 10 years, my parents have been growing further and further apart, fighting more and more frequently and viciously until 2 years ago when the conflict reached a peak. All communication eventually ceased between them. My mother would banter at my father, and the more she bantered, the more he isolated himself from her and from his children. As he isolated himself, she would resort to any means to capture his attention, such as waking him up in the middle of the night and almost literally forcing him to listen to her murmurings into the early hours of the morning—usually mornings where he had to get up at 5:00 or 6:00 A.M. for a 12-hour day of work. She punished him in a variety of ways, including castrating him (figuratively) in front of his children through embarrassment, if he did not do what she wanted. However, if he acceded to her wishes, she would evidence a lack of respect for him.

In any case, my father isolated himself more and more through working hard and seizing the occasions for viable business trips, thus exacerbating my mother's needs and demands for attention. The late nights of listening to her began to seriously undermine his health. With the increased number of business trips, my mother began to imagine that my father had mistresses in every town, representing practically every race. She would then accuse him falsely of infidelity into the early hours of the morning. Finally, one day last January, my mother told him that if he left on Tuesday for his business trip, he was never to return to the house. She was convinced that he was going to see his black mistress in Atlanta (who does not exist except in her mind). My father had to leave for business purposes that day, but she would not listen. So, he took her at her word and moved out of the house, first into a hotel and then into an apartment.

Shortly thereafter, my mother instituted divorce proceedings and had her lawyer serve a divorce petition to my father at his office. Meanwhile, she told her close friends and her children (my younger sister is 13, my younger brother is 18) lies about my father's sex life, including that he was a homosexual (which was patently absurd) and attempted to convince everyone that he was sick, in his second childhood, and that he had abandoned her when she had been a devoted wife for decades.

Both of my parents had been seeing a psychiatrist, who shortly before the separation saw little hope for the marriage. They are continuing to see him at present to facilitate their adjustment to the dissolution of their marriage.

It is clear that much of my mother's recent behavior resulted from a need to justify to herself the fact that my father actually left. Naturally, in the case of a marriage of 26 years, there is a great deal of ambivalence for both parties involved when that marriage breaks up. My father has always been a person who tends to take the responsibility for all that goes wrong. Never once since the separation has my father tried to convince others that he was in the right and that my mother was impossible to live with. He simply says that it did not work out and maybe he could have done something to prevent it. He has maintained a great deal of dignity. Nevertheless, my mother is just as miserable as ever, capitalizing on this separation to gain sympathy from her friends. She calls my father on the telephone at the least excuse and tries to make him feel guilty through asking him why he is so sick and accuses him of devastating all his children through abandoning her.

The trouble is that he does feel guilty that she is unhappy. My mother succeeds very well in manipulating him to come over to the apartment to "face the facts" and endure her accusations through the pretense of various imminent tragedies that her fertile mind produces. When he does come over, this hurts him. It is also bad for my mother because in order to maintain hope for a continuance of the marriage or for her to develop an independent life with a hope for contentment, she must break out of this vicious cycle.

Problem

The specific problem to be dealt with here is that when my father listens to these sessions of self-pity, he only reinforces my mother's play for attention through misery, precludes her development as an independent person, and increases his own guilt.

When my father's situation is considered in terms of an approach--avoidance conflict, the approach gradient for my father consists of freedom, the ability to sleep and lead an independent life when living alone. His avoidance consists of guilt resulting from my mother's misery. The problem is to try to lower the avoidance gradient by decreasing my father's guilt through helping him reduce my mother's misery, if possible. Or at least to make him feel that he is doing his best to help her.

Solution

I decided to devise a solution based on the creation of reactance and the subsequent use of successive approximations to result in my father's determination to stop reinforcing my mother's tendency toward self-pity.

The statement around which the reactance was to be created was: (+7) I feel that I have done my best to take care of your mother during our separation, and I should not feel guilty.

The successive approximation statements devised were:
- −1 Self-pity creates misery and therefore must not be reinforced.
- −2 During the midnight conversations, mother would engage in self-pity.
- −3 Listening can reinforce self-pity.
- −4 If mother did not engage in self-pity, she would be less miserable and more capable of constructively utilizing her energies.
- −5 I would be doing my best for your mother if I did not reinforce her sessions of self-pity.
- −6 If I were doing my best for your mother, I can no longer feel irrationally guilty.

−7 Next time she calls, I will end the conversation when she starts to engage in self-pity.

Implementation of the Solution

I devised this solution after several intensive talks with my father over the phone and at the beginning of a week-long stay in Arizona, where I spent most of my time with him. Due to time factors, the procedure was implemented in two phases.

During the first phase, I created reactance through rather aggressively informing my father that he should feel guilty for causing my mother's misery. He responded quite defensively to the effect that I was crazy and he should not feel guilty because he had done his best to take care of my mother during their separation by being generous monetarily, providing a psychiatrist, and easing her break by seeing her occasionally as a friend (+7). However, he seemed rather perplexed, because he felt, on one hand, that he should see her to help her but, on the other hand, they would only end up fighting when he did take her out. He said that he should not feel guilty because he had tried his best, but he did feel guilty because he saw that she was unhappy while he was enjoying his freedom. This statement evidenced the approach–avoidance conflict mentioned above.

A few minutes later, I said, "You know Dad, self-pity is one of the prime causes of misery, and it really should not be encouraged" (−1). He said that he had never really thought about that, and it made sense. (It must be noted that my father and I both have very analytical minds, and we often have discussions on the whys and wherefores of aspects of human behavior.) Then he said that maybe much of my mother's misery was caused by self-pity, that perhaps his listening and allowing her to wallow in self-pity only increased her misery during their marriage and now (−3, −2). He suggested that when she calls him up on a real or bogus excuse to get him over to the house to solve a problem, when he must go perhaps he should confine their discussion to business, the divorce proceedings, money, and my brother's future.

Then we spent some time discussing the various ways my mother had managed to get him to the house. She had been particularly effective because she had him on a schedule of partial reinforcement. Occasionally he had to come to the house to solve serious viable problems, such as fixing something, when my mother fell down and sprained her ankle, or when my sister was sick. However, often she would blow something relatively minor into catastrophic proportions to get him over there. For instance, once she saw the flames of a fire several miles away from the terrace, and she called him to tell him that she was afraid that her house would burn down. So, my father felt that he must at least go over and check. She seized this particular occasion to speak with my father over a few beers. Alcohol disinhibits my mother's aggressive instincts, which evidence themselves in a viciousness that only aggravates her misery.

After my father and I had reached this stage, several phone calls intervened and dinner was served before I could continue my discussions with him. I felt that this would probably be good anyway, so he could think about our discussion. After dinner (phase two), I suggested that if mother were not reinforced for wallowing in self-pity, she would not be so miserable, and she could probably use her energies more constructively (−4). My father agreed vehemently. He commented on what an intelligent woman my mother really was, and if she put her mind to it, she could accomplish something which would make her a better person. He brought up an example denoting the fact that a few years ago, mother had taken art lessons and was becoming quite good when she stopped because we moved to a different state.

As we were talking the thought occurred to him that as long as he encouraged mother's misery, he was not really looking out for her best interests (-5). Then he said that he really did love her and wanted her to be happy. Then I interjected the comment that if he did his best to help her through avoiding her misery conversations, he would no longer feel guilty. He responded that he was sick of the guilt and so tired of the entire mess.

At that point, my mother called and said that my sister was very sick and needed her father. (She had a case of the flu.) As my father left for the house, he said, "I'll be back soon." Usually that meant a couple of hours at least where my mother was concerned. However, this time he returned an hour later, true to his word. He had visited my sister and spent 15 minutes with my mother. He said that when she started into him, he left. And he seemed rather proud of himself (-6, -7). It was the first time that he had been able to say no to my mother, especially since the separation. She had asked him why had he left when she had always been happy with him. On that cue he left. When I asked him whether he felt he should have stayed, he said, "No, and I don't even feel guilty. It would have been useless and harmful to have stayed with her."

This alleviation of guilt and ability to resist my mother has now persisted for over 3 months. My father usually called mother when away on business trips out of a sense of guilt. He has not called her while on any of his numerous business trips since our talk. And he feels good about that.

I saw my mother for the last 2 days I was in Arizona when she told me that it was definitely over with my father, and now he won't even talk with her. Although she was hostile, she seemed almost relieved because she said that now my father must make it on his own without depending on her, and now she is free of that responsibility. I was not sure that I agreed with her perceptions of the situation, so I said nothing. Before my father started asserting himself in this manner, my mother had been torn because she half believed that he could not survive without her on one hand, but on the other she could not stand a husband who whored around. So in a sense this did alleviate some of her conflict. However, the long-term results remain to be seen.

I must confess that I had been extremely skeptical about the ethics and the efficacy of this particular technique of social technology. However, it seems to have worked on this aspect of my parents' problems. There are other ways I am considering helping my mother through this technique, perhaps through revitalizing her interest in art. When she becomes less self-absorbed, perhaps she will really have a chance to attain peace within herself.

Conclusion

The preceding examples are a small part of the great number of cases that have been attempted and solved by those who have learned how to use social science findings in combination. It will be noted that they all used several findings. Problems do not get solved in general with the use of just one idea or hypothesis. This of course is common to all technologies. However, in general the social sciences have not done this effectively yet. Graduate students at many universities are being taught how to do research rather than to apply what has already been discovered. I am not making a case against research. Had there been no research, there would be no technology. Research must continue. However, it is possible that there is lack of balance. As in other areas, work on the application of research should parallel research itself. The myriad of problems that surround us, crying for solutions, are too tragic to be ignored, particularly when we now have the knowledge and technology to solve many of them.

I repeat that what is included in this chapter is merely one small offshoot of social technology. Social technology has done much other important work in areas such as conflict resolution, group problem solving, and many others. Merely recounting them would take quite some time. It must be noted that at least two of the preceding examples were carried out by persons who lacked prior knowledge of psychology. They nevertheless were able to learn, design, and perform good solutions within one semester. Of course, with much more training more complex action can be undertaken.

Even with short-term courses, results such as those reported here can be obtained. It is my belief that a great deal of good could be accomplished with more extended training in dealing with the serious unsolved human problems we face today.

ACKNOWLEDGMENTS

The author wishes to express his deep appreciation to Roberto D'Aiello, Ariel Joubanoba, Connie Bloch Small, Charles Ortiz, and Virginia Irving for the respective permissions they gave for use of the material they prepared as part of the course passing requirement at the University of Uruguay, New School for Social Research, Columbia University, and New York University.

REFERENCES

Brehm, J. W. *A theory of psychological reactance.* New York: Academic Press, 1966.
Brehm, J. W., and Cohen, A. *Explorations in cognitive dissonance.* New York: Wiley, 1964.
Festinger, L. *A theory of cognitive dissonance.* Stanford University Press, 1957.
Sherif, M., and Hovland, C. *Social judgment.* New Haven: Yale University Press, 1961.
Varela, J. A. *Psychological solutions to social problems.* New York: Academic Press, 1971.
Varela, J. A. Can social psychology be applied? In M. Deutsch and H. Hornstein (Eds.), *Applying social psychology.* Hillsdale, New Jersey: Erlbaum Associates, 1975.
Varela, J. A. Social technology. *American Psychologist,* 1977, 32(11), 914–923.
Varela, J. A. A technology of the social sciences. *Human Nature.* Oct. 1978, Vol. 1. No. 9.

Decision Counseling: Theory, Research, and Perspectives for a New Professional Role

IRVING JANIS AND LEON MANN

"Here I am," says the proverbial middle-aged man, "stuck with a miserable career chosen for me by an uninformed 19-year-old boy." Why do so many young people make poor choices they live to regret? Why do so many middle-aged men and women fail to correct their erroneous decisions of the past and continue to make poor choices? Similar questions can be raised about the ill-conceived decisions made by business executives, public service administrators, and national policy makers. "How could I have been so stupid?" President John F. Kennedy asked after he and his top-level advisors suffered the humiliations resulting from their decision to authorize the CIA's plan for the Bay of Pigs invasion. In recent years research investigators in social psychology, cognitive processes, and organizational behavior have been trying to answer such questions, to explain why people so often make decisions in public or private life that give rise to their personal Bays of Pigs. Some of the theoretical concepts and findings that have emerged point to ways of

IRVING JANIS • Department of Psychology, Yale University, New Haven, Connecticut. LEON MANN • Department of Psychology, Flinders University, Bedford Park, South Australia. This chapter is mainly based on our book, *Decision Making: A Psychological Analysis of Conflict, Choice, and Commitment*, copyright © 1977 by the Free Press, a division of Macmillan Publishing Company, Inc., New York. It also includes some material from the book *Counseling on Personal Decisions*, edited by Irving Janis, to be published by Yale University Press. Most of the studies described in this chapter were carried out as part of a research program supported by a grant from the National Science Foundation to Irving Janis.

preventing gross miscalculations and improving the quality of decision making.

SOURCES OF ERROR

A great deal has been learned during the past 25 years about the cognitive limitations of the human mind in confronting the complexities of selecting among multivalued choice alternatives, including the inability to keep in mind more than about seven chunks of information at one time. (See Carroll and Payne, 1976; Miller, 1956; Shepard, 1964.) More recent studies emphasize other weaknesses and limitations in human information processing, such as the propensity of decision-makers to be distracted by irrelevant aspects of the alternatives, which leads to erroneous estimates of predictable outcomes (Abelson, 1976), and by susceptibility to the illusion of control, which makes for over-optimistic estimates of outcomes that are a matter of chance or luck (Langer, 1975). Tversky and Kahneman (1974) describe various other illusions, some notorious and others not yet widely known, which arise from intuitive assessments of probabilities that may incline all but the most statistically sophisticated of decision-makers to make biased miscalculations in using evidence about the consequences of alternative courses of action. Some of the findings, for example, indicate that sound evidence about the low risks of a given course of action is likely to be ignored when possible unfavorable outcomes are brought to the decision-maker's attention, if it is easy to imagine the ensuing disasters.

Another line of research bearing on sources of error is being pursued by attribution theorists. Some of their studies reveal biases in the way one attributes motives, abilities, and other dispositions to persons whose cooperation might be required to facilitate or implement one's decisions (see Jones and Nisbett, 1971). In studies of policy formation in large organizations, still other common causes of defective decision making have been elucidated, including group conformity pressures and bureaucratic politics (see Etzioni, 1968; Janis, 1972).

Over and above the effects of the individual's cognitive limitations in judging evidence and the social constraints operating on him, a harassed decision-maker is likely to suffer a further decline in cognitive functioning as a result of the anxiety generated by the stress of being confronted with a task too complicated to manage, especially when it can entail serious losses (George, 1974; Janis, 1959; Janis and Mann, 1976, 1977). Our analysis of the ways that people cope with the stresses of making vital decisions emphasizes the tendency of people to short-circuit the essential stages of search and appraisal when they become aware that any choice would lead to undesirable consequences. Decision-makers are often inclined to deceive themselves into thinking they have conducted a complete information search after brief contact with an expert or someone who purports to be an authoritative advisor, and perhaps a few informal discussions with friends. This sometimes happens even when the decision is a vital one—such as quitting college, choosing a career, changing to a different job, getting married, obtaining a divorce, or moving to a different city. In such instances—whenever the decision could entail serious, lifelong consequences—a well-trained counselor can serve a valuable function. Even highly experienced decision-makers might benefit from professional guidance designed to help them to carry out a more effective information search, to correct some of their biased judgments, and to become more aware of the consequences of tempting but inadequate courses of action.

There is undoubtedly room for considerable improvement in the information-seeking and appraisal activities of the average citizen. This has been a neglected social problem for which new solutions, in the form of special counseling services and innovative educational programs, are now being developed to aid people facing fundamental life decisions. A new type of counseling service might also help persons in low-income families to become aware of the hidden consequences of the limited alternatives available to them and to work out personal or collective strategies for opening up more choices.

Our theoretical analysis of defective patterns of coping with decisional conflict (Janis and Mann, 1977) has some direct implications for counseling designed to help people improve the quality of their decision making. In this chapter, we shall discuss those implications after we summarize the theoretical analysis. Included will be several new types of intervention techniques that we have been developing and testing, which are especially applicable when a person is evading the unpleasant cognitive and emotional work of exploring the full range of probable consequences of each of the available alternative courses of action. These interventions appear to be promising aids that a counselor can use when a client seeks advice in making a vital personal decision. Each of the interventions may prove to be equally applicable, with appropriate changes, when a consultant is asked for advice by a chief executive or a group of executives responsible for making policy decisions affecting the welfare of their organization or nation.

WHAT IS DECISION COUNSELING?

We use the term *decision counseling* to refer to the joint work of a consultant and client in diagnosing and improving the client's decision-making efforts. One major type of personal counseling involves helping people to resolve realistic conflicts that arise when they are facing a difficult choice such as whether to be married or divorced, to switch to a different career, or to undergo elective surgery. This type of counseling can be quite nondirective with respect to substantive issues involved in the decision: The counselor abstains from giving advice about which course of action the client should choose and even avoids suggesting in any way that he regards certain choices as good or bad. Instead, the decision counselor tries to help his or her clients make the fullest possible use of their own resources for arriving at optimizing decisions in terms of their own value systems. Much of the counselor's work consists of making clients aware of the decision-making procedures they are using and of alternative procedures that they are not using. The counselor may be somewhat directive, however, in suggesting where to go for pertinent information, how to take account of knowledge about alternative courses of action, how to find out if deadlines need to be taken at face value or can be negotiated, which risks might require preparing contingency plans, and the like.

Decision counseling is currently used to some extent as a component in the treatments offered by psychotherapists, marital counselors, career counselors, and other clinicians who deal with people at a time when they are making important personal decisions (see Baudry and Weiner, 1974; May, 1969; McClean, 1976). It is also similar to an approach that is becoming popular among counselors who attempt to improve the quality of policy making in large organizations (Schein, 1969; Hackman and Morris, 1975). All these various types of counselors generally use a completely improvised approach, relying on their personal sensitivity, intuition, and clinical experience to determine what they say to their clients.

In contrast, we propose a more systematic approach, including a set of standard diagnostic procedures and corresponding interventions based on a theoretical analysis of coping patterns. Although highly structured, the proposed counseling procedures still leave plenty of room for flexibility and improvisation.

The proposed interventions, which usually require only 1 or 2 hours of counseling, obviously cannot be expected to overcome deep-seated neurotic disorders that give rise to chronic procrastination, chronic evasion of responsibility, or chronic denial of unfavorable outcomes. Some persons are probably predisposed to display time and again the same defective coping pattern, irrespective of the issues at stake or the situational opportunities and constraints that uniquely characterize each decision. If so, they require intensive psychotherapy or other psychological treatments far beyond the scope of decision counseling. But for people who occasionally display the more common garden varieties

of defective coping patterns, which presumably are in everyone's repertoire, a session or two with a skilled counselor might bring about a
marked improvement in the quality of their decision-making procedures. It is primarily for such people that the decision-counseling
procedures described in this chapter are intended.

To start with, the counselor must conduct a structured interview
during which the client is asked to express his or her views about
the decisional dilemma and to discuss the steps he or she is planning
to take before making a final choice. To be effective, the decision counselor must apply a variety of clinical skills that help the client overcome
the usual sources of obfuscation—such as efforts to present oneself in a
socially accepted way, to restrict one's conversation to conventional
modes of speech and superficial platitudes that cover up emotionally
explosive conflicts, and to justify one's past and present actions by
rationalizations.

Decision counseling, although different from psychotherapy, is
probably facilitated by standard features of the clinical stance adopted by
many well-trained psychotherapists (see Bergin and Garfield, 1971; Corsini, 1968). One component of this stance consists of making clear that
the counselor has no intention of making moral judgments, or of crit-
icizing or admonishing the client. A second component involves conveying a genuine sense of interest in learning the truth for the purpose of
helping the client become fully aware of the truth about himself, but not
in order to satisfy the counselor's own egotistic needs. A third component, which is especially important when people ask for help in
selecting the best course of action, is consistent renunciation of the role
of an authority figure who will tell the client what to do. Over and over
again, in many different contexts, the counselor can communicate the
prerequisites of nondirective counseling and demonstrate them in his or
her behavior—that the counselor sincerely intends to abstain from making any judgment about what would be the best choice for the client to
make, that the decision is entirely up to the client, and that what the
client does to arrive at it is the client's own responsibility. Nevertheless,
the decision counselor can recommend careful evaluation of alternatives
and effectively use interventions that are directive in order to encourage
a more complete information search, as will become apparent when we
review the evidence from systematic research.

The counselor's procedural interventions are most likely to be accepted and acted upon if his comments foster a relationship that is
socially rewarding to the client. This may require responding to self-
disclosure with genuine acceptance statements, which tend to enhance
the client's self-esteem. It might also require conveying to the client that
the counselor's demands for careful search and appraisal are limited in

scope and that occasional failure to live up to the standards the counselor is advocating will not change his or her basic attitude of positive regard for the client (see Janis, 1975, in press).

A Theoretical Model for Decision Counseling

The specific interventions that we have been developing are based on a theoretical model, which appears to be plausible in the light of evidence from studies of a variety of different types of decisions. The assumptions and the research bearing on them are discussed more fully in Janis and Mann (1977).

We start with the assumption that stress engendered by decisional conflict frequently is a major determinant of failure to achieve high-quality decision making. We postulate that there are five basic patterns of coping with the stresses generated by any agonizingly difficult choice. Each pattern is associated with a specific set of antecedent conditions and a characteristic level of stress. These patterns are derived from an analysis of the research literature on psychological stress bearing on how people react to warnings that urge protective action to avert health hazards or other serious threats. (See, for example, Baker and Chapman, 1962; Coelho, Hamburg, and Adams, 1974; Janis, 1971; Lazarus, 1966; McGuire, 1969; Sarason and Spielberger, 1975.)

The five coping patterns are:

1. *Unconflicted adherence.* The decision-maker complacently decides to continue whatever he has been doing, ignoring information about risk of losses.

2. *Unconflicted change* to a new course of action. The decision-maker uncritically adopts whichever new course of action is most salient or most strongly recommended to him.

3. *Defensive avoidance.* The decision-maker escapes the conflict by procrastinating, shifting responsibility to someone else, or constructing wishful rationalizations to bolster the least objectionable alternative, remaining selectively inattentive to corrective information.

4. *Hypervigilance.* The decision-maker searches frantically for a way out of the dilemma and impulsively seizes upon a hastily contrived solution that seems to promise immediate relief, overlooking the full range of consequences of his choice as a result of emotional excitement, perseveration, and cognitive constriction (manifested by reduction in immediate memory span and simplistic thinking). In its most extreme form, hypervigilance is known as "panic."

5. *Vigilance.* The decision-maker searches painstakingly for relevant information, assimilates information in an unbiased manner, and appraises alternatives carefully before making a choice.

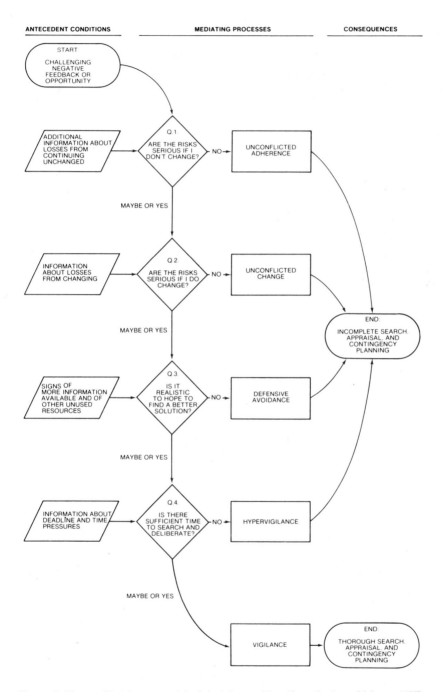

Figure 1. The conflict-theory model of decision making (from Janis and Mann, 1977).

Table 1. Predecisional Behavior Characteristic of the Five Basic Patterns of Decision Making[a]

| Pattern of coping with challenge | (1) Thorough canvassing of alternatives | (2) Thorough canvassing of objectives | (3) Careful evaluation of consequences of | | (4) Thorough search for information | (5) Unbiased assimilation of new information | (6) Careful re-evaluation of consequences | (7) Thorough planning for implementation and contingencies |
			a. Current policy	b. alternative new policies				
Unconflicted adherence	−	−	−	−	−	+	−	−
Unconflicted change	−	−	+	−	−	+	−	−
Defensive avoidance	−	−	−	−	−	−	−	−
Hypervigilance	−	−	±	±	±	−	−	−
Vigilance	+	+	+	+	+	+	+	+

Criteria for high-quality decision making

[a]From Janis and Mann, 1977.
− = The decision-maker fails to meet the criterion
+ = The decision-maker meets the criterion to the best of his ability.
± = The decision-maker's performance fluctuates, sometimes meeting the criterion to the best of his ability and sometimes not.

All evaluation terms such as *thorough* and *unbiased* are to be understood as intrapersonal comparative assessments, relative to the person's highest possible level of cognitive performance.

While the first two patterns are occasionally adaptive in saving time, effort, and emotional wear and tear, especially for routine or minor decisions, they often lead to defective decision making if the person must select a course of action that has serious consequences for himself, for his family, or for the organization he represents. Similarly, defensive avoidance and hypervigilance may occasionally be adaptive but generally may reduce the decision-maker's chances of averting serious losses. Consequently, all four are regarded as defective patterns of decision making. The fifth pattern, vigilance, although occasionally maladaptive if danger is imminent and a split-second response is required, leads to decisions that meet the main criteria for high-quality decision making, which we shall discuss shortly.

The five coping patterns are represented in Figure 1, which we present as a schematic summary of our conflict theory of decision making. This conflict model specifies the psychological conditions responsible for the five coping patterns.

The coping patterns are determined by the presence or absence of three conditions: (1) awareness of serious risks for whichever alternative is chosen (i.e., arousal of conflict), (2) hope or optimism about finding a better alternative, and (3) belief that there is adequate time in which to search and deliberate before a decision is required. We assume that the same five coping patterns are in the repertoire of every person when he or she functions as a decision-maker, that the use of one pattern rather than another is determined by the mediating psychological conditions shown in Figure 1, and that the five patterns lead to distinctive behavioral consequences, which are summarized in Table 1.

The columns of the table represent the major criteria that can be used to judge whether a decision made by a person or a group is of high quality with regard to the problem-solving procedures that lead up to the act of commitment. These criteria were extracted from the extensive literature on effective decision making (see Janis and Mann, 1977, chapters 1 and 2). The seven procedural criteria, named at the head of the columns in Table 1, are as follows. The decision-maker (1) thoroughly canvasses a wide range of alternative courses of action; (2) takes account of the full range of objectives to be fulfilled and the values implicated by the choice; (3) carefully weighs whatever he knows about the costs or drawbacks and the uncertain risks of negative consequences, as well as the positive consequences, that could flow from each alternative; (4) intensively searches for new information relevant for further evaluation of the alternatives; (5) conscientiously takes account of any new information or expert judgment to which he or she is exposed, even when the information or judgment does not support the course of action he or she initially prefers; (6) reexamines the positive and negative consequences of all known alternatives, including those originally regarded as unacceptable, before making a final choice; and (7) makes detailed provisions for implementing or executing the chosen course of action, with special attention to contingency plans that might be required if various known risks were to materialize.

We assume that failure to meet any of these seven criteria is a defect in the decision-making process. The more such defects are present before the decision-maker becomes committed, the greater the chances that he or she will undergo unanticipated setbacks and postdecisional regret, which make for reversal of the decision. Although systematic data are not yet available on this point, it seems plausible to assume that "high-quality" decisions—in the sense of satisfying these procedural criteria—have a better chance than others of attaining the decision-maker's objectives and of being adhered to in the long run.

What is unique about the model is the specification of conditions relating to conflict, hope, and time pressure, which mediate the distinctive coping patterns. We do not claim that the five patterns occur only as a result of the specified conditions. A habitual procrastinator, for example, may almost invariably approach any decision, large or small, in a defensive manner; a flexible person may display vigilance in response to most threats but become hypervigilant each time he reencounters a situation in which he had once been traumatized. Our claim is that the patterns are linked dependably with the conditions specified in Figure 1 —a claim that has testable implications about environmental circumstances that generate vigilance and about deliberate interventions that would counteract the beliefs and perceptions responsible for defective coping patterns. It follows from this theoretical analysis that information inputs and special intervention procedures used by a counselor when consulted by clients about making vital choices can modify the way the clients cope with the stresses of decisional conflict in the direction of improving the quality of their decision-making activity. A number of testable implications of the model have been investigated and at least partially confirmed concerning the conditions that determine whether the decision-makers' information search will be cursory or thorough, whether their deliberations will be biased or unbiased, and whether adherence to their decisions will be short-lived or persistent. (The pertinent studies are reviewed in Janis and Mann, 1977, chapters 4–12.)

COUNTERACTING DEFECTIVE COPING PATTERNS

We propose to use the conflict model as the basis for a systematic approach to decision counseling. From a free-style diagnostic interview centered on the four key questions shown in Figure 1, the decision counselor should be able to diagnose the client's dominant coping pattern. Questionnaires may also prove to be useful in gaining this diagnostic information, particularly self-assessment scales that measure variables related to the client's optimism or pessimism about finding an adequate solution to his or her decisional dilemma—e.g., the social assets scale (Luborsky, Todd, and Katcher, 1973), the social competence schedule (Phillips, 1968), the state of self-esteem scale (Quinlan and Janis, in press). But even without using standardized tests, a skilled interviewer should be able to ascertain the client's expectations about the risks involved in changing and in not changing, as well as his or her degree of optimism about finding a satisfactory solution and expectations concerning deadlines. The counselor would then have to determine whether the client's dominant coping pattern is realistic and adaptive for resolving his or her decisional conflict.

One of the values of the conflict model is that it suggests a number of ways counselors can help their clients avoid defective decision-making patterns. The following prescriptive hypotheses specify counseling procedures for promoting more vigilant search and appraisal.

1. If the counselor ascertains that the client sees no serious risks in continuing in the present course of action and surmises that the client's view is unrealistic, he or she can attempt to prevent unconflicted adherence to whatever course of action or inaction the person has been pursuing. The counselor can raise questions about the potential significance of the negative feedback the client may have already encountered, induce the client to consider possible unfavorable outcomes in the future, and encourage the client to obtain objective information and expert opinion about the costs and risks of not changing.

2. If the counselor ascertains that the client sees no serious risks in adopting an attractive new course of action and surmises that the client's view is unrealistic, he or she can attempt to prevent unconflicted change. This requires encouraging the client to obtain objective information and expert opinion about the risks of making the intended change and inducing the client to consider the unfavorable outcomes he or she may be overlooking, including potential losses from failing to live up to prior commitments.

3. If the counselor ascertains that the client is in a state of acute conflict and that the client believes there is no realistic basis for hoping to resolve the conflict, he or she can try to counteract this pessimistic expectation in order to prevent defensive avoidance. The counselor might encourage the client to discuss the dilemma with respected individuals in his or her personal network of relatives, friends, and advisors who might supply new perspectives, which could help the client to maintain hope. The counselor can also suggest that more information is

available and tell the client where he or she might find it by mentioning pertinent publications or by recommending professional experts who could be consulted. Above all, the decision counselor can convey a sense of optimism about the client's chances of finding a good solution to the problem.

4. If the counselor ascertains that the client is in a state of acute conflict and that the client believes there is insufficient time to find a good solution, he or she can try to counteract the panicky vacillation and premature choice that characterizes hypervigilance. The counselor might give realistic reassurances about what can be accomplished before the final deadline is at hand. Or the counselor might encourage the client to find out if the deadline is negotiable, to see if he or she can obtain an extension without serious costs or risks.

The four prescriptive hypotheses are not necessarily mutually exclusive if we consider the entire time span of the predecisional period. In early sessions the major task may be to establish an understanding of the nature of the alternatives and their associated gains and losses (hypotheses 1 and 2) while in later sessions attention is directed toward resolution, when maintenance of optimism and morale (hypothesis 3) and realistic assessment of deadlines and time pressures (hypothesis 4) become the major concerns. Thus, for example, in the first session after a counselor has successfully applied the first prescriptive hypothesis, he or she may soon discover that the second one has become applicable. In a later session, the other two might in turn become applicable, as the client changes answers to the key questions in response to new information he or she has sought out about probable losses, resources available for working out a good solution, and deadlines.

EXAMPLES OF INTERVENTIONS DESIGNED TO COUNTERACT DEFENSIVE AVOIDANCE

When people are required to make vital decisions, defensive avoidance is probably the most pervasive defective pattern as well as the most difficult to prevent or correct. The combination of conflict and pessimism about finding an adequate solution leads to the all-too-human tendency to seek escape via wishful thinking. Defensive avoidance may take any of three distinct forms: (1) procrastination, based on the wishful belief that nothing will be lost by putting off the decision indefinitely; (2) shifting responsibility, or "buck passing," based on the wishful belief that nothing will be lost by foisting the decision onto someone else; and (3) bolstering, based on wishful distortions of the gains and losses to be expected from adopting the least objectionable course of action. All three result in scanty search and inadequate appraisal. The special conditions that foster the first two forms are governed by cues as to whether the decision can be postponed at no great cost (e.g., absence of a deadline) and whether someone else is willing and able to take responsibility. When neither of these low-effort types of avoidance is available, bolstering, the classic mode of defensive avoidance, becomes the dominant mechanism for coping with the stress of a conflictful decision. Bolstering involves the well-known ways of reducing cognitive dissonance, including distorting, rationalizing, and denying in such a way as to play up the relative merits of the chosen alternative (see Festinger, 1964; Janis and Mann, 1977, chapters 4 and 5).

In our research program, we have been developing some new procedures to reduce defensiveness, all of which are based on the assumption that when defensive avoidance in any of its three forms is the dominant pattern, the person will actively resist new information about risks in an effort to avoid reactivating the distressing conflict, to protect his pseudocalm emotional state.

UNDERMINING RATIONALIZATIONS

In an antismoking clinic, Reed and Janis (1974) developed an "awareness-of-rationalizations" technique that helps to undermine some of the main rationalizations used to bolster the decision to continue smoking. The technique, which is designed to make the heavy smoker more responsive to challenging information that he or she typically discounts, was tested in a field experiment at the Yale Smokers' Clinic on a sample of 74 men and women who wanted to cut down on cigarette consumption. Half the clients were randomly assigned to the experimental group that was given the awareness-of-rationalizations procedure, while the other half received a control treatment that included the same antismoking communications as were presented to the experimental group.

The counselor's introduction to the awareness-of-rationalizations procedure stressed the importance of "honest exploration and frank acknowledgment of basic, deep-down thoughts and feelings" about giving up smoking. The interviewer then presented the client with a list of eight statements (referred to as "excuses") and asked if he or she was aware of using any of the excuses. The list consisted of typical rationalizations made by heavy smokers (e.g., "It hasn't really been proved that cigarette smoking is a cause of lung cancer"; "If I stop smoking I will gain too much weight"). After that the client was given a recorded lecture that refuted the eight rationalizations, followed by two dramatic antismoking films, and then reactions were measured. The same refutation lecture and antismoking films were presented to each client in the control group. Reed and Janis found that the smokers who had received the awareness-of-rationalizations treatment expressed greater feelings of susceptibility to lung cancer and emphysema, stronger belief in the harmfulness of smoking, and more complete endorsement of the anti-smoking films.

Follow-up interviews 2–3 months later revealed that, so far as the reported amount of smoking was concerned, the treatment had a significant effect when given by one psychologist but not by the other. Hence the technique cannot be regarded as an adequate cure for smoking. But the procedure of inducing a decision-maker to acknowledge and explore his or her own tendencies to rationalize appears to have considerable promise for reducing resistance to realistic warning messages. It has much in common with two other successful cognitive confrontation techniques used to undermine defensive attitudes that bolster social prejudices—Katz, Sarnoff, and McClintock's (1956) insight technique and Rokeach's (1971) awareness of inconsistency between values and actions.

Role Playing in Structured Psychodramas

Two types of role-playing procedures have been developed for the purpose of stimulating vigilance at two different stages of decision making, both of which require the client to participate in a psychodrama similar to those widely used for diagnostic and educational purposes. One such technique, known as *emotional role playing*, is intended to make the person more keenly aware of the unfavorable consequences of his current course of action and thereby induce him to consider alternatives. The counselor creates a scenario in which the client is confronted with an "as if" experience of being a victim of a specific disaster. For example, in our initial experiments, we asked each heavy smoker to play the role of a lung cancer patient at the moment when he or she is receiving the bad news from a physician (Janis and Mann, 1965; Mann and Janis, 1968). We soon found that this disquieting psychodramatic experience could be so realistic that heavy smokers would, for the first time, acknowledge their personal vulnerability to the threat of lung disease. The typical cognitive defense "it can't happen to me" or "it is impossible for me to change" can be undermined by this technique.

Sufficient research has been done on emotional role playing in antismoking clinics to show that this technique is capable of producing long-term changes in attitudes of personal vulnerability and in cigarette consumption among heavy smokers (see Janis amd Mann, 1977, pp. 350–360). Additional studies suggest that the technique may prove to be effective for other types of decisions as well—for example, inducing heavy drinkers "to go on the wagon" (Toomey, 1972) and evoking student support for changes in university policy to provide special facilities to meet the needs of disabled students (Clore and McMillan, 1970). Modifications of the technique are now being explored as potentially effective interventions for other types of decisions, including policy decisions by executives.

Another role-playing technique that offers promise for counteracting defensive avoidance and stimulating vigilance is called *outcome psychodrama*. It was devised to aid people when they are approaching the point of making an irrevocable commitment to a final choice, when there is still time to reconsider or to work out contingency plans. The client is asked to participate in a scenario that requires him to project himself into the future and to improvise a vivid retrospective account of what happened as a consequence of choosing each of the leading choice alternatives. The procedure is repeated as many times as necessary to explore the potential risks and consequences of the main alternatives under consideration. In contrast to emotional role playing, the counselor refrains from mentioning any specific consequences, leaving it up to the client to use his or her imagination to improvise the specific losses (or gains) that might be sustained.

Outcome psychodrama as an intervention for use in decision counseling was developed by Janis in a series of pilot studies. It was first used with clients having serious marital problems who came to a family service clinic for aid in making a decision about whether or not to seek a divorce. One woman, for example, in three earlier interviews had consistently described her marriage as nothing but misery and was fully convinced that the only solution was to divorce her unfaithful husband. After the purpose of the psychodrama was explained, she was asked to imagine that 1 year had gone by since she made her decision. She was told that she would be asked to go through the procedure twice, once as if she decided to obtain a divorce and a second time as if she had made a genuine effort to keep her marriage going. She chose to enact the divorce alternative first. When asked during the psychodrama whether she now felt fairly contented living independently, she blurted out, "No, I feel lonely and miserable, I miss my husband terribly, my life is completely empty now," and she burst into tears. This was the first time in any of the counseling sessions that she displayed intense emotion and the first time that she alluded to affectionate feelings toward her husband.

Afterwards, while reviewing what she had said during the psychodramatic enactments, she expressed surprise at the strong feelings that had momentarily overwhelmed her and said, "I have so much reason to hate him I guess I hadn't been willing to admit to myself that I still love him and will miss him." Thus the psychodramatic enactment enabled this client to gain access to deep-seated emotional attitudes toward her husband that she had defensively avoided acknowledging to herself. Once these formerly preconscious components became part of her conscious "balance sheet," she was able to make a more thorough assessment of the alternatives and to work out more realistic plans for implementing her decision. One month later she reported that despite her strong attachment to her husband, his constant mistreatment of her was so intolerable that she decided to obtain a divorce. But she had made a definite plan to avoid the loneliness of the separation by moving into an apartment with a girl friend. It seems probable that this plan was at least partly shaped by the increased awareness she had gained from the psychodramatic enactments of the losses she would sustain from going through with a divorce.

The same outcome psychodrama procedures were used with six other women and two men during the course of marital counseling interviews. In every case the clients showed signs of having become more vigilant, especially by confronting important new considerations regarding the choice alternatives that they had not mentioned in earlier interviews.

A similar psychodramatic procedure was tried out in career counseling with 15 Yale College seniors. Each student enacted two scenarios, dealing with an imagined crisis that occurs 1 year after selecting his most preferred career choice and his second choice. In 12 of the 15 students, new considerations emerged during the psychodrama that affected their evaluation of the alternatives. Four students were so impressed by the undesirable consequences that surfaced during their improvised performance of the psychodrama that they reversed their preferences.

No controlled field experiments on the effectiveness of outcome psychodrama have been reported as yet (one has just been completed by Huba and Janis and is now being analyzed). From the pilot studies we think that the technique will prove useful for clients in the later stages of decision making. In the early stages, this role-playing exercise might have a detrimental effect if it makes the client lose hope of finding an adequate solution to his or her decisional dilemma. But when someone is about to become committed to making a drastic change without having worked out contingency plans, outcome psychodrama might be beneficial in aiding the person to take account of emotionally charged considerations that would otherwise remain outside of his or her conscious deliberations.

FOSTERING VIGILANCE: THE BALANCE SHEET PROCEDURE

Several additional interventions have been developed which are intended to foster the vigilant coping pattern. One is the *balance sheet procedure,* an exercise requiring the person to answer questions about potential risks as well as gains that he or she may not have previously contemplated. Without a systematic procedure, even the most vigilant and well-motivated decision-maker may overlook vital aspects of the choice alternatives, remaining unaware of some of the losses that will ensue from the preferred course and maintaining false expectations about potential gains.

In an earlier analysis of decision-making processes (Janis, 1959), a decisional "balance sheet" of incentives was proposed as a schema to take account of both the cognitive and the motivational aspects of planning for future action. In this schema the expected consequences for each alternative course of action are classified into four main categories: (1) utilitarian gains or losses for self, (2) utilitarian gains or losses for significant others, (3) self-approval or disapproval, and (4) approval or disapproval from significant others.

One of the main hypotheses that has grown out of our subsequent analyses of the balance sheets of persons making stressful decisions (such as choosing a career, getting a divorce, giving up smoking, going on a diet, and undergoing surgery or painful medical treatments) is the following: The more errors of omission and commission in a decision-maker's balance sheet at the time of becoming committed to a new course of action, the greater will be his or her vulnerability to negative feedback when the decision is implemented (Janis, 1959; Janis and Mann, 1977). We refer to this hypothesis as the "defective-balance-sheet" hypothesis. Errors of omission include overlooking the losses that will ensue from the chosen course, which makes the balance sheet incomplete; errors of commission include false expectations about improbable gains that are overoptimistically expected, which are incorrect entries in the balance sheet.

A balance-sheet procedure designed primarily to prevent errors of omission was developed in a series of pilot studies by Janis and was pretested with Yale College seniors several months before graduation, when they were trying to decide what they would do during the subsequent year. At the beginning of each interview, the student is asked to describe all the alternatives he or she is considering and to specify the pros and the cons for each alternative. Then the special procedure is introduced. The interviewer shows the student a balance-sheet grid with empty cells and explains the meaning of each of the four categories. The interviewer helps the student fill in the entries for the alternatives the student had rated as most preferable. Then the interviewer asks the student to examine each cell in the balance sheet again, this time trying to think of considerations that he or she has not yet mentioned. In order to focus on neglected considerations, the student is given a sheet listing the types of considerations that might be involved in a career choice of the type he or she is making (see Table 2). The bulk of the time spent on this cognitive exercise is usually devoted to those categories that start off with few or no entries, most often considerations pertaining to approval or disapproval from the self.

Trial runs with 36 Yale College seniors who were making career choices suggested that the procedure is a feasible way of stimulating

Table 2. List of Considerations that Might Affect Career Choice
Used in the Balance-Sheet Procedure as Tested with College Seniors
Facing a Decision About What to Do After Graduation

1. Utilitarian considerations: gains and losses for self
    a. Income
    b. Difficulty of the work
    c. Interest level of the work
    d. Freedom to select work tasks
    e. Chances of advancement
    f. Security
    g. Time available for personal interests (e.g., recreation)
    h. Other (e.g., special restrictions or opportunities with respect to social life, effect of the career or job demands on marriage, type of people you will come in contact with)
2. Utilitarian considerations: gains and losses for others
    a. Income for family
    b. Status for family
    c. Time available for family
    d. Kind of environment for family (e.g., stimulating, dull, safe, unsafe)
    e. Being in a position to help an organization or group (e.g., social, political, or religious)
    f. Other (e.g., fringe benefits for family)
3. Self-approval or disapproval
    a. Self-esteem from contributions to society or to good causes
    b. Extent to which work tasks are ethically justifiable
    c. Extent to which work will involve compromising oneself
    d. Creativeness or originality of work
    e. Extent to which job will involve a way of life that meets one's moral or ethical standards
    f. Opportunity to fulfill long-range life goals
    g. Other (e.g., extent to which work is "more than just a job")
4. Approval or disapproval from others (includes being criticized or being excluded from a group as well as being praised or obtaining prestige, admiration, and respect)
    a. Parents
    b. College friends
    c. Wife or husband
    d. Colleagues
    e. Community at large
    f. Others (e.g., social, political, or religious groups)

ªFrom Janis and Mann, 1977.

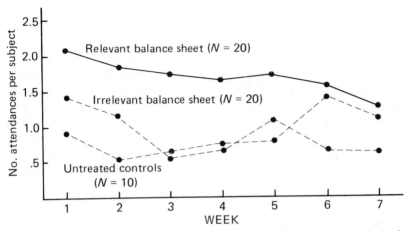

Figure 2. Week-by-week attendance for the relevant balance-sheet group, the irrelevant balance-sheet group, and the untreated control group (from Hoyt and Janis, copyright © 1975 by the American Psychological Association; reprinted by permission).

people to become aware of major gaps in their decisional balance sheets (particularly those pertaining to unfavorable consequences of the preferred courses of action) and can affect their choices. This pilot work was followed up by field experiments on the effectiveness of using the balance-sheet procedure. One study dealt with the choice of a college by high school seniors (Mann, 1972). A second obtained records of weight loss in the setting of a clinic for overweight women who decided to go on a diet (Colten and Janis, in press). In the third study (Hoyt and Janis, 1975), attendance records for healthy women who decided to sign up for an exercise class were unobtrusively collected (see Figure 2). The results of these controlled experiments indicate that the procedure is a promising type of intervention for decreasing postdecisional regret and for increasing adherence to a decision.

Stress Inoculation for Postdecisional Setbacks

Another major type of intervention designed to stimulate vigilance and to make for greater decisional stability is inoculation for subsequent emotional stress, which is usually administered shortly after a decision is made but before it is implemented. Stress inoculation involves exposing the client to preparatory information that vividly describes what it will be like to experience the expected negative consequences of the chosen course of action. Preparatory information functions as a form of inoculation if it enables a person to increase tolerance for postdecisional stress by developing effective reassurances and coping mechanisms (see Janis, 1958/1974, 1971; Meichenbaum, 1977; Meichenbaum and Turk, 1976).

The process is called stress inoculation because it may be analogous to what happens when antibodies are induced by injections of mildly virulent viruses.

We would expect stress-inoculation procedures to be effective for any decision that entails severe short-term losses before substantial long-term gains are attained. Most decisions concerning personal health problems belong in this category, because they usually require the person to undergo painful treatments and deprivations before his or her physical well-being improves. Much of the evidence concerning the effectiveness of stress inoculation comes from studies of such decisions —voluntarily undergoing abdominal surgery, painful medical treatments, and the like. Correlational results from Janis's (1958/1974) studies of surgical patients indicated that those who received information about the unpleasant consequences beforehand were less likely to overreact emotionally to setbacks and adverse events during the postdecisional period. Supporting evidence was subsequently obtained in a number of controlled field experiments with hospitalized surgical patients (Egbert, Battit, Welch, and Bartlett, 1964; Johnson, 1966; Schmidt, 1966; Vernon and Bigelow, 1974). These studies indicate that when physicians or nurses give preoperative information about the stresses of surgery and ways of coping with those stresses, adult patients show less postoperative distress and sometimes better recovery from surgery. Positive results on the value of stress inoculation have also been found in studies of childbirth (Levy and McGee, 1975; Breen, 1975) and noxious medical examinations requiring patients to swallow tubes (Johnson and Leventhal. 1974). Field experiments by Moran (1963) and Wolfer and Visintainer (1975) with children on pediatric surgery wards yielded similar results.

In a completely different area, that of work decisions, there is also evidence that stress inoculation can dampen postdecisional conflict and minimize the tendency to reverse the decision when setbacks are encountered. New employees who are given realistic preparatory information at the time they are offered the job, or immediately after they accept the job, are more likely to stay with the organization (Gomersall and Meyers, 1966; Macedonia, 1969; Wanous, 1973; Weitz, 1956; Youngberg, 1963). All of these findings support the conclusion that many people will display higher stress tolerance in response to undesirable consequences if they have been given warnings in advance about what to expect, together with sufficient reassurances, so that fear does not mount to an intolerably high level.

We know that there are exceptions, of course, such as neurotic personalities who are hypersensitive to any threat cues. But such considerations do not preclude the possibility that techniques of stress inoculation might be developed and used by decision counselors to help mitigate the impact of a wide variety of anticipated postdecisional setbacks, especially when the chosen course of action requires undergoing temporary losses in order to achieve long-term goals.

Laboratory and clinical experiments suggest that stress inoculation probably is worthwhile prior to the onset of any unpleasant event (see Epstein and Clarke, 1970; Meichenbaum, 1977; Meichenbaum and Turk, 1976; Lazarus and Alfert, 1964; Staub and Kellett, 1972). As we have just suggested, however, the more completely the balance sheet is worked out at the time of commitment, the less the need for stress inoculation after commitment. By inducing clients to arrive at an accurate blueprint of the unfavorable consequences that might be in store for them and the coping resources at their disposal, a decision counselor should be able to help each of them to build a basic attitude of self-confidence, to maintain a vigilant approach throughout all the stages of decision making, and to develop realistic reassurances. Acquiring that kind of reassurance can have a dampening effect whenever there is a postdecisional setback that otherwise might incline the person to regret his or her decision and to think about reversing or undoing it.

Coping Devices

A field experiment by Langer, Janis, and Wolfer (1975) illustrates the kind of intervention that can be developed to counteract detrimental effects of defensive avoidance and promote vigilance after a person has already become committed. This experiment assessed the effectiveness of interventions introduced in brief counseling sessions on the surgical ward of a hospital with patients who had recently decided to accept a physician's recommendation to undergo a major surgical operation and were awaiting the operation. In such a setting stress is very high and defensive avoidance is a frequent coping pattern. One intervention tried out in this study consisted of a coping procedure that builds up the patient's hopes by encouraging an optimistic reappraisal of anxiety-provoking events. Without encouraging denial of realistic threats, it encourages the patient to feel confident about being able to deal effectively with whatever losses or setbacks are subsequently encountered. During a brief counseling session the patient is given several examples of the positive or compensatory consequences of his or her decision to undergo surgery (e.g., improvement in health, extra care and attention in the hospital, temporary vacation from outside pressures). Then the patient is invited to think up additional examples that pertain to his or her individual case. Finally, the patient is advised to enumerate these compensatory positive aspects to himself or herself whenever he or she

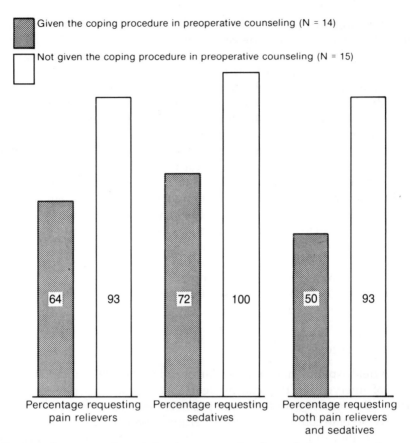

Given the coping procedure in preoperative counseling (N = 14)

Not given the coping procedure in preoperative counseling (N = 15)

| 64 | 93 | 72 | 100 | 50 | 93 |

Percentage requesting   Percentage requesting   Percentage requesting
pain relievers   sedatives   both pain relievers
and sedatives

Figure 3. Percentage of surgical patients requesting drugs during postoperative convalescence: A comparison between control patients and patients given a cognitive reappraisal type of coping procedure in preoperative counseling (based on Langer *et al.*, 1975, p.
161).

starts to feel upset about the unpleasant aspects of the surgical experience. Part of the recommendation is to be as realistic as possible about
the compensatory features so as to emphasize that what is being recommended is *not* equivalent to trying to deceive oneself. The instructions
are designed to promote warranted optimism and awareness of the
anticipated gains that outweigh the anticipated losses to be expected
from the chosen course of action.

Patients about to undergo major surgery were assigned on a random
basis to experimental and control groups that respectively were or were
not given the reappraisal type of coping procedure. As predicted, the
procedure proved to be effective in reducing both pre- and postoperative
stress. The data for testing the predictions were obtained from an analy-

sis of the nurses' blind ratings of preoperative stress and by unobtrusive measures of postoperative behavior—the number of times the patients requested pain-relieving drugs and sedatives. The main findings on postoperative coping, shown in Figure 3, reveal that the coping procedure had a markedly favorable effect on stress tolerance.

We believe there is considerable scope for the development of coping devices to prevent defensive avoidance tendencies and to foster an effective vigilant coping pattern among people facing distressing dilemmas, especially by boosting their hopes about finding satisfactory solutions when even the best available course of action entails undesirable consequences. The cognitive reappraisal device tested by Langer *et al.* represents a step in this direction.

SUMMARY

Recent research indicates considerable room for improvement in the way people arrive at important decisions. A new type of counseling service is described that is designed to help people improve the quality of their search and appraisal procedures when they face choices concerning career, marriage, health problems, or other vital issues. Prescriptive hypotheses for decision counselors have been derived from a theoretical analysis of the conditions making for effective and ineffective coping patterns. Sound procedures of search, appraisal, and contingency planning are most likely to be used, according to the theoretical model, when a vigilant coping pattern is dominant, which requires that the following three mediating conditions be met. The person (1) is aware of serious risks if any of the salient alternative courses of action is chosen, including no change from what he or she has been doing; (2) believes that there is some basis for hoping to find a better solution than the least objectionable alternative; and (3) expects to have sufficient time to search and deliberate before a final choice must be made. When one or another of these conditions is not met, a defective coping pattern will be dominant, which generally leads to inadequate search and appraisal. The four defective patterns are (1) unconflicted adherence to the old course of action despite exposure to a challenging threat or opportunity; (2) unconflicted change to a new course of action without considering its undesirable consequences; (3) defensive avoidance of decisional conflict by procrastinating, shifting responsibility for the decision to someone else, or bolstering the least objectionable alternative with wishful rationalizations while remaining unresponsive to corrective information; and (4) hypervigilance, which takes the form of frantic search for a way out of the dilemma and impulsive choice, without considering the full range of consequences, as a result of paniclike excitement, perseveration, and cognitive constriction.

Evidence from recent research was cited on the effectiveness of specific counseling intervention techniques for fostering vigilance. These include an awareness-of-rationalizations procedure, new forms of role playing in structured psychodramas, a balance-sheet procedure devised to induce awareness of the full range of consequences, stress inoculation for postdecisional setbacks, and a coping device that promotes warranted optimism.

References

Abelson, R. P. Script processing in attitude formation and decision making. In J. S. Carroll and J. W. Payne (Eds.), *Cognition and social behavior*. Hillsdale, N.J.: Erlbaum Associates, 1976.

Baker, G. W., and Chapman, D. W. (Eds.). *Man and society in disaster*. New York: Basic Books, 1962.

Baudry, F., and Weiner, A. The pregnant patient in conflict about abortion: A challenge for the obstetrician. *American Journal of Obstetrics and Gynecology*, 1974, *119*, 705–711.

Bergin, A. E., and Garfield, S. C. (Eds.). *Handbook of psychotherapy and behavior change*. New York: Wiley, 1971.

Breen, D. *The birth of a first child: Towards an understanding of femininity*. London, England: Tavistock, 1975.

Carroll, J. S., and Payne, J. W. (Eds.). *Cognition and social behavior*. Hillsdale, N.J.: Erlbaum Associates, 1976.

Clore, G. L., and McMillan, K. L. *Role playing, attitude change, and attraction toward a disabled other*. Unpublished paper, University of Illinois, 1970. (Summarized in J. S. Wiggins and others, *The psychology of personality*. Reading, Massachusetts: Addison-Wesley, 1971.)

Coelho, G. V., Hamburg, D. A., and Adams, J. E. (Eds.). *Coping and adaptation*. New York: Basic Books, 1974.

Colten, M. E., and Janis, I. L. Effects of self disclosure and the decisional balance-sheet procedure in a weight-reduction clinic. In I. Janis (Ed.), *Counseling on personal decisions*. New Haven: Yale University, in press.

Corsini, R. J. Counseling and psychotherapy. In E. Borgatta and W. Lambert (Eds.), *Handbook of personality theory and research*. Chicago: Rand McNally, 1968.

Egbert, L., Battit, G., Welch, C., and Bartlett, M. Reduction of postoperative pain by encouragement and instruction of patients. *New England Journal of Medicine*. 1964, *270*, 825–827.

Epstein, S., and Clarke, S. Heart rate and skin conductance during experimentally induced anxiety: Effects of anticipated intensity of noxious stimulation and experience. *Journal of Experimental Psychology*, 1970, *84*, 105–112.

Etzioni, A. *The active society*. New York: Free Press, 1968.

Festinger, L. (Ed.). *Conflict, decision and dissonance*. Stanford: Stanford University Press, 1964.

George, A. Adaptation to stress in political decision making: The individual, small group, and organizational contexts. In G. V. Coelho, D. A. Hamburg, and J. E. Adams (Eds.), *Coping and adaptation*. New York: Basic Books, 1974.

Gomersall, E. R., and Meyers, M. S. Breakthrough in on-the-job training. *Harvard Business Review*, 1966, *44*, 62–72.

Hackman, R., and Morris, C. G. Group tasks, group interaction process, and group performance effectiveness: A review and proposed integration. In L. Berkowitz (Ed.), *Advances in experimental social psychology*. Vol. 8. New York: Academic Press, 1975.

Hoyt, M. F., and Janis, I. L. Increasing adherence to a stressful decision via a motivational balance-sheet procedure: A field experiment. *Journal of Personality and Social Psychology*, 1975, *31*, 833–839.

Janis, I. L. *Psychological stress: Psychoanalytic and behavioral studies of surgical patients*. New York: Wiley, 1958. (Reprinted by Academic Press, 1974.)

Janis, I. L. Motivational factors in the resolution of decisional conflicts. In M. R. Jones (Ed.), *Nebraska symposium on motivation*. Vol. 7. Lincoln: University of Nebraska Press, 1959.

Janis, I. L. *Stress and frustration*. New York: Harcourt, Brace & Jovanovich, 1971.

Janis, I. L. *Victims of groupthink*. Boston: Houghton Mifflin, 1972.

Janis, I. L. Effectiveness of social support for stressful decision. In M. Deutsch and H. A. Hornstein (Eds.), *Applying social psychology*. Hillsdale, N.J.: Erlbaum Associates, 1975.

Janis, I. L. (Ed.). *Counseling on personal decisions: Theory and field research on short-term helping relationships*. New Haven: Yale University Press, in press.

Janis, I. L., and Mann, L. Effectiveness of emotional role-playing in modifying smoking habits and attitudes. *Journal of Experimental Research in Personality*, 1965, *1*, 84–90.

Janis, I. L., and Mann, L. A conflict-theory approach to attitude change and decision making. In A. Greenwald, T. Brock, and T. Ostrom (Eds.), *Psychological foundations of attitudes*. New York: Academic Press, 1968.

Janis, I. L., and Mann, L. Coping with decisional conflict. *American Scientist*, 1976, *64*, 657–667.

Janis, I., and Mann, L. *Decision making: A psychological analysis of conflict, choice, and commitment*. New York: Free Press, 1977.

Johnson, J. E. The influence of purposeful nurse–patient interaction on the patient's postoperative course. *A. N. A. Monograph Series #2. Exploring Medical-Surgical Nursing Practice*. New York: American Nurses' Association, 1966.

Johnson, J. E., and Leventhal, H. Effects of accurate expectations and behavioral instructions on reaction during a noxious medical examination. *Journal of Personality and Social Psychology*, 1974, *29*, 710–718.

Jones, E. E., and Nisbett, R. E. The actor and the observer: Divergent perceptions of the causes of behavior. In E. E. Jones *et al.*, *Attribution: Perceiving the causes of behavior*. Morristown, New Jersey: General Learning Press, 1971.

Katz, D., Sarnoff, I., and McClintock, C. G. Ego-defense and attitude change. *Human Relations*, 1956, *9*, 27–46.

Langer, E. J., Janis, I. L., and Wolfer, J. A. Reduction of psychological stress in surgical patients. *Journal of Experimental Social Psychology*, 1975, *11*, 155–165.

Lazarus, R. S. *Psychological stress and the coping process*. New York: McGraw-Hill, 1966.

Lazarus, R. S., and Alfert, E. The short circuiting of threat by experimentally altering cognitive appraisal. *Journal of Abnormal and Social Psychology*, 1964, *69*, 195–205.

Levy, J. M., and McGee, R. K. Childbirth as crisis: A test of Janis's theory of communication and stress resolution. *Journal of Personality and Social Psychology*, 1975, *31*, 171–179.

Luborsky, L., Todd, T. C., and Katcher, A. H. A self-administered social assets scale for predicting physical and psychological illness and health. *Journal of Psychosomatic Research*, 1973, *17*, 109–120.

Macedonia, R. M. *Expectations-press and survival*. Unpublished doctoral dissertation, New York University, 1969.

Mann, L. Use of a "balance-sheet" procedure to improve the quality of personal decision making: A field experiment with college applicants. *Journal of Vocational Behavior*, 1972, *2*, 291–300.

Mann, L., and Janis, I. L. A follow-up study on the long-term effects of emotional role playing. *Journal of Personality and Social Psychology*, 1968, *8*, 339–342.

May, R. *Love and will.* New York: W. W. Norton, 1969.

McClean, P. D. Depression as a specific response to stress. In I. G. Sarason and C. D. Spielberger (Eds.), *Stress and anxiety.* Vol. 3. Wiley, 1976.

McGuire, W. J. The nature of attitudes and attitude change. In G. Lindzey and E. Aronson (Eds.), *The handbook of social psychology.* Vol. 3. Reading, Massachusetts: Addison-Wesley, 1969.

Meichenbaum, D. *Cognitive-behavior modification.* New York: Plenum, 1977.

Meichenbaum, D., and Turk, D. The cognitive-behavioral management of anxiety, anger, and pain. In P. O. Davidson (Ed.), *The behavioral management of anxiety, depression, and pain.* New York: Brunner/Mazel, 1976.

Miller, G. A. The magical number seven, plus or minus two. *Psychological Review,* 1956, *63,* 81–97.

Moran, P. A. *An experimental study of pediatric admission.* Unpublished master's thesis, Yale University School of Nursing, 1963.

Phillips, L. *Human adaptation and its failures.* New York: Academic Press, 1968.

Quinlan, D., and Janis, I. Appendix A: A questionnaire to assess state *versus* trait of self esteem. In I. Janis (Ed.), *Counseling on personal decisions.* New Haven: Yale University Press, in press.

Reed, H. D., and Janis, I. L. Effects of a new type of psychological treatment on smokers' resistance to warnings about health hazards. *Journal of Consulting and Clinical Psychology,* 1974, *42,* 748.

Rokeach, M. Long-range experimental modification of values, attitudes and behavior. *American Psychologist,* 1971, *26,* 453–459.

Sarason, I. G., and Spielberger, C. D. (Eds.). *Stress and anxiety.* Vol. 2. New York: Wiley, 1975.

Schein, E. G. *Process consultation.* Reading, Massachusetts: Addison-Wesley, 1969.

Schmidt, R. L. *An exploratory study of nursing and patient readiness for surgery.* Unpublished master's thesis, Yale University School of Nursing, 1966.

Shepard, R. N. On subjectively optimum selections among multi-attribute alternatives. In M. W. Shelly and G. L. Bryan (Eds.), *Human judgments and optimality.* New York: Wiley, 1964.

Staub, E., and Kellett, D. Increasing pain tolerance by information about aversive stimuli. *Journal of Personality and Social Psychology,* 1972, *21,* 198–208.

Toomey, M. Conflict theory approach to decision making applied to alcoholics. *Journal of Personality and Social Psychology,* 1972, *24,* 199–206.

Tversky, A., and Kahnemann, D. Judgment under uncertainty. *Science,* 1974, *185,* 1124–1130.

Vernon, D. T. A., and Bigelow, D. A. Effect of information about a potentially stressful situation on responses to stress impact. *Journal of Personality and Social Psychology,* 1974, *29,* 50–59.

Wanous, J. P. Effects of a realistic job preview on job acceptance, job attitudes, and job survival. *Journal of Applied Psychology,* 1973, *58,* 327–332.

Weitz, J. Job expectancy and survival. *Journal of Applied Psychology,* 1956, *40,* 245–247.

Wolfer, J. A., and Visintainer, M. A. Pediatric surgical patients' and parents' stress responses and adjustment as a function of psychologic preparation and stress-point nursing care. *Nursing Research,* 1975, *24,* 244–255.

Youngberg, C. F. *An experimental study of job satisfaction and turnover in relation to job expectations and self-expectations.* Unpublished doctoral dissertation, New York University, 1963.

Uses and Abuses of the Polygraph

DAVID T. LYKKEN

The circumstances that led to my becoming an authority on the lie detector were adventitious, to say the least. During the summer of 1958, I was made responsible for the supervision and employment of two freshman medical students who had been awarded summer fellowships. Medical students, in my experience, tend to be very energetic and generally competent. My two summer fellows presented me with an unusual problem. They tore into the work with which I had planned to keep them busy for 3 months and finished in the space of a few weeks. In some desperation, I set them to building a fence around my back garden while I studied the matter. The fence, a week's work for two ordinary persons, was completed in a day and a half but by then I had contrived their next assignment.

We would do an experiment in lie detection. I am a psychophysiologist and therefore had in my laboratory the facilities for recording those physiological responses that are associated with psychological or emotional processes. These include such variables as heart rate, blood pressure, respiration, brain waves, and the subtle electrical signals indicative of muscle tension. I was particularly interested in the *electrodermal* response, a wavelike change in the electrical resistance of the skin of the palms and soles associated with imperceptible sweating in these regions. I would teach my two eager assistants how to measure and record

DAVID T. LYKKEN • Psychiatry Research Unit, College of Medical Sciences, University of Minnesota, Minneapolis, Minnesota.

this phenomenon, known in those days as the *galvanic skin response* or GSR. Then, we would set up an experiment in which summer-school student volunteers would participate in a mock crime. My assistants would use the GSR to attempt to determine which of the subjects were "guilty" of the crime and which "innocent."

In the event, we used two crimes, a "theft" and a "murder." Our subjects were assigned at random to one of four conditions. A subject assigned to the theft group, for example, was met at the lab by Assistant A and given the following instructions. He was to stand outside a certain office in the building until the occupant departed. Then, he was to enter the office and erase his name, which would be found penciled on the appointment calendar. Next, he was to go through the drawers of the desk until he found some specified object he had been assigned to "steal." Finally, he would remove this prize and hide it in an empty locker in the corridor. Subjects assigned to the murder group were marched through a similar charade. One-fourth of the subjects enacted both crimes, hence were doubly guilty. Finally, the last group were innocent of both, being told merely to imagine that they had been picked up for questioning with regard to two matters they knew nothing about.

After a subject had been appropriately indoctrinated by Assistant A, and cautioned against revealing what he had experienced—which crime(s), if any, he was guilty of—he was taken to the lab and introduced to Assistant B whose job it was to conduct the interrogation. B, of course, was kept carefully in the dark as to which subjects belonged in which group. B had to determine this from his examination, specifically, from the galvanic skin responses produced involuntarily by the subject as he was being questioned.

The Nature of Polygraphic Interrogation

How should the interrogation itself be structured? Clearly, it would not do just to let Assistant B ask whatever questions came to mind, in the manner of a police "grilling," because our experiment would tell us merely how skillful or clever B was as an interrogator, not a very important question to answer, particularly since B planned to be a physician rather than a police detective. If our experiment was to tell us something more general, something about the validity of a certain method of detecting lying or guilt, then we must be careful to use that identical test or method in each case. Moreover, since it is an essential requirement of any scientific experiment that it be replicable by an independent investigator, our experiment must use the same question list—and the same method of scoring the responses—in every case.

B. F. Skinner is said to have warned his students against too deep a study of the literature on any problem they were investigating on the grounds that close acquaintance with prior opinion and received doctrine might stifle originality and poison the mind. Being an indifferent scholar, due to a defective memory, I have always found Skinner's (possibly apocryphal) injunction congenial and easy to follow. For this reason, I had not read in 1958 the very limited literature available on lie detection or "polygraphic interrogation" and was therefore not aware that the professionals in this field actually believed that it was possible by physiological measurements to discriminate truthful from deceptive answers. As a psychologist, I was keenly aware of the extent and variety of individual differences. The idea that all liars—or all truth tellers— should feel or behave in the same way seemed obviously incredible to me. Any poker player knows that the symptoms which betray that one opponent is bluffing may be the very clues which indicate that another opponent is holding a strong hand. Therefore, I felt certain that there could be no unique response or pattern of responses that all people show when they are lying but no one shows when telling the truth.

As a psychophysiologist, I was also aware that the same physiological response can have very different meanings, can be associated with different psychological responses, in different individuals. Thus, for example, if two subjects both give the same large GSR in response to a certain question, it may be that one of them is lying—and fearful of being found out—while the other is telling the truth—and fearful or even indignant about being wrongly accused. It was reasonable to suppose that, other things being equal, a subject would be more aroused—and therefore give a stronger physiological response—when he answered a certain question deceptively than he would if he answered truthfully. But, due to individual differences, the fact that Jones gives a larger response than does Smith cannot be safely taken to mean that Jones is lying and Smith is not. Jones may be more physiologically labile than Smith, or more emotionally reactive, or less concerned about being accused. If both suspects have a low opinion of the accuracy of the lie detector test, it might even be that Jones gives a large response because he is innocent, afraid that he will be diagnosed erroneously as lying, while Smith gives his small response because he is guilty, thinking, "I can probably beat this test."

What was needed, obviously, was some sort of control question that would allow us to estimate how this subject would respond to the critical question if he were telling the truth. Then, if he responded, in fact, much more strongly, we might reasonably conclude that he was lying. Alternatively, our control question might be designed to provide us with an estimate of how this subject should respond to the critical question if he were lying. With this sort of control, we would expect that truthful subject's response to be smaller than this estimate. Had I studied the literature, I would have known that professional lie detector people, most of whom are trained as policemen rather than as psychologists, actually claim to be able to devise such necessary controls.

THE CASE OF HARRY K. To illustrate, let us jump ahead some 15 years to a courtroom in Phoenix, Arizona, where a man—call him Harry K.— is on trial for the aggravated rape of a woman we shall refer to as Sally V. Sally's allegations against Harry K. had sounded so strange that even the prosecutor had been dubious, unwilling to bring the case to trial without stronger evidence. So he had offered the defense a proposition. Harry K. was to be given a polygraph test by the State's polygraphist (a polygraph is a machine that measures several different physiological responses simultaneously—GSR, respiration, pulse rate, and "relative blood pressure," in this case). If Harry "passed" the test, the prosecution would agree to drop the charges. Should he "fail," however, the defense would have to stipulate that the results could be used in court as evidence against him. Arizona is one of a growing number of jurisdictions where the courts allow such stipulated lie test results to be admitted into evidence.

Now it happens that Harry K. had already taken a lie test, unknown to the prosecution, and he had passed it. As his attorney explained to me, "Most of my clients are guilty as hell, but I really thought this guy was telling the truth. I had him take a lie test on the quiet just to see if I was right." Therefore, the defense was quick to accept the prosecutor's offer. Harry K. took the second test—and flunked. That test involved three relevant questions: "Did you force your way into Sally V.'s motel room on the night of April 7th?" "Did you threaten to choke Sally V. in her room on April 7th?" "Did you forcibly rape Sally V. in the Buena Vista Motel on the night of April 7th?" Harry K. answered "No" and gave strong physiological responses to all three questions.

The test also included several irrelevant questions: "Is your name Harry K.?" "Are you sitting down?" and so on. These are just filler questions, without any real significance. Finally, the test included several "control" questions. One of these was "Have you ever taken anything that didn't belong to you?" Harry K. answered this question, "Yes," and gave a small physiological response. The polygrapher had hoped that Harry's answer would be "No"; then, since nearly everyone has committed at least one petty theft sometime in his life, we could assume that Harry's answer was a lie. But even a "Yes" answer is useful because here we have Harry answering an emotionally loaded question truthfully. Since his polygraph reaction was much weaker than he gave to the critical questions about Sally, the polygrapher concluded that his answers to the latter questions were deceitful.

Another control question was this: "Have you ever committed an unusual sex act?" Harry K.'s response to this somewhat ambiguous query was, "No." His physiological response was stronger than he gave to "Are you sitting down?" but considerably weaker than when he answered "No" to "Did you rape Sally V. in her motel room?" Having heard of Kinsey and being a man of the world, the polygrapher knew that everybody commits an "unusual sex act" once in a while. Therefore he "knew" that Harry's "No" to this question was a lie. This gave him the second type of control that he was after, an estimate of how Harry should respond to the relevant question, if lying. If he had responded less to the critical questions than he did to this control, he would have passed the test. In fact, of course, he responded more strongly and flunked.

Now the fact is Harry K. was innocent. He had been in Sally's room that night, had gone to bed with her, but all at her invitation. She invented the rape story hours after he had peaceably departed, carrying her address and phone number, which she had pressed upon him. Sally V. was a disturbed, neurotic woman. The reader should try to imagine himself taking this test in Harry's place. You have committed no crime but are suddenly accused of a felony that could ruin your reputation and send you to prison. The results of this polygraph test will put an end to the business—or land you on trial for your freedom. "Did you rape Sally V. in her motel room?"—how would the polygraph pens react if you were the innocent but worried accused? Would either of those alleged "control" questions be as disturbing to you as any question about rape and Sally V.?

What saved Harry K. in this particular instance was an accident. The polygrapher had been told that Harry broke into Sally V.'s room, threatened to strangle her, and then raped her. He used these three facets of the story to frame his three "relevant" questions. But Sally said she had invited Harry K. into her motel room; he had never been charged with having forced his way in. We know that his "No" to this question on the polygraph test was truthful. Since he responded just as strongly to this as he did to the other two relevant questions, it is reasonable to assume that his answers to those two questions were also truthful. That is what I thought and that is what the jury concluded too, and Harry K. was acquitted.

The Guilty Knowledge Test

But in the summer of 1958 I still had not discovered that professional polygraphers really believed they could identify lying as such. I thought the name "lie detector" was just journalistic sensationalism. It seemed obvious that we could hardly expect to think of control questions that would elicit spontaneous lies from all our 40 subjects. Nor could I imagine inventing emotional questions exquisitely calibrated so as to be more disturbing than the critical questions for all innocent subjects and at the same time less disturbing for all guilty subjects. Therefore, for purposes of our experiment, we never seriously considered trying to detect lying. Instead we focused on the more important question, "Who is guilty?"

By definition, the guilty suspect was there at the scene of the crime. He knows what happened because he experienced it. Thus, usually, the guilty suspect possesses "guilty knowledge," the ability to recognize or identify facts, events, people, and objects associated with the crime. This ability no innocent person could share unless he too had been present at the crime or unless he had been exhaustively briefed by, e.g., careless police questioning. This recognition response—"orienting reflex," as the psychophysiologist calls it—can be identified through its involuntary physiological components.

Suppose you were a subject in Group 1 of our experiment, having enacted the mock theft. During the interrogation, Assistant B asks you the following: "The thief stole something from one of the drawers in the desk. If you're the thief, you'll know which drawer you took the object from. I shall mention each of the six drawers at about 10-second intervals. You just sit quietly and repeat each name after I say it. Which drawer was the stolen object taken from? Was it . . . the lower left? . . . the right middle? . . . the upper left? . . . the center drawer? . . . the upper right? . . . the bottom right?" You will probably show a GSR reaction to each of these six alternatives, even though this is a "pretend" situation and nothing important is at stake. Your GSR to the first alternative will likely be fairly large because people tend to respond more strongly to the first item in a series. For this reason, the first alternative in each question was always a dummy and not scored; we never hid the item to be stolen in the lower left-hand drawer.

Suppose Assistant A had placed the billfold in the center drawer in your case and you had taken it from there. The question would cause you to picture that center desk drawer in spite of yourself. When Assistant B got to, "the center drawer?" you would recognize this alternative as the correct one, different from all the others. It is likely that you would show a somewhat stronger physiological response—a larger GSR—to this alternative than to any of the others (except perhaps the first, which is not scored). If you were innocent, and therefore ignorant of which drawer was involved, your responses to the five alternatives should be about equal and only chance would determine which is larger than the others.

In our experiment, there were six such multiple-choice questions for each of the two crimes. Some of them related directly to the crime while others referred to incidental matters. For example: "The thief would have noticed an unusual object on the top of the desk. If you are the thief, you will recognize the object when I name it. Repeat each name after me. Was it . . . a clock? . . . a candy box? . . . a chess set? . . . a baseball glove? . . . a coffeepot? . . . a woman's shoe?" Again, the first alternative is dummy and not scored. For every question there were five scorable alternatives and a subject received a "guilt" score of one for each question in which his largest GSR was elicited by the "correct" alternative.

Now a subject innocent of the theft has about 1 chance in 5—a probability of 0.20—that he will score "guilty " on any particular item. Using the binomial theorem, we can construct a table showing the probability that an innocent suspect, just by chance, might obtain each of the possible scores on a six-item Guilty Knowledge Test (GKT).

From Table 1 we can see that an innocent subject is most likely to get a score of 1 on this test. Nine times out of 10 he will score 2 or less. If we conclude that everyone scoring 5 or more is guilty, we shall misidentify only about 2 innocent subjects out of every 10,000. All this assumes, of course, that we have created a good test, one in which the guilty suspect is likely to recognize the "correct" alternative and in which there is truly only 1 chance in 5 that an innocent suspect would also respond most strongly to this alternative. If the suspect has been questioned earlier by a detective: "How about that box of candy on the desk; did you help yourself to some candy while you were in there?" then the probability that he will "score" on that item of our test is perhaps 0.90, whether he is guilty or innocent.

Similarly, the various alternatives must seem equally plausible to an innocent suspect. If we are trying to determine whether Mr. Fisbee is the masked bandit who held up the bank, we might use a set of photographs

Table 1. Probability That an Innocent Suspect Will Obtain
the Given Score on a Guilty Knowledge Test Having Six Items
with Five Scored Alternatives Each

"Guilt" score	Probability (if innocent)	Cumulative probability
6	.000064	.000064
5	.000154	.000214
4	.0154	.0156
3	.082	.097
2	.25	.35
1	.39	.94
0	.26	1.00

as alternatives in one item of our GKT. "If you're the bandit, you will recognize one of these people as the bank teller who gave you the money. Just look at each picture as I show it to you." If the photographs all depict actual bank tellers standing behind their cages looking worried, then this should be a good item. But if only two are plausibly bank tellers and the others look like movie stars, policewomen, or morgue victims, then the probability of a false-positive score on this item will be 0.5 instead of 0.2.

1958 REVISITED

Our experiment ran off like clockwork due to my superassistants. One of our volunteer subjects had been a resistance fighter in Hungary, twice caught and intensively interrogated by the MKVD. Both times he had successfully maintained his cover and been released. This man happened to be assigned to our Group 3, guilty of both crimes, and he was easily identified as such by Assistant B using neither spotlights, threats, nor torture. (This particular subject felt sure he had defected to a technologically superior society.) Overall, using our objective scoring system and only the briefest of interrogations, we correctly identified who was guilty (or innocent) of which crime 94% of the time. Not one innocent subject was misclassified.

At this point I did begin reading the "lie detection" literature, preparatory to writing up this experiment for publication. I had been calling our method of interrogation the "Guilty Knowledge Test" and I was curious to discover what its accepted name was and what previous research had been done with it. To my considerable surprise, no such method had previously been described. The nearest thing was something called the "Peak of Tension" test, rather like a single item of a GKT in which the examiner hopes to see a buildup of general physiological tension prior to the "correct" alternative, followed by a general relaxation. But a one-item multiple-choice test is obviously not very useful, and my reading revealed that "polygraphic interrogation" in practice consists almost entirely of attempts at actual lie detection of the sort already described. A very few validity studies had been done at that time, laboratory experiments like ours using mock crimes, typically obtaining hit rates on the order of 75% in situations in which half the subjects were lying and half not; i.e., where a 50% hit rate would be obtained by flipping coins.

I was persuaded that the GKT could do much better than that and so we quickly set up a second experiment. In this one, 20 sophisticated subjects—graduate students, psychiatrists—were offered a money prize if they could "beat" the test, by inhibiting their responses (which is very difficult to do), producing false responses by biting their tongues at opportune times (which is much easier), and the like. Since my own money was at stake, I improved the test by using 20 items instead of only 6 and using a scoring system that allowed for the possibility that the subject's largest response might have resulted from self-stimulation after an incorrect alternative. All 20 of these subjects were correctly classified by this strengthened GKT.

A Leading Authority Goes to Washington

The publication of these two experiments (Lykken, 1959, 1960) made me the author of approximately 10% of the scientific literature that had been published on this general topic. My two medical students had not only built me a handsome, sturdy fence, they had also made me into a leading authority. This unexpected status was shortly confirmed by a summons to Washington to participate in a conference on polygraphic interrogation sponsored by the Institute for Defense Analysis (IDA), a "think tank" operated by the U.S. Department of Defense. There I found myself at a table with the other leading authorities—Prof. J. Kubis; John Lacey, Ph.D.; Martin Orne, M.D., Ph.D.; and a few others—encircled by a number of silent, sober men then unidentified but who I now believe to have been professional lie-detector people employed by Army Intelligence, the CIA, NSA, FBI, and sundry other federal agencies who are devoted to the lie detector for screening employees and the like.

Before going to Washington, I had done some last-minute cramming (a leading authority cannot be too careful). Although the scientific literature was very limited, I found two or three monographs and a number of articles on polygraphy in various law and police journals, a literature by and for professional polygraph examiners. And this literature contained some extraordinary claims, claims of 95, 98, 99+% accuracy for the sort of lie detector test that very nearly landed Harry K. in prison. I recall wondering how these claimants could take themselves seriously. Surely, if so prescient a method actually existed, would not the jury system already be an anachronism? With a polygraph built into every witness box, the bailiff who administers the oaths could be retired. Most criminal cases would be decided just by asking the defendant, "Did you do it?"— the polygrapher bringing in his nearly infallible verdict an hour after arraignment, at a prodigious saving of time and expense. Is not a major source of discord among nations a mutual distrust, an unwillingness of each party to believe the pledges and assurances of the other? The marvelous machine I found described by the polygraphist fraternity would not only put most lawyers out of work but half the diplomats as well and bring about world peace into the bargain.

The heavy irony of these reflections seemed transformed to gossamer in that conference room at IDA. Our mission, it developed, was to consider ways in which the polygraph might be employed to solve the problems of the Cold War! One application was to be in nuclear arms control. United States–Russian negotiations had bogged down over the issue of inspection. In 1961–1962 there were no spy satellites that could count ICBM silos from 500 miles up. Could we add clauses to an arms limitation treaty allowing both sides to administer periodic polygraph tests to key personnel on the other side? But the truly mind-bending concept to which the discussion later turned was the brainchild of a distinguished physiologist whose acquaintance with psychology and polygraphy was limited but whose faith in American technology knew no bounds.

We would invest a little R and D to optimize the lie detector. After all, even the polygraphs used by the CIA, carried round the world in suitcases and diplomatic pouches, were 20 years behind the times, still using pneumatically driven pens and so on. (CIA slang for polygraphic interrogation is "fluttering," a rather graphic characterization.) Then, for public relations reasons, we would change the name of the procedure from "lie detection" to "truth verification." Finally, to illustrate the idea at its most dramatic, we were asked to envisage a world leader—John F. Kennedy or then-Chairman Khrushchev—addressing the General Assembly at the U.N. Above and behind the podium would be a giant "truth meter," its pointer-needle bouncing along easily in the white region at the left—as long as the speaker was saying what he believed to be the truth. But, should he attempt to prevaricate, to mislead, to even tell a half-truth, the pointer would swing into the black Lie Zone on the right, his duplicity at once revealed to all the world.

Leaders, government spokesmen, therefore would not lie, schemers and cheaters would have to reform, the sparks of international paranoia would be quickly extinguished. But this utopian vision requires an almost infallible "truth verifier"; 90% accuracy, which would be good performance for any other psychological test, could be disastrous here. What if 10% of Kennedy's assurances scored as lies when they were not? What if 1 world leader out of 10 had an unusual pattern of response which enabled him to perjure himself with impunity? My own experiment had indicated that the GKT could be nearly 100% accurate but the GKT can be used only in certain criminal situations where the culpable subject possesses guilty knowledge and the examiner possesses some of that same knowledge also. The GKT cannot be used in the exotic applications we have been discussing because the GKT does not "detect" lying *per se*. How accurate is the lie detector really?

THE VALIDITY OF THE LIE DETECTOR

It should be understood that the accuracy of any polygraph test can be properly assessed only in the field situation. Student volunteers are not typical of the general run of criminal suspects—or world leaders either. Mock crimes or the offer of money prizes for "passing" the lie test do not engender the same emotional or physiological responses produced in real life in which one's freedom, job, or reputation (or world peace) may hang in the balance. But to study polygraph accuracy in the field, one must have a criterion, some independent means of determining, after the fact, whether each subject had actually been lying or not. Such a criterion is difficult to obtain. Most crimes are never solved and, even when a subject has been adjudicated innocent or guilty by a court, few trial lawyers will pretend that those decisions are absolutely reliable.

For these reasons, only three field studies of lie-detector validity have appeared which meet reasonable scientific standards. Two of these studies used as a criterion the opinion of a panel of experienced trial lawyers or judges who examined all the facts in the case and rendered a judgment—guilty, innocent, or indeterminant—independently of purely legalistic considerations. "Never mind whether he could or should have been convicted; do you think he did it?" In one of these studies (Bersh, 1969), when all four judges agreed as to guilt or innocence, the previously rendered polygrapher's diagnosis matched the unanimous opinion of the judges in 92% of the cases. But when the judges differed 3 to 1, the polygraph agreed with the majority opinion only 75% of the time. And of course no one can say how accurate the polygraph was on those still more difficult cases in which the judges split 2 to 2. One problem with the Bersh study was that his polygraphers all made "global" judgments; their diagnoses were not based on objective scoring of the polygraph charts alone. Instead, his examiners considered the charts, the subject's demeanor and behavior during the test, as well as whatever they knew about the evidence against the suspect at the time of the interrogation. For all we know, these experienced examiners might have diagnosed their subjects' honesty from these other cues just as successfully without viewing the polygraph recordings at all.

In a recent study financed by the U.S. Department of Justice, Barland and Raskin (1976) administered control-question lie tests to 102 criminal suspects. Like Bersh, they also used a panel of legal experts, independently assessing the completed case files, as a criterion of who was truly guilty and who innocent. Barland, who administered the tests, used a method of scoring that emphasized the actual polygraph results and was less influenced by Barland's "clinical" judgments about the suspect or the evidence against him. Excluding cases in which the tests were scored as inconclusive and also those on which a majority of the judges failed to agree, Barland's average accuracy was only 68%. He managed to "detect" 100% of the liars, but this is not too surprising since he scored 91% of all the tests as "deceptive." The distressing feature of the Barland and Raskin study is that 64% of the criterion-innocent suspects were also scored as "deceptive"! Incidentally, this example also illustrates why it is necessary to read research reports carefully, drawing one's own conclusions from the data rather than merely accepting those offered by the authors. Barland and Raskin claimed an average accuracy of 84% rather than 68%. Remember that they were 100% accurate in detecting liars (partly because they classified nearly all the tests as deceptive) but only 36% accurate in detecting the truthful. But it happened that 75% of their suspects were criterion-guilty. By adding 100% of the three-fourths who were guilty and 36% of the one-fourth who were innocent, they got 75 plus 9 equals 84%. But surely the right way to measure the accuracy of a lie test is to average its accuracy on the liars with its accuracy on the truthful; (100 + 36)/2 equals 68%.

Another recent study by Horvath (1977) shows that Barland and Raskin's findings were not exceptional. In the files of a large police department, Horvath located a group of polygraph tests that had been given to suspects who later confessed. Admittedly, suspects who confess may not be typical of suspects in general (e.g., they may be more reactive, easier to identify on the polygraph with that confession trembling on their lips). Still, we know at least that these individuals were in fact lying when they took the test. Horvath also identified another group of suspects who must have been truthful on their polygraph examinations because they were subsequently cleared of all charges by the confession of another person. To avoid contamination by extrapolygraphic sources of information, Horvath had these polygraph charts scored independently by 10 trained polygraphic examiners. These examiners agreed very well with each other (89% of the time, on the average) but they agreed with the criterion—with reality—in only 64% of the cases, very similar to the 68% accuracy obtained in the previous study. Again, Horvath's findings show that lie detector operators make most of their errors on innocent suspects. Horvath found that 49% of the people known to have been truthful on these lie tests were classified erroneously as deceptive.

USE OF THE LIE DETECTOR IN THE UNITED STATES

The accuracy of the polygraph test is a question of more than academic importance. There are at least 4,000 polygraphic examiners currently practicing in the United States. Hundreds of thousands of Americans were subjected to the often harrowing experience of a lie test in 1977, their futures often hanging in the balance. When the lie detector lies (about one-third of the time), someone usually gets hurt. Only a few thousand of these tests were administered by law enforcement agencies to criminal suspects. Most are given for preemployment, or periodic postemployment, screening purposes. Here the examiner has no "specific issue"—no particular criminal charge—to inquire about so his questions are a kind of fishing expedition. "Have you ever used illegal drugs?" "Have you ever stolen from a previous employer?" "Have you ever been involved in homosexual activity?" "In the past 5 years, have you committed any illegal acts without being caught?" and so on. Many Federal agencies—all of the ones concerned with intelligence or security —use lie tests routinely in this way. But most of those 4,000 polygraphers sell their services to employers in the private sector. There has never been a competent field study of the accuracy of this type of lie-test screening. It is certainly no better than the "specific issue" test used in the three studies reviewed above and, indeed, is almost certainly *less* valid because of its generality and diffuseness. Why then is polygraphy such a thriving, growing industry in the United States? Why do hard-headed employers pay for a service of such dubious quality? I think there are two reasons.

The first reason has to do with the lie detector's effectiveness as a deterrent. A supermarket in a small Carolina town, part of a large chain of such stores, had experienced unexplained losses over the past 2 to 3 years. The head office sent in a polygrapher who set up shop in a local motel and "fluttered" all 50 of the store's employees. A few days later, he went back to Charleston with his report: Sam K., the store's assistant manager, had been robbing the till. Mr. K. was fired and that was that. The regional manager of that chain is enthusiastic about the polygraph. "When we're having losses, we just send in the lie detector and then fire somebody and the losses stop." Of course, it would be cheaper, and probably just as effective, merely to pick some employee at random and then shoot him, but that would be impractical. Sam K., a hard-working, deeply religious man with three small children, is alive but he is not very happy. Everyone in town knows he was fired and why. He cannot get another job because other employers find out about his failing the lie test and assume that he is not to be trusted. Sam has been wishing that he had robbed the till because he might then have a nest egg he could use to move his family to another part of the country where they could try to make a new start.*

The second reason that the lie test remains popular—with employers, the police, and the polygraphers—is its ability to induce confessions. The lie test is a kind of painless "third degree" that leaves no visible marks on the victim. A student from my university told me that she had applied for a part-time job with a firm that requires a lie test for

---

* This case provides an illustration of how one can mislead with figures. The polygrapher was mistaken when he concluded that Sam K. was lying. Assuming some other employee was responsible for the store's losses, one of the 49 other lie tests must also have been in error. The lie test not only failed to detect the real culprit, it incriminated an innocent man. Still, only 2 mistakes among the 50 people tested yields an "accuracy" of 96%!

all prospective employees. The examiner went over his questions with her beforehand, pointing out that she must be able to answer confidently or else she would score as deceptive. "If there's anything you've ever done that you think might bother you on any of these questions, better tell me about it now. Then on the test itself I'll ask you, 'Apart from what you've already told me, have you ever . . .,' and you can answer with a clear conscience." After going through the questions once with the young woman hooked up to the machine, the operator shook his head. "You're still showing too much reaction to some of these questions. I think there must be some things you haven't told me yet." Desperately, caught up in the mystique of the test, dreading the thought of "failing," the woman dredged her memory, blurting out her little secrets as though on the rack of the Inquisition. When it was all over she felt violated, hating herself for being so susceptible, hating the operator and the employer for putting her in such a position.

Some polygraphers become very skillful at using this confessional potential of the lie test. In Cleveland in 1975, a man was being examined in regard to the possible theft of $200. After running through the questions once, the examiner looked at the chart dubiously and said, "It doesn't look too good. I'm going to give you a few minutes to think things over and then we'll run through this again." He then left the room but continued to observe his worried subject through a one-way mirror, standard equipment in any good interrogation suite. The subject glowered at the polygraph chart paper for a minute and then, leaning forward, he tore it from the machine and began to eat it, all 3 feet of it. The examiner waited until this strange meal had been completed, then returned to the room and, without comment, began to set up for the next test. Suddenly he looked at the polygraph, leaned his ear down close, and said, "What's that? He ate it?" "My God, you mean it talks, too? I give up!" said the suspect, who then promptly confessed.

It is important to see that neither of these "virtues" of the lie test—the deterrent effect or the confessional impact—is directly related to the validity of the test as such. They would both work just as well if the polygraph were merely a stage prop. P. T. Barnum did not invent the lie detector but he would have appreciated its potential.

The Effect on Lie Test Accuracy of the Base Rate of Lying

As we have already discovered, when scored on the basis of the polygraph charts alone, without help from the examiner's intuitions about the guilt or innocence of the subject, the lie detector is correct less than 70% of the time and strongly biased against the truthful respondent. Although the mystique of the lie detector clearly derives from the scientific aura of the polygraph machine, it turns out that the machine does not provide a very useful means of separating truthful from deceptive answers. But all of us have at least some skill as human lie detectors; those who are less skillful than the norm we refer to as "gullible" or "credulous." When the lie test is scored globally, allowing the examiner's intuitions to compensate for the inadequacies of the machine, then it is my impression that a really skillful examiner can achieve an accuracy perhaps as high as 80%. I have in mind not the average polygrapher but someone with unusual ingenuity, perceptiveness, clinical adroitness, and psychological judgment in manipulating the subject's attitudes and expectations during the pretest interview, in framing the test questions, and in drawing the final inferences from the subject's physiological responses as to his truthfulness or falsity. For this reason, it is unfortunate that so few polygraphers have any real training in psychology or in psychological measurement. Being "fluttered" by an inept, psychologically naive polygraphist, no matter how experienced, is a bit like playing Russian Roulette.

But to say that the lie test may be 80% accurate in really expert hands does not mean that even such an expert will be wrong only 20% of the time in particular, real-life applications. Consider the preemployment screening situation, for example. Here we must be mainly concerned about the "false-positive" errors, the innocent and truthful job applicants who fail the test due to test or polygrapher fallibility. If our true expert tests 1,000 applicants, 80% of the liars will fail the test (these are the true-positives) and 20% of the truth-tellers will also fail, the false-positives. But how many people are involved in each of these categories depends on the base rate of lying in the population being tested (Meehl and Rosen, 1955). And surely no one would contend that half of all the people who apply for jobs in this country are thieves with such a sordid background that they will be forced to answer the lie test questions deceptively. As indicated in Figure 1, it seems reasonable to assume that only a small fraction of job applicants would actually lie on such a screening test, perhaps somewhere between 5 and 30% of the total. And Figure 1 shows us that if less than 20% of job-seekers lie, then more than half of the people who fail the lie test will be honest citizens! That is, if 200 of the 1,000 applicants tested are liars, 80% or 160 of them will fail the test. But 20% of the 800 truthful subjects will also fail the test (be false-positives). Therefore, although this hypothetical polygrapher may be 80% accurate on the average, with respect to the 320 people whom he will fail on the lie test—the ones who will therefore lose all hope of the job for which they may otherwise qualify—for this important third of the total this examiner will be only 50% accurate, as accurate as the personnel manager could be by just flipping a coin.

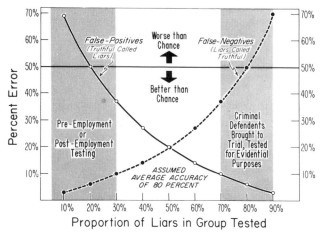

Figure 1. The accuracy of the lie detector varies with the proportion of the group of people being tested who actually try to deceive. Although research indicates that average lie test accuracy is less than 70%, the figure assumes a super lie detector that is correct 80% of the time. If 80% of the people tested are deceptive, then exactly half of those who pass the test will be liars (false-negatives). Similarly, if only 20% among those tested try to deceive, half of those who fail the test and are diagnosed as deceptive will actually be truthful (false-positives). In both cases, the accuracy of the lie test for the subgroups in whom we are most interested will be not 80% but 50%—what one might expect to achieve using a Ouija board.

At the other end of the spectrum, consider the growing practice in some states of permitting criminal defendants to introduce into evidence the results of successful lie detector tests, over the objections of the prosecution. The argument advanced in favor of this procedure is that the defendant should have this opportunity to "demonstrate" his innocence in order to offset the greater resources of the prosecution. Under such a system, of course, we need only to consider those lie tests that are passed since no defendant will offer into evidence the fact that he took such a test and failed it. And we must also consider the base rates for lying in this population of subjects. This is the same thing as asking what proportion of criminal defendants brought to trial are actually guilty, since we can assume that all guilty suspects will try to "beat" the polygraph, try to lie and get away with it. Most criminal lawyers, judges, and other competent authorities will agree that of all those defendants against whom the evidence is strong enough for them to be actually brought to trial, from 70 to 90% are in fact guilty, as indicated on the right in Figure 1. And since here we are concerned only with "passed" lie tests, the only type of error that concerns us is the false-negative, the deceptive subject called truthful by the polygrapher. Figure 1 shows us that if 80% of defendants brought to trial are guilty and must lie on the test, then exactly half of the defendants whom our skilled polygrapher will characterize from the witness box as being truthful will actually be guilty false-negatives. That is, the expert testimony of our 80% accurate polygraphic examiner will have a probative value of exactly zero.

CONCLUSIONS *EX CATHEDRA*

A Leading Authority should have the prerogative of expressing his opinions in the summing up. Here are some of mine.

1. Unlike most other psychological tests, how one performs on the polygraph can have serious and lasting consequences on one's life and future. For this reason, there are many applications of the lie detector which I believe should be proscribed by law. The worst abuse is illustrated by the case of the supermarket manager mentioned earlier. Here are some other examples.

An Indiana minister writes me about one of his parishioners, a college-trained accountant with 6 years' loyal service in the local bank. In 1975, $2,000 disappears from the vault. The bank calls in a private agency, which recommends that the employees be given lie tests. Harold K. is the third person tested. He flunks and he is fired. Community pressure forces the bank to have Harold tested again, by a police examiner. He passes and is temporarily reinstated. But this bank has the polygraph habit by now so Harold is sent to Chicago to be "fluttered" a third time. He flunks again. Harold has never been indicted or charged with any crime. There's not a particle of evidence to prove that this devout family man suddenly changed character and decided to heist the bank vault. There has been no trial before a jury of his peers, no due process. But Harold has been punished. He is out of a job and effectively blacklisted from the profession for which his training and experience equip him. What other bank would hire a man with the reference Harold K. can get from his previous employer?

John K. has worked 8 years for a large chain of freeway restaurant-motels. He has become manager of one of the units, then supervisor over six installations in the Chicago area. Then $2,500 disappears in the accounting. A polygrapher is dispatched from the home office and several employees, including John K., are given lie tests. John K. flunks; John K. is fired. Again, no evidence that would be admissible in court; the company does not bother to bring charges.

Ed K. is a deputy sheriff in a county south of Minneapolis. A prisoner in the county jail is found to have a gun in his possession, accuses Ed of having smuggled it in to him. The sheriff asks both men to take lie tests given by the State Bureau of Criminal Apprehension. The prisoner passes his test; Ed K. flunks. The sheriff tells me, "I always thought these tests were infallible, but I can't believe Ed would do such a thing." I urge the sheriff to investigate; the lie detector is far from infallible. Then the prisoner, who has demanded to be moved to a different jail before naming Ed K., escapes from that more permeable lockup. The sheriff does investigate, secures the confession of a work-release prisoner that he had done the smuggling. Apprehended after his escape, the original accuser admits the hoax. Both lie tests were wrong.

In all of these cases, employers have taken the law into their own hands. In all but the last, a probably innocent employee has been punished, his life blighted, without any semblance of due process. This is wrong, it is truly "un-American," and it should be prohibited by law.

2. Polygraph tests should never be admitted into evidence at trial (Roper, 1975). The polygraphist is unlike other expert witnesses who help the jury to determine certain facts of the case: What was the cause of death; which bullet came from which gun; whose fingerprints were on the knife? The polygraphist presumes to do the jury's job for it; this witness is lying; this defendant is telling the truth. If the lie detector were 99% or even 95% accurate, objective, unbiased, immune to human frailty—well, perhaps it would be a safer route to justice than through the deliberations of the average jury. But the lie detector is none of these things and never will be. The practice of permitting defendants to introduce lie detector evidence in their own behalf must lead to gross abuse. As we have seen, only "passed" lie tests would ever come before the jury, and polygraphers able to produce such happy findings—and stand up well to cross-examination—would command high fees. Every guilty defendant would take a lie test then with nothing to lose and everything to gain. And even if we assume that no polygraphers would even unconsciously bias their tests in favor of the defendants and if we also assume that criminal defendants are not quickly going to learn how to "beat" the lie test,* even then it is probable that about half of the test results presented to the jury will be invalid. The lie test does not belong in the courtroom.

3. The most extensive use of the polygraph by far is in employment screening. As already indicated, I have no doubt that a really skillful

---

* The Backster Zone of Comparison (ZOC) test is widely regarded as the most sophisticated lie test yet devised. Questions 5 and 7 on the ZOC are "relevant" while questions 4 and 6 are "controls." One fails the ZOC if one's responses to question 5 are substantially larger than those to question 4 and if question 7 similarly produces more reaction than does question 6. The best way to try to beat the ZOC is this: Immediately after each control question (nos. 4 and 6), bite your tongue hard, then answer, then tighten the stomach muscles hard for several seconds. These maneuvers will augment your control responses in comparison to your involuntary reactions to the two relevant questions, thus improving your chances of being scored as "no deception indicated" or, at least, as "inconclusive."

examiner will be able to do better than a Ouija board could do in culling out bad apples. It has been argued that none of the other tests or interview procedures currently in use for employee selection are anywhere near to being perfectly valid and that if we bar the use of the lie test, which may be as much as 80% accurate, then we must similarly prohibit all other selection procedures as well and force employers to hire randomly. Here again, however, the base-rate argument seems to me to be very powerful. If an aptitude test is 80% accurate in separating those who can do the job from those who cannot and if at least half of those who apply for the job have the ability required, then at least 80% of those who fail the aptitude test will in fact be people unsuited for the job in question. But, as was illustrated in Figure 1, it is probable that at least 50% of those who fail the lie test part of the job application would have been honest, reliable employees. A Minnesota statute forbids employers from even requesting any employee or prospective employee to take a lie test; I would like to see enacted a Federal statute along similar lines.

4. But why all this criticism of polygraphic interrogation since we have had such good success with the Guilty Knowledge Test—100% accuracy in the second experiment? True, there have been no corroborating field studies of GKT validity under real-life conditions. However, unlike the various forms of lie detector test, the GKT should not be affected by differences in the intensity of emotional involvement. Theoretically, the GKT should work as well in the field as in the laboratory. (Theoretically, it is surprising that the lie test works even as well as it seems to.)

But the attentive reader should have realized by now that the GKT is virtually never used by polygraphy practitioners in this country, and that the GKT could not be used in many applications in which the lie test is employed, in employee screening, in particular.

I believe that the GKT could be used in many criminal investigations as a guide to the police and as a protection for innocent suspects. But this would probably require that the investigating officers themselves be trained in the technique and given the responsibility for constructing the test items. These detectives are first on the scene of the crime and best able to discover the handful of guilty knowledge items required, perhaps photographing scenes or people that the guilty suspect would later recognize. They would have to use good psychological judgment about this. Obviously, no criminal carries away a complete and detailed catalogue of the events and furnishings of the crime scene; the investigator would have to judge which items would probably become part of the suspect's guilty knowledge and which would go unnoticed. He would have to show good judgment in the invention of the incorrect alternatives for each item. As in any multiple-choice test, the object is to make all the alternatives seem equally plausible to someone who doesn't really know the right answer. This task is harder than it looks.

Finally, if the investigating officer is the one who constructs the GKT question list, then he should be more inclined to protect the confidentiality of those bits of information so that the test will remain useful when suspects are finally in hand to be tested. The actual testing could be done by any polygrapher unaware himself of which alternatives are correct and thus unable to give any clues to the subject by his manner or inflection while asking the questions. As the reader can judge by studying newspaper accounts, many of the more important criminal cases tried in our courts would lend themselves to the use of the Guilty Knowledge Test. It is a potentially powerful tool of criminal investigation.

5. I once believed that the conventional lie test also had a legitimate place in criminal investigation but after reading Joan Barthel's *A Death in Canaan* (1977) I have had to change my views. This is a true account of a murder investigation in 1974, quoting at length from the tape recordings of a lie test and subsequent questioning of the victim's 18-year-old son. On the day after discovering his mother's mutilated body, young Peter Reilly gave strong physiological reactions to questions like "Last night did you hurt your mother?" Although such reactions were hardly surprising under the circumstances and provided no rational basis whatever for concluding that Peter was responsible for his mother's death, the police concluded that their case was solved. "We go strictly by the charts. And the charts say that you hurt your mother last night." The transcripts reveal how Peter, shocked and distracted, wanting to cooperate with the kindly policemen, himself came to believe in "the charts" rather than his own memory. "The test is giving me doubts right now. Disregarding the test, I still don't think I hurt my mother." Then, later, "I'm not purposely denying it. If I did it, I wish I knew I'd done it. I'd be more happy to admit it if I knew it. If I could remember it. But I don't remember it." And still later, "Well, it really looks like I did it." So Peter Reilly signed a confession to the murder of his own mother and it was 2 years before that confession was shown to be false, before it became obvious that Peter could not have commited the crime, 2 years during which the trail left by the real killer, still at large, grew icy cold.

I once believed that the single application in which the lie detector might do more good than harm would be in official criminal investigation. I now withdraw that opinion. In every arena in which the lie test is used it is apparently abused. It is time for the lie detector to be retired to those same museums where we keep examples of the rack and the Iron Maiden. As William Styron realized more quickly than I did, it is a "detestable machine."

REFERENCES

Barland, G. H., and Raskin, D. C. Validity and reliability of polygraph examinations of criminal suspects. Report No. 76-1, Contract No. 75-NI-99-0001, Law Enforcement Assistance Administration, U.S. Department of Justice, 1976.

Barthel, J. *A death in Canaan.* New York: Dell, 1977.

Bersh, P. J. A validation of polygraph examiner judgments. *Journal of Applied Psychology,* 1969, *53,* 399–403.

Horvath, F. S. The effect of selected variables on interpretation of polygraph records. *Journal of Applied Psychology,* 1977, *61,* 127–136.

Lykken, D. T. The GSR in the detection of guilt. *Journal of Applied Psychology,* 1959, *43,* 385–388.

Lykken, D. T. The validity of the guilty knowledge technique: The effects of faking. *Journal of Applied Psychology,* 1960, *44,* 258–262.

Meehl, P. E., and Rosen, A. Antecedent probability and the efficiency of psychometric signs, patterns or cutting scores. *Psychological Bulletin,* 1955, *52,* 194–216.

Roper, R. St. J. The search for truth: An argument against the admission of polygraph test results at trial. *Polygraph,* 1975, *4,* 119–138.

SECTION III
CLINICAL
APPLICATIONS
OF BASIC RESEARCH

Introduction

Health Care: Good Intentions Are Not Enough

ALFRED STEINSCHNEIDER

There is little question that society is committed to the reduction of mortality, alleviation of human pain and suffering, and the increased productivity of its members. The number of persons involved in the delivery of health care and the development of improved health care techniques, as well as the amount of money spent, all attest to the strength of this commitment. This is not to deny the continuing debate over the adequacy of allocated resources or the designation of priorities. Nonetheless, because of the massive allocation of resources to the health care system, viewed in its broadest sense, many concerns have been expressed that society is not receiving an adequate return for its investment. One of the criticisms of particular relevance to this discussion stems from the expectation that scientists will discover "almost instant" solutions to problems once they have been identified. Unfortunately, few outside the scientific community fully appreciate the complexities in arriving at solutions. The excellent reviews presented in the following four chapters provide us with insights into some of this complexity.

Obvious as this might seem, fundamental to the solution of any health problem is an objective description of the abnormality to be treated or prevented. For example, Sameroff and Abbe remind us that there has been a long history of concern for the development of low-birth-weight infants. However, the objective measurement of specific behavioral deficiencies had to await the advent of intelligence testing. We sometimes forget the development of objective test procedures is by no means a simple task. Prior to the effective utilization of any test procedure, the developers must deal satisfactorily with issues of reliability, validity, and the size and adequacy of the normative (or standardization) sample.

Rational attempts at evolving therapeutic interventions require an understanding of the pathologic sequence responsible for the symptom complex. In attempting to prevent the consequences of prematurity, it became necessary to elaborate theoretical models adequate to an understanding of those variables (prenatal, infant, and environmental) that influence the characteristics of the growing child. This research has provided for the exciting possibility that some of the observed developmental abnormalities might have resulted from environmental factors and not prematurity. Furthermore, Sameroff and Abbe point out that different intervention approaches stem from differing theoretical models. It has become increasingly clear that, if we are to develop effective preventives for some of the sequelae of prematurity, a much greater understanding of the developmental process will be necessary. Similarly, Aslin and Banks, in their review of animal as well as human infant studies, have demonstrated the importance of early visual experience in the development of adequate binocular function and, consequently, provide the scientific basis for stressing early intervention in the management of infants with esotropia. Conversely, the review by Katkin, Garvey, and Shapiro provides a number of examples in which the failure of a therapeutic approach (biofeedback) might have resulted from an inadequate elaboration of the pathologic process responsible for the clinical symptom.

In addition, it is essential that any proposed therapy be tested under controlled conditions to assess its degree of effectiveness as well as to examine for possible untoward side effects. Katkin, Garvey, and Shapiro's broad, critical review of the clinical use of biofeedback provides sufficient support for this need. It is readily appreciated that the conduct of such studies is by no means easy. Not only must consideration be given to the appropriateness of the research design, allowing for the termination of the clinical trial as soon as a conclusion can be reached, but it is mandatory that sufficient safeguards be introduced to assure the safety of all participants. In the course of developing a clinical trial one can also anticipate the expression of concern for the subjects (patients) in the control group. It will be argued that members of the control group might be deprived of a possible therapy or intervention procedure that could minimize morbidity or prevent long-term functional damage or even death. Although one fully recognizes the emotional impact of this latter argument, it could be tragic if it provided the basis for the decision not to conduct an adequate clinical assessment prior to the general application of a proposed therapy.

The need for strong scientific understanding of the determinants of function, well-developed procedures to assess specific abilities, and methods for evaluating the validity of etiologic formulations is brought into sharp focus in the report by Broen and Jons. These authors provide an in-depth analysis of a single child who presented with a disturbing language problem. It is highly questionable whether this problem could have been resolved without a considerable understanding of speech perception and production, a logical analysis of the component functions, and the availability of technically sound evaluation procedures.

Thus, it should be apparent that the development of approaches directed at improving health care—the early identification of individuals at increased risk, the greater utilization of preventive approaches, and effective therapeutic intervention—requires substantial scientific knowledge of function and process as well as sophisticated technology. In addition, though this is not discussed in any of the subsequent reviews, it is essential that methodologies be elaborated which would allow for the delivery of this improved health care potential to all individuals. All of these efforts leading toward effective application of scientific understanding and technology in the service of humanity require a considerable expenditure of effort, money, and time. Although the intention to improve health is an absolute requirement, it is not sufficient. If we are to avoid the frustrations resulting from unfulfilled expectations, it is necessary that all members of society appreciate the complexities inherent in arriving at scientifically valid solutions.

However, there is also the possibility that the scientific community can do much to facilitate the resolution of health problems. For example, increased consideration could be given to alternative long-range research strategies directed toward the solution of defined complex pathologies. This "problem-oriented" approach, to prove effective, would have to be broadly conceived, allow for theory development and increased understanding of process, and provide for an adequate exploration of divergent formulations and a variety of differing strategies. Obviously, it would be essential to avoid prejudgments and suffer through frequent critical reassessments with an eye toward identifying crucial areas where additional scientific information is necessary. Along this same line, it would be helpful if the scientific community reexamined its own attitude toward differing types of research, often expressed as the dichotomy between "basic" ("pure") and "applied" research. Underlying this dichotomy, and the very choice of terms, is the value judgment that one type of research is "better" or more worthy than the other. At the least this characterization of the value of research is highly debatable. If we are to become more responsive to the needs of society, and we must if we expect to receive continuing support, the scientific community must begin to recognize that all good research is problem oriented.

The Consequences of Prematurity: Understanding and Therapy

ARNOLD J. SAMEROFF AND LAUREN C. ABBE

The birth of an infant before the completion of the normal 40-week gestational period has been postulated to represent a perinatal trauma with detrimental effects upon the health of both the infant and its mother, and upon their social interaction as well. There has been a long history of concern with the intellectual consequences of prematurity. In more recent times, additional concerns have been raised by studies finding that prematurely born children are more frequently abused by their parents than other children (Klein and Stern, 1971). As our understanding of the processes of psychological development has advanced, we have been better able to appreciate the social context for both of these consequences of premature birth and to begin programs for the alteration of both the intellectual and social deficits associated with prematurity.

Attempts have been made to explain the causes of a premature birth and to predict its effects on the child since the time of Aristotle. Labor was thought to begin because of the insatiable hunger of the fetus or an alteration of the position of the infant's head within the mother. Children who were born prematurely in the eighth month of pregnancy were considered to be children of the moon and more susceptible to death: "Because the moon is a cold planet, which has dominion over the child,

ARNOLD J. SAMEROFF and LAUREN C. ABBE • Department of Psychology, University of Rochester, Rochester, New York.

and therefore doth bind it with its coldness, which is the cause of its death" (Aristotle, cited in Fox, 1966).

In contrast, children who were born in the seventh month were considered to have greater chance for survival than the 8-month-old infant because they were not subject to the moon's effects. Even into the 18th century, it was believed that nothing could be done for the premature infant by way of special care.

Medical reports on premature infants written by European physicians in the late 19th century stressed the physical immaturity and inviability of the underweight neonate. There was always a question as to whether it was beneficial for society to maintain the lives of these children who were thought to be at high risk for disease and were considered the "runts" of the social litter in terms of physical and mental development. Premature birth was found most often in the lower social classes and frequently the children were illegitimate, which may have contributed both to the findings of lower intelligence in these children later in their development and to the general attitude of the medical profession that they were a social burden (Peller, 1913).

Little was known about the specific behavioral correlates of premature birth until the beginning of intelligence testing. Reports of intellectual differences up until this point were strictly subjective impressions, usually by a physician called in to help a child who showed some physical or intellectual problem.

After an extensive review of the studies of prematurity and intellectual impairment between 1900 and 1940, Benton (1940) was led to comment upon the wide discrepancies of findings in these studies. The majority were done by physicians who saw a very select subject population, mostly illegitimate children from impoverished environments. The conclusion of the bulk of these early studies was that premature children as a group were retarded in physical and mental development. Capper (1928), for example, wrote: "The immature infant becomes the backward school child, and is a potential psychoneurotic or neuropathic patient and even a candidate for the home for imbeciles and idiots" (p. 447).

This quote expresses the extreme of a general medical and social expectation for the development of the premature infant. Such infants were seen as congenitally weak and their prematurity was considered to reflect and exacerbate their genetic deficiency.

Despite this generally negative outlook for the development of prematurely born children, there were a few who did not find these infants significantly different from normal children. Hess, Mohr, and Bartelme (1934) concluded from their research that premature birth unassociated with intracranial injury did not affect mental development. Gesell (1933) also reported finding no differences between the development of premature and normal infants when the two groups were compared on the basis of conceptual age.

Benton concluded, on the basis of his review, that most of the reliable studies of the intelligence of premature children indicated that these children were not, as a group, any less intelligent than normal children. His views, however, were contrary to the prevalent opinions of that period.

The data on long-term effects of prematurity still do not lead to any clear-cut conclusions. Although Wiener (1962) in a review of 18 studies of prematurity found only 1 that did not report an IQ deficit in the premature group, Parmelee and Haber (1973) argued that it is by no means clear whether the later adverse consequences associated with prematurity were a function of the prematurity itself, the accompanying low birth weight, an extended period of living in an incubator, accompanying perinatal trauma, or the social climate in which the child is raised. A gestationally premature infant who suffers no prenatal, perinatal, or postnatal traumas other than prematurity itself, and is raised in an optimal home environment may, according to these investigators, be no different from a full-term infant raised under the same circumstances. Parmelee and Haber's views are consistent with those studies of prematurity undertaken by Hess, Mohr, and Bartelme (1934), who found generally good childhood outcomes for their subjects. Those premature children who did perform less well than normals were typically those who had evidenced additional neonatal complications as well.

Several large studies that have followed premature infants from infancy through school age did find small intellectual deficits associated with low birth weights. Douglas (1960) reported that when compared with controls the prematures did less well at 8 and 11 years of age. Drillien (1961), in an extensive study of the effects of prematurity, found that the lighter the infant had been at birth, the greater the deficit in developmental quotient at 4 years. The mean IQ scores ranged from 107 for the full-term control group to 89 for a group of infants under 3½ pounds at birth. A complicating factor in the interpretation of these studies is that since a birthweight criterion was used no consideration was given to the possibility that full-term infants who were small-for-date were included in the "premature" sample.

A sample of premature infants initially studied by Knobloch, Rider, Harper, and Pasamanick (1956) were followed up with intelligence testing when they were 6–7 years old (Wiener, Rider, Oppel, Fischer, and Harper, 1965) and again when they were 6–10 years old (Wiener, Rider, Oppel, and Harper, 1968). The prematures, who at birth had weighed between 1,500 and 2,000 grams (approximately 3 lbs. 5 oz. and 4 lbs. 6½ oz.), scored 5 points lower at ages 6 to 7, and 6 points lower at ages 8 to 10. In another study the effects of physical defects were separated from the intellectual deficits in prematures. McDonald (1964) eliminated from her sample infants who were twins or had cerebral palsy, blindness, deafness, or IQs below 50. The resulting sample had an average IQ of 102 when tested at ages 6 to 8, no different from the national mean in Britain. Still, within her sample those infants with birth weights under 3 pounds had an average IQ 5 points less than those with birth weights between 3 and 4 pounds.

It is interesting that the studies of the effects of prematurity have shown consistent, albeit small, IQ deficits, while studies of the effects of perinatal anoxia (oxygen deficiency at birth) have not. A possible explanation is that the premature infant is more easily recognized and labeled by his parent than is the anoxic infant and hence subject to different parental treatment. The parents may not know if their infant had some form of asphyxia, while the premature, and especially the lower-birth-rate premature, is quite easily identified not only by its physical appearance but also by the initial separation from the parents, and the subsequent intense caretaking demands. It will be seen that the parent's perception of the child can play a major role in its deviant development exclusive of any actual deficit that may be present in the child.

Most research on prematurity has attempted to link the single physical cause during the perinatal period with single effects later in development. This research has been generally unsuccessful at demonstrating such links. Moreover, certain facts have been revealed which show the single-cause view to be erroneous. These intrusive facts are that environmental factors play a major role in either modulating or supplementing the effects of any early physical difficulties.

Parmelee, Kopp, and Sigman (1976) cogently argue that the main concern in development is the total adaptation of the infant to the environment regardless of biological problems. A child with motor or sensory handicaps who compensates and makes adequate progress in cognitive and affective development removes himself from the "risk" category. In contrast, infants with similar initial biological problems who continue to do poorly remain in the "high-risk" category for later developmental disability. How is the initial biological problem compensated? Parmelee *et al.* suggest two mechanisms. Either (1) the early apparent risk factor resulted in a transient brain insult rather than permanent brain damage or (2) environmental factors may have a stronger influence on behavioral outcomes than biological events.

Birch and Gussow (1970), in an extensive review of the effects of disadvantaged environments on development, concluded that high risk to infants is associated with both depressed social status and ethnicity. The highest rates of infant loss were found among populations that were both poor and black. Pasamanick, Knobloch, and Lilienfeld (1956) found in their sample that the proportion of infants having some complication increased from 5% in the white upper-social-class stratum to 15% in the lowest white socioeconomic group to 51% among all nonwhites. These data imply that the biological outcomes of pregnancy are worse for those in poorer environments. Birch and Gussow (1970) summarized their review by noting that there was also much data to indicate that the developmental outcomes for these children were often far worse.

Drillien's (1961) data on Scottish premature infants show that for the highest social grades the deficit in developmental quotient for children under 3.9 pounds was reduced from 26 to 13 points between the ages of 6 months and 4 years. For the lowest social grade, the deficit increased from 26 to 32 points. When the same children were tested in school between the ages of 5 and 7, Drillien found that few children from middle-class homes were retarded except when birth weight had been below 3½ lbs., while in poor homes there was a "marked excess of retarded and very dull children" in all weight categories.

McDonald (1964) found that while prematurity affected intelligence in lower social groups, there were no deficits evident in the upper-social-class group in her sample. Similarly, Illsley (1966), who used a large sample of wide social background in Aberdeen, Scotland, found that while in lowest social class IQ scores were seriously depressed in low-birth-weight groups, little effect was noted on IQ scores in the upper social class.

TRANSACTIONAL MODEL

The attempts to predict intelligence or retardation described above have proven inadequate using the single constitutional variable of a premature birth. How are we to understand a situation where prematurity only influences later development for children raised in poor environmental conditions? These poor outcomes are clearly not the result of the prematurity itself, since children with identical gestational periods, raised in good environmental situations, show few consequences of the problem. To answer this question, Sameroff and Chandler (1975) proposed a "transactional model of development" to explain the dynamic process by which children with poor constitutions, such as those resulting from delivery complications, enter into an interaction with their environment which ultimately leads to developmental abnormalities. The commonsense understanding of how children are raised is that society takes them in hand through the agency of their parents or the school system and shapes these children to fit current norms. But many recent studies have demonstrated that in the process of trying to shape these children the caretakers are shaped themselves (Bell, 1968). The specific characteristics of the individual child transact with the caretaker's mode of functioning to produce an individualized ongoing miniature social system. The transactional model adds the reciprocal effect of the organism on the environment.

A clear example of this situation is found in the work of Thomas, Chess, and Birch (1968) in their New York longitudinal study. These investigators were able to classify young infants into two major categories of temperament: the difficult child and the easy child.

The mothers in the New York study were all white, educated, middle-class, with normal child-rearing attitudes. However, when these supposedly "normal" mothers were confronted with a difficult infant, their behavior toward the child was negatively influenced. Most of them became either anxious over their inability to control the child's crying and irregularity or hostile through frustration. The difficult child had converted a formerly normal mother into an abnormal one. The outcome of this disturbed relationship was that nearly three times as many of the infants identified as difficult required some professional help during childhood as compared to nondifficult infants. For our present purposes, the difficult infants in the study who did not have developmental problems are of great importance. The later normalcy of these difficult infants appeared to result from their parents' ability to make allowances for their temperaments. Rather than becoming anxious or hostile, these parents treated the infants' colicky behavior as part of a passing stage. Thus, the fate of these difficult infants appeared to depend on the context in which their behavior was understood by their parents.

A second example of the transactional character of the developmental process can be found in the recent report of the 18-year follow-up of children studied from birth on the island of Kauai (Werner, 1975). At the 10-year follow-up (Werner, Bierman, and French, 1971) children who had learning disabilities, need for long-term mental health service, or a need for short-term mental health service were identified and reports were sent to their parents, their physicians, the local educational guidance office, and the local department of mental health. At the 18-year follow-up, these children were reexamined to determine their developmental progress during the intervening period.

The data revealed that for the overwhelming majority of children who had been diagnosed as having learning disorders at 10, problems persisted throughout adolescence. However, for this same majority, the environment was perceived as not being supportive or understanding. Most of the learning-disorder children were loners, without close friends, who had to rely on a nonsupportive family. In contrast, the few learning-disorder children who improved did so through sustained emotional support of family and friends. In the mental health problem groups, more children showed evidence of improvement, but again the improvement appeared to be a function of environmental support rather than any difference between the children. In other words, children with a diagnosis of minimal brain damage or learning disorder raised in a nonsupportive, nonadaptive environment will continue to show the same deficits, while children with the same initial diagnosis raised in an environment where both institutional and familial support are given will show little evidence of the original disorder.

What we have tried to show in the two examples above is that knowing either the characteristics of the parent alone or the child alone does not permit us to make reliable predictions of developmental outcome. In the New York longitudinal study, parents with normal attitudes were led to behave nonadaptively when confronted with a difficult child. In the Kauai study, children with learning disorders were able to improve when raised in adaptive environments.

MODELS OF INTERVENTION

How would applying such a model to the problems associated with prematurity aid in fostering the positive development of these infants? The results of many studies show that later deviancy associated with prematurity is not a direct consequence of the early birth itself but rather an indirect by-product mediated by the effect on the mother of having a premature infant. In such a model the mother's unusual experience in the hospital, coupled with the problems of caring for an unusual-looking child, interferes with the mother's expected child-rearing performance.

Three kinds of intervention are possible. The first is primary prevention of premature births. However, this primary intervention would require major alterations in society as a whole in order to change the economic and social conditions found in the poorer sectors of our country. In contrast, secondary interventions would focus on the already born premature infant and aim to normalize the experience and the behavior of the infant so that the baby would become a better elicitor of positive caregiving from its mother. The third kind of intervention, and as will be seen probably the most significant, is to change the reactions of the mother to the birth and the child. This kind of intervention would try to focus the mother on the satisfying interactions that can be achieved with any infant, and to help her see that the premature birth need not have consequences for the child's later development. Research that has centered on these last two kinds of intervention will be reviewed in the following sections.

INFANT-ORIENTED INTERVENTION. From an exclusive concern with physical well-being and progress of the premature infant, clinicians have become increasingly concerned with the infant's psychological well-being and progress as well.

The premature infant is characterized by low weight and immature physical systems. Muscle tonus is very weak, the infant is often unable to digest food until a few days after birth and often requires a respirator for regular breathing. Because of these physical problems, severely premature infants are usually placed in isolettes in an intensive-care nursery where their functioning can be constantly monitored by the medical staff and where they can live in an environment carefully controlled for heat, light, oxygen, and bacteria level.

The numerous medical advantages of such an environment are not without disadvantages, however. Living in such a sterile environment eliminates the infant's normal uterine experiences and is also significantly different from the sensory experience of the normal newborn. In addition, the infant is separated from the "mothering" one—a fact that, as we shall see later, may have important effects on the later behavior and attitudes of both mother and infant. There are many consequences that the early isolation of the premature may have for their later development.

Concern with the deleterious effects of living in the anomalous environment of the intensive-care nursery has led researchers to explore a number of techniques for normalizing the premature infant's experience. This normalization has generally been attempted through a variety of stimulation programs.

Returning to the Womb. Working from the assumption that the infant who is born prematurely has been deprived of some important sensory experiences that are necessary for normal development, several investigators have attempted to devise experiences that they feel provide the essential stimulation the child *in utero* receives in the weeks before the expected delivery date.

Neal (1968) postulated that the sensory experience and stimulation the fetus receives from motion within the mother's body is essential for normal development. The vestibular cranial nerve is myelinated by the end of the 24th week of gestation, 3 weeks before the usual age of viability (27 weeks) expected in premature birth. Vestibular responses and myelinization are signs that the vestibular system is functional at an early age and sensitive to specific inputs to the vestibular nerve cells. Neal posited that stimulation of the vestibular apparatus by motion might be of importance to the continuing neural development of the fetal infant.

On the basis of this assumption, Neal ran an intervention program with 31 premature infants and matched controls. Vestibular stimulation was carried out using an apparatus designed to approximate the natural movements of the infant within the mother's body. Beginning on the 5th day after birth and continuing until the 36th week of gestation, infants were placed in hammocks (usually in fetal position) inside their incubator and gently rocked for 30 minutes three times per day. When the two groups of infants were compared at 36 weeks, those infants who had received the stimulation showed (1) higher levels of motor maturation expressed by their ability to raise their heads in a prone position and to demonstrate the crawling reflex in a prone position, by the strength of their grasp, and by the general "vigor" of their muscle responses; and (2) higher levels of activity and visual functioning expressed by their ability to fixate on and follow a stimulus vertically and horizontally. No differences were found between the groups on measures of muscle tension or crying. The infants in the experimental group also showed a greater weight gain than those in the control group.

In another study of the effects of vestibular stimulation, Korner, Kraemer, Haffner, and Cooper (1975) showed that the vestibular stimulation provided by placing the infants on a gently oscillating waterbed mattress significantly decreased the incidence of apnea spells while the babies were in the nursery. The prevention of apnea (transient cessation of breathing) may be highly important in the respiratory well-being of the premature infant.

Barnard (1975) administered two types of sensory stimulation presumed to duplicate *in utero* experience to 15 premature infants. The infants were placed on a "rocker bed" and exposed to a recorded heartbeat for 15 minutes per hour. Infants in the stimulation condition showed greater average weight gain per day than the control infants. Comparisons of the two groups on developmental scales at 8–12 months showed that the stimulated infants had higher scores on mental and language scales.

These studies provide some interesting evidence in support of perinatal stimulation for premature infants. The tendency toward decrease in apnea spells with vestibular stimulation is important (Korner *et al.*, 1975). Other studies have indicated that other forms of kinesthetic stimulation will also assist in regulating the premature infant's breathing (Kattwinkel, Hearman, Fanaroff, Katora, and Klaus, 1975). Another significant effect of "womblike" stimulation during the infant's stay in the premature nursery appears to be increased weight gain, although this effect is found in studies that administer other types of stimulation as well.

Creating a Normal Newborn World. The rationale behind stimulation programs that attempt to alter the premature infant's environment to more closely approximate that of the full-term infant is stated most clearly by Scarr-Salapatek and Williams (1973). They argued that the different functioning of the third trimester fetus in utero and the extrauterine premature infant lead to different experiences. At birth, it seems likely that sensory systems change in their organization and functioning just as the respiratory and digestive systems alter their modes of operation. Forms of stimulation for extrauterine development different from those for intrauterine development may be necessary regardless of maturational age.

Attempts to normalize the extrauterine experience of the premature have used three types of stimulation individually or in combination: (1) sensory-tactile stimulation (touching, rubbing, handling), (2) auditory stimulation (female voice, mother's voice), and (3) visual stimulation (mobiles).

Solkoff, Yaffe, Weintraub, and Blase (1969) studied the effects of handling on the physical and behavioral development of premature infants. They used an extremely small sample, with five premature infants in each of the experimental and control groups. All infants were examined within 12 hours after birth and were determined to be normal by a pediatrician. Both groups were housed in the premature nursery and cared for with usual nursery procedures. The stimulated group while in the isolette was handled in a procedure in which the arms, back, and neck were rubbed for 5 minutes each hour, 24 hours a day for 10 days. The immediate effects of this additional stimulation were that the handled infants regained their initial birth weight faster than controls and were more active during testing. By 6 weeks postnatal age, however, the experimental group had lost its advantage in weight. Solkoff also reported that by 7–8 months there were still indications that the experimental group was performing better on motor tasks and had home environments that were "richer" in terms of stimulation experiences provided for the infant. These findings must be cautiously interpreted because of the small number of infants in the study.

In a study of auditory stimulation, Katz (1971) exposed 31 premature infants to recordings of their mother's voice, six times per day at 2-hour intervals, from birth until a gestational age of 36 weeks. Follow-up measures indicated that the experimental children had higher scores on motor maturity tests and auditory responsive measures at 36 weeks. The design of this experiment does not allow us to conclude whether it was the provision of auditory stimulation that accounted for the advance in the experimental group, or if there was something unique about the mother's voice that was beneficial to the infant. Unfortunately, Katz did not do any further follow-up on the development of these infants, so we do not know how effective this intervention was at producing long-term advantages for the stimulated infants.

Scarr-Salapatek and Williams (1973) employed an intervention procedure with prematures that utilized two modes of sensory stimulation. The experimental group was given visual stimulation that the investigators felt was usually lacking in the premature nursery setting. Each infant had a mobile positioned over its head in the isolette. In addition, these infants were given extra tactile stimulation from the nursery staff. Comparisons of the experimental and control infants at 1 year post-discharge indicated that the infants who had received extra stimulation were more advanced on scales of infant development. Unfortunately, Scarr-Salapatek and Williams were unable to bring all of their subjects back into the lab for testing at 1 year; 7% of their experimental population and 40% of the control group did not return. Therefore, it is possible that the differences they noted in developmental status were due to a statistical artifact in that those control subjects who were doing well did not return for the follow-up testing.

Problems similar to this are common in most of the research in premature infant stimulation programs. We are still unclear on what specific modes of sensory experience are beneficial for development, or indeed, if any stimulation is sufficient for improvement in performance. The research studies that have been done vary widely in the type, combination, intensity, and duration of the stimuli used, as well as the type of relationship between the "stimulator" (nurse, experimenter, mother) and the infant. As a result of these differences, there are many discrepancies within the literature. Cornell and Gottfried (1976) reported in a review of such studies that three of the nine studies measuring weight gain, for example, showed a higher rapidity or overall level of weight gain in the stimulated infant group, while one showed a lower level and five reported no significant differences.

Another area of contradiction is in the increase or decrease of activity level and/or crying in the stimulated groups. Hasselmeyer (1964) found handled infants were more quiescent during testing, while Solkoff et al. (1969) found them more active. Katz (1971) found stimulated infants less active during auditory stimulation.

There are some clear trends that do emerge from this research, however. There is a tendency for premature infants who receive additional early sensory stimulation to perform better on sensorimotor developmental tasks than nonstimulated infants. Cornell and Gottfried (1976) in their excellent critical review of the research on stimulation of premature infants found such a trend. The overall status of infants receiving extra stimulation was better than that of control infants when assessed on Brazelton and Rosenblith neonatal neurobehavioral scales prior to leaving the hospital. There was a tendency for experimental groups to excel on specific items involving motor development, muscle tonus, and responsiveness to auditory stimulation.

While stimulation programs may be effective in raising the developmental performance of prematures, we do not yet know why. Are there factors implicit in these programs which have not been specified by the researchers—for example, the additional concern and attention from the nursery staff involved in the procedures? Is the premature able to process all forms of stimulation or only stimulation in certain specific modalities? Is the premature receptive to sensory input during all or only during certain states, and do these reactivities differ from patterns found in full-term infants? All of these questions are important to consider in further studies of premature status and development.

Altering the hospital environment of the premature infant has had some short-term effects, discussed above. More long-range effects have been found in some studies, but there has generally been a confounding in the subsequent interaction with the home environment. Parents have generally known that their infants have been stimulated and this knowledge may have altered their caregiving behavior. Caregiving behavior in its own right appears to play a major role in influencing the later development of the child. Let us now consider the premature infant as a participant in a social context and examine the effects of variations in caregiver interactions.

MOTHER-ORIENTED INTERVENTION

Social Context of Early Development. The survival of the newborn depends on a caregiving environment. Parental figures are significant in providing the supports of shelter and nutrition to assure the physical survival of the infant. The newborn is completely dependent upon significant adults for the provision and protection of its special environment; because of this, professional concern has been related to the best techniques for assuring the physical well-being of the infant. However, recent trends have shifted from an exclusive concern with physical care of the child to an increasing interest in the psychological care of the infant. The ability of medical technology to minimize the physical disabilities associated with the birth process has permitted us to begin attending to the psychological variables that contribute to normal developmental outcomes.

The natural process of a mother rearing her infant has been so taken for granted as a current social value that attention has been exclusively focused on the "how" of this caregiving rather than on the social and physical factors that produce and maintain this relationship.

Interest in the social environment of the child has been given added impetus by the discovery of two syndromes that seem to be related to poor caregiving practices: "failure to thrive" and the "battered child." These situations, in which the parent does not appear to be interested in the "how" of adequate child rearing, have raised questions now about the "why" of caregiving. As long as one assumes that child rearing is a natural process, one may wonder about its occurrence but one need not be forced to explain it. However, when confronted with a number of situations in which child rearing is approached in an atypical way, one is forced to look at child rearing in a larger context. Only by seeing normal child rearing in the perspective of other possible parenting behavior can one understand "why" parents tend to take care of their infants. Within this larger view one can then attempt to remedy the situations in which deviancies in child rearing occur.

To provide an evolutionary perspective, we will begin with a review of animal studies of parent–infant caregiving behavior. We will then examine those aspects of early child rearing which are distinctly human.

As we go up the evolutionary ladder, the behavioral components associated with attachment between mother and infant assume increasing importance. The young of lower mammals are dependent on their mother for a very brief time and are soon able to follow her, keeping themselves in contact for nourishment and protection. In the lower primates, the infant is able to cling to the mother soon after birth and thus participate in the attachment process by physically insisting upon it. In higher primates, infants are not able to engage in the primary attachment behaviors of the young found in other species; they can neither cling to nor follow the mother. Thus attachment in higher primates must be promoted and maintained transitionally by some other features, either in the mother or the infant or in the social expectations governing the environment surrounding the pair. It is clear that attachment is not inevitable in human cultures. There have been historical epochs in which the drowning, neglect, or abandonment of a newborn not considered valuable by the culture or unwanted by the mother was an accepted practice. There are today certain cultures that engage in such practices of infanticide. It is clear that social values may intervene negatively in the attachment process, and presumably these values could also intervene to promote attachment.

Mother–Infant Bonding in Animals. Attempts to explain the caregiving behavior of the mother toward her young have been based on both physiological and psychological variables. Physiological explanations have focused on the hormonal changes that occur following parturition or in connection with lactation, both of which have been assumed to make the mother more sensitive to her offspring. Rosenblatt (1965), in an extensive analysis of maternal behavior in rats, has shown that although biochemical effects do exist, they are secondary in significance to the effects elicited by the behavior of the infant rats. Groups of ovariectomized (removal of ovaries) and hypophysectomized (removal of pituitary body) females, in addition to intact and castrated males, were exposed to young pups. The typical maternal behaviors of retrieving, crouching to nurse, and nest building appeared in all the groups. The duration of exposure to the infant mice required to elicit the maternal behavior was similar for all of these groups, including the males.

The behavior of the young rats appeared to be a necessary condition for eliciting maternal behavior in their mothers. Rosenblatt found that the mother was most prepared to be maternal during the first few days after parturition (birth process). After that period it was more difficult to elicit maternal behavior. The maintenance of maternal behavior was also most vulnerable to disruption during the first few days after birth. If the pups were removed after the initiation of maternal behavior before the fourth day after birth, the maternal behavior quickly waned. After 3 days there was only a slight reduction of maternal responsiveness to pups when they were reintroduced following a 4-day separation. It appeared to be important for the mother rats to spend time with their offspring in the period immediately following delivery if later maternal behavior was to be maintained in reunions after separation from the young.

It has been difficult to separate the effects of biochemical changes in the mother from those eliciting properties of the offspring in fostering the caregiving relationship. In another attempt to study the effects of the infant's characteristics alone, Noirot (1964) placed infant mice 1 to 20 days of age with virgin adult female mice. The virgin mice responded with the typical maternal behaviors of retrieving, licking, nest building, and crouching in a lactation position. These behaviors occurred at high levels in response to infants of 1 to 10 days of age. Beyond that age there was a decline in these behaviors. Some characteristic of the appearance or external behavior of the newborn mice served to elicit maternal behavior even in these virgin female mice.

Richards (1967) has noted that little is known about the factors that elicit maternal behavior. A variety of studies have pointed to the input provided by the infant through sucking, exteroceptive stimulation, and somatic sensory input. However, other research has indicated that mothers deprived of visual, olfactory, or cutaneous sensation around the snout still retrieve their young. Recent speculation has centered around ultrasonic vocalizations of the young pups as important stimuli for maternal behavior patterns.

The animal research provides an evolutionary context into which human behavior can be placed. Rosenblatt (1965) has hypothesized that a synchrony exists in the activities of mother and infant which follows a transactional model of development. The behaviors of both the mother and the infant mutually affect each other. The infant's initial helpless movements give rise to caregiving in the mother. The caregiving by the mother increases the infant's abilities to suckle and eliminate. As the infant increases in mobility and independent action, he again alters his mother's behavior by reducing the amount of caregiving she engages in. The mother's reduction in maternal behaviors acts to move her offspring more strongly in the direction of independence and maturity.

To draw analogies to the human situation requires the identification of the specific characteristics of the offspring, both physical and behavioral, that elicit maternal behavior. Although the specificity of these characteristics may be quite different for man and animals, the general organizational principles may be quite similar.

Separation in Animals. Studies of separation of mother and infant in lower animals may have special relevance to the treatment of human prematures and their caregivers. Through animal studies, we have been able to investigate the effects of varying degrees of separation on the mother's ability to care for her infant.

Rodent research has demonstrated that separation from the mother shortly after birth strongly reduced the caretaking activities of the mother even after the infants were returned. Another example of the effects of the interruption of the mother–infant synchrony can be found in a study of goats reported by Moore (1968). The typical behavior of goats following birth is for the mother to lick off the amniotic fluid from her newborn kid, after which she pushes the kid toward her udder where suckling is initiated. The mother then establishes a territory including herself and her kid but excluding all other members of her herd. If the kid is removed before having a chance to begin sucking, the mother does not establish this relationship to her own particular infant. If the kid is returned as quickly as an hour later, the mother has already become indifferent to him and will allow herself to be suckled by any kid in the herd. The completion of the initial suckling experience appears to be important for the maintenance of a specific mother–child relationship.

In addition to the immediate reduction of the mother's caregiving produced by separation from her young shortly after birth, there are long-range effects on the offspring's capacity for child rearing. Moore reported that the separated kids were much less effective as mothers after reaching adulthood than kids who had not been separated from their mothers. Much more dramatic evidence of the deleterious effect of having been raised without a mother is seen in the research of Harlow and Harlow (1969). When infant monkeys were separated from their mothers and reared alone, they were severely handicapped in the performance of many adult functions including sexual intercourse and motherhood. As mothers they were indifferent or even brutal to their offspring.

In contrast to the negative effects of separation on the mother's attachment to her infant are the positive effects of a strong mother–infant attachment. In order to establish a strong mother–infant attachment, the care-eliciting behaviors of the infant are extremely important. But once initiated, the absence of these care-eliciting behaviors does not appear to reduce the mother's attachment. Studies of primates have shown that even after the infant has died, the mother will continue to hold it, in some cases even after the body has begun to decompose.

Adoption in Animals. Despite the fact that separation at birth in most mammals will lower the levels of maternal behavior or in some cases eliminate the maternal responses of mothers to the point that they reject their infants upon re-presentation, there is evidence of "adoption," or assumption of maternal care for motherless infants, in most species. This may occur independent of the maternal "readiness" of the adopter but may be facilitated by the state of the adopter if she is close to parturition or has recently given birth. Klaus and Kennell (1976) have concluded, from their review of adoption studies: "(1) There appears to be a sensitive period after birth, distinct for each species, during which females will adopt alien young. (2) In some species, such as goats and sheep, adoption will not take place after the sensitive period without specific conditions (i.e., close contact, isolation, and adequate length of time). (3) Environmental conditions, such as number of young introduced, influence the success of adoptions. (4) Unusual behavior on the part of the infant may interfere with successful adoption" (p. 31).

Thus, there appears to be a period that extends from shortly before to shortly after delivery, during which the mother seems maximally aroused to engage in maternal behaviors elicited by the presence of the young. A label of "critical," however, is somewhat inappropriate as this period is more a time of maximal sensitization in the mother to respond maternally to the young. Adaptations to the needs of the young can clearly be made by maternal animals at other times, or by nonmaternal members of the group (i.e., virgin females or males). Thus, it seems more accurate, and certainly more appropriate in terms of generalizing these results to human behavior, to view this period surrounding birth as one during which the developmental needs of the mother and of the infant are in a state of maximum synchrony. If one considers the period immediately after birth in this fashion, it becomes clear that the results of work with animals cannot be applied directly to the situation of human mother–infant bonding. The needs of the human mother are significantly different in nature from those of the lower mammals in that psychological aspects of her personality and environmental situation may equal or surpass her biological needs in importance. The importance of psychological factors provides a safety device for the survival of a deviant infant as well as a possible interference with otherwise "normal" attachment. If the significance of cultural and personal attitudes is acknowledged in the study of human mother–infant bonding, the "problem" of prematurity becomes a much more complex, but also more hopeful, issue.

Klaus and Kennell (1976) have reviewed an extensive amount of research on mother–infant bonding, the effects of separation (especially that of premature infants from their mothers), and possible interventions to strengthen maternal–infant attachment. They have adopted the "critical period" model of attachment from the animal literature, working from the assumption that the separation of mother and infant at birth has negative consequences in terms of attachment which are exacerbated as the length of separation increases. They feel that this problem can be clearly seen in the relationship between premature mothers and their infants, whose separation is often long and complicated both by maternal feelings of inadequacy and the infant's physical immaturity and extra caretaking needs.

Early Attachment in Humans

As we have seen above, animal studies have indicated that for some species there is a period immediately after birth during which the mother is optimally prepared to "bond" with her infant. Several investigators have postulated that a similar phenomenon is operative in the formation of an attachment relationship between the human mother and her infant. If such a period does exist in human behavior, it is possible that developmental disturbances associated with prematurity are due to the enforced separation of mother and child at birth as well as to problems posed to both by the premature birth itself.

If we regard prematurity as a cause of disturbance in the attachment process, there are two approaches to the problem of ascertaining when this disturbance occurs. Premature birth of the infant may be regarded as an alteration of an attachment process that begins with quickening, i.e., the first perceptible movements of the fetus, and normally extends through the last trimester of pregnancy (Bibring, Dwyer, Huntington, and Valenstein, 1961; Leiderman, 1978). Another theory is that the separation of mother and infant which usually results from premature birth does not allow the mother the essential perinatal contact with her infant needed to form strong bonds of attachment (Klaus and Kennell, 1970).

The procedure of isolating premature infants from their mothers was originally prompted by the need for special regulation of the atmosphere, blood, and heat of the child which could only take place in an incubator. It was also felt that keeping the child in a special unit without visitors would reduce the likelihood of infection, a serious danger to the fragile system of the immature infant. These procedures of isolation have been progressively relaxed in many countries, usually because of economic reasons. Surprisingly, it has been recently found that the admittance of mothers into the premature nursery in American hospitals has decreased, rather than increased, the incidence of infection in premature infants (Barnett, Leiderman, and Grobstein, 1970).

Klaus and Kennell (1976) cited a recent survey of American premature nurseries carried out by Barnett in 1972 which found that this practice, while increasing in frequency, is not yet widely accepted. Mothers were permitted to enter premature nurseries in only 30% of the hospitals surveyed. Despite the changes that may have occurred in the years since this survey was made, it is clear that there is a common practice prevalent in America of separating the mother and her infant, especially if the infant is premature. Some postulate that this separation is the major factor in later problems associated with prematurity rather than any organic factors associated with the early birth itself.

Kennell, Klaus, and Wolfe (1975) have designed a procedure with which they attempt to provide a catch-up period for mothers separated from their premature infants who had been placed in intensive care at birth. In their study of the effects of this program, 15 mothers of premature infants were given a period of close contact with their infants in a "rooming-in" setting for the 3 days prior to the discharge of the infant from the hospital. During this period the infant stayed in the mother's room and the mother provided all caregiving, although a nurse was available outside the room. The father was also allowed unlimited visiting privileges. This intervention procedure was based on observations of the mothering patterns of animals, who will tend to form bonds with infants not introduced at birth, provided they are given special environmental circumstances in which to do so. The mothers in the Kennell *et al.* study tended to alter the rooming-in environment to suit their own personal needs by rearranging the furniture in the room or changing the infant's previous feeding schedule. Mothers tended to have a short initial period of intensive attention to the infant; 13 of the 15 mothers did not sleep during the first night of the "nesting period." Mothers given this experience reported an increased confidence in their caretaking skills, but no differences were found in attachment and caretaking skills when this group was compared at 1 month after discharge to a matched sample who had not had a nesting period. Kennell *et al.* hypothesized that the lack of later differences was due to the fact that the nesting period was initiated too late to have significant effects, i.e., the mother had been separated from her infant for far too long. There was no measure in this study of the maternal response to the experience of the premature birth itself, which may have been a significant factor in the mother's later feelings toward the infant.

In another study of the effects of early contact on later attachment, Klaus, Jerauld, Kreger, McAlpine, Steffa, and Kennell (1972) experimentally increased the amount of contact between mothers and their full-term newborns. The mothers were young, of low socio-economic status, and were predominantly black. Less than one-half were married. Mothers in the experimental group were given contact with their naked newborns for 1 hour during the first 3 hours after birth, and were allowed to play with their babies for 5 extra hours every afternoon during each of the first 3 days postpartum, adding up to a total of 16 hours more than the usual amount of time mothers are allowed to spend with their infant over the first 3 days after birth. A control group of mothers were given normal hospital contact with their full-term infants.

Experimental and control mothers returned to the hospital for three separate assessments 1 month after the birth of their infant. These measures included a standard interview, during which the mother was asked questions pertaining to her health, the baby's behavior, and her attitudes toward the child; a routine physical examination of the infant, during which the mother's behavior was observed and coded in specific behavior categories; and a 15-minute filmed observation of the mother bottle-feeding her infant. Each frame of this film was analyzed separately for 25 specific behaviors relevant to mother–infant attachment, e.g., eye-to-eye contact, smiling, vocalizing, touching.

The mother's scores on the first two measures were combined into a score of maternal attachment behavior, i.e., her unwillingness to be separated from her infant as scored on the questionnaire, and her "hovering" behavior during the physical examination. The mothers who received the extended-contact experience scored as significantly more attached than the control mothers.

The filmed observations were scored for the amount of time the mother spent fondling the infant and the amount of time both spent in *en face*, i.e., face-to-face, interactions. Although the amount of time the mothers in both groups spent looking at their infants did not differ, the extended-contact mothers spent more time in the *en face* positions and fondling their infants. Thus the amount of attention the infants received did not differ, but the nature of the attention did.

One could conclude from these results at the 1-month follow-up that those mothers allowed extended contact with their newborns in the hospital had a much higher level of attachment (behavioral and attitudinal) to their children than they would have had without this extra contact. Unfortunately, Klaus *et al.* were not able to control for the positive effects that the extra staff attention associated with their intervention itself may have had for the experimental group of mothers.

Kennell, Jerauld, Wolfe, Chesler, Kreger, McAlpine, Steffa, and Klaus (1974) retested these mother–infant pairs on the same three measures at 1 year after discharge from the hospital, and tested the infants with the Bayley Scales of Infant Development (Bayley, 1969) as well. The mother's response at 1 year showed a similar pattern on the interview and physical examination scales. Extended-contact mothers reported themselves less willing to leave their babies and as missing them more when they were separated. These mothers also spent a greater amount of time than the control group mothers in assisting the pediatrician during the infant's physical examination and in soothing the infant during crying spells. No differences were found between the two groups of infants on the Bayley scales. It appears that mothers from the extended contact group continued to show more attachment behaviors toward their infants at 1 year. We cannot be certain, however, of the cause of this difference. Was it due to the contact itself or to the interpretation by the mother of her role in this special experience?

Leiderman, Leifer, Seashore, Barnett, and Grobstein (1973) studied premature infants and their mothers in two experimental conditions and compared them with a group of full-term infants with mothers who had similar demographic characteristics. The 20 mothers in each of the two experimental groups were married with husbands in the home, had no previous history of premature births, and had an average age in the early 20s. Their infants were single births and were free of obvious congenital abnormalities.

Mothers in the "separated" group were allowed normal hospital contact with their infant, which consisted of viewing the infant through an observation window during its stay in the intensive care nursery. Mothers in the "contact" group were allowed into the premature nursery to touch and engage in caregiving activities with their infants. In order to control for the possible effects of this additional physical stimulation on the infant, the infants in the separated group were also given extra handling, but by the nursery staff rather than their mothers. Both groups of mothers were allowed to come into the nursery and care for their infants when a weight of 2,100 g was reached. This period lasted until the infant reached the discharge weight of 2,500 g, usually 7–10 days.

The experimental groups were matched as carefully as possible with a control group of full-term mothers. There were no black families in the control group compared to three in each of the experimental groups and the socioeconomic status was slightly higher in the control group, but otherwise, the groups were comparable.

The women in this study were somewhat different from the mothers of a premature infant used in most other investigations, who were young, single, black, poor, and with little education. Such factors considerably increase the burden for the mother of a premature infant. These mothers and infants were given an extensive battery of tests at 1 week after discharge, again at 1 month, at 3 months, and then at 3-month intervals until the babies were 15 months old. When mother–infant interactions were assessed no differences were found between the contact and separated premature groups. Mothers of full-term infants, however, behaved differently from both groups of premature mothers in that they spent more time in front-to-front contact with their babies at 1 week and 1 month after discharge.

However, differences were found between the groups in their level of self-confidence. Mothers who were separated from their infants tended to have lower self-esteem. Powell (1974) studied mothers who were allowed to have differing degrees of contact with their low-weight newborns, varying from routine hospital contact to extra handling and visual contact, or extra visual contact alone. Powell found that mothers allowed to have physical contact with their babies in hospitals were more likely to feel close to their infants and to have higher self-esteem than mothers who were allowed only to look at their infants. Greenberg, Rosenburg, and Lind (1973) in a Swedish study also found that mothers of infants who were given more contact judged themselves more competent to care for their infants.

Mothers in the separated group who were multiparous (had previously given birth) were not as influenced by the separation as were primiparous mothers (who had not previously given birth) (Seashore, Leifer, Barnett, and Leiderman, 1973). The mothers who had already had a successful childbirth experience were able to buffer themselves against the atmosphere surrounding a premature birth which could have acted to undermine their self-esteem.

A complicating factor in the study by Leiderman *et al.* (1973) was that those mothers allowed to have close contact with their infants took little advantage of this privilege. They visited their infant approximately once every 6 days (Leifer, Leiderman, Barnett, and Williams, 1972). Perhaps the mothers in the early-contact group interpreted the opportunity to visit their infants as an expression of confidence on the part of the hospital in the mother's caregiving skills.

The results of Kennell, Trause, and Klaus (1975) can also be reinterpreted in a somewhat different light. Instead of developing a strong attachment to their infants during an early critical period, the mothers allowed contact with their infants at birth may have had a greater level of pride in their ability to care for their infants than those told to "stay away" by the actions of the hospital staff. Thus, it may not be the interaction itself but rather the feeling of competence the mother derives from the hospital staff's acknowledgement of her skills as a mother that leads to the differences in behavior found in the follow-up studies of these subjects.

Leiderman and his associates continued to follow their sample for a 5-year period. Leiderman and Seashore (1975) assessed maternal self-confidence and home interaction of these mothers and infants at 1 year after discharge from the hospital and concluded from their data that the manipulations in the nursery had had almost no effect on infants' behavior and test performance. Although mothers allowed early contact were more likely to touch their infants and tended to have higher levels of confidence than separated mothers, the variables of social status, parity, and sex of infant exerted more influence on the mothers' later behavior than did any of the experimental manipulations.

It may be that those things that most influence a mother's behavior toward her infant, including a premature infant, are related to factors other than a period of actual contact with the newborn. These factors would include the economic and emotional supports available to the mother before, during, and after the birth, the mother's attitudes toward her pregnancy and her role as a mother, and the attitudes directed toward her by the hospital staff.

Prenatal Attachment

Some theorists (Bibring *et al.*, 1961; Cramer, 1976) have postulated that there is a critical period for attachment in human mothers, as there is in other mammals, but that it occurs much earlier in the life of the human infant, that is, during the last 3 months of pregnancy. If one considers the importance of intellectual and emotional factors in human behavior, it seems reasonable that a mother will do a considerable amount of thinking about her infant and form expectations for both their futures long before the infant is born. There may be important developmental steps to be experienced by the mother before as well as after the child's birth which influence her bond to the infant.

The period of pregnancy calls for major developmental accomplishments on the part of the mother. She must accept the pregnancy; prepare for the birth physically, economically, emotionally, and intellectually; acknowledge the independent existence of her growing baby; and after the birth, accept the infant as being separate from herself yet needing her love and support. If one wanted to select a critical period for attachment, the beginning of the third trimester, i.e., the stage of "quickening," would be more appropriate than birth itself. It is at this point that the mother must acknowledge the infant as an organism dependent on her, yet independent as well; part of her yet separate.

From a psychoanalytic perspective (Cramer, 1976), this change in the mother's feeling toward the fetus involves a transition from a narcissistic attachment to the unborn infant to an object love for the infant as one who is intimately linked to herself and yet a separate being. In this model, mothers who have had emotional troubles themselves and have been unable to experience "object love" would be a high risk for attachment difficulties with their newborns.

Prematurity poses an additional stress on the mother. Even if she has had no emotional problems and is able to transfer her love from herself to her normal infant, the premature birth would not allow the mother sufficient time to change from a narcissistic love for the infant as a part of herself to an object love for the infant as a separate entity. The premature infant is not a beautiful baby and may serve as an insult to the self-image of the mother.

Kaplan and Mason (1960) proposed four tasks that the mother of the premature must undertake if she is to make a satisfactory adjustment to her child. The first task is the preparation for the possible loss of the child at delivery via anticipatory grief and emotional withdrawal from the child. The second task is to acknowledge her failure to deliver a normal full-term baby. The grief and depression accompanying these two tasks are positive signs that the mother is struggling with these issues and are healthy responses until the baby's chances of survival are seen as secure. The third task for the mother is to resume the interrupted task of relating to her baby. This task involves her preparation for the baby's home-coming and the now renewed possibility of a positive outcome for her pregnancy. The fourth task concerns her future attitudes and involves understanding the special caretaking needs of the premature infant while at the same time being aware that prematurity is a temporary state that in time will yield to normality. Kaplan and Mason see the comple-tion of these four tasks as requirements for normal adaptation to the stress of the premature delivery.

From this perspective, the mother who has a poor self-esteem, lack of cognitive resources and flexibility, and a lack of experience being a mother or of forming object love relationships will have a more difficult time accepting a premature infant.

Cramer (1976) interviewed a small group of mothers of premature infants at 10 days and at 2 months after birth to determine if their feelings toward themselves and their infant after the birth experience were sim-ilar to those one would expect from mothers of full-term infants who were unable to feel an object love for their babies. He concluded that the birth of the premature infant was a severe blow to the mother's self-esteem, her confidence in her mothering capabilities, and her security in a feminine role. Mothers commonly conceived of the early birth as a loss of a body part, an insult to their bodily integrity, and a sign of inner inferiority. The premature birth enforced a feeling of unreality about the child, who was perceived as alien and thus was more easily rejected by the mother. It is highly conceivable that the mother of a premature infant may have not had sufficient time to develop object love, or may have had other difficulties in establishing an attachment to her unborn child.

Leiderman (1978) notes that pregnancy is frequently an unwanted circumstance for the typical mother of a premature infant. These moth-ers, in other words, have some reason to fight an acknowledgment of the infant's presence and, therefore, may not establish normal attachments. For these mothers in particular, intervention procedures such as the ones used by Kennell and Klaus and their colleagues in their studies of early mother–infant contact (1972) and "nesting periods" (1975) may have a therapeutic effect by offering professional attention and support, and providing these mothers with a special period and environment in which to develop a close relationship with their newborn infant.

We have reviewed a variety of interpretations of the newborn period as a "critical" time for mother–infant attachment. Some have claimed that this period is important because of possible biochemical factors; others have talked about this time as being a sensitive but not critical period. Others have mentioned quickening as a better candidate for a sensitive period. In contrast to all these positions, Dunn (1975) has gone so far as to propose that the period after birth, rather than being a critical period, may offer a kind of physical and psychological buffer zone for both mother and infant. In a longitudinal study of 70 mothers and their children, Dunn interviewed the mother and observed the interactions of the mother and her infant during a feeding session in the first week after birth and again at 8, 14, 20, and 30 weeks. She did not find any significant relationships between the interaction patterns during the first observations and the patterns seen in observations at 8 weeks or later.

This lack of correlation between measures from the early period and later maternal measures led Dunn to hypothesize that the postpartum period, rather than being a sensitive period, may be a time when the relationship between the mother and baby is buffered against difficulties of adjustment. She concludes that it would make good adaptive sense from a biological perspective if problems of adjustment during this early period did not have long-term effects on the patterns of interaction between mother and infant.

In this vein, it is perhaps best to view the postpartum period as one point in a continuous development of the maternal–infant relationship, which is modifiable not only during the first few hours of life but at many points during the early phases of the child's growth.

Summary

We have advanced a long way from the belief that premature birth represents a genetic inadequacy in the infant. We know that the antecedents and consequences of early birth are rooted in the social and emotional conditions of family life. Prematurity is strongly connected to the stress of poor living circumstances, and the developmental outcomes for prematurely born infants also can be attributed to these same factors. Although clinicians alone cannot remake society, we have identified several methods of mitigating some of these deleterious effects.

Interventions that have focused only on the premature infant have had modest successes. Recreating the fetal environment or providing special stimulation has resulted in modest gains in motor behavior and possible accelerations in growth. There are also hopeful signs that some procedures reduce periods of apnea, possibly preventing respiratory problems.

Interventions that have focused on the mother's relation to the child have shown long-range effects on the attachment and caregiving behavior of the mother. The more positive experiences the mother has in competent caretaking of her child, the better she will feel and the more she will be willing to take care of the child. Mothers who are allowed to see and touch their babies immediately after birth are more attached to their infants than mothers who see their babies later. Mothers who have their babies with them longer during the day are more attached to their infants than mothers who see their infants only at feeding time.

During these togetherness experiences the mother, especially the primiparous, has to feel capable of coping with the needs of her infant. The hospital staff has the task of making sure that the mother is prepared, and of being supportive and sympathetic to her efforts. If too many demands are placed on an unprepared mother, the togetherness experience can have negative consequences.

Most nursery practices related to the mother–infant relationship are still based on sentiment and common sense rather than on research data. Although it may be apparent that more contact makes for a different mother–infant relationship later, neither the magnitude nor the duration of these effects is yet known, nor is it known how much of what kind of contact would produce the optimal effects.

POSITIVE AND NEGATIVE RECIPROCAL CYCLES. One of the major stumbling blocks in studying the separate effects of prenatal, delivery, or neonatal variables is that they are frequently confounded. The mother who begins her pregnancy under stressful emotional conditions starts a cycle that may lead to poor attachment after delivery. Her prenatal stress tends to be associated with more delivery complications and a higher incidence of difficult temperament in the offspring. The difficult temperament places more demands on the mother's adaptive ability and caretaking skill and may result in reduced affection and attachment to the child. At what point in this negative cycle interventions should occur, and what kind of interventions are the most effective, are still major research questions.

In contrast to the stress-laden situations described above is the positive reciprocal cycle of the mother prepared for her pregnancy, who suffers a minimum of stress, trains for her delivery and requires a minimum of intervention, immediately begins caretaking for a child with a normal temperament, feels effective in her caretaking, and is able to enter a responsive, affectionate relationship with her infant.

DEALING WITH DEVIANCY. Sameroff (1975) viewed the problem of deviancy in the newborn period as one involving both mother and child as a dyadic unit. In terms of abnormal developmental outcomes, a focus on the characteristics of the infant alone has been the least adequate predictive variable. The crucial factor has been the environmental context in which the child's characteristics are nurtured or hindered. From the perspective of the child's development, deviancy during the newborn period is truly in the eye of the beholder, since the negative consequences for a child who is temperamentally or physically different at birth need not be permanent.

The psychological task is to convert the mother's attitude from one of seeing the child as different from the normal to that of seeing him or her as part of a continuous spectrum of developmental maturity. The professional has two tasks to achieve with the new mother: the first relates to her attitudes toward the child and the second relates to her competence at taking care of her infant. In terms of her attitudes, the mother should feel that the differences between her child and what she would consider a normal child may be only temporary. With age children outgrow their prematurity and colic, and recover from their illnesses. The mother's susceptibility to perceiving her infant as different often goes beyond the child's appearance. Mothers of seemingly normal infants often think of their children as different either through their own ignorance or through some casual remark of the hospital staff. The impulse to treat these fears lightly or even to ignore them may not be helpful to a mother whose future attitudes toward the child may be strongly colored by her initial impressions.

The second task is to assure the mother that she can be a competent caretaker of her infant. The mother's fears and self-doubts about her ability to care for her infant may stem from her lack of experience. These fears occur in nearly every primiparous mother, but having a child in a special care unit would give even an experienced mother pause. The best way to assure a mother of her caretaking competence is not through verbal instruction but rather through the actual experience of caring for her infant. The maximal experience of this kind for the mother of the full-term infant is a "rooming-in" arrangement, while for the mother of the premature infant, similar experiences can be had by being allowed into the special care nursery to tend to her child.

For some mothers even allowing them into the premature nursery is not sufficient contact for promoting the necessary attachment to their infants. An additional period of intensive contact before leaving the hospital may be desirable, with the mother given primary responsibility for the infant's care. The extent to which these effects would carry over into the mother's behavior at home is a subject for further study. Many of the major problems in the mother's response to a premature infant are resolved in this type of setting. The mother has the feeling that the hospital staff has confidence in her ability as she successfully cares for the infant, while at the same time she has resource people readily available.

Until the child does appear and act in accord with the mother's view of normality, there is still the potential of later caretaking problems. For this reason the family requires follow-up care to assure that the mother will not be overwhelmed by a child who may give little satisfaction in return for meeting its many caretaking demands. These problems are most likely to occur in those families with the fewest economic, educational, or emotional resources to deal with such burdens.

The research resulting from our desire to alleviate the problems of premature infants has had an impact on our understanding of normal development as well as deviancy. The study of early mother–infant attachment has enhanced our understanding of the processes by which the child becomes incorporated into the family and the major importance of attitudinal and emotional components in this process. It is this mutual enrichment of both our understanding and our fostering of development that brings satisfaction to those engaged in these research efforts.

References

Bakow, H., Sameroff, A. J., Kelly, P., and Zax, M. *Relation between newborn behavior and mother–child interaction at 4 months.* Paper presented at the Society for Research in Child Development meetings, Philadelphia, 1973.

Barnard, K. *A program of stimulation for infants born prematurely.* Seattle: University of Washington Press, 1975.

Barnett, C., Leiderman, H., Grobstein, R., and Klaus, M. Neonatal separation: The maternal side of interactional deprivation. *Pediatrics,* 1970, *45*(2).

Bayley, N. *The Bayley scales of infant development.* New York: Psychological Corporation, 1969.

Bell, R. Q. A reinterpretation of the direction of effects in studies of socialization. *Psychological Review,* 1968, *75,* 81–95.

Benton, A. L. Mental development of prematurely born children. *American Journal of Orthopsychiatry,* 1940, *10,* 719–746.

Bibring, G. L., Dwyer, T. F., Huntington, D. S., and Valenstein, A. F. A study of the psychological processes in pregnancy and of the earliest mother–child relationship. I. Some propositions and comments, *Psychoanalytic Study of the Child,* 1961, *16,* 9–27.

Birch, H., and Gussow, G. D. *Disadvantaged children.* New York: Grune and Stratton, 1970.

Caplan, G., Mason, E., and Kaplan, D. M. Four studies of crisis in parents of premature infants. *Community Mental Health Journal,* 1965, *1,* 149–161.

Capper, A. M. Fate and development of immature and premature children: A clinical study and review of the literature, and a study of cerebral hemorrhage in the newborn infant. *American Journal of the Diseases of Children,* 1928, *35,* 262, 443.

Cornell, E., and Gottfried, A. Intervention with premature human infants. *Child Development,* 1976, *47,* 32–39.

Cramer, B. A mother's reactions to the birth of a premature baby. In M. H. Klaus and J. H. Kennell, *Maternal–infant bonding.* St. Louis: C. V. Mosby, 1976.

Douglas, J. W. B. "Premature" children at primary schools. *British Medical Journal*, 1960, *1*, 1003–1013.

Drillien, C. M. The incidence of mental and physical handicaps in school-age children of very low birthweight. *Pediatrics*, 1961, *27*, 452–464.

Drillien, C. M. *The growth and development of the prematurely born infant*. Baltimore: Williams and Wilkens, 1964.

Dunn, J. F. Consistency and change in styles of mothering. In *Parent–infant interaction*, Ciba Foundation Symposium 33. Amsterdam: Elsevier, 1975.

Fox, C. *Pregnancy, childbirth and early infancy in Anglo-American culture: 1675–1830*. Unpublished doctoral dissertation, University of Pennsylvania, 1966.

Gesell, A. The mental growth of prematurely born infants. *Journal of Pediatrics*, 1933, *21*, 634–680.

Greenberg, M., Rosenburg, I., and Lind, J. First mothers rooming-in with their newborns: Its impact upon the mother. *American Journal of Orthopsychiatry*, 1973, *43*(5), 783.

Harlow, H. F., and Harlow, M. K. Effects of various mother–infant relationships on rhesus monkey behaviors. In B. M. Foss (Ed.), *Determinants of infant behavior*. Vol. 4. London: Methuen, 1969.

Hasselmeyer, E. G. The premature neonate's response to handling. *American Nurses Association*, 1964, *11*, 15–24.

Hess, J. H., Mohr, G., and Bartelme, P. F. *The physical and mental growth of prematurely born children*. Chicago: University Press, 1934.

Illsley, R. Early prediction of perinatal risk. *Proceedings of the Royal Society of Medicine*, 1966, *59*, 181–184.

Kaplan, D. M., and Mason, E. A. Maternal reactions to premature birth viewed as an acute emotional disorder. *American Journal of Orthopsychiatry*, 1960, *30*, 539.

Kattwinkel, J., Hearman, H., Fanaroff, A. A., Katora, P., and Klaus, M. H. Apnea of prematurity. *Journal of Pediatrics*, 1975, *86*, 585–592.

Katz, V. Auditory stimulation and developmental behavior of the premature infant. *Nursing Research*, 1971, *20*, 196–201.

Kennell, J. H., Jerauld, R., Wolfe, H., Chesler, D., Kreger, N. C., McAlpine, W., Steffa, M., and Klaus, M. H. Maternal behavior one year after early and extended post-partum contact. *Developmental Medicine and Child Neurology*, 1974, *16*, 172–179

Kennell, J. H., Klaus, M. H., and Wolfe, H. Nesting behavior in the human mother after prolonged mother–infant separation. In P. Swyer and J. Stetson (Eds.), *Current concepts of neonatal intensive care*. St. Louis: Warren H. Green, 1975.

Kennell, J. H., Trause, M. A., and Klaus, M. H. Evidence for a sensitive period in the human mother in parent–infant interaction. In *Parent–infant interaction*, Ciba Foundation Symposium 33. Amsterdam: Elsevier, 1975.

Klaus, M., and Kennell, J. Mothers separated from their newborn infants. *Pediatric Clinics of North America*, 1970, *17*, 1015.

Klaus, M., and Kennell, J. *Maternal–infant bonding*. St. Louis: C. V. Mosby, 1976.

Klaus, M., Jerauld, R., Kreger, N., McAlpine, W., Steffa, M., and Kennell, J. Maternal attachment: The importance of the first post-partum days. *New England Journal of Medicine*, 1972, *286*, 460.

Klein, M., and Stern, L. Low birth weight and the battered child syndrome. *American Journal of Diseases of the Child*, 1971, *122*, 15–18.

Knobloch, H., Rider, R., Harper, P., and Pasamanick, B. Neuropsychiatric sequelae of prematurity: A longitudinal study. *Journal of the American Medical Association*, 1956, *161*, 581–585.

Korner, A. F., Kraemer, H. C., Haffner, B. A., and Cooper, L. M. Effects of waterbed flotation on premature infants: A pilot study. *Pediatrics*, 1975, *56*, 361.

Leiderman, P. H. The critical period hypothesis revisited: Mother to infant social bonding in the neonatal period. In F. D. Horowitz (Ed.), *Early developmental hazards: Predictors and preventions.* Washington, D.C.: American Association for the Advancement of Science, 1978.

Leiderman, P. H., Leifer, A. D., Seashore, M. J., Barnett, C. R., and Grobstein, R. Mother–infant interaction: Effects of early deprivation, prior experience and sex of infant. In J. I. Nurnberger (Ed.), *Biological and environmental determinants of early development.* Baltimore: Williams and Wilkins, 1973.

Leiderman, P. H., and Seashore, M. Maternal–infant neonatal separation: Some delayed consequences. In *Parent–infant interaction*, Ciba Foundation Symposium 33. Amsterdam: Elsevier, 1975.

Leifer, A. D., Leiderman, P. H., Barnett, C. R., and Williams, J. A. Effects of mother–infant separation on maternal attachment behavior. *Child Development*, 1972, *43*, 1203–1218.

McDonald, A. D. Intelligence in children of very low birth weight. *British Journal of Preventive and Social Medicine*, 1964, *18*, 59–74.

Moore, A. V. Effects of modified maternal care in the sheep and goat. In G. Newton and S. Levine (Eds.), *Early experience and behavior.* Springfield, Illinois: Charles C Thomas, 1968. Pp. 481–529.

Neal, M. V. Vestibular stimulation and developmental behavior of the small premature infant. *Nursing Research Report*, 1968, *3*(1), 1–5.

Noirot, E. Changes in responsiveness to young in the adult mouse: The effect of external stimuli. *Journal of Comparative Physiology and Psychology*, 1964, *57*, 97.

Parmelee, A. H., and Haber, A. Who is the "risk infant"? *Clinical Obstetrics and Gynecology*, 1973, *16*, 376–387.

Parmelee, A. H., Kopp, C. B., and Sigman, M. Selection of developmental assessment techniques for infants at risk. *Merrill-Palmer Quarterly*, 1976, *22*, 177–199.

Pasamanick, B., Knobloch, H., and Lilienfeld, A. M. Socio-economic status and some precursors of neuropsychiatric disorder. *American Journal of Orthopsychiatry*, 1956, *26*, 594–601.

Peller, S. Der einfluss sozialer Nomente auf der Körperlichen Entwicklugszustand der Neugeborenen. *Wein. Arb. Gebiete Sozial. Med.*, 1913, *5*, 1047.

Powell, L. F. The effect of extra stimulation and maternal involvement on the development of low birth-weight infants and on maternal behavior. *Child Development*, 1974, *45*, 106.

Richards, M. P. M. Maternal behavior in rodents and logomorphs. In A. McLaren (Ed.), *Advances in reproductive physiology.* Vol. 2. London: Logos Press, 1967. Pp. 53–110.

Ringler, N. M., Kennell, J. H., Janvella, R., Navojosky, B. J., and Klaus, M. H. Mother to child speech at two years—effects of early postnatal contact. *Journal of Pediatrics*, 1975, *86*, 141–144.

Robson, K., and Moss, H. Subjective aspects of maternal attachment in man. In M. Lewis and L. A. Rosenblum (Eds.), *The effect of the infant on its caregiver.* New York: Wiley, 1974.

Rosenblatt, J. S. The basis of synchrony in the behavioral interaction between the mother and her offspring in the laboratory rat. In B. M. Foss (Ed.), *Determinants of infant behavior.* Vol. 3. London: Methuen, 1965.

Sameroff, A. J. Psychological needs of the mother in early mother–infant interactions. In G. Avery (Ed.), *Neonatology.* New York: Lippincott, 1975.

Sameroff, A. J., and Chandler, M. Reproductive risk and the continuum of caretaking casualty. In F. D. Horowitz, M. Hetherington, S. Scarr-Salapatek, and G. Siegel (Eds.), *Review of child development research.* Vol. 4. Chicago: University of Chicago, 1975.

Scarr-Salapatek, S., and Williams, M. L. The effects of early stimulation on low birth-weight infants. *Child Development*, 1973, *44*, 94–101.

Seashore, M. H., Leifer, A. D., Barnett, C. R., and Leiderman, P. H. The effects of denial of early mother–infant interaction on maternal self-confidence. *Journal of Personality and Social Psychology*, 1973, *26*, 369–378.

Solkoff, N., Yaffe, S., Weintraub, D., and Blase, B. Effects of handling on subsequent development of premature infants. *Developmental Psychology*, 1969, *1*, 765–768.

Thomas, A., Chess, S., and Birch, H. *Temperament and behavior disorders in children.* New York: New York University, 1968.

Werner, E. E. *The Kauai study: Follow-up at adolescence.* Unpublished manuscript, 1975.

Werner, E. E., Bierman, J. M., and French, F. E. *The children of Kauai.* Honolulu: University of Hawaii, 1971.

Wiener, G. Psychologic correlates of premature birth: A review. *Journal of Nervous and Mental Diseases*, 1962, *134*, 129–144.

Wiener, G., Rider, R. V., Oppel, W. C., Fischer, L. K., and Harper, P. A. Correlates of low birth weight: Psychological status at 6–7 years of age. *Pediatrics*, 1965, *35*, 434–444.

Wiener, G., Rider, R. V., Oppel, W. C., and Harper, P. A. Correlates of low birth weight: Psychological status at eight to ten years of age. *Pediatric Research*, 1968, *2*, 110.

Early Visual Experience in Humans: Evidence for a Critical Period in the Development of Binocular Vision

RICHARD N. ASLIN AND MARTIN S. BANKS

Normal human perceptual systems are highly structured and capable of extremely complex functions. Yet, many persons possess structural anomalies in their perceptual systems which result in functional deficits, or specific perceptual problems. A question of great clinical and theoretical importance is how these functional deficits develop. In the pursuit of answers to this question, basic research concerning normal and abnormal perceptual development has played a major role. This chapter will provide a brief review of basic research concerning the development of binocular vision in animals and then a more complete review of a study that applied the principles uncovered in the animal studies to a population of humans with deficits in binocular vision.

Two opposing views of perceptual development are the nativist and empiricist positions (Hochberg, 1962). Nativists have claimed that perceptual experience has no effect on the development of perceptual abilities. These functional abilities either are present at birth or unfold postnatally according to a genetically controlled maturational plan. Empiricists, on the other hand, have argued that perceptual experience is a necessary prerequisite for the development of normal perceptual abilities and that only very rudimentary abilities are present at birth or unfold

RICHARD N. ASLIN • Department of Psychology, Indiana University, Bloomington, Indiana. MARTIN S. BANKS • Department of Psychology, University of Texas, Austin, Texas. Preparation of this chapter was partially supported by a grant from the Spencer Foundation to Richard N. Aslin.

maturationally. Anastasi (1958) persuasively argued that the nativist and empiricist positions are both untenable, that an organism obviously cannot develop without both a genetic endowment and some experience in its environment. She proposed that the nativist–empiricist controversy be reformulated to ask the question: How much of the variability associated with development can be accounted for by experiential variance and how much by genetic variance? This question acknowledges that both experience and genetic endowment are important, while allowing each a variable role in determining the development of particular perceptual abilities.

To discover the relative importance of genetics and experience, one must be able to control genetic or experiential variation during development. The manipulation of perceptual experience has recently been made possible by perfection of the technique of perceptual deprivation. Using this technique, researchers can deprive a newborn animal of certain types of perceptual experience. Once the animal matures, it is possible to determine the consequences of the deprivation by studying the animal's perceptual abilities. Depending on the type and magnitude of functional deficits found, the importance of experience can be determined. For previously deprived animals, empiricists would expect large deficits whereas nativists would predict only minimal deficits to be observed.

This chapter will show how the perceptual deprivation technique can be applied to study the effects of early experience in humans. Obviously, the experimental manipulation of an infant's or young child's perceptual experience is not possible for ethical reasons. But we will show how studies of a population of subjects with a naturally occurring deprivation can determine the effect that early experience has on later perceptual function.

The particular perceptual ability we investigated is binocular vision. The term *binocular* simply refers to the fact that we have two eyes. One advantage of having two eyes is that while looking at an object located fairly close to ourselves, each eye receives a slightly different view of that object (see Figure 1). The result of this slight discrepancy between two retinal images (called binocular parallax) is that the object is perceived as being located at a particular distance from our eyes as well as having a certain solidity or three-dimensionality. Thus, binocular parallax is an important source of visual information in the perception of three-dimensionality or depth.

A special case of binocular parallax can be generated with flat or two-dimensional patterns that are presented to the two eyes separately. That is, one eye views one pattern and the other eye a slightly different pattern

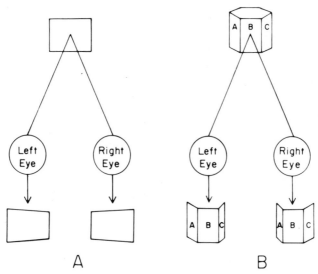

Figure 1. Two examples of binocular parallax in which each retina receives a slightly different image of an object. The resultant percept specifies that the object is three-dimensional and located at a particular distance from the observer.

(see Figure 2). The physical difference between the two patterns is called binocular disparity and the resultant perception of depth or three-dimensionality is called stereopsis. By varying the amount of binocular disparity, one can create the perception of depth that would result if the retinal images had come from a real single object located at different distances from the observer. Furthermore, one can measure the limit or threshold that a person has for reliably detecting the presence of small amounts of binocular disparity. This threshold is called stereoacuity, and it is measured in seconds of arc (see Figure 2).

One important aspect of binocular vision is that the most acute portion of the retina of each eye (i.e., that which most sharply resolves detail), the fovea, must be directed toward the same part of the particular object being fixated (see Figures 1 and 2). Failure to align the eyes appropriately results either in the perception of double images (seeing two objects when only one is present) or in the suppression of information from one eye. Both the presence of double images and suppression result in a large decrease in stereoacuity.

Before describing research concerning the development of human binocular vision, a review of basic neurophysiological research with animals is necessary. This research has provided both theoretical and practical foundations for deprivation studies with humans. The

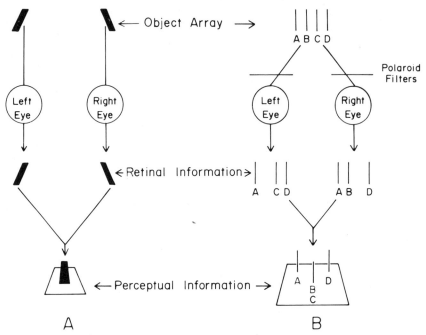

Figure 2. Two methods of stereoscopic stimulus presentation in which the two eyes view separate two-dimensional patterns. In (A) the two patterns are physically separated by an opaque divider. In (B) the observer views two pattern components with both eyes while a third component, differentially located for the two eyes, is viewed by each eye separately. The resultant stereoscopic percept is depicted in the bottom section of each figure. Disparity refers to the difference between the two pattern components that are viewed separately. Stereoacuity refers to the smallest disparity that results in a reliable perception of depth.

pioneering work of Hubel and Wiesel (1959, 1962) demonstrated the existence of single neurons in the cat visual cortex which respond only to the presence of certain configurations of visual stimulation such as edges or bars. These "feature-detecting neurons" are undoubtedly involved in the perception of orientation, size, form, movement, and depth.

Approximately 70–80% of neurons in the adult cat visual cortex respond to stimulation delivered to either of the two eyes. Such neurons are termed *binocular*. The remaining 20–30% respond to stimulation delivered to one eye but not the other. Hubel and Wiesel (1965, 1970) and Wiesel and Hubel (1965) showed that short periods of deprivation early in a cat's life could lead to permanent deficits in several feature-detecting properties of cortical neurons including the property of binocularity. Specifically, they prevented the two eyes of young kittens from working together (viewing the same object at the same time) by occluding or surgically misaligning one eye. The result of such perceptual deprivation was a permanent decrease in the number of neurons that would respond binocularly in the adult cat. The deficit was present only if the perceptual deprivation occurred during the period beginning shortly after initial eye opening (10 days) and ending 14 weeks after birth. Deprivation beginning after 14 weeks of age had little or no permanent effect on the proportion of binocular neurons in the adult visual cortex. The conclusion drawn by Hubel and Wiesel is that normal visual experience (during this 4- to 14-week period) is crucial for the development of normal binocularity. Thus, this period has been called the critical or sensitive period. A quantitative estimate of the cat's relative sensitivity to binocular deprivation at different ages is shown in Figure 3 and can be thought of as a representation of the critical or sensitive period.

Although Hubel and Wiesel demonstrated that cortical neuron binocularity is susceptible to abnormal early experience, one might ask how their measure of binocularity relates to depth perception, i.e., stereopsis. As noted above, a system that detects binocular disparity is required for the stereoscopic perception of depth. The fact that a particular cortical neuron is responsive to visual input delivered to either eye does not necessarily imply that that particular neuron provides information about disparity. However, Barlow, Blakemore, and Pettigrew (1967) and Nikara, Bishop, and Pettigrew (1968) have demonstrated that nearly all binocular neurons in the cortex of adult cats are sensitive to disparity. An entire population of cortical neurons, each neuron responsive to a particular amount of disparity, has been suggested as the neural basis for stereoscopic depth perception. This would permit the visual system to detect the exact degree of disparity in a visual display and thereby determine relative distances from the observer. In sum, cortical neuron binocularity, as measured by Hubel and Wiesel, is a necessary but not sufficient prerequisite for stereopsis.

The responsiveness of cortical neurons to disparity is also susceptible to perceptual deprivation. Pettigrew (1974) has shown that each binocular cortical neuron in kittens is responsive to a wide range of

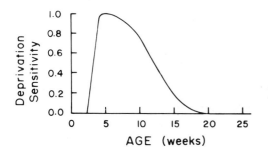

Figure 3. An estimate of the cat's sensitivity to binocular deprivation as reflected in cortical neuron binocularity (adapted from Blakemore, 1975).

disparities, and that this range of disparity responsiveness narrows to an adult level by 6–7 weeks after birth. Failure to receive normal binocular input in early life prevents the development of the precise disparity responsiveness typical of adult cortical neurons. The implication of Pettigrew's neurophysiological findings is that disparity responsiveness becomes more finely tuned or accurate during early life and is also affected by abnormal binocular input. This indicates that normal binocular input is necessary for normal disparity responsiveness in adulthood. Behavioral measures of stereopsis suggest that the functional ability to perceive depth is related to disparity responsiveness among cortical neurons. Blake and Hirsch (1975) and Packwood and Gordon (1975) have shown that the same type and amount of perceptual deprivation that lead to deficits in disparity specificity in the visual cortex also lead to deficits in cats' stereopsis (i.e., stereoscopic depth perception).

There is now compelling evidence that early experience influences later perceptual function in humans. Visual acuity (the ability to resolve fine details) is lower among adults who early in life had degraded visual input due to patching of one or both eyes (Awaya, Miyake, Amaizumi, Shiose, Kanda, and Komuro, 1973) or poor optical image formation by their lens and cornea (Freeman, Mitchell, and Millodot, 1972; Mitchell, Freeman, Millodot, and Haegerstrom, 1973; Fiorentini and Maffei, 1976). Furthermore, persons who have had crossed eyes (esotropia), a condition known to deleteriously affect binocular development in cats, do not develop normal binocular function as indexed by stereoacuity (Mitchell and Ware, 1974; Movshon, Chambers, and Blakemore, 1972).

The clinical importance of such findings is obvious. But the ophthalmologist or optometrist who is concerned about when to prescribe glasses or surgery for esotropia needs to know at what age adequate perceptual experience is most crucial. Two groups of researchers, the present authors and Anne-Marie Hohmann and Otto Creutzfeldt, recently reported initial findings related to this question (Banks, Aslin, and Letson, 1975; Hohmann and Creutzfeldt, 1975). Both studies concern functional deficits in binocular vision. In the remainder of this chapter we will describe our experiment and present Hohmann and Creutzfeldt's data only as a comparison to our own.

Recall that perceptual deprivation produced by misalignment of one of the eyes (surgically induced esotropia) seems to cause a binocular deficit in cats if the misalignment existed during the critical 4- to 14-week period. The aim of our study was to measure the binocularity of subjects who during some period of their lives had had misaligned eyes (esotropia). All of our 24 subjects had since undergone corrective surgery and hence had normally aligned eyes at the time of testing. Thus, as shown in Figure 4, each of the 24 subjects had had abnormal binocular experience due to esotropia during a different period of their lives. By comparing their present level of binocularity to their period of deprivation we could determine if and when a critical period for the development of binocularity is present in humans.

Direct measurement of single neuron binocularity as defined by Hubel and Wiesel (1962) was not possible with our human subjects. However, an estimate of the percentage of binocular neurons present in the visual cortex is provided by measurement of a perceptual aftereffect. Staring at one or more parallel lines tilted slightly from vertical leads to a subsequent alteration in perceived vertical (see Figure 5). This perceptual effect is called the tilt-aftereffect. The aftereffect is usually measured

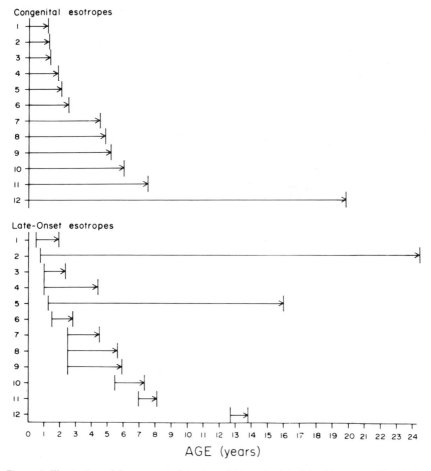

Figure 4. Illustration of the age period during which each of the 24 subjects tested by Banks *et al.* (1975) had abnormal binocular experience due to esotropia.

by having the subject fixate the nonvertical lines (the adapting grating) for a certain period of time and then having him or her adjust another set of lines (the test grating) to perceived vertical. The magnitude of the effect is equal to the angular difference between the adjustments of the test grating made before and after viewing the adapting grating. Of particular interest is the fact that subjects who view the adapting grating with only one eye and subsequently adjust the test grating to vertical using only the other unadapted eye also show a measurable tilt-after-effect. The size of the tilt-aftereffect in this interocular condition is typically 60–70% as great as the effect measured in the intraocular condition (same eye views adapt and test gratings). In order that the inter-ocular measurement be greater than zero, information from one eye must affect the processing of information subsequently delivered to the other eye. Thus, binocular interaction must occur at some level of the visual system. The rationale for using this measure is based on our knowledge that no significant binocular interaction occurs prior to the level of the primary visual cortex in both cats and monkeys. Interocular transfer of the tilt-aftereffect, then, provides us with a measure of the extent of binocular interaction at the level of the visual cortex or higher.

One might argue that interocular transfer of the tilt-aftereffect is a rather contrived method for assessing the level of binocular functioning, especially since other measures of binocularity, such as stereoacuity, are available. Movshon *et al.* (1972) and Mitchell and Ware (1974) have shown that between-subject differences in stereoacuity are highly correlated with interocular transfer of the tilt-aftereffect. In addition, it is known that stereoacuity is affected by monocular acuity or visual clarity. Subjects with normal binocularity but poor acuity in one eye show poor stereoacuity. This confounding of monocular acuity with stereoacuity does not hold for interocular transfer of the tilt-aftereffect. Thus, we chose to concentrate our analysis on the measure we thought best reflected the underlying state of binocular capability.

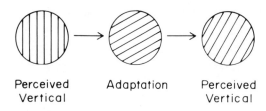

Figure 5. Schematic of the stimulus array used to generate the tilt-aftereffect. The angle of rotation of both the adapting and test gratings (middle and right) have been exaggerated. The actual angle of rotation from vertical of the adapting grating was 15°, and a typical tilt-aftereffect is 3 to 5° (difference between pre- and postadaptation verticals).

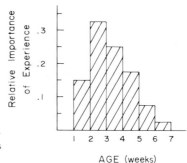

Figure 6. Hypothetical plot of the relative importance of visual experience during the first 8 weeks
after birth.

An explanation of our analysis of the existence and timing of a
critical period for binocularity requires a review of what a critical period
entails. The relative importance of any day, month, or year of visual
experience could be plotted as a bar graph. In Figure 6, for example, we
have simply illustrated the relative importance experience might have
for some particular animal as a function of age. Note that the sum of all
bars is set equal to 1.00, which is assumed to be the optimal amount of
experience that could be obtained. In other words, an organism passing
through weeks 1 to 7 with normal input would have an optimal amount
of experience. An organism deprived during any week between 1 and 7
would lose an amount corresponding to the height of the bar for that
week, and a total of less than 1.00 would result. Recall that the notion of a
critical period requires that deprivation during a certain period of development leads to a permanent deficit. If no critical period exists, then the
height of each bar would be equal for each week of the organism's
lifetime.

Rather than using a bar graph to represent the critical period, we
simply generated a smooth mathematical function to represent the
height of the bars and always set the area under the function equal to
1.00, as in the bar graph example. To find the particular function that best
described the data obtained from our subjects, the following approach
was used. Since we had no idea before the experiment what the critical
period function would look like (where it would start, how peaked it
would be, or where it would end), we used a very general function which
could take on an infinite number of different shapes. For each shape of
the function, a number varying between 0.0 and 1.00 could be calculated
for each of the 24 subjects. This number represents a predicted binocularity score for the particular shape of the function and the particular age
period when deprivation occurred for a given subject. In Figure 7 we
have drawn only one of several thousand functions used, and we have
shaded in the area during which 1 of the 24 subjects had abnormal

binocular input. Age A equals the time when esotropia began and age B
when successful surgery was performed. Age C corresponds to the subject's age at testing and was included since the critical period may have
extended well into adulthood. The estimated amount of normal binocular experience for each subject was computed as the area under the
function from birth to age A plus the area from age B to age C. Each shape
of the function generated a different estimate for each subject. We determined the particular function that best described our subjects' interocular transfer scores by calculating the correlation between the subjects'
actual scores and their estimated scores.

The functions that generated the highest correlations between estimated and measured binocularity are shown in Figure 8. The dashed
line is the best-fitting function from 12 subjects who were born with
esotropia (congenital esotropes). The dotted line is the function for 12
subjects whose esotropia began at some time after birth (late-onset
esotropes). These groups were treated separately because the causes (or
etiology) of congenital and late-onset esotropia were thought to be different. The solid line is from an additional group of late-onset esotropes
who were tested by Hohmann and Creutzfeldt. The dashed and solid
functions fit the data very well, with respective correlations of 0.92 and
0.94 between measured and estimated binocularity. The dotted-line
function fits the data less well (correlation of 0.62), probably due to the
heterogeneous etiological nature of this group.

The conclusion to be drawn from these data is that a critical period
for binocularity as measured by interocular transfer of the tilt-aftereffect
begins several months after birth, peaks during the second year of life,
and declines by 6–8 years of age. Skepticism regarding the use of our
general function is reduced when one considers the fit generated by

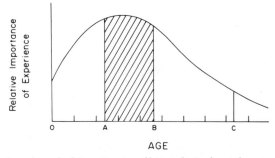

Figure 7. Method used to calculate estimates of binocularity for each esotropic subject. The
function represents a particular critical period indicating the relative importance of binocular experience at different ages. Estimated binocularity consisted of the sum of the areas
under the function from birth to age A, the onset of esotropia, and from age B, the age at
surgical correction, to C, the age at testing. The shaded area from A to B represents the
period of deprivation resulting from esotropia.

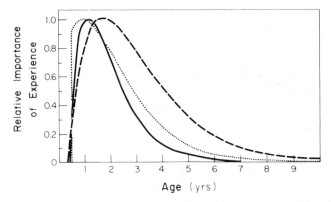

Figure 8. The functions yielding the highest correlations between measured and estimated binocularity for three groups of esotropes. The dashed line represents the best-fitting function for the congenital esotropes studied by Banks *et al.* (1975). The dotted line represents the best-fitting function for the late-onset esotropes studied by Banks *et al.* (1975). The solid line is the best-fitting function obtained for the late-onset esotropes studied by Hohmann and Creutzfeldt (1975). These functions are estimates of the relative importance of abnormal binocular experience from birth to age 10.

other functions. For example, if experience were equally important from birth to 10 years, the correlation between estimated and measured binocularity for the congenital esotrope group would be 0.65. Equal importance from birth to age 20 or from age 10 to 20 for the congenital group generates correlations of 0.21 and 0.02, respectively.

What has been learned from this experiment in conjunction with the Hohmann and Creutzfeldt experiment? First of all, it provides clear evidence that inadequate early experience—specifically, discordant binocular input due to misalignment of the two eyes—has a detrimental effect on the development of a basic binocular function, interocular transfer of information. Deficits in this particular binocular function seem to be related to deficits in other functions such as stereopsis, but the relationship between different functions must be further studied. The experiment also indicates that there is a critical period for binocular development beginning during the first year of life, peaking during the second year, and decreasing in significance by 4 to 8 years. Again, other measures of binocular function should be studied to see if critical period estimates are the same for the development of other important binocular functions. The preliminary message to clinicians is clear. For children born with esotropia, surgical intervention is indicated before age 2 or 3. Early surgery, if successful in realigning the two eyes, can result in minimal functional deficits as measured by our interocular transfer technique. For children who develop esotropia some time after birth, the immediacy of surgery is not as great if the age of onset was later than 5 or 6 years of age.

From a theoretical standpoint, our findings are consistent with an empiricist view of perceptual development. Early experience plays an important role in determining the final integrity of a person's binocular function. But an additional and important question remains before the empiricist and nativist positions as reformulated by Anastasi can really be disentangled: What kind of role does normal experience play? Does normal experience simply serve to maintain the integrity of structures and functions that are specified genetically? If so, then the observed deficits in our subjects occurred because they did not receive this maintaining experience. Or does experience actually facilitate or induce development to proceed along channels that are incompletely specified by genetics? (Classification of the roles that early experience may play in development into maintenance, facilitation, and induction has been delineated by Gottlieb, 1976.) The maintenance view of early experience is, of course, closely related to the nativist position, and the facilitation or induction view to the empiricist position. To distinguish these viewpoints experimentally, one must determine what the state of binocularity is in the young, inexperienced human infant. The maintenance viewpoint would predict that binocular function is present at birth and experience simply serves to maintain its functional integrity. The facilitation and induction viewpoints would predict that binocular function is either absent or very primitive in the young infant. As was the case earlier, important basic research in pursuit of this issue is being done with kittens and young monkeys (Blakemore, 1976; Imbert and Buisseret, 1975; Wiesel and Hubel, 1974; Yinon, 1976). This line of research is providing a foundation for work on human infants' binocular vision (e.g., Aslin, 1977; Slater and Findlay, 1975) which eventually will lead to a better understanding of both normal and abnormal perceptual development.

References

Anastasi, A. Heredity, environment, and the question "how"? *Psychological Review*, 1958, *65*, 197–208.

Awaya, S., Miyake, Y., Amaizumi, Y., Shiose, Y., Kanda, T., and Komuro, K. Amblyopia in man suggestive of stimulus deprivation amblyopia. *Japanese Journal of Ophthalmology*, 1973, *17*, 69–82.

Aslin, R. N. Development of binocular fixation in human infants. *Journal of Experimental Child Psychology*, 1977, *23*, 133–150.

Banks, M. S., Aslin, R. N., and Letson, R. D. Sensitive period for the development of human binocular vision. *Science*, 1975, *190*, 675–677.

Barlow, H. B., Blakemore, C., and Pettigrew, J. D. The neural mechanism of binocular depth discrimination. *Journal of Physiology (London)*, 1967, *193*, 327–342.

Blake, R., and Hirsch, H. V. B. Deficits in binocular depth perception in cats after alternating monocular deprivation. *Science*, 1975, *190*, 1114–1116.

Blakemore, C. Developmental factors in the formation of feature-extracting neurones. In F. O. Schmitt and E. G. Worden (Eds.), *The neurosciences: Third study program.* Cambridge, Massachusetts: MIT Press, 1975.

Blakemore, C. The conditions required for the maintenance of binocularity in the kitten's visual cortex. *Journal of Physiology (London)*, 1976, 261, 423–444.

Fiorentini, A., and Maffei, L. Spatial contrast sensitivity of myopic subjects. *Vision Research*, 1976, 16, 437–438.

Freeman, R. D., Mitchell, D. E., and Millodot, M. A neural effect of partial visual deprivation in humans. *Science*, 1972, 175, 1384–1386.

Gottlieb, G. The roles of experience in the development of behavior and the nervous system. In G. Gottlieb (Ed.), *Neural and behavioral specificity.* New York: Academic Press, 1976.

Hebb, D. O. *Organization of behavior.* New York: Wiley, 1949.

Hochberg, J. Nativism and empiricism in perception. In L. Postman (Ed.), *Psychology in the making.* New York: Knopf, 1962.

Hohmann, A., and Creutzfeldt, O. D. Squint and the development of binocularity in humans. *Nature*, 1975, 254, 613–614.

Hubel, D. H., and Wiesel, T. N. Receptive fields of single neurones in the cat's striate cortex. *Journal of Physiology (London)*, 1959, 148, 574–591.

Hubel, D. H., and Wiesel, T. N. Receptive fields, binocular interaction and functional architecture in the cat's visual cortex. *Journal of Physiology (London)*, 1962, 160, 106–154.

Hubel, D. H., and Wiesel, T. N. Binocular interaction in striate cortex of kittens reared with artificial squint. *Journal of Neurophysiology*, 1965, 28, 1041–1059.

Hubel, D. H., and Wiesel, T. N. The period of susceptibility to the physiological effects of unilateral eye closure in kittens. *Journal of Physiology (London)*, 1970, 206, 419–436.

Imbert, M., and Buisseret, P. Receptive field properties of visual cortical cells in kittens reared with or without visual experience. *Experimental Brain Research*, 1975, 22, 25–36.

Mitchell, D. E., and Ware, C. Interocular transfer of a visual aftereffect in normal and stereoblind humans. *Journal of Physiology (London)*, 1974, 236, 707–721.

Mitchell, D. E., Freeman, R. D., Millodot, M., and Haegerstrom, G. Meridional amblyopia: Evidence for modification of the human visual system by early visual experience. *Vision Research*, 1973, 13, 535–558.

Movshon, J. A., Chambers, B. E. I., and Blakemore, C. Interocular transfer in normal humans and those who lack stereopsis. *Perception*, 1972, 1, 483–490.

Nikara, T., Bishop, P. O., and Pettigrew, J. D. Analysis of retinal correspondence by studying receptive fields of binocular single units in cat striate cortex. *Experimental Brain Research*, 1968, 6, 353–372.

Packwood, J., and Gordon, B. Stereopsis in normal domestic cat, Siamese cat, and cat raised with alternating monocular occlusion. *Journal of Neurophysiology*, 1975, 38, 1485–1499.

Pettigrew, J. D. The effect of visual experience on the development of stimulus specificity by kitten cortical neurones. *Journal of Physiology (London)*, 1974, 237, 49–75.

Slater, A. M., and Findlay, J. M. Binocular fixation in the newborn baby. *Journal of Experimental Child Psychology*, 1975, 20, 248–273.

Wiesel, T. N., and Hubel, D. H. Comparison of the effects of unilateral and bilateral eye closure on cortical unit responses in kittens. *Journal of Neurophysiology*, 1965, 28, 1029–1040.

Wiesel, T. N., and Hubel, D. H. Ordered arrangement of ocular dominance columns in monkeys lacking visual experience. *Journal of Comparative Neurology*, 1974, 158, 307–318.

Yinon, U. Age dependence of the effect of squint on cells in kittens' visual cortex. *Experimental Brain Research*, 1976, 26, 151–157.

The Production and Perception of Speech by a Misarticulating Child

PATRICIA A. BROEN AND SARAH M. JONS

Early research in speech perception sought to identify the acoustic cues used in the perception of speech. This research was made possible by the development of the *sound spectrograph*, the *pattern playback*, and, later, the computer-driven *speech synthesizer*.*

The sound spectrograph transformed spoken speech into a visual display of the energy at various frequencies. From this display possible perceptual cues were identified. The speech synthesizer created synthetic speech in which those cues were varied systematically, independently, and over a wide range of values. Listeners were asked to make judgments of this synthetic speech. In this way, through alternate analysis and synthesis, many cues for perception were identified and explored. Now, after 20 years of research, we know a great deal about the

---

* Two edited volumes were used as basic reference material in the preparation of this chapter. They were *Readings in Acoustic Phonetics*, edited by Ilse Lehiste, and *Contemporary Issues in Experimental Phonetics*, edited by Norman J. Lass. Much of the early research in speech perception was conducted at Haskins Laboratory in New York City, at the Massachusetts Institute of Technology Electronics Research Laboratory, and at the Bell Telephone Laboratories. This early work is presented in *Readings in Acoustic Phonetics*. *Contemporary Issues in Experimental Phonetics* is a description of the current state of research in this area.

PATRICIA A. BROEN and SARAH M. JONS • Department of Communication Disorders, University of Minnesota, Minneapolis, Minnesota. This chapter reflects research supported by the Graduate School, University of Minnesota; the preparation of this chapter was supported in part by grants to the Center for Research in Human Learning, University of Minnesota, from the National Science Foundation (BMS 75-03816).

cues used in the perception of speech and about the production of those cues. Related studies of perception and production have been conducted with adults, with normal children, and with infants. Recently, investigators have been extending that work to describe speech perception and speech production in children and adults with speech problems.

This chapter considers the general problem of speech sound learning and the problems encountered by a specific child who was slow to develop articulate speech. The speech perception skills of this child were explored systematically, using both standard procedures and experimentally based procedures. This single-subject study is representative of the application of speech perception research to the problems encountered by speech pathologists. There are problems with this kind of extension. Perhaps more questions are raised than answered, but it does represent the application of a promising new tool to some old problems.

Introduction

An adult observing a young child who is learning to speak is impressed by the apparent ease with which the child learns. If the adult has ever tried to learn a second language, he may be even more impressed. Speech comes so naturally to the young child. At 3 or 4 a child can pronounce the sounds of his language with an accuracy that the second-language learner may never match. A child learns to articulate the sounds of his language as he learns its vocabulary and its grammar. The speech produced by most young children is intelligible, at least to parents, from the beginning. As the child gains linguistic skill, the accuracy of his speech production increases. By the age of 4, children have mastered most of the sound system of their language. By 8, almost all children produce the sounds of their language as adults do.

In contrast, a small number of children have difficulty learning to produce the sounds of speech. They fail to master the sound system of their language as they learn other language skills. These children may substitute one sound for another, they may distort some sounds, they may omit other sounds altogether. Because of their poor articulation skills, these children are difficult to understand during their preschool years. They may enter kindergarten and first grade with a speech pattern that may make reading difficult and oral communication almost impossible.

Such children are a puzzle. There is often no obvious reason for their failure to learn to produce the sounds of speech. The speech clinicians who work with them sometimes label their problem a "functional" articulation problem because no physical cause can be identified. They hear; at least they respond appropriately to a pure-tone hearing test.

They can use their oral structures in nonspeech tasks such as chewing and sucking and swallowing, but they have difficulty learning to produce articulate speech.

How do children learn to produce the sounds of speech? We do not understand the process completely, but there are some things that we do know. The task is primarily an auditory task. A child will learn the language that he hears. Any child, with exposure, can learn any language. The Korean baby, adopted by American parents, will learn English. The child raised in a bilingual home will probably learn two languages. The deaf child, that is, the child who is denied auditory input, will not learn to speak without extraordinary teaching, while the blind child, the child who is denied visual input, will learn with relative ease.

The task is also a pattern recognition task. Speech is carried by a complex acoustic signal, produced when a column of air, originating in the lungs, is modulated, constricted, and obstructed in various ways as it moves from the lungs, past the vocal cords, and out through the nose or mouth. That acoustic signal is then transmitted through the air to the ears of the listener. The sounds that fall upon the listener's ears are transformed from acoustic to mechanical energy at the eardrum and ultimately to nerve impulses; the message is extracted from those nerve impulses. In learning to speak, the child must learn the relationship between the physical process that generates speech and the form of the acoustic signal that carries speech. He must identify the important cues in the speech that he hears and he must produce those cues in his own speech. The particular cues that are important will vary from one language to another. The organization of those cues will also vary from one language to another. There will be other aspects of the speech signal, related to the speaker or the environment, that have nothing to do with the message. The child must learn to disregard those aspects of the message.

The process of extracting important cues from the acoustic signal and matching those cues in production can break down at several points. One child may not produce the sounds of his language correctly because he has difficulty with the analysis of speech. He may not perceive or correctly identify the important cues. Because he fails to perceive a cue, he also fails to produce it. Another child may identify the appropriate cues but he may have difficulty with the synthesis, that is, he may not be able to produce the cues that he has identified.

In working with a misarticulating child, it would be helpful to separate the child who fails to perceive a cue from the child who can hear and identify the cues but cannot produce them. As a first step, it would be useful to describe the child's speech perception skills in a systematic way.

Speech clinicians, working with misarticulating children, have always been concerned about the speech perception skills of those children. Tests of speech sound perception have been a part of the speech clinician's stock-in-trade for years. These tests, though, are relatively imprecise. They provide a rough estimate of a child's ability to distinguish among the sounds of the language, but they do not give an exact description of the child's skills and weaknesses. They do not describe, in any precise way, the important distinctions that the child can and cannot make. Recent studies in the field of speech perception provide a more detailed account of the auditory cues used by normal adults and children in the perception of speech. These studies of normal speech perception may offer new tools for the speech clinician faced with a child who may have problems with the perception of speech. This chapter will describe the speech production of a misarticulating child and a systematic exploration of his speech perception skills through standard procedures, natural speech perception tasks, and synthetic speech perception tasks.

THE PROBLEM

When John was first seen at the University of Minnesota Speech and Hearing Clinic he was 3½ years old. His productive language skills were those of an 18- to 20-month-old child. He was able to speak 25 single words. These words were difficult to understand. He used no sentences.

In contrast, John seemed to have no difficulty understanding speech. He responded to questions and directions, he interacted appropriately with his mother, and he performed at an appropriate level for his age on standardized tests of receptive language. His hearing, as measured by a pure-tone hearing test, was normal. His problem seemed limited to the production of speech.

John was enrolled in a remedial speech and language program. Within a year he could produce sentences that were as long and as complex as the sentences produced by other children of the same age, but often John's speech could not be understood. His speech was unintelligible because he substituted one sound for another. This pattern of misarticulation was resistant to the usual therapy procedures.* Table 1 describes John's production of initial consonant sounds when he was 4½ years old. The data presented here come from his imitation of single-syllable, consonant-vowel-consonant (CVC) words. The three letters in the substitution column describe his production when he attempted to say the target sound in three different CVC words. For example, when

---

* John was enrolled in a remedial program designed to teach the production of initial *t* in syllables and in words. There was no change in the accuracy of his productions after 10 weeks of therapy. When it became apparent that John had difficulty hearing the difference between *t* and *d*, his usual substitution, he was enrolled in a program designed to teach him to discriminate auditorily between *t* and *d*.

Table 1. John's Imitation of a Series of Consonant-Vowel-Consonant (CVC) Words.[a]

Target consonant	Substitution	Target consonant	Substitution
Stop consonants		Fricative Consonants	
m	m,m,m	v	d,d,d
n	n,n,n	ð	d,d,d
b	b,b,b	z	d,d,d
d	d,d,d	f	d,d,d
g	g,g,g	Θ	d,d,d
p	p,p,b	s	d,d,d
t	d,t,d	š	d,d,d
k	g,g,k	Approximant Consonants	
		w	w,w,w
		l	w,w,w
		r	r,r,r
		y	y,y,y

[a] The sounds listed in the substitution column represent his production of the target sound in the initial position in those words.

ð = voiced *th*   Θ = voiceless *th*   š = *sh*

the target sound was *t*, John produced a *t* in one word and a *d* in two other words. He said *ten* correctly, but substituted a *d* for the *t* in *tooth* and *tongue*. John made other errors when more than one consonant occurred at the beginning of a word or when consonants occurred at the end of a word. Here we will only consider sounds that occur at the beginning of a CVC word.

It is apparent in Table 1 that John's errors were not random, they were quite systematic. A small number of sounds—*m, n, b, d, g, w, r, y*— were always correct, the sounds *p, t, k* were sometimes correct, and *d* was substituted for almost all other sounds.

When the underlying structure of English is considered, John's errors appear even more systematic. The sound system of any language is organized and the sounds that occur in any language can be described by a small number of features. These features describe either the physical process that generates speech or the acoustic characteristics of speech. The four features used in the analysis of John's speech describe the physical process that generates speech (Table 2). These features include the degree of constriction in the oral tract, the presence or absence of voice, the presence or absence of nasal airflow, and the location of the constriction within the oral tract or place of articulation. These features are relatively independent. They can and do occur in various combinations to form the consonants of English.

The first feature, constriction of the oral tract, can take one of three values: *stop, fricative,* or *approximant.* The stop consonants are produced

Table 2. Four Distinctive Features Used in the Analysis of John's Speech"

Dimensions	Speech sound																		
	m	n	b	d	g	p	t	k	v	ð	z	f	Θ	s	š	w	l	r	y
Constriction of the oral tract	s	s	s	s	s	s	s	s	f	f	f	f	f	f	f	a	a	a	a
Voice	+	+	+	+	+	–	–	–	+	+	+	–	–	–	–	+	+	+	+
Nasal	+	+	–	–	–	–	–	–	–	–	–	–	–	–	–	–	–	–	–
Place of articulation	1	3	1	3	5	1	3	5	1	2	3	1	2	3	4	5	3	3	4

"This model is derived from a model proposed by Ladefoged (1971, 1975).

s = stop
f = fricative
a = approximant

1 = lips (labial)
2 = teeth (dental)
3 = alveolar ridge
4 = hard palate (palatal)
5 = soft palate (velar)

+ = presence of a feature
– = absence of a feature

ð = voiced *th*
Θ = voiceless *th*
š = *sh*

with an obstruction in the oral tract that momentarily stops the flow of air. John generally produced the stop consonants correctly (Table 1), although, in the case of *p, t, k*, he sometimes substituted one stop for another.

The fricative consonants are produced with a constriction, but not an obstruction, at some point in the oral tract. Air is forced through that constriction and turbulence or noisiness occurs at the point of constriction. The consonants *f, v, s, z, th*, and *sh* are examples of fricative consonants. John substituted the stop consonant *d* for all fricative consonants.

The approximant consonants are produced with little constriction in the oral tract. The airstream is only shaped in the production of approximants. John either produced the approximants correctly or, in one case, he substituted one approximant consonant for another; he substituted *w* for *l*.

The second feature in Table 2 is the feature voice. This feature is binary; consonants are either voiced or they are voiceless. A voiced consonant is produced with a rapid opening and closing of the vocal folds that produces a periodic excitation of the vocal tract. A voiceless consonant is produced without this periodic excitation of the vocal tract. Both stop consonants and fricative consonants occur in voiced and voiceless pairs. For example, *p* is voiceless while *b* is produced in exactly the same way but is voiced; *f* is voiceless and *v* is voiced. When John made an error in the production of stop consonants, he substituted a voiced stop for a voiceless stop. He substituted *b* for *p*, *d* for *t*, and *g* for *k*. John made no distinction between the voiced and voiceless fricatives. The approximant consonants and the nasal consonants are always voiced in English. Therefore, the only voiceless consonants produced by John were a few voiceless stop consonants.

The third feature is nasal. The feature nasal is also binary; consonants are either nasal or nonnasal. Nasal consonants are produced with the velum or soft palate lowered so that air can escape nasally (Figure 1). Nonnasal consonants are produced with the velum raised so that no air can escape through the nose. John always produced the feature nasal correctly. That is, nasal sounds were always nasal and nonnasal sounds were always nonnasal.

The fourth feature in Table 2 is place of articulation. In the production of consonants, some degree of constriction occurs, somewhere in the vocal tract. The place of articulation feature identifies the location of that constriction. In the feature system used here, five places of articulation are identified: lips (*labial*), teeth (*dental*), alveolar ridge, hard palate (*palatal*), and the soft palate (*velar*). Figure 1 presents a drawing identifying each of these structures. The consonants *p, b, m, f, v* have a labial place of articulation. They are all produced with an obstruction or a constriction at the lips. The two "th" sounds, ð and ϴ , have a dental place of articulation. They are produced when air is forced through a slit between the tongue and the back of the upper teeth. Place of articulation can be described in this way for each of the consonants. John used the correct place of articulation for all stops and nasals. He made no place distinction among the fricatives.

Thus two major errors occurred in John's production of initial consonants. He substituted the stop *d* for all fricatives, and almost all consonants were voiced. He sometimes voiced the voiceless stop consonants and always voiced the voiceless fricative consonants.

THE ASSESSMENT OF AUDITORY PERCEPTION

John was enrolled in a remedial program designed to teach him to produce speech sounds correctly. In designing a program for John it seemed reasonable to begin teaching sounds that he could produce some of the time rather than to begin teaching sounds that he never produced. For this reason teaching began with the voiceless stops *p, t, k*. Specifically, the remedial program was designed to teach him to use the voiceless stop *t* and its voiced cognate *d* correctly in a variety of contexts. It did not work! After a reasonable period of time John was still sometimes substituting the voiced stop *d* for *t*. What is more, there was some indication that he confused *d* and *t* in the speech of the clinician. Asked to point to *doe*, he might point to *toe*. Asked to point to *T* he might point to *D*. The errors that he made in picture identification and in other receptive language tasks seemed to indicate that he had difficulty distinguishing between voiced and voiceless stop consonants. In addition to *t* and *d*, he also seemed to have difficulty distinguishing between *p* and *b* and between *k* and *g*. He seemed to have difficulty with the auditory discrimination or the auditory perception of the cue for voicing within this set of consonant sounds. At this point a series of auditory tasks were employed to determine if John had a specific problem with the cue for voicing or if he had a more general auditory discrimination problem.

First, a standard test, the *Goldman–Fristoe–Woodcock Test of Auditory Discrimination* (1970), was administered. This was an identification task, as were all of the tasks used in assessing John's auditory perception. In the investigation of speech perception, speech scientists generally make a distinction between a discrimination task and an identification task. In a discrimination task, the subject is presented with two or more stimuli and asked to determine if two stimuli are alike or, perhaps, which two of three stimuli are alike. In an identification task the subject is presented with one stimulus and asked to label it in some way. The label may be a letter name, a nonsense syllable, or a real word. The subject may say the name, point to a picture, or write his response. But basically, he hears one stimulus and labels it.

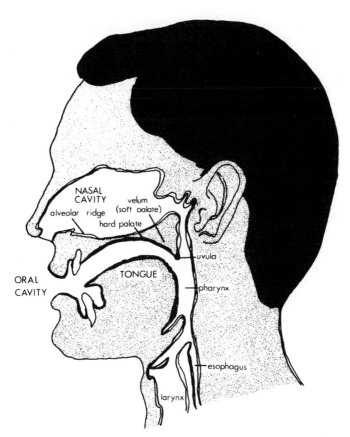

Figure 1. The airstream carrying speech may be set into vibration at the larynx by the vocal folds, directed through the mouth or allowed to pass through the nose by raising or lowering the velum, and shaped or constricted or stopped by the movement of the tongue and the lower lip. Various combinations of these modifications are made in rapid succession as we produce the sounds of speech.

Speech scientists are interested in the systematic relationship between auditory discrimination and identification. They carefully distinguish between the two tasks. Speech pathologists, using the test instruments available to them, have not systematically made that distinction. Some tests labeled tests of "auditory discrimination" use *identification* tasks and some use *discrimination* tasks. The *Goldman-Fristoe-Woodcock Test of Auditory Discrimination* (G-F-W) uses an identification task. The subject is presented with a single word and a page containing four pictures. He is asked to point to the picture that depicts the word. In this way he labels or identifies the word. The four pictures on the page represent four words that are minimally different. They differ in either the initial sound or the final sound and are otherwise alike. For example, the pictures on a page might depict the words *pea, tea, bee,* and *key.* The child hears *bee* and is expected to point to the picture of the *bee*. The child must identify the word *bee* in the presence of pictures representing three similar words. The pictures, in a sense, define the confusions that are possible. In another example, the child might be shown pictures depicting words that differ only in the final sound: *core, coal, comb,* and *cone*. The child is asked to point to the picture of *cone*. The child is thus asked to label or identify final *n* in the presence of *r, l,* and *m*.

The G-F-W samples from the wide range of consonant sounds that occur in English. It provides an overall score for each child, a score that compares his performance to that of other children of the same age. It provides an estimate of the child's general ability to distinguish every sound from every other sound.

John had no difficulty with this test, he performed as other 4- to 5-year-old children do. He did not appear to have a general auditory discrimination problem, but his performance in therapy raised questions regarding his ability to distinguish specifically between voiced and voiceless consonants. This ability is not systematically sampled in the G-F-W.

A new test was constructed using the model of the G-F-W but testing only the voicing contrast (Jons, 1976). The new test had four, separately administered, subtests. The subtests tested the voicing contrast in four different consonant pairs: p:b, t:d, k:g, and f:v. Five word pairs were identified for each consonant pair. One word in the pair began with the voiced consonant and one word began with the voiceless consonant. The word pairs used in this test are listed in Table 3. A picture was drawn to represent each word. During the initial teaching phase, John was taught to point to pictures representing the words in a particular subtest in the absence of the corresponding confusable word. He was, for example, taught to point to a picture for *dent* and a picture for *tent*, to a picture for *time* and a picture for *dime*, and so on. During this phase the pictures representing both members of a pair were not presented together. He never had to point to the picture for *time* with the picture for *dime* present. He never had to point to the picture for *dent* with the picture for *tent* present.

Table 3. Pairs of Words Used to Test John's Ability to Distinguish Between Voiced and Voiceless Consonants

p:b	t:d	k:g	f:v
pea—bee	tear—deer	cap—gap	face—vase
pad—bad	tent—dent	kill—gill	fan—van
pear—bear	ten—den	cold—gold	fine—vine
park—bark	time—dime	coon—goon	few—view
pole—bowl	tot—dot	curl—girl	fern—Vern

John learned the picture names easily. He could consistently point to the word spoken by the examiner. At this point he was presented with a page containing four pictures representing two word pairs. Now both the picture for *tent* and the picture for *dent* were present, and both the picture for *time* and the picture for *dime* were present. During this testing phase John's performance fell from 100% correct to between 72% and 95% correct, depending on the particular consonant pair being tested.

This test was repeated twice during the following 4 months and each time his performance was about the same. He could point to the correct picture 100% of the time when the picture representing its voiced or voiceless mate was not present. With the paired picture present his performance was poorer. John's errors always involved choosing the word that differed from the target word in the voicing of the initial sound. His errors were bidirectional. That is, he sometimes chose the voiced sound when presented with the voiceless sound and he sometimes chose the voiceless sound when presented with the voiced sound. In contrast, his production errors always involved the substitution of a voiced sound for a voiceless sound. On this new test the velar stops k and g and the fricatives f and v were consistently more difficult than the labial stops p and b or the alveolar stops t and d.

During this period an attempt was made to teach John to discriminate between voiced and voiceless stop consonants using a spoken discrimination task. A number of strategies were employed. The general plan was to add a cue to either the voiced or the voiceless consonant. When he could make the distinction with the additional cue, the cue was faded. For example, voiced sounds were produced at a low pitch and voiceless sounds were produced at a high pitch. John could use this additional or exaggerated cue to distinguish between words beginning with voiced and voiceless stop consonants. When the pitch difference was decreased so that the production of voiced and voiceless stops became more normal, he could no longer make the distinction. When any cue was added, his performance improved. When that cue was faded, he could no longer make the distinction.

At this point John was still a puzzle. On a general test of auditory discrimination, John looked like a normal child. When a similar test was constructed that examined only the contrast between voiced and voiceless sounds, his performance was poorer but he could still make the discrimination most of the time. If he could perform the task most of the time, why didn't his performance improve with teaching? Why couldn't he be taught to make the distinction all of the time?

The testing procedures used with John up to this point reflect the problems inherent in speech perception testing done in most clinical situations. The stimuli, the words, used in testing are relatively uncontrolled. In the test that we constructed, the words were presented to John "live voice." That is, the examiner spoke the word and John responded. The stimuli in this kind of presentation are difficult to specify and nearly impossible to control. The production by the examiner may vary from one presentation to the next. The examiner may add either visual or auditory cues that could aid the child in his identification. It was apparent from the attempts at teaching a voicing contrast that if additional cues were available, John would use them.

The G-F-W attempts to circumvent this problem by using a standard tape recording of a human speaker to present the stimulus words. This eliminates the variability but does nothing to specify the exact nature of the production. This makes the production of a given word the same for all of the children who take the test but that production still represents one of many possible productions.

In the case of voicing among the stop consonants, it seemed that we might do better than that. The voicing distinction, particularly among the stop consonants, has been studied extensively. It is possible to specify the cues used to distinguish between voiced and voiceless stop consonants in a very exact manner. It seemed that if we could borrow some of the techniques used in speech perception research, we could explore John's ability to use the voicing cues in a more controlled situation and could, perhaps, describe his problem better.

THE NATURE OF VOICING

Let's go back and reexamine the voice feature and the distinction between voiced and voiceless stop consonants. Earlier, voiced consonants were described as being "produced with a rapid opening and closing of the vocal folds that produces a periodic excitation of the vocal tract." Voiceless consonants were described as being "produced without this periodic excitation." This assumes that the critical distinction between *p, t, k* and *b, d, g* is that the first set of consonants is produced without vocal fold vibration while the second set is produced with vocal fold vibration. It also makes the implicit assumption that this is the cue listeners use in distinguishing between *p* and *b* or between *t* and *d*.

Not everyone agrees with this position. At least two other cues have been proposed as critical in making the distinction between voiced and voiceless stop consonants: *aspiration* and *force of articulation*. Voiceless stop consonants are said to be aspirated or produced with an extra puff of air following the consonant. Voiced stop consonants are said to be unaspirated. Voiceless stops are also said to be produced with greater articulatory force while voiced stop consonants are produced with less force. Force of articulation is sometimes said to be the critical cue used in distinguishing *p, t, k* from *b, d, g* while voicing is a related but less important cue.

Prior to the late 1940s and the early 1950s these hypotheses were made by listening to speech and describing what was heard. While the ears of the linguists and the phoneticians who were describing speech were finely tuned, there was no way to validate their claims. There was no way to determine if voiced consonants were, in fact, voiced or un-aspirated or less forcefully articulated. There was also no way to deter-mine which of the cues were actually used by listeners to distinguish between voiced and voiceless stop consonants. The acoustic signal that carries speech is a complex signal. The relevant information in that signal is buried and could not be extracted easily.

In the 1950s a device called the sound spectrograph became avail-able. The spectrograph seemed to offer a particularly useful trans-formation of the acoustic signal. A spectrograph provides a visual "pic-ture" of the speech signal called a spectrogram (Figure 2). A spectrogram both simplifies the speech signal and highlights possible cues used in the perception of speech. In a spectrogram the vertical axis represents frequency and the horizontal axis represents time. The intensity of the stimulus at a given frequency is indicated by the darkness of the trace.

To produce a spectrogram, speech is passed through a wide-band (300-Hz) filter of variable center frequency. The energy pattern displayed on the spectrogram is the output of that filter. In this way the fine spectral detail is masked while broad energy patterns are enhanced. Figure 2 contains a spectrogram of the sentence "She began to read her book." Notice that there are broad bands of energy that move or change in frequency over time. These concentrations of energy reflect the vocal-tract resonances or "formants" and they are labeled or numbered from the bottom to the top. The lowest band of energy is the first formant, the next is the second formant, and so on. Sometimes these formants contain vertical striations, sometimes they contain less regular energy patterns. The spectrogram also contains sections in which energy appears more or less randomly across a wide range of frequencies and sections in which there is no energy at any frequency.

The pattern of energy displayed on a spectrogram is related to the physical process of speaking. Most of the information describing that relationship comes from a series of studies conducted at the Haskins Laboratory in New York. The relationship between the articulation of speech and the spectrographic display can be organized in terms of the features described earlier in this chapter. Place of articulation, for exam-ple, is reflected in the frequencies at which formants occur. Formants reflect the resonance characteristics of the vocal tract. The natural reso-nance of a cavity such as the vocal tract is determined by its size and shape. As the tongue, lips, and jaw move from the position required for the articulation of one sound to the position required for the articulation of another sound, the size and shape of the vocal tract change, the

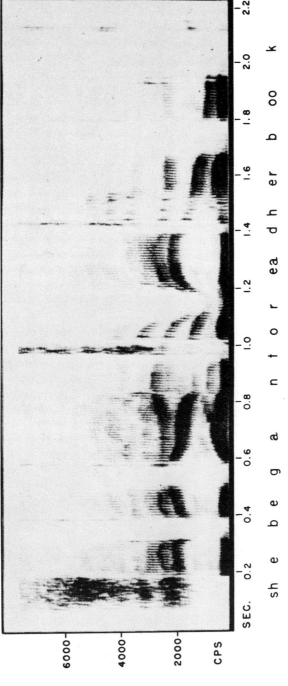

Figure 2. Spectrogram of a natural utterance: *She began to read her book.* Frequency is plotted against time, with relative intensity represented by the degree of blackness (from Studdert-Kennedy, 1976).

resonance characteristics of the vocal tract change, and so the locations of the formants change. In Figure 2 notice the movement of the second formant from time 0.6 to time 0.8 as the oral structures move from the articulation of *g* through the vowel *a* to the articulation of *n*.

A spectrogram also provides information about the nature of the sound source. The energy that appears in the formant structure must be generated somewhere. Sometimes it will be vocal fold vibration that causes the vocal tract to resonate, sometimes it will be turbulence resulting from air being forced through a narrow opening as in the production of fricatives. Vocal fold vibration, a periodic sound source, will be represented in a spectrogram by vertical striations, particularly in the first formant (Figure 2, 0.6 to 0.8). Frication, a random sound source, will be represented by a stippled pattern that may still show evidence of formants, as with *h* (Figure 2, 1.4), or that appears as simply a wide-band noise without obvious formants, as with the *sh* (Figure 2, 0.1).

The momentary obstruction of the oral tract associated with stop consonant production appears on a spectrogram as a brief period with no energy at any frequency or with energy only in the first formant. Notice the production of *b, g, t, d, b,* and *k* in Figure 2.

Two questions were raised by speech scientists regarding the voice feature and the distinction between voiced and voiceless stop consonants. First, are the old hypotheses true? Are voiced consonants produced with vocal fold vibration and voiceless consonants produced without vocal fold vibration? Second, is voicing the cue used by listeners in distinguishing between *p, t, k* and *b, d, g*? Armed with the sound spectrograph, it seemed possible to answer these questions. It was possible to observe and describe the relationship between voicing and consonant production in natural speech in a very exact way. It was possible to determine if voiced consonants were produced with vocal fold vibration, to determine the relationship between aspiration and voiceless stop consonant production, and so on.

The strategy used in the investigation of voicing was to identify the segment of the speech spectrogram that corresponded to a consonant and determine if that segment contained the vertical striations that indicated that the consonant was voiced. The first surprise was that stop consonant segments did not appear to exist, at least not independent of the vowel that followed. For example, it was not possible to cut a section of audiotape so that it contained only the stop consonant and no vowel. As soon as there was enough tape for listeners to identify the consonant, the vowel could also be identified. How could one determine if voicing accompanied the production of a stop consonant if the consonant could not be separated from the vowel?

The second surprise was that the same stop consonant in the context

of two different vowels often presented two very different spectrographic patterns. This can be seen in the two productions of the stop
consonant *b* in Figure 2. For a further discussion of this phenomenon see
Liberman, Cooper, Shankweiler, and Studdert-Kennedy (1967).

Nevertheless, there did seem to be a systematic relationship between the spectral pattern of voicing in initial stops and the listener's
identification of the consonant as voiced or voiceless. That pattern could
not be described as the absolute presence or absence of voicing during
the stop consonant segment; rather, it had to be described relative to
other aspects of the speech signal.

In producing a stop consonant, the breath stream is stopped momentarily. During that brief closure, pressure builds up within the oral
cavity so that the pressure within the oral cavity is greater than the
pressure outside of the oral cavity. When the stop consonant is released,
there is a momentary "burst," visible on the spectrogram as a short burst
of random energy across a wide range of frequencies. This reflects the
equalization of air pressure at the release of the consonant. In Figure 2
notice the short burst of energy across a wide range of frequencies
following the silent period in the production of *b* (0.4) and the production
of *g* (0.6). If the onset of voicing is described relative to the onset of that
burst, rather than in some absolute sense, a systematic difference between voiced and voiceless stop consonants emerges. When producing
an initial voiced stop, most English speakers begin voicing or vocal fold
vibration simultaneous with or shortly after the release of the stop. When
producing an initial voiceless stop, English speakers typically begin
vocal fold vibration some time after the release of the stop. During the
relatively long period between the release of a voiceless stop and the
initiation of voicing, the vocal tract is excited or caused to resonate by
energy generated when air is forced through the partially closed vocal
folds. This causes turbulence or frication at the level of the vocal folds,
seen in a spectrogram as random energy. This is aspiration. Aspiration
and the onset of voicing are, then, directly related. Aspiration fills the
time between the release of a stop and the beginning of voicing. The
production of *t* in Figure 2 (about 1.0) shows aspiration.

The temporal relationship between the onset of burst for a stop
consonant and the onset of voicing has been called voice onset time or
VOT. When voicing precedes the release of the stop as sometimes happens, VOT is reported as a negative value. For example, a VOT of −85
msec indicates that voicing preceded the release of the stop by 85 msec. A
VOT of 15 (+15) indicates that voicing began 15 msec after the release of
the stop. In English, the voiced stops *b* and *d* are typically produced with
a VOT of about +10 msec and the voiced stop *g* with a VOT of about +20
msec. The voiceless stop consonants are all typically produced with a
VOT of about +70 msec (Zlatin, 1974). The exact VOT values used by a

particular speaker will vary over a fairly narrow range from one production of a consonant to another and the VOT values for a particular consonant will vary from one speaker to another. The VOT values observed in voiceless stop productions are distributed in a normal pattern centering on +70 msec while the distribution of voiced stop productions is skewed, with most productions occurring at or near a VOT of +10 to +20 but with some productions occurring with VOTs as great as −100 to −150. It appears that speakers produce and listeners hear a range of VOT values for both voiced and voiceless stops.

Voice onset time has been shown to vary systematically with the identification of the target consonant as voiced or voiceless. But VOT is a complex cue, more complex than the absolute presence or absence of vocal fold vibration. VOT includes both the temporal relationship between the onset of voicing and the release of the consonant and the excitation of the vocal tract by a random noise source, aspiration, when voicing begins after the release of the consonant. The next step in exploring VOT as a cue for the voicing distinction was to determine if listeners could use VOT to distinguish between voiced and voiceless stop consonants.

Abramson and Lisker (1965) sought to determine if VOT was, in fact, a sufficient cue for making a distinction between the voiced stops *b, d, g* and the voiceless stops *p, t, k*. This kind of study requires that only VOT be varied while the rest of the production remains constant. It is difficult if not impossible to achieve this kind of control with natural speech. Speakers cannot monitor and control their production closely enough. Such control can be obtained, however, through the use of artificial or synthetic speech, speech produced not by a person but by a device called a speech synthesizer.

Speech synthesizers used in the study of the perception of speech are called *terminal analog* synthesizers because they model the end product of speech rather than the process of speaking. They accept as input the kind of information obtained from a spectrogram, information regarding the location and the movement of formants, the nature of the sound source, and the presence or absence of energy. The early terminal analog synthesizer was called a pattern playback. Schematic spectrograms were literally painted and played on the synthesizer. Current speech synthesizers are computer driven but still accept as input parameters abstracted from a spectrographic display.

To test the usefulness of VOT as a cue for voicing, a series of synthetic speech stimuli were created that matched the formant structure of a labial stop plus -*a* syllables such as *pa* or *ba*. The series varied in 10-msec steps from a VOT of −100 to a VOT of +100. Figure 3 presents a spectrogram of two such synthetic speech syllables.

When this series was randomized and played to listeners, a some-

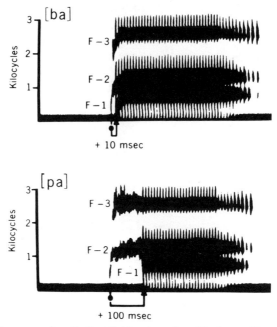

Figure 3. Spectrograms of synthetic syllables, *ba* and *pa*. The interval between release and voicing (vertical striations) (VOT) is 10 msec for *ba*, 100 msec for *pa*. During this interval, F1 is absent and the regions of F2 and F3 are occupied by *aspirated* noise (after Lisker and Abramson; from Studdert-Kennedy, 1976).

what surprising pattern of response was observed. Listeners identified all syllables with a negative VOT or a positive VOT up to about +25 msec as *ba*. At about +25 msec half of the productions were identified as *ba* and half were identified as *pa*. The remaining higher positive VOT values were identified as *pa*. The same procedure was repeated for the alveolar (*ta-da*) and the velar (*ka-ga*) stop series. In both cases the speech tokens were identified as the voiced cognate whenever the VOT value was negative or for positive values up to about a VOT of +35 for the alveolar series and a VOT of +45 for the velar series (Abramson and Lisker, 1965). At those points there was a fairly abrupt change and the remaining tokens were identified as the voiceless cognate. This study has been repeated using word pairs pear:bear, peas:bees, time:dime, and coat:goat (Zlatin, 1974). The crossover values were slightly different, but the general result was the same. Words up to some VOT were identified as voiced, beyond that value they were identified as voiceless. The study was repeated with children as young as 2½ years of age who correctly articulated the stop consonants (Zlatin and Koenigsknecht, 1975). All of these subjects could identify consonants as voiced or voiceless based on

VOT. All of the subjects could use VOT to distinguish between *p, t, k* and *b, d, g*. The young children had a slightly wider crossover (or boundary) area between the two cognate consonants, but they could perform the task. It appears that VOT is a cue that both adults and children can use to distinguish between voiced and voiceless stop consonants.

THE CLINICAL USE OF SYNTHETIC SPEECH

It seemed appropriate to use this synthetic speech, voice onset time, task with John. It would provide a controlled sample of speech and it might isolate a distinction in speech that John was unable to make. VOT is a temporal cue. It requires the listener to make a judgment regarding the temporal relationship between the release of the consonant and the onset of voicing. All of the cues that had been previously added during the attempt to teach John a voicing distinction were frequency or intensity cues. When frequency or intensity cues were added, John could distinguish between voiced and voiceless consonants. When these cues were faded, he could no longer make the distinction.

VOT is only one of the cues for the distinction between voiced and voiceless stop consonants, but it appears to be an important cue. Perhaps John could make the voicing distinction based on other inconsistent cues, cues that required him to make, for example, a frequency or an intensity judgment, but he could not distinguish between voiced and voiceless stop consonants when the only cue was the temporal one, VOT. This would account for the pattern of performance that was observed and for the difficulty he had in learning to make consistently a distinction that he seemed able to make some of the time. Perhaps when other cues were available, he could make the voicing distinction, but when he had to make the distinction based on VOT alone, he made errors.

To test this hypothesis, we used a labial VOT series (Abramson and Lisker) that ranged from −100 msec VOT to +100 msec in 10-msec steps. The task was "identification," similar to the task used in the earlier studies of voicing. John was presented with a synthetic speech token from the labial VOT continuum. The token would be heard as either *pa* or *ba*. Prior to testing, John was taught to point to a picture of a lamb for the word *ba* and a picture of an old man (grandpa) for the word *pa*. In the test situation John was seated at a small table with the picture for *pa* and the picture for *ba* in front of him. Ten different randomizations of the 21-item synthetic speech VOT series were presented to John through a speaker. When he heard a token, he pointed to one of the two pictures. He received a chip for each response and later pennies for the chips.

Three other children about John's age were also tested. One of the children was enrolled in the Speech and Hearing Clinic for articulation therapy. He made errors in articulating speech sounds but not on the stop consonants. The other two children had articulation skills that were appropriate for their age. Zlatin and Koenigsknecht (1975) tested children as young as 2½ years of age on a similar task but with different words.

On the task used with John, adults would be expected to respond in the following way. They would identify all of the words with negative VOT values and all positive values up to a VOT of about +20 msec as *ba* and all positive VOT values greater than +30 msec as *pa*. The crossover would occur abruptly at about +25 msec.

The performance of the four children is presented in Figures 4 and 5. It is apparent from the pattern of performance that the three children who produced the stop consonants correctly had no difficulty with the task. They performed much as adults would. It is also apparent that John was not able to perform this task. He was not able to identify voiced and voiceless stop consonants based on VOT; his performance was es-

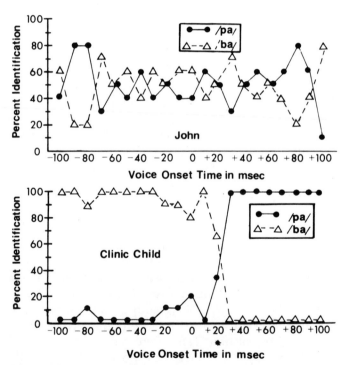

Figure 4. John and three other children were asked to identify synthetic speech tokens that ranged from −100 VOT to +100 VOT as either *ba* or *pa*. Here John's performance is compared with that of another child who was enrolled in articulation therapy. The clinic child made no errors in his speech on the feature voice (Jons, 1976). John could not distinguish among the synthetic speech tokens; the clinic child could. (Data points marked with an asterisk are based on 9 rather than 10 trials by the child.)

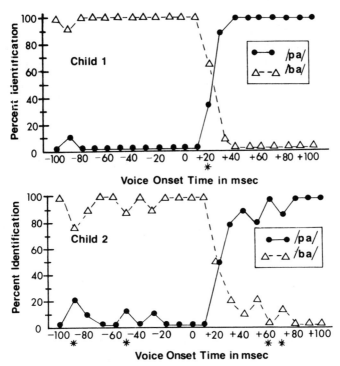

Figure 5. Two normally articulating children identified almost all synthetic speech tokens with VOT values of +20 or less as *ba* and almost all synthetic speech tokens with VOT values greater than +30 as *pa*. This performance is like the performance of adults on this task. (Data points marked with an asterisk are based on 9 rather than 10 trials by the child.)

sentially random. He identified almost every word as voiced half of the time and voiceless half of the time. The tokens at the extremes seem to be as difficult for him as the tokens near the crossover point.

The pattern in Figure 4 contrasts with his performance on the live-voice test of the distinction between voiced and voiceless stop consonants. In that task, he made errors, but his performance was not random. John's performance on the synthetic speech is at least consistent with our hypothesis. The synthetic speech VOT identification task is much more difficult than the live-voice identification task. Whatever the source of the difficulty, it was peculiar to John. Three other 4- to 5-year-old children could perform on this task. Children as young as 2½ could perform on a similar task. We have hypothesized that it was the temporal nature of the cue that made the task difficult for John. It is possible, however, that it was some other aspect of the task or situation we aren't aware of.

During the next year John learned to produce the voicing distinction first among the stop consonants and later among the fricative consonants.* This same labial VOT series was administered after he had mastered voicing in the stop consonants (Figure 6, Time A) and again after he had mastered voicing in the fricative consonants (Figure 6, Time B).

When John could consistently produce both voiced and voiceless stop consonants, he could also distinguish between voiced and voiceless synthetic stops on the basis of VOT (Time A). At that time it appears that his identification of the stimuli changed from the voiced *ba* to the voiceless *pa* at a VOT of about +35 msec. This is somewhat higher than the crossover point for the other children (Figures 4 and 5) or for adults on this series. He also seems to have a wider crossover boundary than the other children. This was typical of some of the younger children in the Zlatin and Koenigsknecht (1975) study also.

When John could produce the voicing distinction in the fricative consonants as well as the stop consonants, his performance on this synthetic speech identification task looked much like the performance of other children (Figure 6, Time B). His crossover boundary is lower and steeper.

IMPLICATIONS

The materials and procedures used in this study allowed us to identify and describe a specific perceptual problem in a child with multiple articulation errors. They also provided a way to monitor the changes that occurred in that child's perception of speech over time. This particular procedure seems to provide a way for the speech clinician to distinguish between the child who fails to perceive the cues for voicing and thus does not produce them and the child who can hear and identify the cues for voicing but cannot produce them.

It appears from this study that VOT is not the only cue for the distinction between voiced and voiceless consonants, at least for this child. In a live-voice speech task this child could often distinguish between voiced and voiceless stop consonants. He could not make that distinction all of the time, and his performance did not improve with teaching. On the VOT task it appears that he was completely unable to distinguish between the voiced and voiceless stop consonants *b* and *p*. His performance was random. In the live-voice task he must have used some cue other than the relationship between the release of the consonant and the onset of voicing.

---

* While there was no immediate reason for the changes observed in John's speech production, they probably represent the cumulative effect of a year and a half of speech therapy. John was enrolled in a speech therapy program during this study.

It may be possible to use synthetic speech as a teaching device. Speech tokens can be created with any VOT value. A series could be constructed, for example, that would present stimuli from the ends of the VOT continuum. The child who fails to perceive the voicing distinction could be taught to distinguish those tokens. As the child became proficient in making that distinction, tokens closer to the boundary could be added. Such a procedure would provide a controlled set of speech stimuli that could be changed systematically. This kind of control cannot be obtained with natural speech.

Voice onset time is only one of the many cues used in distinguishing one speech sound from another. As we learn more about the perception of speech, it may be possible to create a set of testing and teaching materials that will identify a variety of specific perceptual deficits and will teach perceptual distinctions to individuals who fail to make them. The testing and teaching procedures promise to be more precise than any currently available.

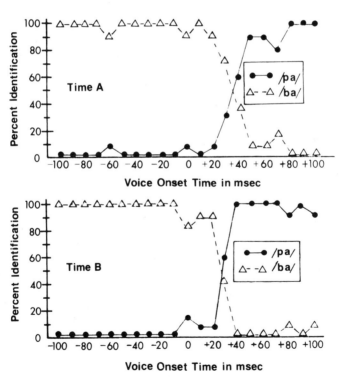

Figure 6. John's performance on the Labial VOT series A when he could produce a voicing distinction among the stop consonants and B when he could produce a voicing distinction among both stop and fricative consonants.

We have proposed that both the materials and the procedures developed for the study of speech perception in adults and normal children can be applied to the study of perception in children with articulation problems. This kind of investigation provides a much more controlled method of examining perception in the misarticulating child and it raises interesting questions regarding basic speech perception skills, questions that might not be raised if only normal adults and children were studied.

Acknowledgments

We would like to thank Arlene Carney for help in constructing the audiotape used in this study, and Joanna Moore, Jill Jacobsen, and Christine Bremer for help in the follow-up testing of this child.

References

Abramson, A. S., and Lisker, L. Voice onset time in stop consonants: Acoustic analysis and synthesis. 5th International Congress on Acoustics, Liège, Belgium, 1965.

Cooper, F. S., Liberman, A. M., and Borst, J. M. The interconversion of audible and visible patterns as a basis for research in the perception of speech. *Proceedings of the National Academy of Sciences,* 1951, *37,* 318–325.

Flanagan, J. L. Note on the design of terminal analog speech synthesizers. *Journal of the Acoustical Society of America,* 1957, *29,* 306–310.

Fromkin, V., and Rodman, R. *An introduction to language.* New York: Holt, Rinehart & Winston, 1974.

Goldman, R., Fristoe, M., and Woodcock, R. W. Goldman–Fristoe–Woodcock test of auditory discrimination. Circle Pines, Minnesota: American Guidance Service, 1970.

Jons, S. M. *The relationship of articulation performance to the ability to perform on voice onset time and live voice identification tasks.* Unpublished master's thesis, University of Minnesota, 1976.

Koenig, W., Dunn, H. K., and Lacy, L. Y. The sound spectrograph. *Journal of the Acoustical Society of America,* 1946, *17,* 19–49.

Ladefoged, P. *Preliminaries to linguistic phonetics.* Chicago: University of Chicago Press, 1971.

Ladefoged, P. *A course in phonetics.* New York: Harcourt Brace Jovanovich, 1975.

Lass, N. J. (Ed.). *Contemporary issues in experimental phonetics.* New York: Academic Press, 1976.

Lehiste, I. (Ed.). *Readings in acoustic phonetics.* Cambridge: M.I.T. Press, 1967.

Liberman, A. M., Cooper, F. S., Shankweiler, D. S., and Studdert-Kennedy, M. Perception of the speech code. *Psychological Review,* 1967, *74,* 431–461.

Lisker, L., and Abramson, A. S. A cross-language study of voicing in initial stops: Acoustic measurements. *Word,* 1964, *20,* 384–422.

Lisker, L., Cooper, F. S., and Liberman, A. M. The uses of experiment in language description. *Word,* 1962, *18,* 82–106.

Studdert-Kennedy, M. Speech perception. In N. J. Lass (Ed.), *Contemporary issues in experimental phonetics.* New York: Academic Press, 1976.

Wakita, H. Instrumentation for the study of speech acoustics. In N. J. Lass (Ed.), *Contemporary issues in experimental phonetics.* New York: Academic Press, 1976.

Zlatin, M. A. Voicing contrast: Perceptual and productive voice onset time characteristics of adults. *Journal of the Acoustical Society of America,* 1974, *56,* 981–994.

Zlatin, M. A., and Koenigsknecht, R. A. Development of the voicing contrast: Perception of stop consonants. *Journal of Speech and Hearing Research,* 1975, *18,* 541–553.

Clinical Applications of Biofeedback: Current Status and Future Prospects

EDWARD S. KATKIN, CATHERINE R. FITZGERALD, AND DAVID SHAPIRO

During the past decade there has been a surge of interest in the feasibility of applying new techniques in "biofeedback" to the alleviation of psychosomatic and psychiatric disorders. In addition, there has been a proliferation of advertising in the lay press and in some professional journals describing the development of centers devoted to the enhancement of personal growth and creativity through the utilization of biofeedback techniques. The purpose of this chapter is to review the current state of research on the efficacy of biofeedback as a therapeutic tool for psychosomatic and psychiatric disorders and to evaluate the degree to which the use of biofeedback as a growth and creativity facilitator is justified by the research results.

Biofeedback refers to any technique that uses instrumentation to provide a person with immediate and continuing signals concerning bodily functions of which that person is not normally conscious. Usually, biofeedback connotes external feedback from visceral organs such as the heart or blood vessels, but it also refers to feedback from any physiological function, including central nervous system activity (brain

EDWARD S. KATKIN and CATHERINE R. FITZGERALD. • Department of Psychology, State University of New York, Buffalo, New York. DAVID SHAPIRO • Department of Psychiatry, University of California, Los Angeles, California. Preparation of this chapter was supported in part by a grant from James McKeen Cattell Fund and National Institute of Mental Health fellowship MH06042 awarded to Edward S. Katkin, and by National Institute of Mental Health research grant MH26923 and Office of Naval Research Contract N00014-75-C-0150, NR201-152, awarded to David Shapiro.

waves) and peripheral striate muscular activity, which may not be providing normal feedback (after a stroke, for instance). Miller (1975) has
pointed out that learning to control visceral responses may be likened to
learning to shoot a basketball. Whereas the muscles used to shoot baskets
provide the learner with immediate and usable feedback, the smooth
muscles, glands, and blood vessels that are the typical target organs of
biofeedback researchers do not provide readily usable feedback. With
electronic interfaces, usable feedback can be obtained which the learner
can ideally employ in modifying previously uncontrollable functions,
according to the same principles used in increasing one's field goal
percentage.

Just as the origins of behavior therapy may be linked rather directly
to learning theory and the experimental analysis of behavior, biofeedback may be seen to derive from these fields and from psychophysiology as well. Specifically, a review of the scientific background of
current work in biofeedback reveals that it emerged from the exciting
milieu of basic research on the instrumental conditioning of autonomically mediated behavior (Crider, Schwartz, and Shnidman, 1969; Katkin
and Murray, 1968; Katkin, Murray, and Lachman, 1969).

SCIENTIFIC BACKGROUND

The question of whether or not responses mediated by the autonomic nervous system (ANS) could be conditioned instrumentally had
been a subject of continuing controversy. Traditionally, learning theorists had assumed that "for autonomically mediated behavior, the evidence points unequivocally to the conclusion that such responses can be
modified by classical, but not instrumental, training methods" (Kimble,
1961, p. 100). Explanations for the apparent inability to condition ANS
responses instrumentally usually were founded upon the observation
that because the ANS did not interact directly with the external environment, it was incapable of functioning instrumentally. It was also thought
that the ANS was solely a motor system and that, lacking an afferent
function, it was therefore incapable of learning by reinforcement principles (Smith, 1954).

Yet, despite all this testimony, a number of empirical investigations
carried out in both the United States and the Soviet Union suggested that
autonomically mediated responses could be shaped by instrumental
conditioning (see Kimmel, 1967). The key to these early studies was the
employment of appropriate technology to allow the autonomic response
to interact with the environment directly. With the use of electronic
devices and logic circuitry it was possible to create situations in which
changes in skin resistance or heart rate or blood flow could be detected,

differentially reinforced, and conditioned. Early reports from the laboratories of Kimmel (Kimmel and Kimmel, 1963; Kimmel and Hill, 1960; Kimmel and Sternthal, 1967); Shapiro (Birk, Crider, Shapiro, and Tursky, 1966; Crider, Shapiro, and Tursky, 1966; Shapiro, Crider, and Tursky, 1964); and Miller (DiCara and Miller, 1968; Miller, 1969; Miller and DiCara, 1967) all signaled the end of a scientific era in which the distinction between motor learning and autonomic learning was considered fundamental.

The new findings were not accepted without controversy, however, and the most intense scientific controversy focused on the so-called mediation issue. Katkin and Murray (1968) argued that there were no unequivocal data on the instrumental conditioning of ANS responses that could be shown to be independent of skeletal or cognitive mediators, and they suggested further that it was probably impossible to design experiments to obtain such data. Although Miller and his colleagues had successfully demonstrated instrumental conditioning in rats anesthetized with curare, a finding that seemed to effectively rule out the possibility that such responses were skeletally mediated, recent reports (Dworkin and Miller, 1977; Miller and Dworkin, 1974) indicate that the findings on curarized rats have not been successfully replicated. This failure to replicate has been discussed in terms of certain undesired peripheral autonomic and central nervous system effects of curare and of difficulties in maintaining a stable animal preparation with artificial respiration (Hahn, 1974; Roberts, 1974). Moreover, curare does not affect the central nervous system linkage between cardiovascular or other autonomically mediated behaviors and somatomotor behaviors (Black, 1974). That is, central somatomotor activity may initiate peripheral autonomic and skeletal motor activity, but the latter cannot be observed because the muscles are paralyzed. With respect to this central linkage, therefore, the use of curare cannot provide a critical experimental test of the role of central somatomotor processes in learned visceral control (Obrist, Howard, Lawler, Galosy, Meyers, and Gaebelein, 1974).

While investigators such as Miller attempted to develop strategies to demonstrate the instrumental conditionability of ANS responses independent of potential mediators, other investigators argued that the mediation issue was totally irrelevant to the issue of using reinforcement to modify autonomic responses (Crider et al., 1969). Black (1974) pointed out that a distinction must be drawn between the *conditioning* of ANS responses (a theoretical concept) and the *controlling* of ANS responses (a technological problem); and Katkin and Murray, while arguing strongly that instrumental ANS conditioning could not be demonstrated, nevertheless suggested that the technology that had emerged from the controversial research was already on its way to making a clinical, applied contribution: "For those researchers whose primary goal is to gain control over ANS function, and for whom theoretical problems concerning possible mediators and underlying phenomena are less important, it may be unnecessary to demonstrate the pure phenomenon of instrumental conditioning" (Katkin and Murray, 1968, p. 66). Later, Katkin (1971) suggested a strategy for clinicians that would exploit possible mediators rather than trying to eliminate them, saying that "for those who want to control autonomic activity for clinical or therapeutic reasons an alternative procedure would be first to determine accurately the relationship between certain voluntary skeletal actions and their associated autonomic response patterns, and then to reinforce the voluntary responses. Similarly, . . . relationships between cognitive activity and autonomic responses can be determined, and subjects may then be reinforced for certain specified thoughts" (p. 23).

Out of this background there emerged an approach to the problem of instrumental control of autonomic functions which was pragmatic and based upon the "skills acquisition" model (Lang, 1974) implied by Miller's analogy of learning to throw a basketball through a hoop.

Armed with this skills acquisition model of visceral learning and with rapidly developing technology, researchers and clinicians have set out to use biofeedback to attempt to teach people to control their brain waves, heart rate, blood pressure, peripheral blood flow, muscle tension, and various other phenomena, in order to try to treat a variety of clinical syndromes, including epilepsy, essential hypertension, cardiac arrhythmias, migraine, tension headache, stuttering, and impotence. In this chapter, we will review the existing clinical and research literature in an attempt to assess the current state of these treatments. The areas to be reviewed include feedback from electrical activity of the brain, cardiovascular responses, and peripheral skeletal–muscular behavior.

CRITERIA FOR EVALUATION

Melzack (1975) has suggested that investigators who have been using biofeedback for therapeutic purposes should be required to pass muster on four criteria of effectiveness—criteria that we believe are sound and represent minimal demands for evidence of legitimate therapeutic effectiveness:

1. Controlled experimentation should demonstrate that the biofeedback treatment effect is greater than a placebo effect.

2. The therapeutic effect must be of sufficient magnitude to have clinical significance for the alleviation of pathology. (This point is essential for clinical evaluations; a treatment group of hypertensives, for instance, may show a reduction in blood pressure of three to five mmHg,

which may be statistically greater than the reduction shown by a control group, and yet have no clinical significance for the hypertensive patient.)

3. The therapeutic effects should be transferable from the laboratory to the natural environment.

4. The therapeutic effects should be relatively long-lasting.

Although we believe that all four of these criteria are important, we shall emphasize the first criterion in this review. There are, of course, instances in which carefully described case studies, without control groups, provide substantial support for belief in the efficacy of a treatment; in such cases the latter three criteria for evaluation should be employed, and the case histories should provide motivation to carry out appropriate controlled studies.

ELECTRICAL ACTIVITY OF THE BRAIN

One of the most widely investigated, and widely publicized, applications of biofeedback involves control of the electrical rhythms of the brain. Much public attention has been focused on the specific application of biofeedback to the control of alpha rhythm, a rhythm of approximately 8–12 Hz which is produced in relaxed, waking states, and which is recorded most easily from the occipital surface of the skull. Early interest in enhancing alpha rhythm was spurred by reports that high percentages of alpha were found in the electroencephalogram (EEG) records of Yoga and Zen masters (Anand, Chhina, and Singh, 1961; Kasamatsu and Hirai, 1966). Subsequent investigations in American biofeedback laboratories indicated that subjects reported sensations of pleasure, well-being, relaxation, and "letting go" as they learned to increase their percentage of time in alpha (Brown, 1970a,b; Kamiya, 1969; Nowlis and Kamiya, 1970). Outside of the research laboratory these findings were often seen as ushering in a new era of mind–body unity, and many centers sprang up around the country (usually near campuses) promising that the feats of Eastern Zen and Yoga masters—who had practiced for decades—might soon be possible for anyone with a feedback machine and a few days of training.

Several years and many research articles later, reports of alpha biofeedback sound much more cautious. Researchers have found that it is difficult for subjects to increase alpha above the levels spontaneously produced under normal relaxed conditions (Paskewitz and Orne, 1973). After conducting a series of alpha feedback studies, Lynch, Paskewitz, and Orne (1974), for instance, concluded that "the data do suggest that alpha densities observed in the feedback situation have less to do with feedback per se or a learning process than with the experimental situation and Ss' own natural alpha densities" (p. 399).

It now appears, also, that some of the early reports of universally pleasant experiences with alpha may not be replicable. Travis, Kondo, and Knott (1975), for example, reported that 50% of their subjects found alpha enhancement "pleasant" but that the other 50% found it "unpleasant" or "neutral." Other experimenters have reported that instructional set (Walsh, 1974) and subject expectations (Valle and Levine, 1975) can have a profound influence on subjective reports of the feedback experience. In conclusion, it appears that although subjects may be capable of learning to control their alpha waves, there is little reason to believe that such control results in universally pleasant life-enhancement or in any profound phenomenological changes.

Finally, Plotkin (1976) and Plotkin and Cohen (1976) have recently reported carefully controlled experiments on the effects of different control strategies for occipital alpha production, in which they have been unable to find any evidence for a relationship between the strength of alpha and the occurrence of the "alpha experience." Plotkin and Cohen (1976) concluded that "the 'alpha experience' as a whole is not directly or intrinsically associated with enhanced occipital alpha strength" (p. 17). Plotkin's unusually careful experiments suggested that the primary attribute of the "alpha experience" is reduced eye movement activity, or "not looking" (Mulholland, 1968, 1972).

While many lay centers have been "experimenting" with alpha feedback for "growth experiences," a number of investigators in research laboratories have also been attempting to evaluate the potential effectiveness of brain wave feedback for the alleviation of disorders such as headache, epilepsy, chronic pain, and a variety of psychiatric disorders such as anxiety and insomnia.

HEADACHE. In a case study, Gannon and Sternbach (1971) used alpha feedback in an attempt to reduce a patient's severe headaches, which occurred subsequent to head injuries. After 64 sessions, their patient still reported having painful headaches that he could not relieve, although he could sometimes prevent them. McKenzie, Ehrisman, Montgomery, and Barnes (1973) reported successful treatment—an average reduction of 79.4% in hours of headache—in seven tension headache patients, using a combination of relaxation training and alpha feedback. The specific effects of the feedback were questionable, however, for eight control subjects who received only relaxation training with no feedback also experienced symptom alleviation, although not as quickly as the experimental group.

EPILEPSY. The earliest mention of brain wave feedback as a treatment of epilepsy was made by Miller (1969), who claimed there was "some success" in training epileptic patients to suppress abnormal paroxysmal spikes in their EEG. Lang (1970) also reported that Forster and his associates had successfully treated a patient who had developed photic seizures (those induced by flashing light). But the most comprehensive program of research on the treatment of epilepsy by brain wave feedback has been in Sterman's laboratory.

Sterman and his associates (Sterman, 1973, 1977a,b; Sterman and Friar, 1972; Sterman, Macdonald, and Stone, 1974) have trained epileptics to increase the amount of a brain rhythm that they call "sensorimotor rhythm" (SMR) and define as a rhythm of 12–14 Hz recorded above the central part of the cortex. Training in SMR as a treatment for epilepsy was suggested initially by the finding that SMR-trained cats were resistant to seizures. Over a period of 3–18 months, Sterman and his associates used SMR feedback in patients with whom chemotherapy had failed to control seizure activity. Although seizure activity during the biofeedback training period was markedly reduced in these patients, within a few weeks after the cessation of biofeedback training there was a sharp increase in symptoms, suggesting either that the treatment must be considerably longer to be effective or that biofeedback offers a treatment that can only temporarily control, but not cure, seizure activity in epileptics.

In a similar attempt to control seizures with SMR training, Kaplan (1975) found that she could achieve some success (two out of three patients) when employing feedback of brain wave activity in the 6–12 Hz range, rather than the SMR range reported by Sterman. Kaplan suggested that Sterman's and her own results may be caused by the nonspecific relaxation induced by EEG feedback, and that it may therefore be premature to assume that the outcome was attributable to a specific effect of SMR feedback. Sterman (1977a) has noted that Kaplan's failure to obtain positive results, as well as Kuhlman and Allison's (1977) findings that feedback in the alpha range seemed to be associated with reduced seizure frequency, suggests that there are unresolved technological problems involved in the appropriate detection and reinforcement of specific brain wave frequencies. Sterman's most recent conclusion (1977a) is that EEG feedback training of central cortical activity anywhere between 9 and 20 Hz may reduce seizures.

CHRONIC PAIN. Melzack (1975) reported controlled experimental attempts to alleviate chronic pain caused by injuries, cancer, arthritis, etc., in 24 patients. He assigned patients to one of three conditions: alpha feedback, alpha feedback plus hypnosis, and hypnosis alone. Alpha feedback plus hypnosis was successful in reducing pain in 58% of his patients; alpha feedback alone, however, was the least successful treatment, and hypnosis alone had intermediate success.

PSYCHIATRIC AILMENTS. In addition to attempts to alleviate neurological and medical problems through brain wave feedback, there have been a number of applications of such feedback to symptoms of more clearly psychogenic disturbances. Budzynski and Stoyva (1973), for instance, attempted to use alpha biofeedback as an aid to systematic desensitization. With alpha feedback, subjects first learned to increase their percent of alpha. However, since visual imagery resulted in immediate suppression of alpha, alpha feedback could not be used effectively during the presentation of desensitization scenes. The authors then switched to muscle potential feedback and obtained more successful results.

In an uncontrolled study, Budzynski (1973) reported that a sequence of electromyogram (EMG) and theta wave (6–8 Hz) feedback training sessions was effective in treating sleep-onset insomnia in 6 out of 11 patients but failed for the remaining 5. Using the same treatment sequence, also without controls, Sittenfeld (1972) was successful in treating only 4 out of 7 sleep-onset insomniacs.

SUMMARY. Despite all the time and money spent on alpha research, there is no study that can meet our evaluative criteria and demonstrate the efficacy of alpha feedback for any clinical complaint. In addition to its disappointing results as a clinical treatment, there is also decreasing interest in alpha training as a life-enhancement experience. In contrast to early reports of subjective rapture, some subjects are now reporting that alpha enhancement is neutral or unpleasant for them.

In general, all forms of EEG biofeedback have produced few positive clinical results. Sterman's work with epileptics presents an exception, in that his case reports are dramatically suggestive of important benefits for seriously impaired epileptic patients. Although Sterman and his associates have only reported on a small group of epileptics who have been treated to date, their chronicity of symptoms and their failure to respond to chemotherapy offer strong support for at least the transitory effectiveness of EEG training treatment. Nevertheless, there are no carefully controlled experiments to support Sterman's case reports, and Kaplan's (1975) suggestion concerning the nonspecific relaxation associated with such training should lead the reader to be cautious in making any conclusions about its clinical effectiveness. Critical experimental tests are now in progress (Sterman, 1977a).

CARDIOVASCULAR RESPONSES

HEART RATE. There has been a great deal of experimental work aimed at controlling the human heart rate response, much of it done with normal subjects. A typical experimental design for this research consists of subjects attempting to raise or lower their heart rate with a variety of different kinds of feedback reinforcement—lights, oscilloscope patterns, slides of landscapes, pictures of nudes, etc. These studies have typically shown that normal subjects can raise and lower their heart rate to some extent and can decrease heart rate variability. There are some limitations on how the results of these studies may be interpreted. They usually involved very few sessions and rarely took measurements outside of the laboratory to measure transfer of learning. Moreover, it is difficult to assess whether the small decreases in rate obtained were the results of the feedback process itself or could be accounted for by general relaxation or could possibly be more efficiently obtained by other methods. Studies of physiological changes associated with transcendental meditation (Wallace, 1970; Wallace and Benson, 1972) and progressive relaxation (Paul, 1969), for instance, have found heart rate decreases that equal and sometimes exceed changes obtained in biofeedback experimentation.

Typically, however, the clinician has not adopted cardiac rate bio-feedback techniques for the purpose of raising or lowering heart rate in and of itself. Rather, the strategies more commonly employed have been to use cardiac rate feedback to treat a specific type of cardiac dysfunction, such as cardiac arrhythmias and cardiac neurosis.

CARDIAC ARRHYTHMIAS. Engel and his associates (Engel and Melmon, 1968; Weiss and Engel, 1970, 1971) were the first to report work involving a clinical population suffering from cardiac arrhythmias (irregular changes in heart rate and pressure). Their series of case reports dealt with the treatment of eight patients with premature ventricular contractions (PVCs). Weiss and Engel (1971) reported that five of these eight patients showed a decrease in PVCs after biofeedback treatment; follow-ups showed that four patients had maintained a low PVC frequency. Unlike the studies with normal subjects mentioned earlier, Weiss and Engel devoted a great many sessions to treatment and did extended follow-ups (up to 21 months). A later report from the same laboratory (Engel and Bleecker, 1974) presented the case history of another patient who had successfully decreased the number of PVCs with the help of biofeedback. The same report also documented the successful treatment of three tachycardia patients. In yet another case study, Bleecker and Engel (1973) reported on the biofeedback treatment of a patient with Wolff-Parkinson-White syndrome, a heart conduction defect. The patient learned to increase and decrease the occurrence of normal and Wolff-Parkinson-White condition and could eventually maintain normal conduction without feedback.

Additional case report evidence of successful work with cardiac patients is accumulating from other laboratories. Scott, Blanchard, Edmunson, and Young (1973) reported successful treatment of two tachycardia patients, and "Pickering . . . has replicated learned specific voluntary control (of premature ventricular contractions) on two patients he is training. It seems unlikely that such specific voluntary control could be a nonspecific placebo effect" (Miller, 1974, p. 685).

CARDIAC NEUROSIS. In an interesting application of the use of heart rate feedback, Wickramasekera (1974) reported the treatment of a chronic case of cardiac neurosis (an unwarranted fear of heart attack) which had not responded to previous medical and psychological interventions. The patient was taught to reduce his heart rate and could reliably do so after 6 weekly sessions of 30 minutes each. A combination of self-administered desensitization and therapist-administered flooding was then combined with the heart rate self-control procedure, and dramatic improvement was reported after 16 sessions. It is obvious that such a combination of biofeedback with desensitization and flooding therapies makes it difficult to use Wickramasekera's (1974) case report as an empirical test of the specific value of biofeedback as a treatment for cardiac neurosis; the absence of any control conditions also makes it difficult to tease out the possible placebo effects.

BLOOD PRESSURE CONTROL. It is estimated that 15% of the American population suffers from hypertension—chronically elevated arterial blood pressure accompanied by increased risk of coronary artery disease, atherosclerosis, and cardiovascular accidents. Between 90 and 95% of hypertension cases are labeled "essential," which means that they have no demonstrable biological cause (Shapiro, 1974), nor are they cases of hypertension secondary to renal or endocrine disturbance. This high rate of incidence of a potentially dangerous "psychosomatic" syndrome has provided the incentive for biofeedback researchers to devote considerable effort to developing blood pressure control procedures. As with heart rate experimentation, the initial biofeedback research with blood pressure was done with unaffected (or normotensive) college students, who were taught to raise and lower their blood pressure (Brener and Kleinman, 1970; Shapiro, Schwartz, and Tursky, 1972; Shapiro, Tursky, Gershon, and Stern, 1969). Differences were found between groups trained to raise or to lower blood pressure, but the differences were small.

Shapiro and his colleagues, while reporting a series of successful attempts to train normotensives to control their blood pressure, have obtained mixed results with hypertensives (see Shapiro, Mainardi, and Surwit, 1977; Shapiro and Surwit, 1976). In the first published study on the clinical treatment of essential hypertension with biofeedback, Benson, Shapiro, Tursky, and Schwartz (1971) taught five out of seven hypertensive patients to lower their systolic blood pressure 16 to 34 mmHg. Similar attempts to train patients to lower their diastolic pressure, however, were not as successful. Schwartz and Shapiro (1973) found that only one of seven patients was able to learn to reduce diastolic pressure. To confound the meaning of the above data even further, Elder, Ruiz, Deabler, and Dillenkoffer (1973) found opposite results; they reported that they had more success in training hypertensives to reduce diastolic pressure than to reduce systolic pressure.

Miller (1975) has reported one relatively successful case of treatment of a partially paralyzed hypertensive woman who achieved good control of her blood pressure in the laboratory but had to be restored to anti-hypertensive drugs after some personal emotional stresses. According to Miller, this patient was able to regain control a few years later; other of his patients fared considerably worse. Attempts to achieve similar success on 27 patients in his laboratory have produced "considerably poorer, not really promising, results" (p. 244).

None of the clinical studies reported has presented evidence that the magnitude of blood pressure decrease obtained by biofeedback is greater than could be obtained by simple methods of suggestion, relaxation, or merely adapting to the training situation. Relaxation and placebo effects in blood pressure biofeedback should be taken seriously. Grenfell, Briggs, and Holland (1963) have detailed the enormous power of placebo and expectancy effects in the pharmacological treatment of hypertension; there is little reason to believe that biofeedback treatment is less vulnerable. Patel (1973) reported, for instance, that she was able to obtain significant blood pressure reductions among hypertensive patients in her clinical practice by providing them with skin resistance feedback, and training them to modify their skin resistance level. Since skin resistance is generally regarded as a reasonably useful index of overall autonomic arousal level, it is likely that Patel was helping to train her patients to relax. For instance, in a later study, Patel (1975) reported that with a combination of yoga exercises and biofeedback, patients were able to lower their systolic and diastolic pressures both during rest and in response to everyday emotional stresses. Along similar lines, Datey, Deshmukh, Dalvi, and Vinekar (1969) reported the successful use of yoga in the treatment of renal and essential hypertension. The results of these studies indicate that it is possible, and perhaps likely, that a combination of treatment modes such as relaxation training, biofeedback, and hypnosis may provide a potential nonmedical treatment for essential hypertension. They do not attest to the relative value of biofeedback per se in the treatment process.

Kristt and Engel (1975), on the other hand, have reported results with five patients that provide somewhat stronger evidence for a specific biofeedback treatment effect. Their patients, all of whom suffered hypertension of at least 10 years' duration, were given training in alternately raising and lowering systolic blood pressure and then were asked to monitor their systolic blood pressure at home and report the results to the experimenters. Kristt and Engel reported that their patients were able to reduce systolic pressure significantly at home using the techniques they had learned in the laboratory, and that the blood pressure reductions were independent of changes in heart rate, alpha activity, breathing rate, and triceps brachii muscle tension. These findings, in contrast to earlier ones, are less likely to be explained as a by-product of general relaxation. Nevertheless, the Kristt and Engel study does not constitute controlled experimental evidence. The components that led to its successful outcome remain to be analyzed.

PERIPHERAL VASOMOTOR CONTROL. There has been increasing interest in the biofeedback control of specific peripheral vasomotor responses. This form of control has been used in an attempt to reduce migraine and tension headaches and has also been employed in an effort to alleviate symptoms of Raynaud's disease, a condition that affects the parts of the body that are particularly influenced by exposure to cold (usually the hands and sometimes the feet, ears, or nose). Normally, when the body is exposed to cold, surface blood vessels are narrowed; in Raynaud's disease, however, because of a local abnormality of small peripheral vessels, the blood vessels become completely closed and circulation stops, resulting in numbness and potential tissue damage. To date, two general strategies for increasing vasomotor control have been investigated: (1) modifying peripheral blood volume and (2) modifying peripheral skin temperature.

Blood Volume. The first reported attempt at instrumental modification of an autonomic response was Lisina's (1958/1965) experiment on voluntary control of peripheral vascular dilatation. It was followed a decade later by Snyder and Noble's (1968) successful demonstration of peripheral vascular instrumental conditioning. Yet, despite the fact that instrumental vascular conditioning was among the earliest and perhaps the most successful of the attempts at instrumental autonomic conditioning, there has been very little systematic basic research on it. There have been, however, an increasing number of clinical reports using peripheral finger blood volume control to treat clinical problems. Shapiro and Schwartz (1972) obtained mixed results with two patients who had Raynaud's disease. Recently, Rosen, Shapiro, and Schwartz (1975) reported a successful attempt to increase penile tumescence using biofeedback of penile blood flow. This study, which has implications for the "rehabilitation" of functionally impotent males, was controlled with a group who received similar instructions and incentives but no biofeedback.

Skin Temperature. In addition to the attempts to treat vascular disorders with blood volume feedback there have been a number of attempts to use skin temperature feedback as an indirect way to teach patients to control their vascular processes. The rationale for the use of skin temperature feedback as a treatment for vascular disorders such as Raynaud's disease or migraine is simple: there is a high correlation between peripheral blood volume and skin temperature, and therefore the voluntary control of temperature leads to voluntary control of blood volume. Symptoms in Raynaud's disease are associated with peripheral vasoconstriction, symptoms in migraine headache with cranial vaso-dilatation and peripheral vasoconstriction. It is hypothesized that in-creased skin temperature of the hand will reflect increased peripheral vasodilatation there, which will counteract the vasoconstriction of both Raynaud's disease and migraine headache.

Jacobson, Hackett, Surman, and Silverberg (1973) reported the suc-cessful treatment of one Raynaud's patient and Surwit (1973) achieved considerable success in the biofeedback treatment of one patient. Re-ports of clinical treatment of Raynaud's disease by skin temperature feedback, as with blood volume feedback, are limited to single, uncon-trolled case studies.

Results are somewhat mixed with regard to the skin temperature treatment of migraine headaches. Sargent, Green, and Walters (1973) reported on a pilot treatment in which 2 migraine patients were treated, one wholly successfully and the other with partially beneficial results. An uncontrolled skin temperature feedback program with 28 headache patients (Sargent et al., 1973) had mixed results, with half of the patients generally considered "improved" and the other half questionable or unimproved. Weinstock (1972), in an uncontrolled study in which a combination of self-hypnosis, EMG, and skin temperature training was used, successfully treated 7 chronic migraine and tension headache patients; and Wickramasekera (1973b) detailed the successful skin tem-perature training treament of 2 migraine patients.

SUMMARY. The results of biofeedback treatment of cardiovascular dysfunction are promising but inconclusive; the positive clinical litera-ture consists almost entirely of case reports. One controlled experiment (Elder et al., 1973) obtained small magnitude decreases in diastolic blood pressure, a finding that has not been confirmed in other laboratories. Although the work of Engel and his associates and the work of Shapiro and his colleagues on cardiac arrhythmias and on blood pressure control have resulted in dramatic and clinically significant results for some patients, the fact remains that "there is not one well-controlled scientific study of the effectiveness of biofeedback and operant conditioning in treating a particular physiological disorder" (Shapiro and Surwit, 1976, p. 113).

The Skeletal–Muscular System

Biofeedback of electrical activity from the skeletal–muscular system is somewhat different in character from feedback of brain or cardiovascular functions. Whereas the patient usually has had no prior continuous awareness of the daily functioning of the cardiovascular system, and no inner knowledge of the electrical state of the cortex, it is likely that the average patient will have had a lifetime of experience in receiving and being aware of feedback from striate muscles (traditionally known as kinesthesis and proprioception). From a theoretical viewpoint, therefore, it is apparent that striate muscular feedback exploits already existing patterns of sensorimotor control and may not require as extensive a reeducational process as autonomic or brain wave feedback might. Clinically, there have been three main foci of interest in skeletal muscular biofeedback: (1) rehabilitation of patients who have lost normal muscular control, (2) headache treatment, and (3) anxiety reduction and relaxation enhancement.

Rehabilitation. Successful use of muscle electrical potential feedback in rehabilitation medicine has been reported by several investigators, who have used three general treatment strategies:

1. Detecting and feeding back neuromuscular electrical potentials in currently nonfunctional muscles, in conditions such as hemiplegia, nerve injury, and reversible physiological block.

2. Inhibiting undesired motor activity and increasing voluntary control of desired movement, in conditions such as spasmodic torticollis and various kinds of spasticity.

3. Coordinating and controlling a series of muscle actions, in conditions such as chronic fecal incontinence.

Several researchers (Andrews, 1964; Brudny, Korein, Levidow, Grynbaum, Lieberman, and Friedmann, 1974; Johnson and Garton, 1973; Marinacci and Horande, 1960) have reported case studies of successful individual treatment of hemiplegic patients by use of feedback from needle or skin EMG electrodes placed in or over the affected muscles. Booker, Rubow, and Coleman (1969) also reported a case study in which they successfully trained a patient afflicted with paralysis of one side of the face to control the facial muscles by teaching him to match a signal from the unaffected side.

In a series of case studies Brudny, Grynbaum, and Korein (1974), Brudny *et al.* (1974), and Cleeland (1973) have reported successful treatments of spasmodic torticollis, a disease in which the finely tuned movement and postural control of the head and neck are disturbed. Using a combination of both conventional physical therapy and biofeedback, Swaan, van Wieringen, and Fokkema (1974) reported improvement in 7 patients who had undesirable muscle contractions of the knee caused by hemiplegia or poliomyelitis. In a somewhat related application, Jacobs and Felton (1969) were successful in training 10 patients with neck injuries to relax rigid neck muscles. Finally, Engel, Nikoomanesh, and Schuster (1974) taught 6 patients with chronic fecal incontinence to control the functioning and synchronization of external and internal anal sphincter muscles, producing relief of clinical symptoms that was maintained for 5 years.

The use of electromyogram feedback for muscular rehabilitation is impressive in that many of the patients treated were from a chronically disabled population in which traditional rehabilitation efforts had been partially or completely unsuccessful. Yet the successful reports all take the form of case studies, and there are no well-controlled experimental evaluations of the specific efficacy of biofeedback. For a review of current developments, see Basmajian (1977).

TREATMENT OF TENSION HEADACHE. Although muscular feedback has met with little success in the treatment of migraine (Sargent et al., 1973; Wickramasekera, 1973b), electromyographic feedback from the frontalis muscle of the forehead has been reported to be effective in relieving tension headache. The failure to treat migraine effectively with muscle tension feedback is not surprising, since muscle action is probably not involved in the migraine syndrome, which is most likely a vascular disorder. The successful reports of muscle tension feedback to relieve tension headache have more face validity, since it is widely believed that the source of pain in "tension" headache is head and/or neck muscle tension. Budzynski and his associates (Budzynski and Stoyva, 1973; Budzynski, Stoyva, and Adler, 1970), Wickramasekera (1972, 1973a), and Raskin, Johnson, and Rondestvedt (1973) have reported successful cases of treatment of chronic tension headache. A report by Epstein, Hersen, and Hemphill (1974) also detailed the treatment of a headache patient who responded well to muscle tension biofeedback but who had difficulty sustaining low headache levels without continuous feedback. In addition, Budzynski, Stoyva, Adler, and Mullaney (1973) reported the results of a controlled experiment in which a group of subjects receiving EMG biofeedback showed greater headache reduction than a control group who received pseudofeedback.

Thus, good results have been reported for treatment of tension headaches both in case reports (Budzynski et al., 1970) and in one controlled study (Budzynski et al., 1973). However, the particular role of biofeedback has not been clarified by the case studies, as the successful technique usually included both laboratory feedback training and home relaxation practice. Even in the controlled outcome study of Budzynski et al. (1973), one of the "pseudofeedback" controls who regularly practiced home relaxation experienced a significant decline in headache activity, and the authors emphasized that they considered daily practice outside of the laboratory setting "critical." Further research is clearly needed to investigate the specific versus the interactive effects of muscle tension biofeedback and relaxation.

ANXIETY REDUCTION AND RELAXATION ENHANCEMENT. Muscle tension feedback has been used, with mixed results, in a number of attempts to reduce anxiety and/or enhance relaxation. Raskin *et al.* (1973), for example, reported little success of frontalis muscle feedback treatment of 10 chronically anxious patients, although accompanying symptoms of tension headache and insomnia showed some improvement. In other uncontrolled studies, Sittenfeld (1972) used muscle feedback with theta EEG feedback to successfully treat 4 out of 7 insomniacs; and Budzynski (1973) achieved success with 6 out of 11 sleep-onset insomnia patients, with a similar treatment combination of muscle tension feedback and theta EEG feedback. Budzynski and Stoyva (1973) asserted that systematic desensitization is more successful when aided by muscle tension feedback, although they provided no empirical data to support their assertion.

In a controlled study, Davis, Saunders, Creer, and Chai (1973) used frontalis muscle feedback combined with relaxation in severe and non-severe (as indicated by strength of medication required) asthmatic children. In the nonsevere patients, relaxation training with biofeedback resulted in a greater reduction of asthma symptoms than relaxation training alone or a control procedure in which patients were told to "relax." None of the experimental procedures was effective with the severely asthmatic children.

SUMMARY. Although there is considerable face validity for the effective treatment of skeletal muscular disorders with electromyographic feedback, as well as a considerable number of clinical case reports to support its use, there are still no adequately controlled experiments to document the specific effectiveness of such treatment. The evidence to date supports an optimistic view, however, about the use of muscle tension feedback for the treatment of specific disorders such as hemiplegia, torticollis, and nonpathological problems such as unnecessary subvocalization in reading (Aarons, 1971; Hardyck, Petrinovich, and Ellsworth, 1966; McGuigan, 1967)—a habit that prevents people from increasing their reading speed. On the other hand, there appears to be no conclusive evidence that muscle tension biofeedback treatment is effective in reducing anxiety. As with studies of tension headache treatment, those studies reporting positive results used other procedures, such as EEG theta feedback, relaxation, or systematic desensitization, combined with muscle tension feedback to achieve positive results. Thus, the specific role of muscle tension feedback in the alleviation of anxiety remains unclear.

Discussion and Conclusions

At the beginning of this review, we listed Melzack's (1975) four criteria for evaluating the effectiveness of biofeedback as a clinical treatment. It is apparent that there is simply no body of substantive experimental evidence to satisfy the first criterion, that biofeedback has a greater effect than a placebo treatment. Shapiro and Surwit (1976) have concluded that there is "not one" well-controlled experiment to demonstrate the clinical effectiveness of biofeedback for specific disorders, and we must agree with that somber assessment. To be sure, one can find careful experiments that demonstrate some effect of biofeedback as compared to a control procedure, but those experiments were conducted with normal populations and serve only to demonstrate that the technique is feasible. These positive reports encourage clinical researchers to keep searching for specific therapeutic applications of biofeedback; however, they should not be mistakenly construed (by professional psychologists or laymen) as evidence of clinical success. To be fair, it should be noted that therapy outcome research has been continuously faced with trying to find adequate experimental designs, and biofeedback is no exception. One possible research strategy might be to test therapeutic combinations such as suggestion, relaxation, and biofeedback against control treatments that include all ingredients except biofeedback. Such an approach would be able to evaluate the relative therapeutic utility of biofeedback in the context of the total treatment employed by the average practitioner.

The reports of the treatment of premature ventricular contractions (Engel and Bleecker, 1974) and those of seizure reduction with sensorimotor rhythm feedback (Sterman, 1973) have been carefully performed, and it is highly unlikely that a placebo effect might be responsible. Engel's patients, in addition, did not show relapses; they did show changes that were clinically significant in terms of their pathology, and they also showed effects that were relatively long-lasting. Thus, of all the research reviewed, Engel's work on cardiac arrhythmias and systolic blood pressure comes closest to satisfying the criteria for demonstrating a specific therapeutic effect of biofeedback. Nevertheless, not all of the other case studies can successfully meet the remaining three of Melzack's criteria. Sterman's patients, for instance, showed serious relapses after the feedback was terminated.

It is noteworthy that the cardiac arrhythmia with which Engel and his associates have dealt is among the most specific and clearly defined syndromes to which biofeedback has been applied. Yet Weiss and Engel (1971) have noted that the mechanisms of such control are quite complex and involve at least two underlying physiological processes: sympathetic and parasympathetic control. The implications of this are clear. If a patient produces premature contractions only through a sympathetically mediated route, and the biofeedback of heart rate leads to learned control of heart rate through *parasympathetic* vagal control, then it is unlikely that the biofeedback will have any effect on the reduction of premature ventricular contractions. Shapiro and Surwit (1976) have aptly noted that precise knowledge of the underlying mechanisms of a symptom have clear implications for treatment choice. If a cardiac symptom, for instance, is exacerbated by increased sympathetic tone, then the object of treatment might be to reduce sympathetic tone, and cardiac feedback may not be the most efficient means to that end.

The lack of knowledge of the relationship of underlying process to clinical symptom may underlie much of the failure to develop adequate empirical evidence about the effectiveness of biofeedback. For instance, although there are numerous reports of the positive effect of frontalis muscle feedback on tension headache (Budzynski *et al.*, 1970), Engel (1975) reported evidence that curarization of the frontalis muscle has virtually no positive effect on tension headache reduction. It seems impossible to explain the positive effects of frontalis feedback in known biological terms, when its complete drug-induced relaxation does not lead to similar positive effects. Similarly, although there are some reports of successful treatment of migraine by temporal artery biofeedback (Friar and Beatty, 1976), it is not clear that the temporal artery is involved in the migraine syndrome, and there is still considerable controversy among neurologists about the precise vascular phenomena that produce the migraine headaches (Wolff, 1963). Some investigators are not convinced that migraine is vascular and have suggested the hypothalamus as the source of the headache symptoms (Herburg, 1967), and other investigators have suggested that if migraine is vascular, the underlying cause of the vascular disturbance may be best understood by analyzing serotonin levels (Anthony, Hinterberger, and Lance, 1967).

In addition to the obvious difficulties created by the tendency of biofeedback research to either ignore or oversimplify the problem of correct analysis of the underlying process, there is the related problem of appropriate technology. The development of sophisticated electronic equipment was a prerequisite for the initiation of biofeedback research; the miniaturization and decreasing cost of this equipment has contributed to the widespread use of biofeedback, both in laboratories and by private users. The multiplication of both commercial and privately built devices, however, has created its own set of problems specific to the new field, for there has been no set of standards developed (see Schwitzgebel and Rugh, 1975). Lack of standardization exists even in EEG feedback devices where the basic signal being fed back is well defined. In addition, the technology in biofeedback is rapidly growing and changing; equipment and techniques become rapidly outdated, making comparisons of research results quite difficult.

Assuming that all of the technical problems can be overcome, and assuming further that future controlled experimental research demonstrates that biofeedback can, in fact, be used as effective treatment, the question remains whether it will prove to be an efficient form of treatment. For example, if it were demonstrated conclusively (which it has not been) that biofeedback training of increased hand temperature and decreased forehead temperature results in migraine reduction, could it not also be shown that similar and more easily obtained results might be achieved with simultaneous application of a heating pad to the hands and ice to the head? By the same token, is there any reason to believe that successful treatment of tension headache by biofeedback would be any more direct or productive than the use of aspirin already is? Conversely, is there any reason to believe that headaches that are resistant to simple pharmacological analgesia treatments (aspirin) should be any less resistant to biofeedback-induced analgesia? Nonetheless, the possibility that biofeedback and other behaviorally oriented treatments may be useful in reducing required drug dosage and the undesirable side effects of drugs in some patients continues to be an important reason for further clinical biofeedback research.

CURRENT STATUS AND FUTURE PROSPECTS. It is clear that much of the current interest in the clinical application of biofeedback has focused on the treatment of physiological symptoms of medical or psychosomatic disorders; problems of a more traditional psychological or psychiatric nature have not received as much attention from clinical biofeedback research. This is ironic, since the early excitement about biofeedback was generated by investigators who saw new ways of approaching traditional philosophical and psychological issues about the nature of consciousness and transcendent experiences. While there are still many investigators concerned with these issues, it remains clear that the bulk of therapeutic research with biofeedback has been addressed to cardiovascular problems, central nervous system disease, and rehabilitation medicine. Biofeedback has become a central focus of the discipline that Birk (1973) has called "behavioral medicine" more than it has for behavioral psychology. Indeed, the more successful and more significant contributions to date have been in areas of behavioral medicine—muscular rehabilitation, epilepsy control, headache treatment, and cardiac dysfunction. Applications to more traditional psychological areas such as

altered states of consciousness, anxiety reduction, and relaxation enhancement have yielded less promising results. Yet, whatever promise
biofeedback holds for the evolving discipline of behavioral medicine, it
will be lost unless there is tighter experimentation and more systematic
attempts to tease out the active treatment effects from the placebo effects
(see Stroebel and Glueck, 1973).

We would like to make a final comment concerning the enormous
attention that biofeedback has received within the professional community. Despite the clear lack of experimental evidence to support asser-
tions of the effectiveness of biofeedback as therapy (see Melzack, 1975;
Miller, 1974; Schwartz, 1973; Shapiro and Surwit, 1976), increasing numbers of clinicians are incorporating biofeedback into their practice.
Workshops to train clinical biofeedback practitioners are heavily at-
tended, and a new network of cassette-tape-trained biofeedback practitioners are working from one end of the continent to another. It is not
uncommon to see secondary sources describe Miller's and Shapiro's
remarkable success in treating essential hypertension, even as these
authors (Miller, 1975; Shapiro and Surwit, 1976) take great pains to
publish clear statements of caution about the actual effectiveness of their
treatments. The pattern of enthusiasm is similar in some ways to the
enthusiasm shown about the introduction of projective testing, various
forms and varieties of psychotherapy, and, within modern medicine, the
flirtations with vitamin treatments for cancer and cholesterol reduction
for the prevention of heart disease. There is a powerful desire among
health and health-related professionals to be able to provide treatment. It
is incumbent upon the serious scientist to temper that noble desire with
an equally noble appreciation for the value of hard evidence, and the
need for caution and patience. Biofeedback may provide future generations with important new weapons against disease. The current state of
evidence neither supports nor denies that hope. There are many tough
questions yet to be asked and no shortcuts to meaningful answers.

References

Aarons, L. Subvocalization: Aural and EMG feedback in reading. *Perceptual and Motor Skills*, 1971, *33*, 271–306.

Anand, B. K., Chhina, G. S., and Singh, B. Some aspects of electroencephalographic studies in yogis. *EEG and Clinical Neurophysiology*, 1961, *13*, 452–456.

Andrews, J. M. Neuromuscular re-education of hemiplegic with aid of electromyograph. *Archives of Physical Medicine and Rehabilitation*, 1964, *45*, 530–532.

Anthony, M., Hinterberger, H., and Lance, J. W. Plasma serotonin in migraine and stress. *Archives of Neurology*, 1967, *16*, 544–522.

Basmajian, J. V. Learned control of single motor units. In G. E. Schwartz and J. Beatty (Eds.), *Biofeedback: Theory and research*. New York: Academic Press, 1977.

Benson, H., Shapiro, D., Tursky, B., and Schwartz, G. E. Decreased systolic blood pressure through operant conditioning techniques in patients with essential hypertension. *Science*, 1971, *173*, 740–742.

Birk, L. (Ed.). *Biofeedback: Behavioral medicine*. New York: Grune and Stratton, 1973.

Birk, L., Crider, A., Shapiro, D., and Tursky, B. Operant electrodermal conditioning under partial curarization. *Journal of Comparative and Physiological Psychology*, 1966, *62*, 165–166.

Black, A. H. Operant autonomic conditioning: The analysis of response mechanisms. In P. A. Obrist, A. H. Black, J. Brener, and L. V. DiCara (Eds.), *Cardiovascular psychophysiology*. Chicago: Aldine, 1974.

Bleecker, E. R., and Engel, B. T. Learned control of cardiac rate and cardiac conduction in the Wolff–Parkinson–White syndrome. *New England Journal of Medicine*, 1973, *288*, 560–562.

Booker, H. E., Rubow, R. T., and Coleman, P. J. Simplified feedback in neuromuscular retraining: An automated approach using EMG signals. *Archives of Physical Medicine and Rehabilitation*, 1969, *50*, 621–625.

Brener, J., and Kleinman, R. A. Learned control of decreases in systolic blood pressure. *Nature*, 1970, *226*, 1063–1064.

Brown, B. B. Awareness of EEG-subjective activity relationships detected within a closed feedback system. *Psychophysiology*, 1970a, *7*, 451–464.

Brown, B. B. Recognition of aspects of consciousness through association with EEG alpha activity represented by a light signal. *Psychophysiology*, 1970b, *6*, 442–452.

Brudny, J., Grynbaum, B. B., and Korein, J. Spasmodic torticollis: Treatment by feedback display of the EMG. *Archives of Physical Medicine and Rehabilitation*, 1974, *55*, 403–408.

Brudny, J., Korein, J., Levidow, L., Grynbaum, B. B., Lieberman, A., and Friedmann, L. W. Sensory feedback therapy as a modality of treatment in central nervous system disorders of voluntary movement. *Neurology*, 1974, *24*, 925–932.

Budzynski, T. H. Biofeedback procedures in the clinic. *Seminars in Psychiatry*, 1973, *5*, 537–547.

Budzynski, T., and Stoyva, J. Biofeedback techniques in behavior therapy. In D. Shapiro, T. X. Barber, L. V. DiCara, J. Kamiya, N. E. Miller, and J. Stoyva (Eds.), *Biofeedback and self-control 1972: An Aldine annual on the regulation of bodily processes and consciousness*. Chicago: Aldine, 1973.

Budzynski, T., Stoyva, J., and Adler, C. Feedback-induced muscle relaxation: Application to tension headache. *Journal of Behavior Therapy and Experimental Psychiatry*, 1970, *1*, 205–211.

Budzynski, T. H., Stoyva, J. M., Adler, C. S., and Mullaney, D. J. EMG biofeedback and tension headache: A controlled outcome study. *Psychosomatic Medicine*, 1973, *35*, 484–496.

Cleeland, C. S. Behavior techniques in the modification of spasmodic torticollis. *Neurology*, 1973, *23*, 1241–1247.

Crider, A., Schwartz, G. E., and Shnidman, S. On the criteria for instrumental autonomic conditioning: A reply to Katkin and Murray. *Psychological Bulletin*, 1969, *71*, 455–461.

Crider, A., Shapiro, D., and Tursky, B. Reinforcement of spontaneous electrodermal activity. *Journal of Comparative and Physiological Psychology*, 1966, *61*, 20–27.

Datey, K. K., Deshmukh, S. N., Dalvi, C. P., and Vinekar, S. L. "Shavasan": A yogic exercise in the management of hypertension. *Angiology*, 1969, *20*, 325–333.

Davis, M. H., Saunders, D. B., Creer, T. L., and Chai, H. Relaxation training facilitated by biofeedback apparatus as a supplemental treatment in bronchial asthma. *Journal of Psychosomatic Research*, 1973, *17*, 121–128.

DiCara, L. V., and Miller, N. E. Changes in heart rate instrumentally learned by curarized rats as avoidance responses. *Journal of Comparative and Physiological Psychology*, 1968, *65*, 8–12.

Dworkin, B. R., and Miller, N. E. Visceral learning in the curarized rat. In G. E. Schwartz and J. Beatty (Eds.), *Biofeedback: Theory and research*. New York: Academic Press, 1977.

Elder, S. T., Ruiz, Z. R., Deabler, H. L., and Dillenkoffer, R. L. Instrumental conditioning of diastolic blood pressure in essential hypertensive patients. *Journal of Applied Behavior Analysis*, 1973, 6, 377–382.

Engel, B. *Evaluation of the clinical use of biofeedback techniques*. Symposium discussion at the meeting of the Society for Psychophysiological Research, Toronto, October, 1975.

Engel, B. T., and Bleecker, E. R. Application of operant conditioning techniques to the control of the cardiac arrhythmias. In P. A. Obrist, A. H. Black, J. Brener, and L. V. DiCara (Eds.), *Cardiovascular psychophysiology*. Chicago: Aldine, 1974.

Engel, B. T., and Melmon, L. Operant conditioning of heart rate in patients with cardiac arrhythmias. *Conditional Reflex*, 1968, 3, 130.

Engel, B. T., Nikoomanesh, P., and Schuster, M. M. Operant conditioning of rectosphincteric responses in the treatment of fecal incontinence. *New England Journal of Medicine*, 1974, 290, 646–649.

Epstein, L. H., Hersen, M., and Hemphill, P. Music feedback in the treatment of tension headache: An experimental case study. *Journal of Behavior Therapy and Experimental Psychiatry*, 1974, 5, 59–63.

Friar, L. R., and Beatty, J. Migraine: Management by trained control of vasoconstriction. *Journal of Consulting and Clinical Psychology*, 1976, 44, 46–53.

Gannon, L., and Sternbach, R. A. Alpha enhancement as a treatment for pain: A case study. *Journal of Behavior Therapy and Experimental Psychiatry*, 1971, 2, 209–213.

Grenfell, R. F., Briggs, A. H., and Holland, W. C. Antihypertensive drugs evaluated in a controlled double-blind study. *Southern Medical Journal*, 1963, 56, 1410–1416.

Hahn, W. W. The learning of autonomic responses by curarized animals. In P. A. Obrist, A. H. Black, J. Brener, and L. V. DiCara (Eds.), *Cardiovascular psychophysiology*. Chicago: Aldine, 1974.

Hardyck, C. D., Petrinovich, L. F., and Ellsworth, D. W. Feedback of speech muscle activity during silent reading: Rapid extinction. *Science*, 1966, 154, 1467–1468.

Herburg, L. J. The hypothalamus and the aetiology of migraine. In R. Smith (Ed.), *Background to migraine*. London: Heinemann, 1967.

Jacobs, A., and Felton, G. S. Visual feedback of myoelectric output to facilitate muscle relaxation in normal persons and patients with neck injuries. *Archives of Physical Medicine and Rehabilitation*, 1969, 50, 34–39.

Jacobson, A. M., Hackett, T. P., Surman, O. S., and Silverberg, E. L. Raynaud phenomenon. Treatment with hypnotic and operant technique. *Journal of the American Medical Association*, 1973, 225, 739–740.

Johnson, H. E., and Garton, W. H. Muscle re-education in hemiplegia by use of electromyographic device. *Archives of Physical Medicine and Rehabilitation*, 1973, 54, 320–323.

Kamiya, J. Operant control of the EEG alpha rhythm and some of its reported effects on consciousness. In C. Tart (Ed.), *Altered states of consciousness*. New York: Wiley, 1969.

Kaplan, B. J. Biofeedback in epileptics: Equivocal relationship of reinforced EEG frequency to seizure reduction. *Epilepsia*, 1975, 16, 477–485.

Kasamatsu, A., and Hirai, T. An electroencephalographic study of the Zen meditation (Zazen). *Folia Psychiatrica et Neurologica Japonica*, 1966, 70, 315–336.

Katkin, E. S. *Instrumental autonomic conditioning*. New York: General Learning Press, 1971.

Katkin, E. S., and Murray, E. N. Instrumental conditioning of autonomically mediated behavior: Theoretical and methodological issues. *Psychological Bulletin*, 1968, 70, 52–68.

Katkin, E. S., Murray, E. N., and Lachman, R. Concerning instrumental autonomic conditioning: A rejoinder. *Psychological Bulletin*, 1969, *71*, 462–466.

Kimble, G. A. *Hilgard and Marquis' conditioning and learning* (2nd ed.). New York: Appleton-Century, 1961.

Kimmel, E., and Kimmel, H. D. A replication of operant conditioning of the GSR. *Journal of Experimental Psychology*, 1963, *65*, 212–213.

Kimmel, H. D. Instrumental conditioning of autonomically mediated behavior. *Psychological Bulletin*, 1967, *67*, 337–345.

Kimmel, H. D., and Hill, F. A. Operant conditioning of the GSR. *Psychological Reports*, 1960, *7*, 555–562.

Kimmel, H. D., and Sternthal, H. S. Replication of GSR avoidance conditioning with concomitant EMG measurement and subjects matched in responsivity and conditionability. *Journal of Experimental Psychology*, 1967, *74*, 144–146.

Kristt, D. A., and Engel, B. T. Learned control of blood pressure in patients with high blood pressure. *Circulation*, 1975, *51*, 370–378.

Kuhlman, W. N., and Allison, T. EEG feedback training in the treatment of epilepsy: Some questions and some answers. *Pavlovian Journal of Biological Science*, 1977, *12*, 112–122.

Lang, P. J. Autonomic control or learning to play the internal organs. *Psychology Today*, 1970, *4*, 37–41.

Lang, P. J. Learned control of human heart rate in a computer directed environment. In P. A. Obrist, A. H. Black, J. Brener, and L. V. DiCara (Eds.), *Cardiovascular psychophysiology*. Chicago: Aldine, 1974.

Lisina, M. I. The role of orientation in the transformation of involuntary into voluntary reactions. In L. G. Voronin, A. N. Leontiev, A. R. Luria, E. N. Sokolov, and O. S. Vinogradova (Eds.), *Orienting reflex and exploratory behavior*. Moscow: Akad. Pedag. Nauk RSFSR, 1958 (in Russian); Washington: American Psychological Assoc., 1965 (in English).

Lynch, J. J., Paskewitz, D. A., and Orne, M. T. Some factors in the feedback control of human alpha rhythm. *Psychosomatic Medicine*, 1974, *36*, 399–410.

Marinacci, A. A., and Horande, M. Electromyogram in neuromuscular re-education. *Bulletin of Los Angeles Neurological Society*, 1960, *25*, 57–71.

McGuigan, F. J. Feedback of speech muscle activity during silent reading: Two comments. *Science*, 1967, *157*, 579–580.

McKenzie, R. E., Ehrisman, W. J., Montgomery, P. S., and Barnes, R. H. The treatment of headache by means of electroencephalographic biofeedback. *Headache*, 1973, *13*, 164–172.

Melzack, R. The promise of biofeedback: Don't hold the party yet. *Psychology Today*, 1975, *9*, 18–22; 80–81.

Miller, N. E. Learning of visceral and glandular responses. *Science*, 1969, *163*, 434–445.

Miller, N. E. Biofeedback: Evaluation of a new technic. *New England Journal of Medicine*, 1974, *290*, 684–685.

Miller, N. E. Clinical applications of biofeedback: Voluntary control of heart rate, rhythm, blood pressure. In H. I. Russek (Ed.), *New horizons in cardiovascular practice*. Baltimore: University Park Press, 1975.

Miller, N. E., and DiCara, L. Instrumental learning of heart rate changes in curarized rats: Shaping, and specificity to discriminative stimulus. *Journal of Comparative and Physiological Psychology*, 1967, *63*, 12–19.

Miller, N. E., and Dworkin, B. R. Visceral learning: Recent difficulties with curarized rats and significant problems for human research. In P. A. Obrist, A. H. Black, J. Brener, and L. V. DiCara (Eds.), *Cardiovascular psychophysiology*. Chicago: Aldine, 1974.

Mulholland, T. Feedback electroencephalography. *Activitas Nervosa Superior,* 1968, *10,* 410–438.

Mulholland, T. Occipital alpha revisited. *Psychological Bulletin,* 1972, *74,* 176–182.

Nowlis, D. P., and Kamiya, J. The control of EEG alpha rhythms through auditory feedback and the associated mental activity. *Psychophysiology,* 1970, *6,* 476–484.

Obrist, P. A., Howard, J. L., Lawler, J. E., Galosy, R. A., Meyers, K. A., and Gaebelein, C. J. The cardiac-somatic interaction. In P. A. Obrist, A. H. Black, J. Brener, and L. V. DiCara (Eds.), *Cardiovascular psychophysiology.* Chicago: Aldine, 1974.

Paskewitz, D. A., and Orne, M. T. Visual effects on alpha feedback training. *Science,* 1973, *181,* 360–363.

Patel, C. H. Yoga and biofeedback in the management of hypertension. *Lancet,* 1973, *7837,* 1053–1055.

Patel, C. 12-month follow-up of yoga and biofeedback in the management of hypertension. *Lancet,* 1975, *7898,* 62–64.

Paul, G. L. Physiological effects of relaxation training and hypnotic suggestion. *Journal of Abnormal Psychology,* 1969, *74,* 425–437.

Plotkin, W. B. On the self-regulation of the occipital alpha rhythm: Control strategies, states of consciousness, and the role of physiological feedback. *Journal of Experimental Psychology: General,* 1976, *105,* 66–99.

Plotkin, W. B., and Cohen, R. Occipital alpha and the attributes of the "alpha experience." *Psychophysiology,* 1976, *13,* 16–21.

Raskin, M., Johnson, G., and Rondestvedt, J. W. Chronic anxiety treated by feedback-induced muscle relaxation. *Archives of General Psychiatry,* 1973, *28,* 263–267.

Roberts, L. E. Comparative psychophysiology of the electrodermal and cardiac control systems. In P. A. Obrist, A. H. Black, J. Brener, and L. V. DiCara (Eds.), *Cardiovascular psychophysiology.* Chicago: Aldine, 1974.

Rosen, R. C., Shapiro, D., and Schwartz, G. E. Voluntary control of penile tumescence. *Psychosomatic Medicine,* 1975, *37,* 479–483.

Sargent, J. D., Green, E. E., and Walters, E. D. Preliminary report on the use of autogenic feedback training in the treatment of migraine and tension headaches. *Psychosomatic Medicine,* 1973, *35,* 129–135.

Schwartz, G. E. Biofeedback as therapy: Some theoretical and practical issues. *American Psychologist,* 1973, *28,* 666–673.

Schwartz, G. E., and Shapiro, D. Biofeedback and essential hypertension: Current findings and theoretical concerns. *Seminars in Psychiatry,* 1973, *5,* 493–503.

Schwitzgebel, R. L., and Rugh, J. D. Of bread, circuses, and alpha machines. *American Psychologist,* 1975, *30,* 363–378.

Scott, R. W., Blanchard, E. B., Edmunson, E. D., and Young, L. D. A shaping procedure for heart rate control in chronic tachycardia. *Perceptual and Motor Skills,* 1973, *37,* 327–338.

Shapiro, D. Operant-feedback control of human blood pressure: Some clinical issues. In P. A. Obrist, A. H. Black, J. Brener, and L. V. DiCara (Eds.), *Cardiovascular psychophysiology.* Chicago: Aldine, 1974.

Shapiro, D., Crider, A. B., and Tursky, B. Differentiation of an autonomic response through operant reinforcement. *Psychonomic Science,* 1964, *1,* 147–148.

Shapiro, D., Mainardi, J. A., and Surwit, R. S. Biofeedback and self-regulation in essential hypertension. In G. E. Schwartz and J. Beatty (Eds.), *Biofeedback: Theory and research.* New York: Academic Press, 1977.

Shapiro, D., and Schwartz, G. E. Biofeedback and visceral learning: Clinical applications. *Seminars in Psychiatry,* 1972, *4,* 171–184.

Shapiro, D., Schwartz, G. E., and Tursky, B. Control of diastolic blood pressure in man by feedback and reinforcement. *Psychophysiology*, 1972, *9*, 296–304.

Shapiro, D., and Surwit, R. S. Learned control of physiological function and disease. In H. Leitenberg (Ed.), *Handbook of behavior modification and behavior therapy*. Englewood Cliffs, New Jersey: Prentice-Hall, 1976.

Shapiro, D., Tursky, B., Gershon, E., and Stern, M. Effects of feedback and reinforcement on the control of human systolic blood pressure. *Science*, 1969, *163*, 588–590.

Sittenfeld, P. *The control of the EEG theta rhythm*. Paper presented at the meeting of the Biofeedback Research Society, 1972.

Smith, K. Conditioning as an artifact. *Psychological Review*, 1954, *61*, 217–225.

Snyder, C., and Noble, M. E. Operant conditioning of vasoconstriction. *Journal of Experimental Psychology*, 1968, *77*, 263–268.

Sterman, M. B. Neurophysiologic and clinical studies of sensorimotor EEG biofeedback training: Some effects on epilepsy. *Seminars in Psychiatry*, 1973, *5*, 507–525.

Sterman, M. B. Clinical implications of EEG biofeedback training: A critical appraisal. In G. E. Schwartz and J. Beatty (Eds.), *Biofeedback: Theory and research*. New York: Academic Press, 1977a.

Sterman, M. B. Effects of sensorimotor EEG feedback training on sleep and clinical manifestations of epilepsy. In J. Beatty and H. Legewie (Eds.), *Biofeedback and behavior*. New York: Plenum Press, 1977b.

Sterman, M. B., and Friar, L. Suppression of seizures in an epileptic following sensorimotor EEG feedback training. *EEG and Clinical Neurophysiology*, 1972, *33*, 89–95.

Sterman, M. B., Macdonald, L. R., and Stone, R. K. Biofeedback training of the sensorimotor electroencephalogram rhythm in man: Effects on epilepsy. *Epilepsia*, 1974, *15*, 395–416.

Stroebel, C. F., and Glueck, B. C. Biofeedback treatment in medicine and psychiatry: An ultimate placebo? *Seminars in Psychiatry*, 1973, *5*, 379–393.

Surwit, R. S. Biofeedback: A possible treatment for Raynaud's disease. *Seminars in Psychiatry*, 1973, *5*, 483–490.

Swaan, D., van Wieringen, P. C. W., and Fokkema, S. D. Auditory electromyographic feedback therapy to inhibit undesired motor activity. *Archives of Physical Medicine and Rehabilitation*, 1974, *55*, 251–254.

Travis, T. A., Kondo, C. Y., and Knott, J. R. Alpha enhancement research: A review. *Biological Psychiatry*, 1975, *10*, 69–89.

Valle, R. S., and Levine, J. M. Expectation effects in alpha wave control. *Psychophysiology*, 1975, *12*, 306–310.

Wallace, R. K. Physiological effects of transcendental meditation. *Science*, 1970, *167*, 1751–1754.

Wallace, R. K., and Benson, H. The physiology of meditation. *Scientific American*, 1972, *226*, 85–90.

Walsh, D. H. Interactive effects of alpha feedback and instructional set on subjective state. *Psychophysiology*, 1974, *11*, 428–435.

Weinstock, S. A. *A tentative procedure for the control of pain: Migraine and tension headaches*. Paper presented at the meeting of the Biofeedback Research Society, 1972.

Weiss, T., and Engel, B. T. Voluntary control of premature ventricular contractions in patients. *American Journal of Cardiology*, 1970, *26*, 666. (Abstract)

Weiss, T., and Engel, B. T. Operant conditioning of heart rate in patients with premature ventricular contractions. *Psychosomatic Medicine*, 1971, *33*, 301–321.

Wickramasekera, I. Electromyographic feedback training and tension headache: Preliminary observations. *American Journal of Clinical Hypnosis*, 1972, *15*, 83–85.

Wickramasekera, I. Effects of EMG feedback training on hypnotic susceptibility: More preliminary observations. *Journal of Abnormal Psychology,* 1973a, *82,* 74–77.

Wickramasekera, I. Temperature feedback for the control of migraine. *Journal of Behavior Therapy and Experimental Psychiatry,* 1973b, *4,* 343–345.

Wickramasekera, I. Heart rate feedback and the management of cardiac neurosis. *Journal of Abnormal Psychology,* 1974, *83,* 578–580.

Wolff, H. G. *Headache and other head pain* (2nd ed.). New York: Oxford University Press, 1963.

SECTION IV
APPLICATION OF PSYCHOPHYSICS AND HUMAN PERFORMANCE INFORMATION

Introduction

HERSCHEL W. LEIBOWITZ

The distinction between basic research and applied research is in a sense artificial. As we gain insight into processes and mechanisms, applications of this knowledge to societal problems follow almost automatically. Similarly, when we are faced with an applied problem it is often because we lack basic information. It is not surprising that research carried out for theoretical reasons turns out to have unanticipated and valuable practical applications. Frequently, research directed toward a specific applied problem uncovers fundamental generalizations that increase our knowledge of basic science.

The four chapters in the present section all represent outstanding research by psychologists whose work illustrates both of these approaches. The chapter by Gunnar Borg has its roots deep in the history of experimental psychology. In the middle of the 19th century, Gustav Fechner proposed that the philosophical dichotomy between mind and body could be "solved" if one could write a mathematical equation quantifying the relationship between the energy in the physical stimulus and the magnitude of perceived sensation. This proposal was a contributing factor in establishing psychology as an independent science and led not only to the classical psychophysical methods but also to the evaluation of sensation magnitudes by scaling techniques. During the last 50 years, scaling has developed into a fundamental approach of psychophysics, as exemplified by the work of the late S. S. Stevens and his collaborators. Gunnar Borg, an experimental psychologist who is director of the Institute of Applied Psychology in Stockholm, has successfully applied these methods to the quantitative evaluation of perceived exertion. His innovative program typifies the application of a sophisticated methodology, developed originally for theoretical purposes, to a wide variety of problems in exercise physiology, sports medicine, occupational health, and rehabilitation medicine. The successful application of these scaling methods to such a broad spectrum of applications could not have been anticipated by the early psychophysicists. It does, however, illustrate well the fact that progress in psychology frequently follows innovations in methodology. (For the reader interested in the broad impact of Borg's work, the recent book *Physical Work and Effort,* Wenner-Gren Symposium, Vol. 28, G. Borg (Ed.), Pergamon Press, Oxford, 1976, is recommended.)

The chapter by Willem A. Wagenaar illustrates the versatility of experimental psychologists in solving problems arising within modern technology. One of Wagenaar's many interests is the application of mathematics to the behavioral sciences. The Institute for Perception, where the research described in the chapter was carried out, is a unique organization staffed by physicists, engineers, and psychologists who carry out basic as well as applied studies. In the United States, research groups tend to be more specialized, but in the smaller Netherlands it is feasible to combine these various disciplines into one national organization. In the 28 years since its founding, this group has produced an enviable record of accomplishments, some of which would be classified as basic, some applied, while many would be recognized as making a dual contribution. The research on maneuvering of supertankers required the contributions of a broad psychologist such as Wagenaar who understands the limitations and capabilities of human beings faced with the difficult task of playing a critical role in a complex man–machine control system. The development of a simulator such as Wagenaar describes involves a number of decisions as to which features of the real life situation must be included in order for the operator to acquire the proper skills in training. The fact that the design of this system was so successful is a tribute to the skill and insights of Wagenaar and his organization.

The development of signal detection theory and its applications represents one of the best examples of the artificiality of any distinction between basic and applied research. The development of classical psychophysics had all but ignored the fact that responses are influenced by decision processes as well as by physical stimuli. Whereas the specification of the physical stimulus can be accomplished readily within the framework of physics, the role of the subject's decision criterion had been essentially ignored until a group at the University of Michigan approached this problem in the early 1950s. John A. Swets, David M. Green, and W. P. Tanner were members of this innovative and productive group. The history of signal detection theory and the role of allied disciplines and collaborators is detailed in their chapter. Of major significance is the fact that these techniques have been successfully utilized in countless studies investigating sensory function and, at the same time, have found an amazing variety of applications in diverse fields ranging from medicine to the military. As if to parallel the versatility of signal detection theory, John Swets has been associated during most of his career with Bolt Beranek and Newman, Inc., a major research and consulting firm in Cambridge, Massachusetts, where he is currently chief scientist. David Green taught for a number of years at the University of California, San Diego, and is currently professor of psychophysics at Harvard University.

The research by Conrad L. Kraft was formulated within the context of aviation safety. This field represents the convergence of a number of disciplines and skills to which experimental psychology has contributed significantly in the past. Standardized checklists, instrument standardization and coding, and computer stimulation of air traffic control all represent significant advancements in which psychologists have played a major role. Kraft, a student of the late Paul M. Fitts, a pioneer in this field, joins this tradition with a rich background in human engineering and the experimental psychology of vision and visual perception. The present account describes his successful efforts in identifying a visual height illusion implicated as a possible cause of a series of night visual approach accidents. His contribution has been recognized by many of the major airlines of the world who immediately incorporated the implications of this research into their standard operating procedures. Along with his collaborator, Charles L. Elworth, he was honored in 1969 for contributions to air safety by *Aviation Week* magazine and by the International Flight Safety Foundation. In 1973, the American Psychological Association awarded him their first Distinguished Contribution Award for applications to society.

Maneuvering the Mammoth

WILLEM A. WAGENAAR

Reeling as a Drunk

Imagine yourself driving a car on a perfectly straight and lonely two-lane highway. You can switch to the left lane without any danger of colliding with opposing traffic, since the return can be easily executed when another car comes into sight. Now consider how you would feel if changing lanes required at least ten minutes, and if opposing traffic could appear in either lane. A captain on a Very Large Crude Carrier (VLCC) or "supertanker" is faced with this very situation: sailing through restricted waters he may be on a collision course without knowing it, and the appropriate action should have been taken minutes ago.

Let us look at the situation a bit closer. Rotterdam Harbor is one of the major crude oil harbors in the world. Oil is brought in from the Persian Gulf in large tankers. The modal dimensions of VLCCs are nowadays a length of 300 m, a width of 50 m, and a draft of 21 m (Figure 1), with a capacity of some 300,000 tons of crude oil. The entrance to Rotterdam is through a channel 400 m wide, 23 m deep, dredged in the bottom of the sea. The walls of the channel produce a suction effect: when the ship comes too close it is irresistibly drawn to one side. Can the captain keep the ship away from the walls? What happens if there is other traffic across the channel or from the opposite direction?

WILLEM A. WAGENAAR • Institute for Perception TNO, Soesterberg, The Netherlands.

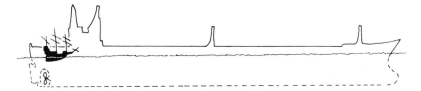

Figure 1. The Mayflower compared to a VLCC of 300,000 tons. The Mayflower required a crew of 26; supertankers are sailed by a crew of 40.

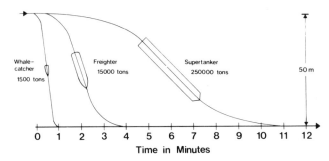

Figure 2. It takes a tanker of 250,000 tons about 12 min to make a translatory shift of 50 m.

For a full appreciation of the problem, we will discuss the maneuverability of VLCCs in more detail. Changing from one lane to the other (a shift of 50 m) is pictured in Figure 2. A small ship can perform the maneuver in 1 minute, but it takes a 300,000-ton tanker at least 12 minutes. This means that avoidance maneuvers must be initiated about 10 minutes before the expected collision. If not, the collision will occur unless some emergency maneuver is performed which will almost certainly lead to a grounding. As groundings are generally less harmful than collisions, a captain will prefer an emergency maneuver in case of uncertainty. In Rotterdam Harbor groundings occur about 10 times a year, and in other harbors the score will not be much better. The situation is complicated by the fact that large ships tend to follow an oscillatory path. The amplitude of the oscillation can, under bad visibility conditions, amount to a total of 400 m, which is the total width of the channel. Imagine yourself driving your car in a heavy fog swaying from one side of the road to the other, with opposing traffic to be expected any time!

It is no surprise that, according to the American Hull Insurance Syndicate, 85% of the shipping accidents can be traced to human error. A list of major factors causing casualties, published by the Panel on Human Error in Merchant Marine Safety (sponsored by the Maritime Transportation Research Board of the National U.S.A. Research Council), include inattention, inefficient bridge design, fatigue, high level of calculated risk, inadequate design of shore-based signals, and misuse of radar. Clearly safety problems in maritime transportation are related to the fact that man is included in the system. To be more specific, problems emerge because the system is not geared toward man's limited performance capabilities. Adapting the task to the operator is the basic aim of human factors research. This chapter will discuss the work that has been done in the area of maneuvering large vessels.

SIMULATORS FOR THE STUDY OF STEERING SUPERTANKERS

First of all, human factors specialists need a research tool. No ship-owner will put his fully laden oiltanker at the disposal of a psychologist experimenting with accidents in busy harbors! A first attempt was made to simulate large ships by using small ships. In a project sponsored by EXXON, a model of 1:25 scale was laid out in a pond near Grenoble, France, to be used for training purposes (Figure 3). Unfortunately, psychological research disclosed that training obtained in this small-scale world does not always transfer to a large-scale reality; the reverse might even be the case, as first-shot transfer appeared to be negative. How could this happen? The explanation is quite simple. In a 1:25 scale model, time is going five times faster than in reality; hence, all velocities (including rate of turn) are increased by a factor of five. Now, human perception is not infallible; there is a whole range of very slow ship motions that cannot be detected by a human observer. But in a simulation with an increased time scale, all sorts of otherwise invisible motions become visible. Once a shipmaster is used to seeing all relevant motions, he will come to rely upon them; set back in reality, he is bound to make severe mistakes because he will interpret the absence of motion cues as absence of motion. An illustration of this effect is presented in Figure 4; a simple maneuver (shifting one lane) is executed in three time scales—1:1, 1:5,

Figure 3. Captains training in the scale model facility in Grenoble, France.

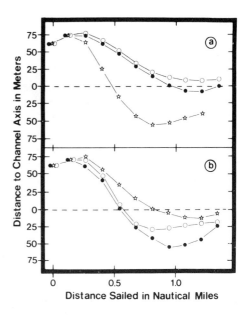

Figure 4. (a) A maneuver to reach the axis of a channel that is 60 m to starboard, executed in 1:1 (+——+), 1:5 (●——●), and 1:7 (○——○) time scales. The large overshoot in the 1:1 condition is absent when the time scale is reduced. (b) The same maneuver in a 1:1 scale, without (○——○) and with (●——●) training in a 1:5 time scale. It is seen that the overshoot is increased by training. The overshoot did not occur in the 1:5 training sessions (+——+).

and 1:7. These scales correspond with spatial scales 1:1, 1:25, and 1:50. It is clearly seen that the maneuver, which is hard in reality (as judged by the large overshoot), becomes increasingly easy when the time scale is reduced. The first-shot transfer, after training in a 1:5 situation, appears to be negative. The conclusion is that the behavior of physical systems, like ships and river basins, can be studied in scale models, but behavior of man cannot.

The alternative to using scale models is development of a computer-based simulation, such as is used in air and space flight. The problems involved are more complicated in the marine application of simulators. A large visual field is required, somewhere between 180° and 360°, whereas flight simulators usually provide a field of 20° at a maximum. The crew should be allowed to walk around in a wheelhouse of at least 6 × 4 m without the occurrence of obvious distortions, whereas in a flight simulator the pilot is strapped to his chair. The simulators cannot be limited to night conditions (as many flight simulators are), and quite unlike flight simulators, the representation of other realistic moving and interacting traffic is essential in many conditions.

The earliest ship maneuvering simulators were constructed about 10 years ago in Japan (2 simulators) and in Holland (1). Since then the number of simulators has increased to 17: 2 in the USA, 7 in Europe, and 8 in Japan. The visual display of the outside world is accomplished by sophisticated combinations of slides, TV projectors, computer-generated images, and shadow projectors. As I was involved in producing one of the first simulators, I would like to describe a very simple, easily constructed system.

The silhouette of a harbor is painted in color on a vertical sheet of Plexiglas, with small iron piers protruding horizontally. Important inland marks, like towers or factory chimneys, are attached to the Plexiglas as shown in Figure 5. A small bright light (Xenon arc; for the purpose of demonstration a normal car light bulb will do) is placed in front of the Plexiglas so as to project the silhouette of the scene on a large translucent screen. An observer is looking at the screen through the windows of a simulated wheelhouse (Figure 6). When the light is moved toward the glass, the projection on the screen appears to come closer; the observer experiences an effect of approaching the harbor. When the light moves parallel to the glass, the observer gets the impression of a translation

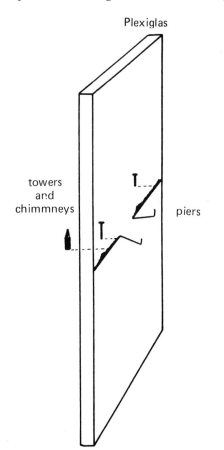

Plexiglas

towers
and
chimmneys

piers

Figure 5. How to produce a visual environment in a maneuvering simulator. The piers, chimneys, and towers are mounted perpendicular to the Plexiglas.

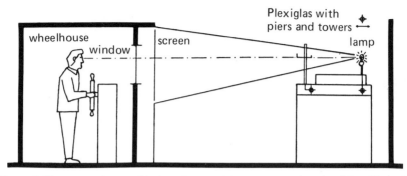

Figure 6. How to produce a visual environment in a maneuvering simulator. Through a window the observer is watching a screen on which the scenery is projected. Motions of the lamp and of the lamp + Plexiglas imitate all possible motions of the ship in the horizontal plane.

parallel to the coastline. When finally the Plexiglas and the light are moved parallel to the screen simultaneously, the projection on the screen will move such that the observer perceives a heading or orientation change. The motions of the light and the Plexiglas are controlled by a small computer, continuously computing the heading and the position of the simulated ship. Changes in heading and position are effected by the observer turning the wheel. This system is fairly simple and the total cost in 1967 was around $5,000. A quite complicated simulator based on the same principles cost about $1.5 million and is situated at the Neth-

Figure 7. Interior of the maneuvering simulator at The Netherlands Ship Model Basin.

erlands Ship Model Basin (Figure 7). An even more expensive simulator is CAORF (approximately $24 million), which is now in operation at the Maritime Administration at King's Point, New York.

The Psychologist's Point of View

Now what does all this have to do with psychology? The issue is simple. After the simulators had been developed, psychologists could prove their claim that maneuvering the mammoth is a primarily psychological problem and not a technical one. By this we mean that with increasing ship sizes we reach human limitations, not technical ones. We will illustrate this point of view by two simulator experiments.

We have seen before that maneuvering of scale models is much easier than maneuvering the full-size ship; our tentative explanation was that rate of turn was more readily detected in the model situation. Can more evidence be collected showing that rate of turn is key information to the operator? The following experiment was conducted.

Pilots were asked to steer a VLCC through a channel with a 30 bend in it. The radius of the curve was either 5,000 m or 1,600 m, or the bend was a sharp kink (Figure 8a). The effect of these three layouts was to impose low, medium, and high rates of turn (Figure 8b). During these maneuvers heart rate was recorded; as is shown in Figure 8c, heartbeat interval was shortened markedly as soon as the ship started to turn. In the extreme case (rate of turn about 0.2°/sec, which amounts to a full turn in half an hour) heartbeat intervals as compared to the control scores are reduced by about 100 msec. As a rule heart rate is used to measure mental load imposed by a task, or simply task difficulty. Leaving aside the lengthy discussions on the measurement of mental load we take Figure 8 to mean that the difficulty of the control task is proportional to the rate of turn of the ship. This conclusion cannot easily be arrived at without physiological measurements because of the captain's attempt to maintain constant efficiency during all maneuvers. Until the operation of the system reaches its limits, levels of difficulty can be established only by measuring in some way how much effort is spent. The insight that task difficulty is related to rate of turn was nicely utilized to solve the next problem.

Large vessels frequently display a nasty property called *course instability;* this means that there is no unique relation between rudder angle and the resulting turning direction and turning velocity. Figure 9 shows that a course-unstable tanker might turn either to starboard or to port with a rudder angle between plus or minus 4°. Such a ship will never sail straight when the rudder is 0° amidships; the helmsman, in order to stay on a straight course, is forced to make the ship turn to one or the

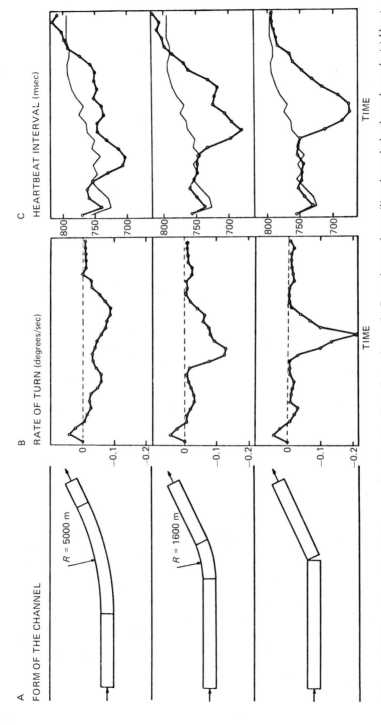

Figure 8. (a) Three channels used in an experiment on the effect of rate of turn. (b) Rate of turn when sailing through the three channels. (c) Heart rate occurring during the maneuvers. The drawn line represents the heart rate in a control condition in which no course changes were required.

other side all the time. The actions of the helmsman will always result in high turning rates (about 0.17°/sec outside the hysteresis loop) and we have shown already that this may contribute considerably to task difficulty. Clearly, course instability is undesirable and should be redressed as much as possible.

Two solutions present themselves. The first solution is based upon the notion that instability is a property of the ship, and that removal of the bad consequences of instability should be achieved by changing the ship. In practice, this will mean that the ship is to be brought into a dry dock; there the hull is changed by the addition of an extra skeg area, the rudder is enlarged, and the steering mechanism is changed accordingly. The whole operation involves millions of dollars, and even then the effect is unpredictable.

The second solution evolves from the idea that steering the unstable ship is just a difficult task, not an impossible task; the ship could follow a prescribed path, but man cannot make her do so. The information man needs to control the ship is simply not presented adequately. Instability prohibits accurate control of rate of turn but, as we noticed before, rate of turn should be kept well under control in order to prevent severe oscillation. Small differences in rate of turn are not easily detected by unaided human observers; a rule of thumb says that acceleration of angular movement can be detected only if the velocity at least doubles every 5 sec. The accelerations of large vessels are never that high; as a consequence it is impossible for operators, unaided by instruments, to tell whether rate of turn is increasing or decreasing. Rather he will wait until the course error has accumulated to, for instance, one degree, which may happen in about 35 sec. Correction of the error will take another 120 sec. During that period the deviation from the prescribed path (at cruising speed) will have increased to 60 m, and correction of that error if at all possible takes about 15 min. It is not unreasonable to assume that the adverse effect of

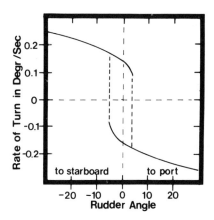

Figure 9. The effect of course instability. When the rudder is set at 30°, the ship will make a turning circle with a constant rate of turn of 0.25°/sec. When the rudder is set back to 20°, 10°, and finally 0°, the resulting rate of turn is 0.22°, 0.20°, and 0.17°/sec. With the rudder amidships, the ship keeps turning. Only when the rudder is switched to −5° is a sudden change of the turning direction observed.

instability can be counteracted by simply presenting rate of turn on a separate dial. This is easily done as rate of turn is already provided to the autopilot used in the deep sea.

An experiment to check our line of reasoning was conducted as follows. Pilots of the Dutch Pilotage were asked to perform a series of maneuvers in the simulator, which was programmed to behave like a 250,000-ton oil tanker. The degree of course instability, as defined by the distance between the two curves in Figure 9, was varied between 0 and 9, not an unrealistically extreme case. The maneuvers consisted of course keeping and making some small course changes (up to 25). All maneuvers were performed with and without a rate-of-turn indicator.

The results of the course-keeping maneuvers (Figure 10) show that the unstable ship gets into an oscillatory sway fairly soon, provided that the rate of turn is not presented to the master. However, introduction of

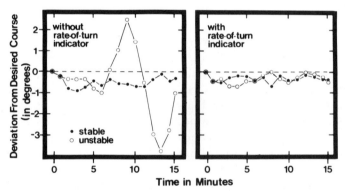

Figure 10. Results of course-keeping maneuvers with stable and unstable tankers. The unstable tanker follows an oscillatory path, unless the operator is allowed to use a rate-of-turn indicator.

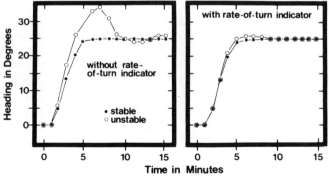

Figure 11. Results of a 25° heading change with stable and unstable tankers. The unstable tanker makes a large overshoot, but only when no rate-of-turn indicator is used.

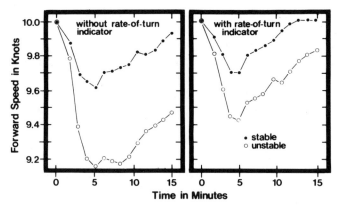

Figure 12. Results of a 25° heading change with stable and unstable tankers. The unstable ship loses 8.5% of its original forward velocity, whereas the stable ship loses only 4%. When a rate-of-turn indicator is used, this difference is considerably reduced.

the rate-of-turn indicator almost removes the oscillation. Similar observations were made in the course-changing maneuvers (Figures 11 and 12). Large overshoots and considerable speed loss occur as a result of badly adjusted steering motions on unstable ships; the rate-of-turn indicator helps to reduce these effects considerably. The meaning of this is evident: course-unstable ships can maneuver like stable ships *if the operator has the necessary information*. The positive effects of a rate-of-turn indicator occur because it improves the man–machine interface and not because of a technical improvement in the maneuverability of the ship.

The Man–Machine Interface

A task that becomes too difficult for human operators should be either automated or adapted to human limitations. Adapting man by training or selection to meet the requirements of the task is a final resort that implies a failure on the part of the designer. Quite often a control task can be simplified by a proper design of the man–machine interface, which is the channel through which all information passes from machine to man and vice versa. In the case of entering a harbor with a large tanker, the interface should pass information on actual position, course, rate of turn, and speed to the master, and information on desired values to the ship. Human engineering in ship handling is not limited to the classical field of knobs and dials; we also study the design of channels before they are dredged, of piers and bridges before they are constructed, of traffic control systems before they are imposed.

In Holland push-barges are locked through 24-m-wide locks, while the barges themselves have a width of 22.80 m. The captain, some 175 m behind the bow, is faced with the impossible task of steering the ship into the lock with a 60-cm margin on each side. If the angle between the axis of the ship and the lock surpasses 0.5°, the ship will get irrevocably stuck, a common problem when locks were designed as in Figure 13a. One guide wall provided continuous information on the position of the lock chamber, whereas the opening between the two walls was made very wide to facilitate the entrance. From our studies it became clear that captains tended to overlook the asymmetry of this design. As a result they sailed on a course that bisected the angle between the guide walls, which is only correct in the case of a symmetrical design. Somehow the guide walls, as they were perceived by the captains, did not convey the information necessary for a correct approach. The solution was not to train the captains to do something against their nature, nor to change the main dimensions of either the ship or the lock chamber. Instead we suggested a new design for the guide walls, so as to form a symmetrical

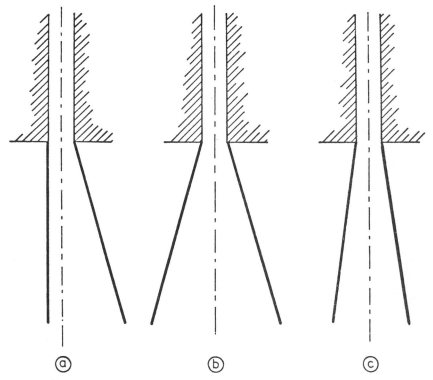

Figure 13 (a). Guide walls as originally used in Dutch locks (not to scale). (b) Symmetric guide walls appear to be much better, as captains tend to sail over the bisectrix. (c) A narrow opening enhances estimation of distance to both sides, resulting in a more precise localization of the lock chamber axis.

entrance (Figure 13b). With respect to the angle between the guide walls, we found in our studies that it is easier to enter the locks through a narrow opening (Figure 13c) because estimation of the distances to both sides is much more accurate if the walls are close by. Knowledge of the exact location of the main axis of the lock chamber is essential for entering the lock; this information should be provided by the man–machine interface in an easy and natural way. A redesign of the locks served this purpose: narrow, symmetrical guide walls are more informative than wide asymmetrical ones. No specific training or any additional aids like guiding lines of lights or radiographic positioning equipment were needed. All this happened about 10 years ago, and no further problems have emerged in these and similar locks.

CONCLUSION

Jobs can be designed in many ways. The choice is not merely a technical problem but also a psychological one; the design of the job should fit in with human possibilities and limitations. It is the psychologist who can assist in the creation of conditions under which a job can be done by ordinary people like you and me. Quite often the solutions he will propose are much simpler than technical solutions that tend to complicate situations rather than to simplify them.

Applications of Signal Detection Theory

JOHN A. SWETS AND DAVID M. GREEN

Introduction

There are hundreds of situations that require one to discriminate between two alternatives under conditions of uncertainty. The pilot is
trying to detect the airport beacon on a foggy night—is that faint light the
tower or not? The radiologist is inspecting an X-ray film—is that shadow
a tumor or not? A witness to a robbery is looking at a lineup—is the third
man from the end the culprit or not? The driver of a car is entering the on-
ramp of a busy freeway—is there an opening in the traffic or not? In all
such cases the problem arises because the information is not perfect and
confusion among the potential alternatives can occur.

Signal detection theory (SDT) provides a means of analyzing choices
and evaluating how effectively they are made. The advantage of the
theory is that it provides a means of separating two aspects of performance in such decision situations. The first aspect is the decision-maker's
capacity to discriminate between the two alternatives. Usually the alternatives can be confused—the light from a shopping center may be
confused with the airport beacon, radiographic mottle may be confused
with a tumor. Indeed, if the alternatives are perfectly discriminable, the
decision problem is often trivial. The second aspect is the decision-
maker's bias or criterion for selecting one alternative over another, as

JOHN A. SWETS • Bolt Beranek and Newman, Inc., Cambridge, Massachusetts.
DAVID M. GREEN • Laboratory of Psychophysics, Harvard University, Cambridge,
Massachusetts.

influenced by his assessment of the probability of an alternative or the utility of a given decision outcome. The pilot would like to see the airport beacon, and the radiologist would like to make a firm diagnosis. By distinguishing between these two aspects, (1) discrimination capacity and (2) decision bias or criterion, and by providing independent measures of both, SDT provides a means of evaluating the performance of man, man–machine systems, or, indeed, fully automated systems, in these discrimination tasks.

EXAMPLE: AN INSPECTION TASK. A concrete example will facilitate a description of basic components of the discrimination task. Suppose you are inspecting some manufactured item and trying to decide whether it is acceptable (say, whether or not it will function 500 days without failure) or faulty. You perform some test on the item, and on that basis must label the item as acceptable or faulty. Obviously, the first thing you must establish is some criterion or standard. If the item is better than the standard, you accept it; if it is worse, you reject it. Now, if the standard is set too low, it is useless, because everything will then be accepted. Conversely, if the standard is set too high, nothing will ever be accepted. So some middle level is required—but what should determine the standard's exact value?

FACTORS AFFECTING THE DECISION CRITERION. Two factors are obviously relevant in setting a standard, or a decision criterion. First, there is the *a priori* probability that the product is faulty. If most items are faulty, then a high or stringent criterion is needed to ensure that an item that passes the criterion is truly acceptable. The converse is also true. If most items are good, then a relatively lenient criterion will still ensure that a large percentage of the items passing the criterion are acceptable. A second factor is the utility of the decision—the values and costs associated with correct and incorrect decisions of both kinds. Suppose that the item is part of a rocket. If the rocket will carry a man to the moon, then a stringent criterion should be employed; if the rocket is part of an inexpensive and harmless fireworks display, then a lenient criterion is appropriate. These two considerations—*a priori* probabilities and the values and costs associated with the decision outcomes—are the main variables that influence the selection of the decision criterion.

THE DISCRIMINABILITY OF THE TWO ALTERNATIVES. The second aspect of the decision problem is the quality of the evidence or information upon which the decision is based. What is the capacity of the inspection test to discriminate good from bad items? What is the likelihood that a good item, when inspected, will be labeled faulty? In all discriminations of this kind, performance is strongly influenced by the quality of the information. If the information is poor, then the selection of a less-than-optimal decision criterion may make very little difference.

SCOPE OF THIS CHAPTER. The remainder of this introduction first describes the means of analysis of decision making in these simple discrimination situations. It concludes with a brief history of signal detection theory and its introduction into psychology. In following sections we consider the application of SDT to the areas of military and industrial monitoring, medical diagnosis, and information retrieval. Finally, we review some additional areas where the application has not been as extensive but has just begun or has only been suggested, including driving behavior, product evaluation, and forensic situations. Important in all these situations is a simple graph, called the relative, or receiver, operating characteristic (ROC) curve, which uniquely describes performance in these discrimination tasks. This curve provides a basis for separating the two important aspects of performance: discriminatory capacity and decision criterion.

ANALYSIS OF DISCRIMINATION AND THE ROC CURVE. Formally, all two-alternative tasks can be represented by the intersection of the two possible stimulus situations and the two possible responses. In the inspection example we discussed earlier, the two stimulus alternatives, or "states of the world," are acceptable and faulty items. The two responses are to label the item as acceptable or faulty. Thus performance can always be summarized completely in terms of a 2 × 2 matrix. The stimulus alternatives are columns of the matrix and the two possible responses are the rows of the matrix. Figure 1 presents such a matrix. The entries in the matrix are the conditional probabilities of a particular

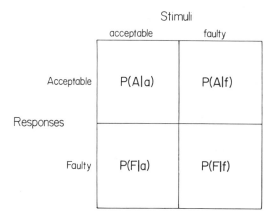

Figure 1. A 2 × 2 matrix, with the terminology of the illustrative inspection problem. In general, two states of the world are considered, and one is selected. Repeated trials yield estimates of the conditional probabilities of the four possible decision outcomes. Two of these probabilities are independent and yield estimates of discrimination capacity and the decision criterion, as indicated in later figures.

response given a particular stimulus. The response or decision is labeled by a capital letter, A or F, and the states of the world by corresponding lower-case letters. Thus, when a capital letter is followed by the same lower-case letter, the response is correct; when the letters are different, the responses are incorrect.

Although one generally views the inspection situation as an effort to detect faulty items, our example treated the acceptance of an acceptable item as a "true positive" and the acceptance of a faulty item as a "false positive." In common practice, a true-positive response is called a "hit" and a false-positive response is termed a "false alarm."

If one performs the inspection task repetitively and the decisions are independent, then the 2 × 2 matrix is a complete representation of the discrimination task. The entries of the matrix completely specify the inspector's behavior. It is important to realize that the quantities in the matrix are not independent of one another. In fact, each column adds to 1:

$$P(A \,|\, a) + P(F \,|\, a) = 1.0$$

$$P(A \,|\, f) + P(F \,|\, f) = 1.0$$

These two equations indicate that a particular item, whether acceptable or faulty, must be labeled one way or the other by the inspector. The important point, confirmed by these equations, is that there are really only two independent probabilities in two-alternative decision tasks, not four, as the entries of the matrix might imply. Thus we can completely represent decision-making behavior by only two probabilities. Conventionally we use the false-positive or false-alarm probability $P(A \,|\, f)$ and the true-positive or hit probability $P(A \,|\, a)$ and plot them as x and y coordinates of a graph. Figure 2 shows such a hypothetical graph, and a single point located on a smooth curve. The point represents one possible decision criterion in the discrimination task; the curve represents the locus of possible points for a given discrimination capacity.

As indicated, we have represented a particular behavior, or decision criterion, as a single point on a line. But potentially one could alter the decision criterion and hence alter the hit and false-alarm probabilities. Such changes might move the probabilities along the smooth line shown in Figure 2. That is, if one adopted a very stringent criterion, then very low false-alarm and hit probabilities would result. Conversely, if one adopted a very lenient criterion, then very high false-alarm and hit probabilities would result. These criteria represent the extremes. The ROC curve represents all potential discrimination performances.

The major diagonal is indicated as a dotted line in Figure 2. Points on that diagonal correspond to a hit probability that is equal to a false-alarm probability. They represent situations in which the inspection pro-

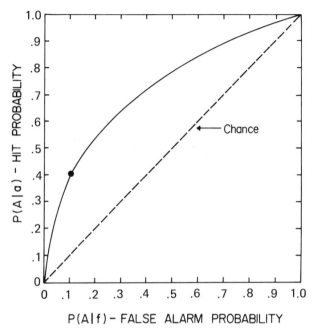

Figure 2. An ROC graph. The point represents a decision criterion; the curve represents the locus of possible decision criteria for a given discrimination capacity. In general, the slope of the ROC curve decreases monotonically, and the slope at any point can serve as a measure of the decision criterion that produced that point.

cedure is so poor that it cannot discriminate between good and bad items at a better than chance level. In this case, one could simply ignore the inspection test and make the two responses at random; one would still achieve a point somewhere along the dotted line. In the case we have considered, i.e., the solid curve of Figure 2, we assume that the inspection procedure is able to discriminate between good and bad items to some extent, and so the hit probability exceeds the false-alarm probability for every point along the curve.

Figure 3 shows a set of three hypothetical ROC curves that represent different degrees of discrimination capacity. This fact can easily be appreciated if we take a single false-alarm probability, for example, a 0.1 false-alarm probability, and note that the hit probabilities for these three curves are 0.2, 0.6, and 0.9, respectively. This same ordering is true no matter what false-alarm probability we take. Other ways of looking at this situation are to observe that the topmost curve encompasses the greatest area in the ROC space and more closely approaches the upper left corner representing perfect discrimination; thus one can conclude that the discrimination capacity is better for this curve than for either of the other two curves.

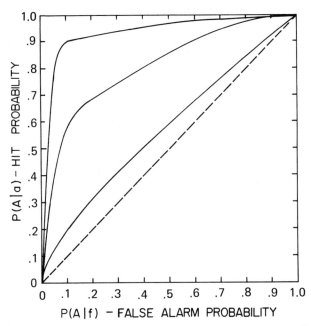

Figure 3. Three ROC curves, representing different discrimination capacities. Capacity can be indexed in several ways; it is evident that higher curves have larger hit probabilities for a given false-alarm probability, lie further from the positive diagonal, and contain more area than the lower curves.

This, then, is the distinctive contribution of SDT—a means to separate two potentially independent aspects of simple discrimination tasks. One aspect is the criterion used to make one or the other response. This criterion determines the hit and false-alarm probability for a single point along the ROC curve. The false-alarm probability or, alternatively, the slope of the curve, at that point is a measure of whether the criterion is strict or lenient. The second aspect is the capacity to discriminate between the alternatives, which can be measured by the area under the ROC curve or by some measure of the distance of the curve from the major diagonal.

   This distinction between these two aspects of uncertain decision making provides a means of evaluating performance in discrimination tasks. Performance may be good or poor with respect to the location of the decision criterion, or it may be good or poor with respect to the ability to discriminate among the alternatives. Any recommendation to change the performance of a man, a man–machine system, or an automatic system must distinguish between these two aspects of performance.

BRIEF HISTORY OF SIGNAL DETECTION THEORY. SDT was first applied in psychology to a visual detection task by Tanner and Swets (1954). They induced observers to alter their willingness to say they had detected a weak flash of light and found variation in the hit probability and false-alarm probability that followed an ROC curve such as that shown in Figure 2.

Tanner and Swets were applying a theory developed by their colleagues at the University of Michigan, Peterson and Birdsall (1953), whose main area of application was the detection of weak radar signals. At about the same time, Van Meter and Middleton (1954), at Harvard, had also seen the way to apply statistical decision theory to electronic communication problems. Neyman and Pearson (1933) and Wald (1950) had earlier shown how decision problems were amenable to statistical and probabilistic analysis.

The original theory proposed by Tanner and Swets was similar to some earlier ideas on psychometric scaling expressed by Thurstone (1927). For a more complete description of this history and a recent review of SDT's applications within psychology, see an article by Swets (1973). Several books have also appeared on the topic: Green and Swets (1966/1974) have written a general introduction, Egan (1975) has written about ROC curves, and McNicol (1972) has written a primer on the subject.

MILITARY AND INDUSTRIAL MONITORING

We proceed now to consider several applications of SDT to problem areas outside of psychology proper. The first is to human monitoring performance. Military monitoring of radar and sonar signals—indicating planes and submarines, respectively—gave the initial impetus to the development of SDT during World War II. Engineers were interested in equipment design and hence in the best possible detection performance (or in the "ideal receiver") for a given signal and a given background of interference, or noise. Psychologists were interested in the behavior of the human as sensor and decision-maker, for although the engineer's equipment sometimes replaced the human lookout, it often merely extended the range of the human's senses while leaving the human with a difficult detection or discrimination task. It was clear to the engineers that they could set a threshold or decision criterion for their devices, relative to each device's inherent noise level, in order to achieve any balance between hits and false alarms that a given signal-to-noise ratio would permit. Psychologists studying sensory and cognitive processes then learned that humans were not constrained by a fixed sensory threshold but could similarly adjust their decision criterion for sensory data.

Application of the ROC analysis to military monitoring is represented in upwards of 50 studies beginning in the early 1960s (reviews are given by Broadbent, 1971; Mackworth, 1970; Swets, 1977; Swets and Kristofferson, 1970). Through most of this time the task was conceived as one of vigilance for low-probability signals. The need for vigilance characterizes also the industrial inspector who views item after item looking for a flaw. The ROC analysis has been applied to such industrial quality-control problems, in perhaps 20 studies, since about 1970 (Drury and Fox, 1975a; Swets, 1977).

The psychologist's interest in military vigilance behavior was initially stimulated by a commonly observed change over time in the human's detection performance, namely, by a substantial decline in the probability of a correct, positive detection response (or "hit") beginning almost at the start of a watch. This change was viewed as a decrement in performance, and specifically as a decrement in sensitivity. At least five theories, and many studies, focused on a host of variables thought to affect alertness, including work–rest cycle, intersignal interval, irrelevant stimulation, incentives, knowledge of results, introversion–extraversion, temperature, drugs, age, and sex (e.g., Frankman and Adams, 1962).

The application of SDT revealed that the probability of a false alarm dropped along with the probability of a hit, and that in most cases the declines in the two probabilities were of a relative magnitude. This indicated a change only in the decision criterion, with sensitivity remaining constant. Specifically, of 42 studies recently considered by Parasuraman and Davies (1977), 14 showed a sensitivity decrement as well as a criterion shift, and the remainder showed only a criterion shift. Meanwhile, emphasis has shifted to new variables, such as values and costs of decision outcomes and changing subjective probabilities of signal occurrence, that influence the decision criterion. Indications are that training can produce a criterion that will remain constant over time.

A taxonomic analysis of the displays used in the 42 studies showed a clear difference between those that yielded only a criterion shift and the 14 that showed both a change in criterion and a change in sensitivity. The latter displays required a successive comparison (of the two stimulus alternatives) at a high rate (greater than 24 comparisons per minute). The identification of those displays that yield a sensitivity decrement is clearly an advance, even in instances in which one cannot substitute other displays for them.

The same taxonomic analysis has served to revise opinions about individual differences in vigilance tasks. Whereas formerly the quality of the performances of different observers apparently had no pattern from one task to another, and so individual differences were assumed to be "task-specific," now relative individual performances are seen to have a consistency across tasks of a given type. Individuals especially capable in tasks requiring rapid successive comparisons maintain that proficiency, independent, say, of sensory modality. The taxonomy thus brings an order to this area of research and practice and suggests that selection tests can be devised for people doing monitoring tasks, and that performance data can be extrapolated from laboratory to practical tasks (Parasuraman and Davies, 1977).

Though vigilance is required by industrial-inspection tasks, research on inspection has tended not to show the "decrement" found in psychological experiments on military vigilance. Perhaps this difference arises because the investigating engineers have usually employed well-practiced inspectors, working on familiar tasks, as subjects. The application of SDT in this context has been motivated by the usefulness of the theory as a general framework for analysis. Thus, several authors have suggested that it offers a framework to integrate alertness, search, and memory with discrimination and decision in complex monitoring (Adams, 1975; Buck, 1975; Drury and Fox, 1975b). "Since the use of SDT permits the study of both stimulus and response variables, the entire inspection task may, at least in theory, be studied. The use of ROC curves should permit the comparison of viewing conditions, inspectors, equipment used, or visual target used to signal a defect" (Adams, 1975, p. 65). SDT "is most attractive as the vehicle for integrating human factors data with established quality control models. . . . Certainly in attempting to conceptualize the role of physical and organizational factors . . . it is invaluable and provides a rationale which makes the importance of these factors indisputable" (Drury and Fox, 1975b, p. 98).

The economic value of the ROC as an analytic tool for management has also been cited. The ability to predict various combinations of error probability along an ROC curve permits management to select the appropriate decision criterion for its inspectors. An "acceptable quality limit" can be selected in accordance with the *a priori* probabilities and with the relative costs of misses and false rejections, and the need or not for a further check on the rejects can be assessed (Wallack and Adams, 1969; Drury, 1973; Drury and Fox, 1975c). The ROC analysis aids in training inspectors to establish new criteria and in apprising them of inappropriate criteria, and it emphasizes the desirability of informing the inspectors of changing fault probabilities (Sheehan and Drury, 1971).

Of course, there is often more to human monitoring in both military and industrial settings nowadays than mere vigilance for a relatively simple signal. In semiautomated military systems for command, control, and communication, and in a largely automated industrial system for process control, the operator must infer "signals" from complex patterns of events, which may indicate failure of a subsystem or the presence of a new situation outside the capabilities of the automatic equipment. In both cases the operator may be responsible for taking whatever action is required. Often, too, the operator has much else to do and must decide when and where to make observations of the several displays showing aspects of the system's status.

The application of SDT to such complex tasks, involving monitoring in the interests of supervisory control, is young, but some directions are emerging. In general, the operator uses probabilities and values in establishing response strategies that govern the decisions made about the signal data obtained from observations. Also, the operator makes decisions about when and where to observe, with the goal of predicting and adapting well enough to reduce reaction time and processing load (Moray, 1976; Young, 1969). More of the power of SDT is being used to deal with simultaneous detection and classification of signal patterns that develop over time (Swets, 1976a). The distribution of attention and effort among various perceptual and control tasks is being studied with the aid of the ROC—sometimes called an "attention" or "performance" operating characteristic in this application (Sperling, 1976; Norman and Bobrow, 1976). At this juncture, SDT gives promise of helping to merge the analysis of attention and perception with the analysis of skilled motor and cognitive performance, and so to facilitate quantitative treatment of complex behaviors in practical settings (Sheridan, 1970; Welford, 1968; Wickens, 1976; Wickens and Gopher, 1975).

MEDICAL DIAGNOSIS

ROC analysis was introduced in medicine by Lusted (1968). Most of the applications since then have been to evaluation of radiographic and other imaging systems (e.g., Starr, Metz, Lusted, and Goodenough, 1975), but the ROC has also been used in cost-benefit analyses of other diagnostic techniques, not involving perceptual judgments (e.g., McNeil, Varady, Burrows, and Adelstein, 1975). A recent review describes use of the ROC in some 20 medical studies (Swets, 1976b).

In the evaluation of imaging systems, the ROC first does what it usually does. It provides a measure of the perceptual, diagnostic accuracy afforded by a system (in conjunction with the radiologist or other reader) that is independent of the reader's decision criterion—in this context, the reader's tendency to "underread" or "overread."

However, for medical application one usually wants to go beyond the accuracy afforded by an imaging modality to an assessment of its usefulness, including an evaluation of its medical efficacy, risks, and cost-effectiveness. Here, one can use the ROC to determine the probabilities of decision outcomes (true and false positives and negatives) at the "optimal" point on the ROC, as determined by the probabilities, values, and costs of the particular diagnostic–therapeutic situation. That is to say, the evaluator can follow diagnostic decisions through a decision flow diagram to their medical outcomes. The first choice point in the diagram can have (as best he can tell) *appropriate* probabilities attached to it, not just the probabilities he happened to obtain from his test readers. (If the new imaging system proves to be sufficiently useful to continue in practice, readers can presumably be induced to adjust their decision criteria to approximate the optimum.)

At present, the National Cancer Institute is supporting at Bolt Beranek and Newman, Inc., the development of a standard protocol for the evaluation of medical diagnostic techniques, with special reference to imaging techniques in cancer diagnosis, that is based largely on the ROC analysis. The protocol is being applied first to the evaluation of computed tomography versus radionuclide brain scans and the more invasive radiographic techniques (angiograms, pneumoencephalograms), based on data collected at five medical centers, and to Xeromammography versus regular and low-dose film mammography, based on data collected at three medical centers. The intention is to evaluate the diagnostic accuracy of the various techniques relative to their medical efficacy, hazard, and financial cost.

A way in which the ROC analysis facilitates interpretation of results on imaging-system accuracy and associated decision strategies is illustrated by Lusted's (1968) reanalysis of the two classical studies of radiological performance (Garland, 1949; Yerushalmy, Harkness, Cope, and Kennedy, 1950). One study examined the accuracy of a team of two readers and counted either positive responses from both readers or a positive response from one reader as a positive team response. The other study examined the effect of repeated readings by a single reader—first with a conservative, then with a liberal, criterion for a positive response. Both variations, of course, led to movement in the ROC space, though the data from the two studies do not overlap in that space. Analysis in terms of the probability of a correct decision (of both kinds), a metric still frequently used, led to values ranging from the 0.70s to the 0.90s, suggesting different degrees of discrimination. The ROC analysis, on the other hand, showed that all the data fell along one curve, representing a single discrimination capacity but differences in decision criteria.

Straightforward applications of ROC analyses have been made to remote viewing of images. Television degrades chest X-ray films somewhat but appears worthy of further investigation (Kundel, 1972; Andrus, Dreyfuss, Jaffer, and Bird, 1975). Picturephones seem not to detract from radionuclide scans (Anderson, Mintzer, Hoffer, Lusted, Smith, and Pokorny, 1973). Also, ROC analysis has been applied to training of paramedics to read film—training programs for nonprofessionals enabled them to reach the professionals' level of performance for mammography (Alcorn and O'Donnell, 1969) and chest X-rays (Sheft, Jones, Brown, and Ross, 1970).

One testimony to the value of the ROC in roentgenology appeared recently as an editorial in a medical journal. The authors begin by pointing out that the ROC enables comparison of the accuracy of inter- and intraobserver readings. They say: "The former variation is widely known but personally suppressed. The latter is virtually denied and seldom studied (especially by radiologists)." They conclude: "Receiver operating characteristic curves offer: (1) an excellent way to help us all face the issue of variations in roentgenographic interpretations . . . ; (2) a stimulating technique to practice self-assessment; (3) an objective method to quantitate the learning rate of the resident in radiology; and (4) a striking approach to the establishment of diagnostic criteria in roentgenographic disease" (Andrus and Bird, 1975, pp. 378, 379).

The medical application of SDT has instigated several extensions of the theory by members of the Center for Radiologic Image Research at the University of Chicago. One extension deals with the case where more than one signal may be present, allowing prediction of human performance in a multiple signal detection task from the ROC curve obtained in a simple detection task (Metz, Starr, Lusted, and Rossmann, 1975). Another extension deals with the evaluation of combinations of diagnostic tests and derives optimal decision criteria for successive tests in "screening" and "follow-up" (Metz et al., 1975). A third extension of SDT relates an ROC representing correct localization as well as correct detection to the simple detection ROC (Starr et al., 1975).

This third development is an exciting one because it provides the first substantial results in the attempts over two decades to relate not only localization but, more generally, "recognition," or "classification"—the selection of one alternative from a set of many—to the two-alternative detection task. This new ability to treat multiple alternatives seems destined to have important implications in several applications and in the basic areas of psychology as well.

The final application in the medical context to be mentioned here is an evaluation of the systems for delivering emergency medical services at two large hospitals, primarily of the systems' response to ambulance need. It was found that the system's accurate discrimination of ambulance need was high with young and old patients but lower with 20- to 64-year-olds. The decision criterion, on the other hand, was relatively lenient for young patients and strict for old patients. The decision criterion was also related to category of insurer, with Medicare patients showing an even lower ambulance utilization than the uninsured, and appreciably lower than patients covered by other insurers. According to the authors, SDT allowed a "peek inside" the decision process of emergency medical services, relative to its degree of difficulty and its inherent value structure (Drury, Barnes, and Rakower, 1976).

INFORMATION RETRIEVAL

Conventional systems retrieve documents from their shelves, and facts from their documents. Budding computer systems retrieve messages according to descriptors and give answers to questions. We must know, at least in considering alternative systems, how effectively these systems separate the desired or relevant items from the chaff.

The appeal of one or another of the discrimination measures drawn from the ROC as an index of retrieval performance stems from four properties of such a measure: (1) It is a measure of "effectiveness" only, leaving for separate consideration factors related to cost or "efficiency"; (2) it is not confounded by the relative willingness of the system to emit items, whether the "acceptance criterion" is characteristic of the system or adjusted by the user; (3) it is a single number—rather than, for example, a pair of numbers that covary in a loosely specified way, or an empirical curve representing several pairs of numbers; (4) its metric is a scale with a unit, a true zero, and (practically) a maximum value. Other measures proposed, as far as we know, including 10 reviewed elsewhere (Swets, 1963), possess no more than two of the four properties, usually the first two or the last two.

The validity of the SDT model for the retrieval task was initially tested against three large sets of experimental data: (1) data generated by Cyril Cleverdon and Michael Keen at the Association of Special Libraries and Information Bureaux in Cranfield, England; (2) data generated by Gerald Salton and Michael Lesk at Harvard and Cornell Universities; and (3) data obtained by Vincent Giuliano and Paul Jones at Arthur D. Little, Inc., in Cambridge, Massachusetts. In the first case, document analysis was manual, and variables examined included type of index language, specificity of index terms, and amount of intelligence applied in formulation of search rules. In the second case, document analysis was fully automatic, and variables examined included the parts of documents used in analysis, vocabulary normalization by thesaurus or statistical word

association, hierarchical or syntactical relations between subject iden-
tifiers, and degree of user control of search. In the third instance, document analysis was both manual and automatic, and variables examined
included length of query, coordinate methods, statistical word association, and human intervention.

The SDT model passed these tests very well. Some 80 empirical
ROCs, with an average of about 10 points each, were exceptionally well
fitted by theoretical curves (Swets, 1969).

Together, these results give a clear appraisal of the state of the
retrieval art, at least in the 1960s and probably today, and indicate that
the information retrieval problem is difficult indeed. None of the 82
empirical ROCs exceeded a d'_e of 2.5 (ranging as low as 1.0) or, equiv-
alently, an $A = 0.96$ (ranging as low as 0.74). (These indices are measures
of sensitivity. The first index, d'_e, is the normal–deviate measure taken at
the negative diagonal of the ROC, and the second index, A, is the
proportion of area beneath the curve, which equals the probability of a
correct choice among two alternatives.) To appreciate these numbers
more fully, consider a file of 3,000 items. For each of a given set of
queries, assume that 10 items are relevant. Then, to retrieve 3 of the 10
items, one must accept, on the average, 3 false drops as well. To retrieve 6
of the 10 relevant, 30 false drops will occur, and to retrieve 9 of 10
relevant, 300 false drops will occur. In short, a user desiring reasonably
high hit rates will have to do considerable winnowing of the items he
receives.

Other articles examining the application of SDT to the problem of
information retrieval include those by Bookstein (1974), Brookes (1968),
Cooper (1974a,b), Farradane (1974), Heine (1973, 1974, 1975), Kraft
(1973), and Robertson (1969).

OTHER APPLICATIONS

The preceding sections have described fairly extensive applications
of SDT in three areas. The theory has also been applied less extensively to
a number of other topics. These other areas deserve mention, however
brief, simply to illustrate the range of present and potential application.

DRIVING, ROAD SIGNS, AND TRAFFIC INJURIES. Automobile drivers
often select one mode of response over another. Cohen and Ferrell (1969)
presented tasks in which the subject had to guide an object, traveling at a
fixed speed, between two obstacles. In one case the operator controlled
the deflection of a recorder pen; in the other, the operator drove a car
between two objects. ROC curves obtained for these tasks showed decision behavior to be influenced by a priori probabilities and utilities in a
way that one would expect.

The ROC analysis enabled separation of the effects of the operator's prediction ability, the operator's skill, and the factors of value and cost. This analysis also provided a test of the validity of the simulation of the real driving task. In general, if the same ROC is obtained in real and simulated environments, the simulator subjects need not be induced to act as if real-world utilities applied, because the range of operating points can be determined. More extensive work on driver behavior in this theoretical context was recently reported by Allen, Schwartz, and Jex (1976). Earlier experiments include those of Chinnis (1972) and Newsome (1974).

A second area of application related to automobile transportation is the evaluation of traffic signs or markers. Drivers must acquire information quickly from these signals, under conditions of uncertainty, so SDT can be used in evaluating the best signal design. ROC curves have been obtained from observers in simple tasks requiring the action called for by the sign. Curved versus flat stop signs, for example, were investigated in one study at various angles of regard. The proportion of area under the ROC curve was approximately 0.78 for the flat road sign and about 0.94 for the curved road sign. Thus, the curved road sign would achieve more appropriate responses, independent of the prevailing tendency to stop or not stop at the sign (Ladan, Heron, and Nelson, 1974). Extensive use of ROC analysis for road sign evaluation was also made by Markowitz, Dietrich, Lees, and Farman (1968) and by Dietrich and Markowitz (1972).

A third, potentially important, area of application under this heading is the study of traffic injuries. A central problem here is the lack of a well-accepted scale for "degree of injury." Although fatality is one well-defined result of a traffic accident, the border between slight and serious injury can be defined in many and diverse ways. The fact that fatality is a well-defined category is of little assistance, since one hopes that category will have very few occurrences, and whatever policy is adopted should attempt to make those occurrences even fewer. For the same reason, one does not want to wait a long time so that many fatalities will occur before initiating some change; rather, one would hope to make use of data when more prevalent but less serious accidents can be used to dictate policy. So one problem is to extrapolate from less serious accidents, however defined, to an estimate of the percentage of fatalities. Of course, some estimate of the fatality percentage must be made to yield any realistic policy analysis, for fatalities have much more weight than even fairly serious accidents in a cost-benefit analysis.

An interesting approach to this problem has been made by T. P. Hutchinson of the Traffic Studies Group of University College, London (Hutchinson, 1974). The central theme of Hutchinson's analysis is what he calls a Relative Injury Frequency (RIF) curve, patterned after an ROC curve, which shows numbers of "serious injuries" as a function of numbers of fatalities, as the definition of "serious" is made more strict or more lax. Points on the curve are obtained by considering accident statistics under different conditions such as time of day or weight of vehicle, for which the percentage of fatalities and percentage of serious injuries tend to covary. Suggested applications include (1) describing the effectiveness of some device that reduces injury, irrespective of different definitions of injury terms; (2) predicting the effectiveness of an injury-reduction measure in one locale from a knowledge of its effect, under different conditions or definitions, elsewhere; (3) compensating for initial level of injury severity when comparing the effectiveness of injury reduction in two circumstances (say, of seat belts in large and small cars); as well as (4) estimating the reduction in fatalities from a small sample in which only serious and slight injuries can be accurately estimated.

PRODUCT EVALUATION. Evaluation of different products is often complicated by the substantial response biases of the judges. Often the mere fact that one has had extensive experience with a given product leads one to feel natural with that product and prefer it to any alternatives. Also, this experience may make discrimination among alternative products difficult. Again, a judge's assignment of an adjective to one product is meaningful only in the context of how often that judge uses that adjective for other products. Panels differing in some respect, say in training, may differ widely in the stringency of the criterion for judging a product to have a given degree of an attribute, but differ little in discerning two degrees of that attribute.

One area in which response biases are particularly acute is in preferences for food. In some circumstances it is very important to distinguish and preserve whatever differences among products are discriminable and real from the tendencies to lump together as unpalatable those products that differ from one's own preferences. A study of Angus and Daniel (1974) on the richness of ice cream is one example of this approach.

Although application in this area is just developing, we anticipate a considerable increase in the use of ROC analysis in the fields of taste and smell preferences. Moreover, food scientists have recently extended their concern beyond "flavor" to include visual, tactile, thermal, and auditory correlates (Pangborn, 1969). The results of better measures of these attributes are expected to be useful in food science and in the development of standards of quality.

FORENSIC SITUATIONS. Three potential applications of SDT to forensic situations deserve mention. One is eye-witness testimony—the witness of a lineup may correctly identify the person or make an incorrect (false-positive) identification. The witness's willingness to decide in one way or the other depends strongly on a host of variables besides his perception and memory of the crime. In a recent article in a popular magazine many of these factors are summarized. "We are using the ROC function to test various hypotheses about how environmental conditions, stress, mental set, bias in interrogation, age, sex, and social, ethnic and economic group affect the accuracy and reliability of eyewitnesses" (Buckhout, 1974, p. 31).

Spectrographic analyses of speech recordings—commonly called voiceprints—are sometimes used in an attempt to identify the unknown speaker. The problem shares many similarities with the problem of eye-witness identification. Often the investigator is asked to pick one suspect from a set of many, as in the "lineup" identification. There is some hope that the relation between recognition and detection, as studied in radiology and discussed earlier, might be helpful in understanding and evaluating both this new means of identification and that of eye-witness testimony.

The final application of SDT mentioned here is to the detection of "guilty knowledge" through physiological means, by measurement of the galvanic skin response. The guilty-knowledge technique (see chapter by Lykken, this volume) was designed to avoid the problematic concept of "lying," and, in fact, the subject sits quietly throughout a session without responding. As in conventional lie detection, a series of questions (or items) is read, including some with neutral content and others for which relevant knowledge is incriminating. As pointed out by Shakhar, Lieblich, and Kugelmass (1970), the appropriate decision criterion for the inference of guilt will vary from one situation to another, and SDT can be used to calculate the various criteria. Until such procedures become almost infallible, errors will occur and it is important to understand the cost associated with these errors. Security screening and criminal cases are but one pair of examples where very different decision criteria may be appropriate. Once more, SDT can help evaluate the fallibility of the lie-detection process and determine where appropriate decision criteria should be set.

Summary

In the quarter century since the development of modern signal detection theory, several hundred papers have been published on the topic in the field of psychology. These papers have led to many applications outside of psychology, even more diverse than we have indicated —including, for example, the baseball batter's decision to swing or not (Newell, 1974). In some areas—human monitoring, medical diagnosis, and information retrieval—the applications have been substantial. In other areas—transportation, product evaluation, and forensics—we see more potential than achievement. It seems likely that in still other areas where people, people and machines in combination, or machines alone face decisions based on uncertain information, signal detection theory will aid the analysis and evaluation of these tasks.

REFERENCES

Adams, S. K. Decision making in quality control: Some perceptual and behavioral considerations. In C. G. Drury and J. G. Fox (Eds.), *Human reliability in quality control.* New York: Halsted Press, 1975. Pp. 55–69.

Alcorn, F. A., and O'Donnell, E. The training of nonphysician personnel for use in a mammography program. *Cancer,* 1969, *23,* 879–884.

Allen, R. W., Schwartz, S. H., and Jex, H. R. Driver decision-making research in a laboratory simulation. Presented at NATO Conference on "Monitoring Behavior and Supervisory Control," Berchtesgaden, (F.R.) Germany, March 8–12, 1976. Preprints pp. 49–59.

Anderson, T. M., Mintzer, R. A., Hoffer, P. B., Lusted, L. B., Smith, V. C., and Pokorny, J. Nuclear image transmission by Picturephone. *Investigative Radiology,* 1973, *8* (4), 244–250.

Andrus, W. S., and Bird, K. T. Radiology and the receiver operating characteristic (ROC) curve. *Chest,* 1975, *67* (4), 378–379.

Andrus, W. S., Dreyfuss, J. R., Jaffer, F., and Bird, K. T. Interpretation of roentgenograms via interactive television. *Radiology,* 1975, *116,* 25–31.

Angus, R. C., and Daniel, T. C. Applying theory of signal detection in marketing: Product development and evaluation. *American Journal of Agricultural Economics,* 1974, *56,* 573–577.

Bookstein, A. The anomalous behavior of precision in the Swets model, and its resolution. *Journal of Documentation,* 1974, *30,* 118–122.

Broadbent, D. E. *Decision and stress.* New York: Academic Press, 1971.

Brookes, B. C. The measures of information retrieval effectiveness proposed by Swets. *Journal of Documentation,* 1968, *24*(1), 41–54.

Buck, J. R. Dynamic visual inspection: Task factors, theory and economics. In C. G. Drury and J. G. Fox (Eds.), *Human reliability in quality control.* New York: Halsted Press, 1975. Pp. 165–186.

Buckhout, R. Eyewitness testimony. *Scientific American,* 1974, *231*(6), 23–31.

Chinnis, J. O. An application of the theory of signal detectability to drivers' passing decisions in a simulated task. (Doctoral dissertation, University of Michigan, 1972). *Dissertation Abstracts International,* Series B, 1973, *33,* 4535–4536.

Cohen, H. S., and Ferrell, W. R. Human operator decision-making in manual control. *Institute of Electrical and Electronics Engineers, Transactions on Man-Machine Systems,* 1969, *10* (2), 41–47.

Cooper, W. S. On selecting a measure of retrieval effectiveness: Part I. The "subjective" philosophy of evaluation. *Journal of the American Society for Information Science,* 1974a, *March–April,* 87–100.

Cooper, W. S. On selecting a measure of retrieval effectiveness: Part II. Implementation of the philosophy. *Journal of the American Society for Information Science,* 1974b, *November–December,* 413–424.

Dietrich, C. W., and Markowitz, J. Investigation of new traffic signs, markings, and

signals. Vol. I, Laboratory Experiments and Road Tests. Report #1762 prepared by Bolt
Beranek and Newman, Inc. for the Federal Highway Administration, United States
Department of Transportation, Washington, D.C., 1972.

Drury, C. G. The effect of speed of working on industrial inspection accuracy. *Applied
Ergonomics*, 1973, 4(1), 2–7.

Drury, C. G., and Fox, J. G. (Eds.). *Human reliability in quality control*. New York: Halsted
Press, 1975a.

Drury, C. G., and Fox, J. G. Models of inspector performance: Conclusions. In C. G. Drury
and G. J. Fox (Eds.), *Human reliability in quality control*. New York: Halsted Press,
1975b. Pp. 97–98.

Drury, C. G., and Fox, J. G. The imperfect inspector. In C. G. Drury and J. G. Fox (Eds.),
Human reliability in quality control. New York: Halsted Press, 1975c. Pp. 11–15.

Drury, C. G., Barnes, R. E., and Rakower, S. A. *A decision-making perspective for system
response to ambulance need*. Unpublished paper, 1976.

Egan, J. P. *Signal detection theory and ROC analysis*. New York: Academic Press, 1975.

Farradane, J. The evaluation of information retrieval systems. *Journal of Documentation*,
1974, 30 (2), 195–209.

Frankman, J. P., and Adams, J. A. Theories of vigilance. *Psychological Bulletin*, 1962, 59,
257–272.

Garland, L. H. Scientific evaluation of diagnostic procedures. *Radiology*, 1949, 52, 309–327.

Green, D. M., and Swets, J. A. *Signal detection theory and psychophysics*. New York: Wiley,
1966; Huntington, New York: Robert E. Krieger, 1974.

Heine, M. H. The inverse relationship of precision and recall in terms of the Swets model.
Journal of Documentation, 1973, 29, 81–84.

Heine, M. H. Design equations for retrieval systems based on the Swets model. *Journal of
the American Society for Information Science*, 1974, May–June, 183–198.

Heine, M. H. Measures of language effectiveness and the Swetsian hypotheses. *Journal of
Documentation*, 1975, 31 (4), 283–287.

Hutchinson, T. P. A new theoretical framework for assessing injury reduction. London:
Traffic Studies Group, University College. 1974.

Kraft, D. H. A decision theory view of the information retrieval situation: An operations
research approach. *Journal of the American Society for Information Science*, 1973, September–October, 368–376.

Kundel, H. L. Factors limiting roentgen interpretation—physical and psychologic. In E. J.
Potchen (Ed.), *Current concepts in radiology*. St. Louis: C. V. Mosby, 1972.

Ladan, C. J., Heron, R. M., and Nelson, T. M. A signal-detection evaluation of flat vs.
curved marker performance. *Perceptual and Motor Skills*, 1974, 39, 355–358.

Lusted, L. B. *Introduction to medical decision making*. Springfield, Illinois: Charles C
Thomas, 1968.

Mackworth, J. F. *Vigilance and attention: A signal detection approach*. Middlesex, England,
and Baltimore, Maryland: Penguin, 1970.

Markowitz, J., Dietrich, C. W., Lees, W. J., and Farman, M. An investigation of the design
and performance of traffic control devices. Report #1726 prepared by Bolt Beranek and
Newman, Inc. for the Federal Highway Administration, United States Department of
Transportation, Washington, D.C., 1968.

McNicol, D. *A primer of signal detection theory*. London: George Allen & Unwin, 1972.

McNeil, B. J., Varady, P. D., Burrows, B. A., and Adelstein, S. J. Measures of clinical
efficacy: Cost effectiveness calculations in the diagnosis and treatment of hypertensive
renovascular disease. *New England Journal of Medicine*, 1975, 293(5), 216–221.

Metz, C. E., Starr, S. J., Lusted, L. B., and Rossmann, K. Progress in evaluation of human
observer visual detection performance using the ROC curve approach. In C. Raynaud

and A. Todd-Pokropek (Eds.), *Information processing in scintigraphy*. Orsay, France: Commissariat à l'Energie Atomique, Departement de Biologie, Service Hospitalier Frederic Joliot, 1975. P. 420.

Moray, N. Attention, control, and sampling behavior. Presented at NATO Conference on "Monitoring Behavior and Supervisory Control," Berchtesgaden, (F.R.) Germany, March 8–12, 1976. Preprints pp. 160–182.

Newell, K. M. Decision processes of baseball batters. *Human Factors*, 1974, *16*(5), 520–527.

Newsome, L. R. Risk taking as a decision process in driving. Supplementary Report 81 #UC, Transport and Road Research Laboratory, Crowthorne, England, 1974.

Neyman, J., and Pearson, E. S. On the problem of the most efficient tests of statistical hypotheses. *Philosophical Transactions of the Royal Society of London*, 1933, Series A, 289.

Norman, D. A., and Bobrow, D. G. On the analysis of performance operating characteristics. *Psychological Review*, 1976, *83*(6), 508–510.

Pangborn, R. M. Factors influencing responses to chemical and physical stimuli. In B. Drake (Ed.), *Proceedings of the International Symposium on Sensory Evaluation of Food: Principles and Methods, Kungälv, Sweden, September 9–13, 1968*. Göteborg: A. Rydberg, 1969. Pp. 34–35.

Parasuraman, R., and Davies, D. R. A taxonomic analysis of vigilance performance. In R. R. Mackie (Ed.), *Vigilance: Theory, Operational Performance, and Physiological Correlates*. New York: Plenum, 1977.

Peterson, W. W., and Birdsall, T. G. The theory of signal detectability. University of Michigan: Electronic Defense Group, Technical Report No. 13, 1953.

Robertson, S. E. A statistical analysis of retrieval tests: A Bayesian approach. *Journal of Documentation*, 1969, *30*(3), 273–282.

Shakhar, G. B., Lieblich, I., and Kugelmass, S. Guilty knowledge technique: Application of signal detection measures. *Journal of Applied Psychology*, 1970, *54*(5), 409–413.

Sheehan, J. J., and Drury, C. G. The analysis of industrial inspection. *Applied Ergonomics*, 1971, *2*, 74–78.

Sheft, D. J., Jones, M. D., Brown, R. F., and Ross, S. E. Screening of chest roentgenograms by advanced roentgen technologists. *Radiology*, 1970, *94*, 427–429.

Sheridan, T. On how often the supervisor should sample. *Institute of Electrical and Electronic Engineers, Transactions on System Science and Cybernetics*, 1970, 140–145.

Sperling, G. *Attention operating characteristics for visual search*. Presented at Ninth Annual Mathematical Psychology Meetings, New York University, September 1976.

Starr, S. J., Metz, C. E., Lusted, L. B., and Goodenough, D. J. Visual detection and localization of radiographic images. *Radiology*, 1975, *116*, 533–538.

Swets, J. A. Information-retrieval systems. *Science*, 1963, *141*, 245–250.

Swets, J. A. Effectiveness of information retrieval methods. *American Documentation*, 1969, *20*, 72–89.

Swets, J. A. The relative operating characteristic in psychology. *Science*, 1973, *182*, 990–1000.

Swets, J. A. Human monitoring behavior in a command/control/communication system. Prepared as a section in a report from Bolt Beranek and Newman, Inc. to the Advanced Research Projects Agency, U.S. Department of Defense, October, 1976a.

Swets, J. A. Signal detection theory applied to the evaluation of imaging techniques in clinical medicine. In H.-G. Geissler and Yu. M. Zabrodin (Eds.), *Advances in Psychophysics*. Berlin: VEB Deutscher Verlag der Wissenschaften, 1976b. Pp. 427–448.

Swets, J. A. Signal detection theory applied to vigilance. In R. R. Mackie (Ed.), *Vigilance: Theory, Operational Performance, and Physiological Correlates*. New York: Plenum, 1977.

Swets, J. A., and Kristofferson, A. B. Attention. *Annual Review of Psychology*, 1970, *21*, 339–366.

Tanner, W. P., Jr., and Swets, J. A. A decision-making theory of visual detection. *Psychological Review*, 1954, *61*, 401–409.

Thurstone, L. L. A law of comparative judgment. *Psychological Review*, 1927, *34*, 273–286.

Van Meter, D., and Middleton, D. Modern statistical approaches to reception in communication theory. *Transactions of the Institute of Radio Engineers, Professional Group on Information Theory*, 1954, *4*, 119–141.

Wald, A. *Statistical decision functions*. New York: Wiley, 1950.

Wallack, P. M., and Adams, S. K. The utility of signal-detection theory in the analysis of industrial inspector accuracy. *American Institute of Industrial Engineers Transactions*, 1969, *1*, 33–44.

Welford, A. T. *Fundamentals of skill*. London: Methuen, 1968.

Wickens, C. D. The effects of divided attention on information processing in manual tracking. *Journal of Experimental Psychology*, 1976, *2*(1), 1–13.

Wickens, C. D., and Gopher, D. *Strategies and attention allocation in dual task performance*. Presented at Psychonomic Society Meeting, Denver, Colorado, 1975.

Yerushalmy, J., Harkness, J. T., Cope, J. H., and Kennedy, B. R. Role of dual reading in mass radiography. *American Review of Tuberculosis*, 1950, *61*, 443–464.

Young, L. On adaptive manual control. *Institute of Electrical and Electronics Engineers, Transactions on Man-Machine Systems*, 1969, *10*, 292–332.

Subjective Effort in Relation to Physical Performance and Working Capacity

GUNNAR BORG

"Two things make my heart beat faster: walking upstairs and watching pretty girls."

This confession makes an important point, namely, that an increase of the heart rate, which is the most important and simplest physiological effort variable, can mean different things. The increase may mean that the individual has been doing some heavy work, but not necessarily so, since the heart rate is sensitive to emotional stimulation as well. If, instead, perception of effort and fatigue is used to distinguish the two situations, the difference is obvious. Perception of these feelings is high for walking upstairs but indeed not for watching pretty girls.

The many experiments on work and effort carried out during the last decade have had the rather surprising result that the subjective perception of effort or exertion is sometimes a better indicator of the degree of physical strain than is the objective heart rate. Our ability to use perceptual cues to estimate the intensity of physical strain is astonishingly good. Indeed, we may speak of a separate perceptual modality composed of the sensations of effort.

The human body is built for physical and not only for mental work. This rather trivial truth is often ignored because the main demands in industrialized societies of today are mental. We are overwhelmed by sensory stimuli and we must carefully select and heed the ones most

GUNNAR BORG • Institute of Applied Psychology, University of Stockholm, Stockholm, Sweden.

relevant for performance. We must often do so in the midst of stress, as, for example, when driving in heavy traffic. We are called upon to learn and to remember more and more as the stream of information becomes greater and greater. We are forced to solve difficult problems and to make crucial decisions, frequently without having the necessary information. If we commit errors, the consequences may sometimes be drastic, not only for ourselves but also for others.

As the mental load becomes higher and higher, we strain ourselves to the utmost. The heart rate increases, the blood pressure rises, and the general state of arousal is heightened. Since we share the physiology of our ancestors of several thousand years ago, we react to stress in a Stone Age manner by straining our muscles for fight or flight. This state of arousal is quite suitable for simple muscular performances like running, but not for solving mental problems or for making sound decisions.

The ability to perceive muscular effort and fatigue correctly must have been of great importance thousands of years ago. To survive in and adapt to a hostile environment, man had to be able to mobilize his physical energy at a moment's notice and use it efficiently. It was of vital importance to know one's resources and to be alert to the continuous information about effort and fatigue in order to moderate the perfor-mance to exactly the right intensity level. Wasting too much energy on a minor problem or exerting too little energy for a major one could mean disaster. A current example of man's ability to use his perception of effort and fatigue to regulate his muscular performance is the long distance runner, who knows well how to pace himself for a maximal achievement.

In modern society those of us who do not aspire to such achieve-ments as those of the long distance runner may find ourselves in poor physical condition; first of all, we have been relieved of much of the hard physical exertion on the job and at home which was the lot of our grandparents. Moreover, the industrialization that has decreased the demand for physical work has also created a surplus of food for large affluent societies. We have paid for these changes not only by a decline of physical fitness but also by an increase in certain diseases, such as circulatory diseases and psychological stress symptoms. Since the hu-man body is built for physical exertion, poor physical fitness leads to feelings of effort, discomfort, and fatigue, even performing such ordi-nary tasks as carrying suitcases or walking up the stairs.

BACKGROUND TO OUR STUDIES ON WORK AND PERCEPTION OF EFFORT

The studies described in this chapter have purported to shed light upon psychological aspects of physical work, such as the relation between perceived effort and physical performance and the dependence of this relation on working capacity. The very first question, whether it was even possible to measure perceived exertion during heavy work, has evolved into the more difficult and sophisticated question of whether comparisons can be made between different individuals' subjective experiences. Ultimately, we have pursued the question of whether it would be possible to discriminate among different kinds of subjective symptoms and thereby obtain quantitative, reliable measurements for diagnostic purposes or for predictions of maximal working capacity.

On one hand, the program entails basic methodological and theoretical work concerning how human beings act in their complicated role as a "working machine" against the backdrop of their capacities for thinking and feeling; on the other hand, the program consists of applied research and development studies within the areas of ergonomics, clinical and diagnostic practice, sports, and preventive health. Problems concerning effort and exertion are treated from three different angles, corresponding to the three effort continua: the perceptual, the performance, and the physiological. The program is of necessity interdisciplinary, rooted mainly in psychology but also embracing physiology and medicine.

The decision to devote ourselves to this field of research was spurred by several circumstances. One of these was a clinical observation pertaining to persons engaged in heavy manual labor; namely, the individual's own evaluation of his working capacity did not agree very well with that made by his doctor. A 50-year-old lumberjack might complain that his working capacity had gone down by at least 50%, while a clinical examination involving ergometer tests might point to a decrease of only 25%. This lack of correspondence disturbed the communication between the doctor and his patient, the latter sometimes being suspected of imitating a decreased working capacity in order to gain insurance or retirement benefits. Closer investigation seldom revealed any serious deception but rather indicated that the patient was making a sincere effort to rate himself. The idea was then put forth that the subject's judgment might be "distorted" in a primitive, sensory way due to a general "error" in the perceptual process. The result would be that the relation between the subjective change and the objective change would not remain constant. Since the individual's judgment of his working capacity during a work test must be based to a great extent upon cues related to how heavy he experiences his daily physical work to be, we started to study how perception of effort and exertion varies with physical work load.

Another factor that led us to launch this research program was an article in a daily newspaper about the relation between perceived reward and perceived effort, published by the Swedish professor of psychology, Gösta Ekman. Ekman had introduced psychophysical methods in Sweden and had made many important contributions to them (Ekman, 1958, 1959, 1961). In his article, Ekman discussed the different relations between objective economic reward and objective measurements of work. He considered the relations between, on the one hand, the subjective reward (subjective value or perceived economic utility) and the physical reward and, on the other hand, the subjective effort and the physical performance. He found that if a person must expend a lot of effort to increase his performance, he will perceive the increase in the subjective reward as being disproportionately small to the effort. Ekman's article was fascinating and his reasoning elegant. However, at that time the accumulated knowledge did not permit conclusions as to what kind of function could best describe the relation between subjective effort and objective performance. The idea of searching for such a function intrigued us.

BACKGROUND OF PSYCHOPHYSICAL RESEARCH

In the 1950s the new psychophysics gained more and more momentum thanks to S. S. Stevens and his collaborators at Harvard (Stevens, 1953, 1957, 1966). Psychophysical questions such as how subjective, or perceived, intensity (e.g., "perceived" radio volume) grows with objective, or physical, intensity (e.g., radio volume measured in dB) could be studied for the first time with methods classified as *ratio-scaling methods*. Such methods yield measurements on a ratio scale with a zero point and equidistant scale values, such as length and weight scales. A fascinating field was thus opened due to the possibility of measuring the intensity of a perception. Previously, it had only been possible to place differences in perceptual intensities in rank order, i.e., to say, "This radio volume is greater than that one." Now intensities could be assessed quantitatively, and one could say, "This volume is approximately three times as intensive as that one." Mathematical functions were then presented which showed the perceived intensity variation to be analogous to mathematical descriptions of physiological responses. Stevens found that a power or "exponential" function could best describe the psychophysical relation in most sensory modalities. In its simplest form the function was written:

$$R = c \times S^n$$

where R is the intensity of the perception, c a measure constant, S the physical intensity, and n the exponent.

In the late 1950s the new psychophysical methods were applied to problems of subjective effort and exertion during physical work. The first concerned whether or not it would be possible and, if so, meaningful to assess perception of effort quantitatively and to describe its variation mathematically. Borg and Dahlström (1959, 1960) showed that such measurements could in fact be made. They found that subjective effort grew according to a "positively accelerated" function, as did perceived speed in driving a car. That is, at a high speed, a small increase in speed is perceived as greater than the same increase at a low speed. Similarly, at a strenuous work level, a small increase in physical performance is perceived as requiring a larger subjective effort than the same increase at an easy work level.

In the 1960s the psychophysical methods met some criticism. For example, they were found to fall short of being absolutely true ratio-scaling methods. Nevertheless, they proved to suffice for rough descriptions and for comparisons between sensory modalities. Physiological validations attested to the method's value, e.g., subjective taste intensities showed a very high correlation with neural responses from the taste nerve (Borg, Diamant, Ström, and Zotterman, 1967).

Perception of Effort During Work of Short Duration

In the ratio-setting method known as halving, the subject must first perceive a standard intensity for a certain amount of time, e.g., half a minute, after which he must set a variable intensity that he perceives to be half as strong as the standard intensity. While this is very simple and, in many modalities, convenient, it is fettered with some errors. "Time order errors" and "adaptation effects" are but two examples; in these cases halvings often have to be complemented by doublings. These and other difficulties notwithstanding, the method has worked well with many perceptual continua and has given results comparable to those yielded by other methods. The method has proven to function very well in experiments on perception of effort involving work of short duration (less than 1 min) on the bicycle ergometer (Borg and Dahlström, 1959, 1960). Reliable results have been obtained and a psychophysical power function has proven suitable for describing the intensity variation.

An example from an experiment on the perception of speed while driving a car will elucidate how this psychophysical method of halving works. This experiment was performed by the author at about the same time as the first studies on perceived effort during heavy muscular activity. The subjects had to perceive a certain standard speed, e.g., 50 mph for about 20 sec, when driving an ordinary car on a straight, flat road. The speed was then slowly reduced until the subjects perceived it

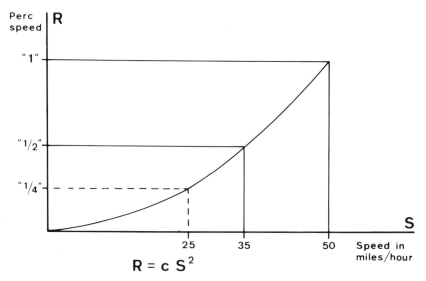

Figure 1. Variation of perception of speed when driving a car.

to be half the standard speed. This procedure was repeated using several different standard speeds. The experiment revealed that the half value set by the subject is consistently much higher than the physical half; e.g., the perceived "half value" of 50 mph will correspond to about 35 mph, and the physical half of 25 mph will correspond to about one-fourth of the perceived speed at 50 mph. In short, the subjective or perceived speed grows by about the square of the physical speed (see Figure 1).

The results of the experiment on perceived effort during work on the bicycle ergometer yielded a psychophysical function of the same kind as shown in Figure 1 for perceived speed. The exponent was slightly smaller than that for perceived speed but still above 1, meaning that the function is positively accelerated. The following equation describes the function:

$$R = a + c \times S^n$$

where R is the intensity of the perception, a is a small perceptual "noise" constant, indicating a slight subjective intensity when no actual work is being performed, c is the measure constant, S is the physical intensity in watts, and n is the exponent, which in this case is equal to 1.6.

Later experiments on perception of effort on the bicycle ergometer using other psychophysical methods have also yielded an exponent of about 1.6 (Borg, 1962; Borg, Edgren, and Marklund, 1970). Experiments on subjective force of handgrip while squeezing a dynamometer and experiments on subjective foot pressure have revealed psychophysical functions with exponents of 1.7 (Stevens and Mach, 1959) and 1.6 (Eisler, 1962), respectively. Many other experiments on other muscular activities have shown an exponent of about the same size (see review by Stevens, 1972).

In experiments on subjective heaviness in weight lifting, exponents of about 1.45 have been obtained (Stevens and Galanter, 1957). When estimating the heaviness of different objects, one must learn to correct for this information error. Otherwise, one can easily be fooled, e.g., when comparing produce by the feeling of weight in a grocery store.

GENERAL STUDIES OF WORK OF LONGER DURATION

Hard work lasting for more than several minutes and involving large muscle groups places a great strain upon the cardiovascular system. The demands on the individual are then different from those made upon him during short-time work, in which case his perception of effort, to a high degree, is related to peripheral sensations in the muscles and joints. During work of longer duration in an experimental or clinical context, the individual usually advances to a heavier and heavier workload, spending some minutes on each. This routine allows the circulatory system to attain steady-state. Work of longer duration gives rise to many stress responses and symptoms of diagnostic value and renders possible the determination of aerobic work capacity, i.e., capacity to do heavy work lasting several minutes. The variation of perceived exertion during such work has been studied in several experiments using different psychophysical methods. All experiments have given positively accelerated functions with exponents around 1.6 (Borg, 1961, 1962).

The most general function for describing the results of experiments on work and effort, and, for that matter, many biological experiments, should include two more constants than expressed in the simple power law:

$$R = a + c(S-b)^n$$

where R is the intensity of the response, S is the physical intensity, a is the basic perceptual "noise" constant, which, together with a physical constant b, describes the starting point of the curve, and n is the exponent that describes the shape of the curve (Borg, 1961, 1962). One example of a physiological variable describable by this general function is the increase of lactic acid concentration with increasing work loads on the bicycle ergometer. The best function to describe perceived exertion during heavy physical work on a bicycle ergometer has a positive a-value and with $b = 0$. This function was earlier proposed by Ekman (1961a,b) to describe variation in taste perception.

A psychophysical estimation method has been introduced to determine individual functions of exertion and to enable direct comparisons of individual intensity levels (Borg, 1972). The subjects were instructed to estimate the degree of perceived exertion in relation to their notion of maximal exertion, which was designed "100."

The psychophysical functions obtained were positively accelerated with exponents of 1.5–1.6. The following equation was found to describe the data on the largest group of subjects, who managed to work up to 200 watts on the bicycle ergometer:

$$R = 4 + 0.001 \ S^{1.6}$$

where S is measured in watts and the constant 4 denotes a basic "noise" value of 4% of a maximal exertion. This "noise" constant means that subjects perceive a small degree of exertion even while just being awake and relaxing. Ordinary daily activities will impose a slightly increased state of arousal and effort upon the individual in heart rate, blood pressure, and other physiological stress variables associated with the perception of exertion. Some people may enter a rather high state of exertion without doing any heavy work, while others in the same situation might be close to a resting "zero."

The treadmill is another ergometer often used for exercise tests. When being tested on the treadmill, the individual has to walk or run, usually at stepwise increased speeds or slopes. The physical strain and the perception of exertion are similar to those brought on by the bicycle ergometer. In one experiment, the subjects had to walk on a flat surface (zero grade) for 4 min at several different speeds varying from about 1 to 6 mph. The following power function was obtained:

$$R = 1 + 0.066(S-1)^3$$

where R is the intensity of perceived exertion while walking, the number 1 denotes the value of the perceptual noise level, which is equal to the R-value arbitrarily set at 1 for $S = 1$ mph, 0.066 is the measure-constant, S is the physical speed in mph, the parenthetic number 1 shows the starting point of the curve, and 3 is the exponent (Borg, 1973). This general function is depicted in Figure 2. As can be seen from the figure, perceived exertion undergoes but little increase when speed is increased from 0 to 3 km $\times$ hour^{-1}. After that point, however, the intensity of the perception increases greatly. Individual differences are of course large. Less fit subjects as well as persons walking in a natural outdoor setting will have leftward-moved curves.

That the psychophysical functions described in this section are highly reliable and valid is shown by the fact that the heart rate grows almost linearly with the work load on the bicycle ergometer, while it

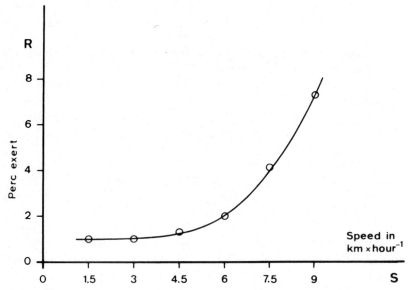

Figure 2. Variation of perceived exertion with physical speed during work on a treadmill. Perceived exertion measured by a ratio scale R and expressed in relative units while physical speed S is expressed in km $\times$ hour^{-1}. The R value at $S = 1.5$ km $\times$ hour^{-1} is set at "1." $R = 1 + 0.0125 \, (S\text{-}1.5)^3$ (from Borg, 1973).

grows with about the square of the physical speed when walking. The relation between the exponents for perceived exertion and for heart rate, then, is about the same for walking as for pedaling the bicycle.

DIFFERENTIAL STUDIES

If an individual rides a bicycle slowly for about 10 min, he might perceive the physical effort to be "rather light." If he has to run the same distance in the same amount of time, he will perceive the effort to be much greater, e.g., "very hard." Toward the end of the exercise, his heart rate will correspond well with his verbally expressed perception of effort. If he were to compare the second activity with the first, he might say that it was "about three times as hard." Such a numerical comparison has the advantage of giving measurements on a ratio scale, in turn permitting mathematical descriptions of the kind outlined in previous sections. A disadvantage is that subjects feel more uncertain when they have to make ratio comparisons than when they may merely express their feelings in common language. A still more serious disadvantage of the ratio-scaling techniques is that they do not give us any information about the strength of the perception in a more "absolute" sense. We do not know if a subject's perception is very intensive or fairly weak. In the example given above, an individual might perceive the 10-min run to be three times as hard as the 10-min bicycle ride but still perceive the run as requiring only a moderate degree of effort, i.e., if he is a trained distance runner in top physical condition.

The problem exemplified above—that the psychophysical ratio-scaling methods give only ratios between percepts and not intensity levels that would enable direct comparisons between the perceived intensities of individuals—is of great concern. The extent to which we can rely on our senses and assume that other people perceive the same things (e.g., the same sourness and color) as we do is a classic philosophical–psychological question. Our inability to creep under the skin of another person means that we can never be quite sure of that person's subjective view of reality.

Philosophical and psychological difficulties notwithstanding, a model was presented which would enable rough comparisons between individuals regarding the quantitative aspects of perception (Borg, 1961, 1962). In the model, it is assumed that subjective range and perceptual intensity at a maximum intensity level are about the same for all subjects in spite of the fact that the performance range, or the stimulus range, from zero or a just noticeable intensity to a "maximal" intensity might differ very much. In the general psychophysical equation presented above the values of the denominator can be determined experimentally for each individual and the measure constant c can be solved for each individual in the following way:

$$c = \frac{R_T - a}{(S_T - b)^n}$$

where R_T is the subjective intensity at the maximal (terminal T) level and $R_T - a$ is assumed to be equal for all subjects (and can arbitrarily be set at "1" or "100"). In Figure 3 the content of this model is visualized. The two curves may represent two individual functions, e.g., the subjective effort in weightlifting. One of the subjects is assumed to be stronger and can therefore lift a heavier weight S and reach a higher maximal S value ($S_{T2} > S_{T1}$). In the figure, the perceptual intensities at these S_T values are arbitrarily set to be equal ($R_{T2} = R_{T1}$). This idea, namely, that all subjects will perceive the effort to be equally strong at their maximal effort level, is one of the main foundations of the model. The model renders possible the comparison between individuals at various submaximal intensity levels as well as calculations of relative response RR and relative stimulus RS values (see Figure 3).

Figure 3. Variation of perceived exertion (R according to a ratio scale, see text) with the physical work load (S in watts) during work on a bicycle ergometer. The curves represent two individuals (subjects 1 and 2). The curves start at a very low intensity level represented by the constants a and b. The highest load at which subject 1 can manage to work is denoted S_{t_1} and the corresponding load for subject 2 is S_{t_2}. These maximal (or terminal) t levels are proposed to be perceived as equally intensive (R_{t_1} R_{t_2}). With this assumption, comparisons

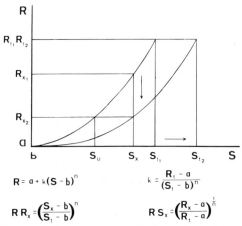

$$R = a + k(S - b)^n \qquad\qquad k = \frac{R_t - a}{(S_t - b)^n}$$

$$R\,R_x = \left(\frac{S_x - b}{S_t - b}\right)^n \qquad\qquad R\,S_x = \left(\frac{R_x - a}{R_t - a}\right)^{\frac{1}{n}}$$

can be made between subjects for the same submaximal intensity levels (e.g., S_x), and relative response (RR_x) and relative stimulus (RS_x) values can be determined. The figure also shows how much perceived exertion for a certain submaximal level (S_x) decreases as a result of training for the one individual, until he can manage the same highest load as the other individual (from Borg, 1961, 1970).

One often important goal of training and learning as a whole is not to increase the maximal capacity *per se* but to increase the ease in performing daily tasks of moderate difficulty. That the perception of effort will diminish as an effect of training is self-evident. The model in Figure 3 allows us to go a step further, namely, to predict how much the subjective effort will go down with training for a given submaximal work load. Our prediction is based upon how much the maximal work capacity has risen. Of course we can also make predictions in the opposite direction, i.e., say how much more demanding a task will be for a subject whose working capacity has been impaired because of age or disease. This model has been validated against physiological criteria such as heart rate.

In most applied studies, a simple method is needed that can be used by everyone, not only by subjects who have a superior capacity to handle numbers and express perceptual relations in ratios. One such method has been developed. It involves a category rating scale called the RPE scale (Ratings of Perceived Exertion). The scale varies from 6 to 20 to match the heart-rate variation from 60 to 200 beats/min. Every second number is anchored with such verbal expressions as "fairly light," "somewhat hard," etc. (see Table 1).

The RPE scale has been used in many studies in several different countries for different kinds of work, different age groups, and different clinical groups. In one of the first validation studies, a correlation of 0.85 was obtained between ratings (RPE) and heart rates (HR) during ergometer work. In later studies correlations of the same magnitude have been obtained whenever a wide range of stimulus variation (physical strain) has been used (see Borg and Noble, 1974).

In fairly young to middle-aged people (25 to 45 years old), working at moderate to high intensity levels, the HR roughly corresponds to 10 times the RPE value. Compared to young adults and middle-aged persons, teen-agers give lower RPE ratings and older people higher RPE ratings for the same HR. If we assess physical strain in an age-heterogenous group by looking at HR only, we will obtain values that mislead us to conclude that the younger people are in a higher state of exertion than the older ones. That such is not the case is revealed by looking at the ratings or by calculating the relative HRs, i.e., by transforming a certain HR to a percentage of the range from a resting to a maximal HR. As a matter of fact, the latter goes down from about 195 beats/min for 20-year-old persons to about 175 for the 50-year-olds.

Figure 4 depicts the relation between RPE and HR, which is linear in all age groups. The RPE scale was intentionally constructed to match a psychological scale to a highly reliable and valid physiological variable, so that its values follow the physiological variation very closely. Since HR grows linearly with the physical work load, RPE does so as well. Figure 4 also demonstrates a clear-cut age-related difference in that older people rate the degree of exertion to be higher in relation to HR.

Table 1. The Category Scale for Ratings of Perceived Exertion[a]

6	
7	very, very light
8	
9	very light
10	
11	fairly light
12	
13	somewhat hard
14	
15	hard
16	
17	very hard
18	
19	very, very hard
20	

[a]RPE-scale according to Borg (1970).

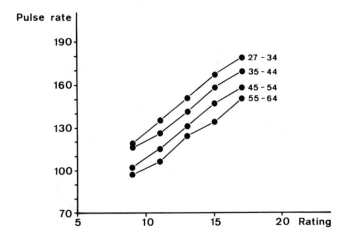

Figure 4. Pulse rate in relation to perceived exertion during work on a bicycle ergometer in various age groups (from Borg and Linderholm, 1970).

Estimates of perceived exertion have proven to be of value in several sports in which it is important to moderate exertion to just the right intensity level in training or in competition. The risk for accidents that to some degree are caused by effects of fatigue (e.g., accidents in downhill skiing) also constitutes a special situation in which subjective feelings of exertion and fatigue may be a vital signal to the individual to be more careful.

SUBJECTIVE SYMPTOMS

An individual experiences many different kinds of symptoms when suffering from some disease or when under physical or mental stress. Under the physical stress of performing heavy work he may perceive aches or pains in the muscles or joints, aches in the chest, breathing difficulties, headache, etc. The overall perception of exertion, with which we have mainly been dealing up to now, may then be looked upon as a kind of "gestalt" or complex configuration of many different sensations. If the subject is asked to express how he feels and which symptoms he perceives, he may in addition to overall ratings of exertion speak of sensations of the nature mentioned above.

Two classes of sensations have been found during heavy physical work. One class consists of sensations from the peripheral muscles and joints. Such sensations are easily studied during short-time work and work with small muscle groups. Sensations of another class are engendered by heavy work of longer duration. Such work entails more

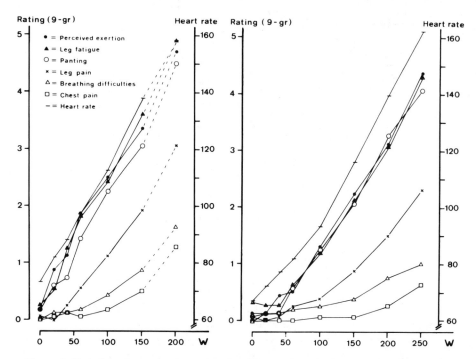

Figure 5. Variation of perceived exertion, leg fatigue, panting, leg pain, breathing difficulties, chest pain, and heart rate during a work test on a bicycle ergometer according to a nine-graded rating scale. The subjects consisted of healthy middle-aged men with about normal working capacity (left) and very fit subjects (right) (from Borg *et al.*, 1976).

stress on the cardiovascular system for which reason perceptions of exertion and fatigue have predominantly central and general circulatory origin (Borg, 1962). Ekblom and Goldbarg (1971) point out that in work with small muscle groups, local factors seem to be dominant for the perception of effort, while in work with large muscle groups, a central factor comes into play in addition to the local strain. In a systematic experimental study of many subjective symptoms and their correlation during heavy work, Weiser and Stamper (1977) found two main dimensions labeled "general fatigue" and "leg fatigue," and also a component labeled "task aversion."

Subjective symptoms during exercise tests are routinely recorded in clinical examinations. One important purpose of physical work tests is to arouse symptoms of diagnostic interest. Besides such symptoms as general exertion and aches and pains in different parts of the body, the subjects may experience panting as well as feelings of dizziness, sickness, or fear and anxiety related to their health status.

A study has been performed on the subjective variation of the following symptoms during work on the bicycle ergometer: (1) overall perception of exertion, (2) leg fatigue, (3) leg pain, (4) chest pain, (5) panting, and (6) breathing difficulties (Borg, Karlsson, and Lindblad, 1976). The subjects consisted of healthy middle-aged men who were tested at a submaximal load. The test was interrupted when the subjects reached a HR of about 170 beats/min or rated the exertion to be "very hard." The results of the study are shown in Figure 5.

The results on the left side of Figure 5 refer to a group of less fit subjects and those on the right side to a group of more fit subjects. Overall perception of exertion, leg fatigue, and panting, as an effect of the increase in work load, increases in a very simple linear way, as does HR. The feeling of leg pain is not as intense; breathing difficulties and chest pain show only a very small increase. When the two groups are compared, a striking difference in the absolute subjective intensity values is seen for certain work loads, but no marked difference in relative values emerges (i.e., subjective symptoms are related to the heart rates).

The subjective symptoms were assessed according to the following simple rating scale: 0 = nothing whatsoever, 1 = very, very weak, 2 = very weak, 3 = fairly weak, 4 = somewhat hard, 5 = hard, 6 = very hard, 7 = very, very hard, 8 = maximal.

Some Clinical Studies

During clinical examinations it has been the practice for several years to collect ratings of perceived exertion together with physiological data during an ordinary exercise test. In groups of patients, the increase of subjective symptoms during physical stress will be quite different from that in groups of healthy subjects. Depending upon which disease the individual is suffering, certain symptoms will dominate, as can be seen from the symptom profiles. In one study, the relation between heart rate and ratings of general exertion was calculated for three different groups of patients (Borg and Linderholm, 1970). All three groups showed a smaller increase in heart rate in relation to the increase of perceived exertion than was the case in groups of healthy persons of the same age. The results of the study are shown in Figure 6.

The two continuous lines in this figure refer to two different groups of healthy subjects, one younger group (the upper line) and one older group (the lower line). The previously demonstrated age difference in the relation between HR and RPE is clearly seen in this figure. The upper dashed line of the figure refers to a group of patients with a vaso-regulatory asthenia syndrome and the lower dashed line to a group of patients with coronary heart disease. In comparison with the healthy

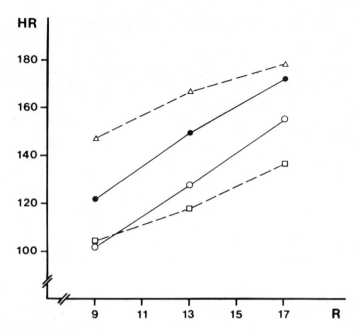

Figure 6. Relation between heart rates (HR) and ratings of perceived exertion (R, according to an older 21-graded RPE scale) in a group of healthy young men (●———●), and a group of healthy middle-aged men (○———○), a group of young male patients with the vasoregulatory asthenia syndrome (△———△), and a group of middle-aged men suffering from coronary insufficiency (□———□) (from Borg and Linderholm, 1970).

subjects of the same age, the patients with the vasoregulatory asthenia syndrome rated exertion to be less in relation to HR, especially at low intensity levels. Also compared to healthy subjects, the patients with coronary heart disease rated exertion to be higher in relation to HR, especially at high intensity levels. A third group of patients with arterial hypertension (not included in the figure) was somewhat similar to the group with vasoregulatory asthenia but the difference between the former and the healthy subjects was less marked.

In another study, two groups of young men at a rehabilitation center, one group consisting of mentally retarded patients and the other of psychiatric patients, performed a work test on the bicycle ergometer during which both HR and RPE were recorded. Compared to "normal" men of the same age, the patients had a lower physical fitness coupled with a higher RPE in relation to work load. The patients' low physical working capacity and high degree of subjective stress probably resulted from institutionalization in general and inadequate programs for fitness training in particular (Borg, Egerman, Freeman, and Gust, 1969; Borg, 1970).

Sanne (1973) studied exercise tolerance and physical training in patients after myocardial infarction (MI). One of the purposes of the study was to evaluate the effect of physical training on certain physiological variables and perceived exertion as well as on the working capacity of the individual. Exercise after an infarction is a decisive factor in the patient's struggle to restore his heart function and to resume his social, professional, and leisure-time activities. Patients with a low respiratory efficiency (defined as the ratio between oxygen uptake and pulmonary ventilation) perceived exertion during exercise to be exceptionally high. After training, the pulmonary ventilation and the perception of exertion were normalized. When the patients were first tested, their perception of exertion in relation to HR was significantly higher than that of the healthy control groups. This difference disappeared after repeated testing. The training also had a positive effect on several physiological variables and resulted in a decreased perceived exertion. One of the important factors was the patients' growing confidence in their ability to have good physical fitness.

Several other studies in this area have been or are being performed. One such study is that of Turkulin, Zamlić, and Regan (1977), in which patients were studied convalescing after a myocardial infarction. Two groups of healthy people were also studied, one consisting of untrained subjects and the other of athletes. While the subjects performed ordinary ergometer tests, data were collected on a number of physiological variables and RPE was recorded. A high correlation between RPE and work load was observed in all three groups, but RPE was higher in the group of patients with myocardial infarction. The correlation between RPE and HR was high in the two healthy groups but not in the group of MI patients. The MI patients rated exertion to be higher than would be expected from HR, a finding similar to that described by Borg and Linderholm (1970) in a group of patients with coronary insufficiency but not infarction. The young athletes rated exertion to be lower than would be expected from HR. Turkulin *et al.* (1977) concluded that the RPE scale was a suitable clinical instrument to define the subjective exercise tolerance limit of MI patients. Sargeant and Davies (1973, 1977) compared one-leg exercise with two-leg exercise, left-leg exercise with right-leg exercise, and normal healthy subjects with patients who were suffering a loss of function in one leg due to immobilization following fracture. They found that the differences in muscle mass involved during exercise caused differences in RPE, whereupon the relationship between RPE and HR shifted. When work load was expressed in relative terms, i.e., oxygen uptake as a percentage of maximal oxygen uptake, the variability of RPE was reduced. The authors concluded, "In patients who had suffered a loss of function in one leg due to immobilization following fracture, the perception of exertion was accurately related to the new reduced function level." They also pointed out that RPE measurements seem to be of value for advising patients on desirable exercise levels.

In clinical examinations it is sometimes difficult to know when to interrupt an exercise test. The patients must work hard enough to provoke the symptoms needed for diagnostic information, but at the same time they of course should not be subjected to too much strain. A certain submaximal HR level (e.g., 150 beats/min), geared to the age and the illness of the subject, is often used. Because of the great variability in maximal HR, it cannot be ideal to have a certain fixed level to signal interruption of the test. Instead, a combination of RPE assessments, HR measurements, and other physiological data may serve to enable the patient to reach an optimal intensity before the test is interrupted (Grimby, Aurell, Bjure, Ekström Jodal, and Wilhelmsen 1972; Sanne, 1973). RPE values may also indicate the appropriate times for making stepwise increases of the work load during the testing program.

Ratings of perceived exertion may also provide information as to how rigorous a physical training program should be. A man who has been hospitalized for some disease and then sent home for convalescence is often given some vague instructions to the effect that he should exercise moderately or the like. It is easy to tell a man that he should walk for an hour or run or swim for half an hour, but it is not easy to tell him at what intensity level he should exercise. The HR might of course be a good indicator of the degree of physical strain but some people have difficulties in counting their own HR. Another drawback is that they might become so obsessed with counting their HR that they dare not make a move without doing so. In most cases it is better to advise people to use their subjective feelings of effort to adjust their exercise intensity. Granted, not everybody is as adept as an athlete in knowing how hard to strain himself, when to slow down, or when to make a harder effort. Some people may need training, which may begin at the clinic or laboratory with walking or running on the treadmill or pedaling on the bicycle ergometer. They should rate their degree of exertion during this exercise and compare it to the HR. Most individuals will then learn to recognize the feeling that arises when the exercise intensity is at just the right level.

Quantitative assessments of the perception of exertion have also been applied to the evaluation of the effectiveness of physical training programs. In one study, patients with rheumatic fever participated in a therapeutic program that included physical fitness training. The program was difficult, even painful, for the patients and it did not cure the disease. However, as a result of the physical training, the patients' fitness increased and the degree of perceived exertion and pain for a certain amount of physical work decreased substantially (Ekblom and Lövgren, 1974).

Some Special Laboratory and Industrial Studies

In work studies, human factors engineering and improvement of man–machine systems, the focus is often upon productivity criteria, e.g., the speed and error of performance. Besides technical aspects and physiological responses of man at work, the psychological "costs" in the form of the perception of effort and difficult subjective stress and fatigue should be studied to enable us to understand the relationship between human beings and their work.

Most psychophysical studies have dealt with thresholds, such as absolute thresholds and differential thresholds, and have arrived at functions describing the variation between very low and very high intensity levels. In daily life, however, other intensity levels are of interest, such as levels to which the individual might be forced to adapt, stress levels, and the like. When a person tries to adapt himself to a work situation, the load and the difficulty of the task should be of just the right intensity level, not too low and not so high as to bring him too near the stress zone in relation to his maximal working capacity. To identify which industrial tasks will be too strenuous for the individual, percep-

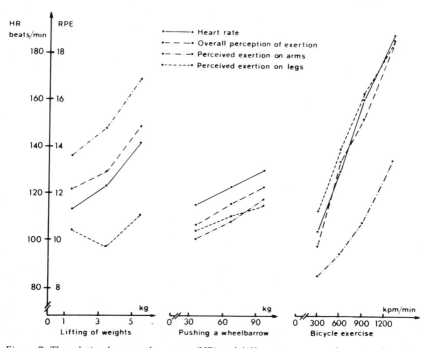

Figure 7. The relation between heart rate (HR) and different measures of perceived exertion (RPE) for submaximal exercise in lifting weights and pushing the wheelbarrow and for submaximal and maximal exercise on a bicycle ergometer. Each point is a mean value of 12 subjects.

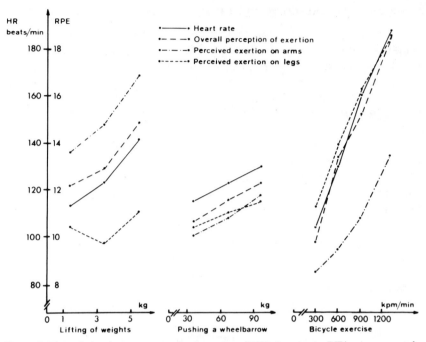

Figure 8. The relation between perceived exertion (RPE), heart rate (HR), oxygen uptake (V_{O_2}), and blood lactate concentration for submaximal exercise in lifting weights and pushing the wheelbarrow and for submaximal and maximal exercise on a bicycle ergometer. Each point is a mean value of 12 subjects.

tual measurements of effort and difficulty may be used for a quantitative evaluation of the degree of stress and thus complement physiological and performance measures.

In a study by Gamberale (1972), subjects had to do three different kinds of work, while the perception of overall exertion and peripheral exertion in the working muscles was studied together with some physiological variables. The tasks consisted of (1) lifting heavy parcels from a lower shelf to a higher one, (2) pushing a wheelbarrow, and (3) working on a bicycle ergometer. The results of the study can be seen in Figures 7 and 8.

It is evident from the first figure that the subjects could differentiate very well among the different sensations and feelings of exertion evoked by the different tasks. The physiological responses are seen in the second figure. The overall perception of exertion, heart rate, oxygen uptake, and blood lactate during the bicycle work are arbitrarily placed as closely together as possible so that the differences in these variables during the other two tasks can be clearly seen. The physiological differences obtained should be viewed against the backdrop of the perceptual differences presented in the previous figure. The physiological data in this study may be viewed to some extent as a validation or rough explanation of the psychological results.

In an industrial work situation, people sometimes have to carry out heavy physical work while under high heat stress. Experiments on the perception of effort evoked by such work must therefore combine exercise and heat stress. In a study by Pandolf, Cafarelli, Noble, and Metz (1972), no significant differences in the perception of exertion were found when temperature changed, as long as work load was constant, even though HR was significantly increased by heat stress. HR was sensitive both to the work load and to the heat, while the RPE values followed the actual work load but not HR (see Figure 9).

A similar result was obtained by Gamberale and Holmér (1977) in a study on the effects of heat load during simulated fire fighting, gas accident practice, and exercise on a bicycle ergometer while wearing an

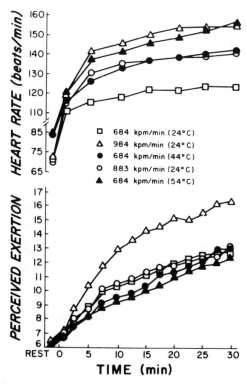

Figure 9. Heart rate (beats/min) and perceived exertion (according to the RPE scale) as a function of time for various physical work loads and environmental temperatures (from Pandolf *et al.*, 1972).

unventilated gas-protective suit. The increase in HR brought about by the heat load was not followed by a corresponding increase in RPE. The authors suggest that this "incongruity" between the RPE and HR during work with a high heat load might be a decisive factor in bringing on exhaustion and collapse in emergencies.

In a study by Costa and Gaffuri (1977) RPEs were collected and several physiological variables were measured in nurses employed in shift work and in students exposed to high volumes of noise. In the shift workers, HR was lower at night than during the day, while RPE was higher at night. In the students, high volumes of noise did not seem to influence RPE during physical work.

Estimates of Physical Working Capacity from Perceived Exertion

There is some evidence that the general fitness level of people in a number of countries has gone down during the last decades. This decline seems to be coupled with an increase of certain illnesses such as circulatory diseases and certain mental disturbances. Most people will also agree that good physical fitness is important for a good mental performance and a general feeling of well-being. It is certainly not desirable to become so exhausted from just walking, playing with children, or gardening that not much energy is left for various mental activities.

Faced with these developments, authorities and other groups have launched an extensive campaign to persuade people to improve their physical fitness. Many physiological tests have been worked out to measure physical fitness. The most important ones concern aerobic capacity, i.e., capacity to do heavy work lasting several minutes. This capacity is studied by measuring an individual's maximal oxygen uptake during work with large muscle groups. The tests may be performed on a bicycle ergometer or a treadmill. The work load W (in watts) increased stepwise till the subject cannot work any more. The maximal intensity at which an individual can work for some specified time, e.g., 6 min, gives a measurement of the working capacity (W_{max}) that is very highly correlated with maximal oxygen uptake $(V_{0_2\ max})$.

In most exercise tests, it is not necessary to have the individual work to his maximum or even close to it. There may also be medical or other reasons for not stressing the individual to such a degree. A submaximal test is then performed and discontinued when a medium intensity level is reached, e.g., about 80% of the working capacity of the individual.

An excellent simple and direct measurement of the degree of physical strain is the heart rate. If the HR-W relation is studied for an individual, estimates of his physical working capacity can be made. When testing an individual, several work loads are often administered with a stepwise increase.

HR is recorded just prior to the transition to a new work load (e.g., each load may last for 6 min as in the descriptions by Sjöstrand, 1947; Wahlund, 1948). The test may be continued until the subject has reached a predetermined HR, e.g., 170 beats/min for young men and 150 beats/min for middle-aged subjects. As a measurement of the working capacity, the work load at a certain HR is taken and denoted, e.g., W_{170} or W_{150}. This value correlates highly with the maximal oxygen uptake, V_{O_2max}, and the maximal performance, W_{max}.

RPE values may be used in analogy to the way in which HR is used during a work test. As an estimate of the working capacity, the work load at a certain rating value—e.g., when the subject rates the work to be "very hard" (RPE = 17)—is determined and denoted W_{R17}. In several studies, measurements based on such ratings have proven to be highly reliable and valid (Borg, 1962; Borg and Linderholm, 1970; Edgren, Marklund, Nordsjö, and Borg, 1976). The reproducibility is about as good for the W_R measurements as for the W_{HR} measurements.

To check the validity of the W_R measurements, they have been compared to other measurements of working capacity, such as performance measurements and physiological measurements. In a study on lumberjacks in Sweden (Borg, 1962), both W_{170} and W_{R17} measurements were made. Wages from piecework were used as a rough gauge of working capacity. A moderate correlation ($r_{xy} = 0.54$) was obtained between the W_{R17} measurements and the wages, whereas a lower correlation was found between the W_{170} values and wages ($r_{xy} = 0.23$). In a study by Morgan, Raven, Drinkwater, and Horwath (1973) maximal performances on a bicycle ergometer (W_{max}) were predicted from HR and from RPE. The predictions based on the ratings were slightly better than those based on HR. Sargeant and Davies (1973, 1977) used the relationship between RPE and V_{O_2} during submaximal exercise to predict maximal aerobic capacity (V_{O_2max}) in normal subjects and in patients suffering from leg injury. This method gave rather rough estimates of the subjects' capacity but such estimates were judged to be fruitful for the therapist when used in conjunction with other indicators.

In some later studies the W_R measurements have been shown to be as good as the W_{HR} measurements. These two kinds of measurements have been shown to complement each other (Edgren et al., 1976).

In age-heterogeneous groups the W_R measurements have been shown to yield better estimates of the working capacity than have the W_{HR} measurements. This depends upon the great individual difference in maximal HR and upon the decline of the maximal value with age. If an individual's maximal HR is known from previous tests, a prediction of his working capacity based upon submaximal data may be corrected for the individual deviation from the normal maximal reference value for his age. In a group of middle-aged people, the maximal HR might vary between 150 beats/min and 200 beats/min. A certain fixed HR value will hence have different meanings with regard to the degree of physical strain of an individual. The ratings of perceived exertion do not fall prey to the same range problem since the individual makes a direct rating in relation to a maximal intensity. If instead of a fixed reference HR level (e.g., 170 beats/min) a relative HR level is determined as a percentage (e.g., 80%) of the HR range from a minimal to a maximal HR (e.g., 65 beats/min to 195 beats/min in young men) and above the minimal value, more valid W_{HR} measurements (as W_{p80}) will be obtained. This value will have greater power for predicting W_{max} and maximal oxygen uptake and will have a higher correlation with the W_R measurements.

Figure 10 shows the variation of physical working capacity with age according to some of the types of W measurements discussed above. As can be seen from the figure, the W measurements based on relative HR (in this case W_{p80}) go down with age in about the same way as does the maximal oxygen uptake. The W_{130} values do not decline with age, erroneously indicating that the working capacity should not decline with age. The W_{R13} (= W at rating "13") drops with age in very much the same way as does the oxygen uptake.

In a study by Bar-Or (1977), HR and RPE were collected from more than 1,000 people of different ages from school age to old age while they exercised. In this study the W measurements based on RPE values changed with age according to what we know about actual changes in working capacity, whereas the W measurements based on HR did not. It can thus be concluded that RPE values are a valuable complement to HR whenever information about the maximal HR of an individual is not available and a submaximal work test has to be carried out. The RPE values give W measurements a higher validity.

SOME FURTHER PSYCHOPHYSIOLOGICAL STUDIES

In the previous sections, several psychophysiological studies have been described, most of which have confirmed the relation between RPE and HR. For a full understanding of the complex overall perception of exertion, many different physiological variables should be measured and correlated to each other as well as to various peripheral and central sensations of exertion. The knowledge available at the moment does not suffice to "explain" physiologically what causes the variation of perceived exertion.

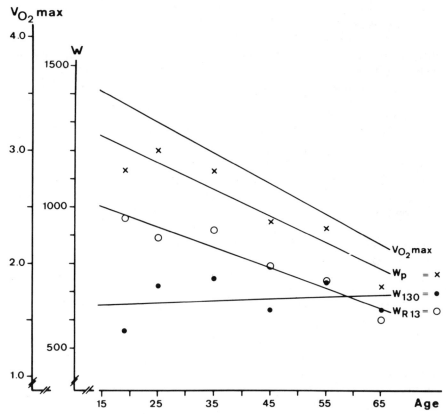

Figure 10. Change in physical working capacity with age. The uppermost line shows the decline of maximal V_{O_2} (from Astrand and Rodahl, 1970). The next three lines show estimates of aerobic capacity based on submaximal tests (from Borg and Linderholm, 1970). The top line of these three (adjusted to crosses) shows estimates of aerobic capacity according to W_P, i.e., the work load at which the subject can work at 80% of his heart rate range. The next line (adjusted to open circles) shows the variation of the W_{R13} measurements, i.e., the work load at which the subject rates the perceived exertion to be rather hard. The lowest line (adjusted to filled circles) shows the variation of W_{130} measurements, i.e., the work load at which the subject has a heart rate of 130 beats/min.

The very high correlation between HR and RPE (0.80–0.90) over a wide range of work loads shows that HR and RPE share a high percentage of common variance. No simple causal relation has been suggested to exist between them but in middle-aged men the RPE value is about 0.1 of the corresponding HR. The surprisingly good relation between HR and RPE has been found in samples from many different countries, as can be seen by comparing results reported by Borg (1962), Skinner, Borg, and Buskirk (1969), Borg and Linderholm (1970), Bar-Or, Skinner, Buskirk, and Borg (1972), Bar-Or (1977), and others.

The relationship between HR and oxygen uptake (V_{O_2}) is known to be linear, for which reason RPE can also be assumed to be linearly related to V_{O_2}. With training, both HR and RPE are reduced for the same work loads. The relation between HR and RPE seems to remain unchanged with training but the V_{O_2}–RPE relationship is altered in terms of raw values, since maximum V_{O_2} is increased with training. If the V_{O_2} values are expressed in relative terms, their relation to RPE remains constant (Ekblom and Goldbarg, 1971).

Skinner *et al.* (1969) studied young men, about 20 years old, who differed in activity levels and body sizes. The sedentary men perceived a higher degree of exertion and had a higher HR than the active men for the same work loads. The lean subjects had a higher HR than the heavier subjects but did not differ from them in perception of effort. For given percentages of maximum working capacity, no differences arose with regard to either HR or RPE between the activity and body size sub-groups. The important factor for the differences in RPE and HR was thus the working capacity of the men.

Other physiological variables that are correlated to changes in RPE are ventilation, blood lactate, and catecholamine excretion. The variation of blood lactate, like RPE, follows a positively accelerated function when measured with psychophysical ratio scales. Catecholamine excretion has been proposed as a factor in RPE during heavy work (Frankenhaeuser, Post, Nordheden, and Sjöberg, 1969).

The relation between RPE and HR is shifted from the normal when subjects exercise under the influence of autonomic nervous system blocking agents. After administration of propranolol RPE is increased for the same HR level and after administration of atropine it is decreased (Ekblom and Goldbarg, 1971).

More studies are necessary for a better understanding of the variation of perceived exertion and its relationship to the physiological factors mentioned here as well as others. The dependence of RPE upon different situations, different kinds of physical and mental stress, and differences in the working capacity of the individual also needs further elucidation.

References

Astrand, P. O., and Rodahl, K. *Textbook of Work Physiology,* McGraw-Hill: New York, 1970.

Bar-Or, O. Age-related changes in exercise perception. In G. Borg, (Ed.), *Physical work and effort* (Wenner-Gren Center International Symposium Series, Vol. 28). New York: Pergamon Press, 1977. Pp. 255–266.

Bar-Or, O., Skinner, J. S., Buskirk, E. R., and Borg, G. Physiological and perceptual indicators of physical stress in 41- to 60-year-old men who vary in conditioning level and in body fatness. *Medicine and Science in Sports,* 1972, 4, 96.

Borg, G. Interindividual scaling and perception of muscular force. *Kungliga Fysiografiska Sällskapets Förhandlingar*, 1961, *12*, 117–125.

Borg, G. Physical performance and perceived exertion. Gleerup, Lund, 1962.

Borg, G. Perceived exertion as an indicator of somatic stress. *Scandinavian Journal of Rehabilitation Medicine*, 1970, *2*(3), 92–98.

Borg, G. A ratio scaling method for interindividual comparisons. *Reports from the Institute of Applied Psychology, University of Stockholm*, 1972, No. 27, 12.

Borg, G. Perceived exertion during walking: A psychophysical function with two additional constants. *Reports from the Institute of Applied Psychology, University of Stockholm*, 1973, No. 39, 10.

Borg, G., and Dahlström, H. Psykofysisk undersökning av arbete på cykel-ergometer. *Nordisk Medicin*, 1959, *62*, 1383–1386.

Borg, G., and Dahlström H. The perception of muscular work. *Umeå Vetensk, Bibl. Skriftserie*, 1960, *5*, 1–26.

Borg, G., and Linderholm, H. Exercise performance and perceived exertion in patients with coronary insufficiency, arterial hypertension and vasoregulatory asthenia. *Acta Medica Scandinavica*, 1970, *187*, 17–26.

Borg, G., and Noble, B. J. Perceived exertion. In J. Wilmore (Ed.), *Exercise and sport science reviews*. New York: Academic Press, 1974. Pp. 2, 131–153.

Borg, G., Diamant, H., Ström, L., and Zotterman, Y. The relation between neural and perceptual intensity: A comparative study on the neural and psychophysical response to taste stimuli. *Journal of Physiology*, 1967, *192*, 13–20.

Borg, G., Edgren, B., and Marklund, G. A simple walk test of physical fitness. *Reports from the Institute of Applied Psychology, University of Stockholm*, 1970, No. 18.

Borg, G., Edström, C.-G., and Marklund, G. A new method to determine the exponent for perceived force in physical work. *Reports from the Institute of Applied Psychology, University of Stockholm*, 1970, No. 4, 7.

Borg, G., Egerman, K., Freeman, E., and Gust, T. A study of exertion. *Report from the Pennsylvania Rehabilitation Center*, 1969, No. 6, Vol. 4, 25 pp.

Borg, G., Karlsson, J.-G., and Lindblad, I. Quantitative variation of subjective symptoms during ergometer work. *Reports from the Institute of Applied Psychology, University of Stockholm*, 1976, No. 72.

Costa, G., and Gaffuri, E. Studies of perceived exertion rate on bicycle ergometer in conditions reproducing some aspects of industrial work (shift work; noise). In G. Borg (Ed.), *Physical work and effort* (Wenner-Gren Center International Symposium Series, Vol. 28). New York: Pergamon Press, 1977. Pp. 297–305.

Edgren, B., Marklund, G., Nordsjö, L.-O., and Borg, G. The validity of four bicycle ergometer tests. *Medicine and Science in Sports*, 1976, *8*(3), 179–185.

Eisler, H. Subjective scale of force for a large muscle group. *Journal of Experimental Psychology*, 1962, *64*, 253–257.

Ekblom, B., and Goldbarg, A. N. The influence of physical training and other factors on the subjective rating of perceived exertion. *Acta Physiologica Scandinavica*, 1971, *83*, 399–406.

Ekblom, B., and Lövgren, O. Fysisk träning av patienter med reumatoid artrit. *Läkartidningen*, 1974, *71*(39), 3663–66.

Ekman, G., Two generalized ratio scaling methods. *Journal of Psychology*, 1958, *45*, 287–295.

Ekman, G. Weber's Law and related functions. *Journal of Psychology*, 1959, *47*, 343–352.

Ekman, G. A simple method for fitting psychophysical power functions. *Journal of Psychology*, 1961a, *51*, 343–350.

Ekman, G. Methodological note on scales of gustatory intensity. *Scandinavian Journal of Psychology*, 1961b, *2*, 185–190.

360 Gunnar Borg

Frankenhaeuser, M., Post, B., Nordheden, B., and Sjöberg, H. Physiological and subjective reactions to different physical work loads. *Perceptual and Motor Skills*, 1969, *28*, 343.

Gamberale, F. Perceived exertion, heart rate, oxygen uptake and blood lactate in different work operations. *Ergonomics*, 1972, *15*, 545.

Gamberale, F., and Holmer, I. Heart rate and perceived exertion in simulated work with high heat stress. In G. Borg (Ed.), *Physical work and effort* (Wenner-Gren Center International Symposium Series, Vol. 28). New York: Pergamon Press, 1977. Pp. 323–332.

Grimby, G., Aurell, M., Bjure, J., Ekström Jodal, B., and Wilhelmsen, L. Work capacity and physiological response to work. The men born in 1913 study. Department of Clinical Physiology I, and Unit of Preventive Cardiology, Medical Clinic I, University of Göteborg, 1972.

Morgan, W. P., Raven, P. B., Drinkwater, B. L., and Horwath, S. M. Perceptual and metabolic responsivity to standard bicycle ergometry following various hypnotic suggestions. *International Journal of Clinical and Experimental Hypnosis*, 1973, *21*, 86–101.

Noble, B. J., and Borg, G. Perceived exertion during walking and running. In R. Piret (Ed.), *Proceedings of the 17th International Congress of Applied Psychology* (Vol. 1). Brussels, 1972. Pp. 387–392.

Pandolf, K. B., Cafarelli, E., Noble, B. J., and Metz, K. F. Perceptual responses during prolonged work. *Perceptual and Motor Skills*, 1972, *35*, 975.

Sanne, H. Exercise tolerance and physical training of non-selected patients after myocardial infarction. *Acta Medica Scandinavica*, 1973, Suppl. No. 551.

Sargeant, A. J., and Davies, C. T. M. Perceived exertion during rhythmic exercise involving different muscle masses. *Journal of Human Ergology*, 1973, *2*, 3–11.

Sargeant, A. J., and Davies, C. T. M. Perceived exertion of dynamic exercise in normal subjects and patients following leg injury. In G. Borg (Ed.), *Physical work and effort* (Wenner-Gren Center International Symposium Series, Vol. 28). New York: Pergamon Press, 1977. P. 345.

Sjöstrand, T. Changes in the respiratory organs of workmen at an ore smelting works. *Acta Medica Scandinavica*, 1947, *196*, 687–699.

Skinner, J. S., Borg, G., and Buskirk, E. R. Physiological and perceptual reactions to exertion of young men differing in activity and body size. In D. Franks (Ed.), *Exercise and fitness–1969*. Chicago: The Athletic Institute, 1969.

Stevens, J. C., and Cain, W. S. Effort in isometric contractions: Buildup and recovery. In R. Piret (Ed.), *Proceedings of the 17th International Congress of Applied Psychology* (Vol. 1). Brussels, 1972. Pp. 399–407.

Stevens, J. C., and Mach, J. D. Scales of apparent force. *Journal of Experimental Psychology*, 1959, *58*, 405–413.

Stevens, S. S. On the brightness of lights and the loudness of sounds. *Science*, 1953, *118*, 576.

Stevens, S. S. On the psychophysical law. *Psychological Review*, 1957, *64*, 153–181.

Stevens, S. S. Matching functions between loudness and ten other continua. *Perception and Psychophysics*, 1966, *1*(1), 5–8.

Stevens, S. S., and Galanter, E. H. Ratio scales and category scales for a dozen perceptual continua. *Journal of Experimental Psychology*, 1957, *54*, 377–411.

Turkulin, K. B., Zamlić, B., and Regan, U. Exercise performance and perceived exertion in patients after myocardial infarction. In G. Borg (Ed.), *Physical work and effort* (Wenner-Gren Center International Symposium Series, Vol. 28). New York: Pergamon Press, 1977. Pp. 357–366.

Wahlund, H. Determination of the physical working capacity. *Acta Medica Scandinavica,*
   Suppl., 1948, *132,* 215.

Weiser, P. C., and Stamper, D. A. Psychophysiological interactions leading to increased
   effort, leg fatigue, and respiratory distress during prolonged, strenuous bicycle riding.
   In G. Borg (Ed.), *Physical work and effort* (Wenner-Gren Center International Symposium Series, Vol. 28). New York: Pergamon Press, 1977. Pp. 255–266.

Weiser, P. C., Kinsman, R. A., and Stamper, B. A. Task specific symptomatology changes
   resulting from prolonged submaximal bicycle riding. *Medicine and Science in Sports,*
   1973, *5,* 79.

A Psychophysical Contribution to Air Safety: Simulator Studies of Visual Illusions in Night Visual Approaches

CONRAD L. KRAFT

It is often asked how the work of engineering psychologists is applied. There are many examples demonstrating how an improved design can increase performance with displays and controls, or how the redesign of controls has avoided repetitive errors. There are numerous systems studies in which the flow information per unit has been accelerated by the application of principles from the behavioral sciences. This chapter is an account of an experimental laboratory investigation that provided the aircraft industry with an explanation for a number of accidents. This series of experiments changed the interpretation of these accidents and avoided a possible redirection of effort that would have taken the industry away from the most successful of the second-generation jet aircraft.

THE PROBLEM

The Boeing Company introduced the first of the second-generation jets, the 727 (100 series) in the fall of 1965. This airplane had shown great promise in flight test and acceptance by the pilots was immediate and enthusiastic. However, a series of four accidents occurring in late 1965 and early 1966 appeared to indicate that there were some problems with the design of this aircraft.

1. A 727 being flown by United Airlines into Chicago from the northeast left 22,000 feet altitude, started a steady descent (about equiv-

---

CONRAD L. KRAFT • Crew Systems, Boeing Aerospace Company, Seattle, Washington.

alent to a 3-degree glide slope), and continued descending until it literally flew into the water of Lake Michigan 19 miles off shore (Figure 1, No. 1).

2. About a month later, another 727 approaching runway 12 at Cincinnati was just ahead of a storm front to the west, traveling east from Indiana into Ohio. This American Airlines flight to Boone County Airport on the Kentucky side of the Ohio River had to pass over a relatively dark area to the west of the business district of Cincinnati. The aircraft then passed over the dark banks of the Ohio approaching the steep south bank on top of which the threshold of runway 18 began. Unfortunately this airplane struck the ground some 12 feet below the runway elevation (Figure 1, No. 2).

3. In January 1966, a United Airlines 727 traveling from Denver to Salt Lake City, approaching from the south, made too rapid a descent that was only partially checked, and the aircraft landed short of the runway. This approach was also over dark land with the runway and the lights of Salt Lake City out ahead of the airplane and to the right (Figure 1, No. 3).

4. It was only a short time later in Japan that a 727, operated by All

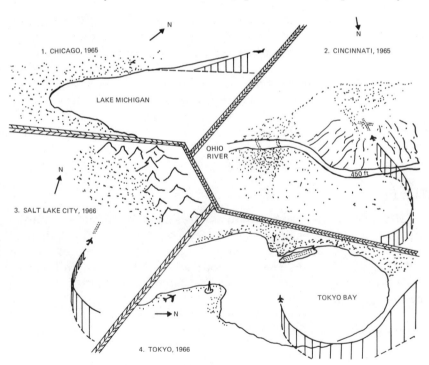

Figure 1. Four night approach accidents of 1965–1966.

Nippon Airlines, bringing a full load of tourists back to Tokyo from the north, left an altitude of about 23,000 feet while flying south and east of Tokyo Bay. Normally, when making a radio-radar-controlled letdown, the aircraft would have proceeded on south, and while east of the bay would have turned to the right about 135 degrees and passed over a radio range on the west bank of the peninsula, making good a final heading of 300 degrees while crossing a portion of the bay to the runway at Tokyo International Airport. This particular evening the pilot could see the lights of Tokyo very clearly to the right of the airplane and called the tower to request permission to make a visual flight rules approach (VFR) instead of an instrument flight rules approach (IFR). The tower granted the pilot's request and the 727 started a descending approach, gradually turning to a due westerly heading. While the airplane was making this descent, Tokyo tower informed the pilots to watch out for another aircraft making an approach to the same runway. The end of this flight occurred as the aircraft struck the water 6½ miles due east of the runway. It was flying at 240 knots with a perfectly "clean" airplane—that is, the wheels were up, the flaps had not been extended, and the configuration was that of an airplane proceeding along an approach path and not in the final phases of landing. It could therefore be assumed that the pilots were not aware of the rapidness of descent nor their proximity to the water. The airplane actually skipped like a flat rock and then, on the second impact with the water, dug a wing in and spun itself to destruction.

Accident Analysis

Analysis of these four accidents, as well as others, revealed a pattern of common factors. In every case the flights were operating under visual flight rules (VFR), which assumes that visibility is adequate to permit the pilot to fly by reference to cues from outside the cockpit. If this were not the case, and instrument flight rules (IFR) were in effect, the pilot would be required to depend on instruments for orientation. Secondly, there is no indication in any of these accidents that the altimeters in the planes were malfunctioning. In all cases the pilots flew too low, which in view of the fact that they were not required to monitor their altimeters, suggests that they were relying on visual cues outside the cockpit which somehow misled them to a dangerously low altitude. If the pilots had been on instrument flight rules, or had frequently monitored their altimeters, it is unlikely that any of these accidents would have occurred.

This analysis suggests that the cause of these accidents is an error in space perception, i.e., a visual illusion. Further analysis revealed that all of the accidents occurred at night and that in making the approach to the airports the planes were flying over a dark area, either water or unlighted land. In all cases, lights were visible in the distance.

A Hypothesis

It may be inferred from this analysis that the pilots were confident of their ability to judge altitude without reference to their altimeters, and that somehow the combination of flying over a dark area into a region where lights were visible produced an illusion of height which caused the pilots to estimate that they were at a higher altitude than was actually the case. If these assumptions are true, there is still the question of why the pilots did not refer to the altimeters, since knowledge of altitude is such a critical factor in the final phase of landing. One possibility, which is confirmed by data from some of the accidents, is that there was a distracting factor that competed for the pilots' attention and caused them to assign a lower priority to reading the altimeters than to the many other factors involved in approach and landing.

In view of this hypothesis, consider the Tokyo Bay accident. It is not unreasonable to assume that both the captain and the copilot were, in response to the instructions from the tower, searching for visual confirmation of the other aircraft in their vicinity. If this were the case, they probably depended upon the lights forward of the aircraft and to its left as an altitude reference and were looking away from the large flat plane of lights that represented Tokyo proper (see Figure 1, No. 4). The lights ahead of them and to the left were those of Yokahama and the lights along the shoreline to the west of Tokyo Bay and south of Yokahama. This narrow pattern of lights is on a slope. The lights to the west are on higher ground than on those on the immediate shore of the bay. Is it possible that this spatial configuration was responsible for the inferred illusion of height?

As a further step in this analysis, consider a plane flying at 10,000 feet of altitude 20 miles from a coastal city with the airport on the near side of the city. Beneath the airplane is dark water, a condition often referred to by pilots as the "dark hole." From the cockpit, the pilot can see the sequence lights leading to the runway, the runway edge lights, the runway end lights, and beyond that almost 16 miles of city lights. In this case the city extends north and south of the airport about 10 miles in each direction, producing in all a configuration 20 miles wide and 16 miles deep.

Assume the coastal plane is flat and that the pilot, instead of landing, is maintaining the same altitude and flying over the city. As the pilot approaches the city, the angle subtended by the nearest and furthest lights progressively increases in size (see Figure 2) until the airplane is over the city. On the other hand, if the pilot were in a helicopter descending along a vertical path, the visual angle would decrease systematically as altitude was reduced until all of the lights appeared to form a horizontal straight line. For an airplane making a landing at the airport

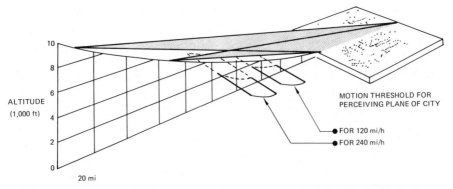

Figure 2. Zero change visual angle approach paths and thresholds for perceiving motion.

the normal approach combines both forward motion and vertical motion. If this forms a straight line, the angle subtended by the city lights might approximate a nonchanging visual angle. This would result from the fact that the horizontal component makes the angle larger but this might be exactly compensated by the vertical component, which simultaneously makes the angle smaller.

It turns out that the mathematical expression of a nonchanging visual angle is the arc of the circle whose center is high in the air above the center of the city lights. For this example, in which we use a 16-mile-deep city, the center of this arc would be 192 miles in the air, so that if the pilot were in fact following this visual null the approach descent would follow a very shallow arc.

ADDITIONAL OBSERVATIONS

It should be noted that this discussion is concerned with the possibility that some factor may have led the pilots into descending to a dangerously low altitude. This assumption implies that an unknown visual illusion could have contributed to a major series of aircraft accidents. A frequent cause of accidents, especially with new aircraft, is a design or structural failure in the plane itself and these possibilities were naturally considered in the original accident investigations. The fact is that the aircraft did have something to contribute but it was neither a structural nor a design failure. Rather, the superior design of this aircraft resulted in unusually stable performance, which did not provide the usual auditory, kinesthetic, or vibratory cues. Normally, such cues would have provided feedback to warn the pilot of his very rapid descent. This was dramatically demonstrated to the author who was able to participate in some operational flights in 727 aircraft and to experience their handling characteristics under experimental conditions. In one case, the author was in a 727 that was descending from 16,000 feet to 8,000 feet at a rate greater than 6,000 feet per minute (the average rate encountered in commercial operations is approximately 800 feet per minute for a 3-degree glide slope). The skill of the instructor pilot and the stability of the aircraft were such that this unusually rapid descent rate provided no indication as to how fast the aircraft was descending. The only cue to the speed of the aircraft was the sound of the wind rushing by, which was indistinguishable from that which would occur if the aircraft were traveling at high speed in level flight. (On this plane the engines are located at the rear of the fuselage.) Under operational conditions, a smoothly accelerated descent could easily become a very high rate of descent without providing a visual warning to the pilot, who is looking through the windscreen. In a less well-designed aircraft, the lack of stability would produce vibratory cues and would force the pilot to make a series of control adjustments in order to fly the aircraft properly. In another case, the author was aware that a student pilot had set up a too-rapid rate of descent, 2,100 feet per minute rather than 500 feet per minute. This awareness, however, did not come from the visual scene but from the sudden inhalation of breath by the senior pilot and his immediate instructions to the student pilot to correct the excessive sink rate. The inability to be aware of excessive sink rates from the instability of the aircraft or the visual scene was apparently a factor in the accidents with this new aircraft.

As part of the background leading up to the experimental phase of this program, the records of previous accidents involving jet aircraft were examined. By December 1967, there had been 234 jet accidents, 82 of which had occurred on approach and landing; of these, 38 occurred at night over water or dark land while approaching lighted cities. Another interesting statistic was that approximately 17% of all fatal jet accidents over a period of 8 years had occurred during night visual approaches. It is well known that a disproportionate number of accidents occurs during approach and landing (see Figure 3), but the fact that so many of these had occurred under visual flight conditions was both a surprise and a challenge for engineering psychology.

SIMULATOR STUDIES

Based on these observations, and with a background in the experimental psychology of vision, the author attempted to formulate a reasonable hypothesis regarding the cause of these accidents, and to design an experiment that would test these ideas. The obvious experimental approach was to utilize an aircraft simulator, i.e., a device that provides the pilot with a reasonable replica of the controls, instruments, and visual

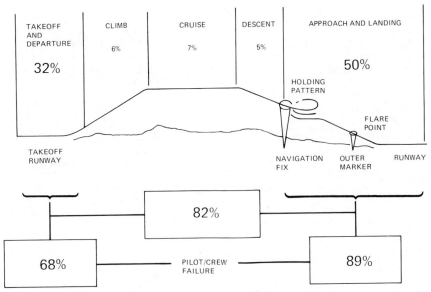

Figure 3. Operational hull loss accidents and distribution of probable causes, 1959 through 1973.

scene that are normally encountered in operational flights. Simulators have become an integral part of pilot training and have been developed to the point where they are very sophisticated indeed. Simulators currently under development for the Air Force are supported by budgets as high as $18 million, with the simulation of visual scenes costing almost half this amount. In the present case, a relatively simple simulator was constructed for about $12,000. The simulator was built into a dark room to permit control of illumination. The cab itself, mounted on a firm platform, had walls and windows cut from "foam-core," which is a blown plastic between two layers of paper. These were shaped to duplicate the visual areas of a 727 series Boeing aircraft (see Figure 4).

The pilot looking through the windows of the simulator viewed a pattern of lights representing a hypothetical city. The platform on which these lights were mounted could be moved so that the visual scene, from the pilot's position, appeared very similar to an actual night visual approach. Movement of the platform was controlled by a small homemade computer that produced a visual effect similar to that which would be experienced in a 727 aircraft weighing about 136,000 pounds. Fortunately, from the point of view of simulation technology, the changes in appearance of the visual scene are essentially the same irrespective of whether the motion is produced by movement of the visual pattern or, as is the case in actual flight, by movement of the aircraft itself.

Figure 4. Night visual approach simulator and Nightertown scene.

The movement in this simulator consisted of changes corresponding to approach, climb, and descent. The simulator was always "flown" by the pilot sitting in the left forward seat. From this position, the pilot's right eye was aligned with the runway and this position was maintained by a combination head- and chin rest. The headrest supported an occluder before the left eye of the pilot so that he could see all the instruments with both eyes, but when he looked up to view the scene, out the forward window, the left eye line of sight was blocked by this occluder. This arrangement allowed the experimenters to depict the city on a scale of 6 inches to a mile and make it look like a real-world scene. For the pilot, the realism was good. When viewing the instrument panel he had to converge and accommodate as he would in a real-world situation, but when he looked at the city scene the effort required for accommodation or convergence was so weak that no extraneous oculomotor cues were introduced to provide a clue to distance.

Considering the scale of the city, it was important that the eye height be controlled precisely. Since 1 millimeter of vertical movement would be equivalent to a change in altitude of 23 feet, it was also important to maintain the eye-to-city distance. Both of these controls were accomplished by a headrest. Built into the forehead portion of the rest was a switch that operated in such a manner that if the pilot had to sneeze or for some other reason remove his head from the standard position, all the lights in the city would be extinguished. This was necessary to avoid cues from head motion, since slight lateral shifts in head position would have given a strong parallax cue. This also meant we could not carry out studies with two crew members, since the visual scene as seen by the copilot would have been equivalent to a position 7½ miles to the right of the pilot. The copilot's position was occupied by the in-cockpit experimenter.

The instrument panel contained a replica of all the instruments in a 727 aircraft but only two of the instruments were active: true airspeed and the vertical-speed indicator, which measured rate of climb or descent in feet per minute. The active controls included the column and yoke (with the trim tab operated by the left thumb) and the throttles on the center column. The column had a spring and hydraulic dampening to make the "feel" similar to a real 727 series aircraft. These aspects of the control situation are shown in Figure 4. As the pilot operated the control he changed his apparent approach speed and his rate of climb or descent. Actually, of course, he was controlling the movement of a platform in the darkness before him.

Above this platform, like a large table with extendable and contracting legs, was the transilluminated model of the city. It consisted of an 8'×10'×1' light box containing fluorescent lights, some independently controlled tungsten lights, and some special purpose lights in cylinders with holes around the circumference of the cylinder. On the outside of the cylinder and facing the position of these holes were fiber optics. As the cylinder was rotated by a motor drive, light was obscured from the fiber optics until a hole appeared between the light source and the fiber optics. The other end of the fiber optic came up through the ground map and was pointed toward the pilot's eye. By this mechanism we could simulate rotating beacons, flashing lights on the ground, and moving vehicles. The 7-watt tungsten lights were generally covered by an 8"×8" frosted diffuser and were pulsed to provide light shimmer as though there was atmosphere between the pilots and the city. The fluorescent lights were arranged among baffles so they could be illuminated or turned off to give the impression of cities of different dimensions. All the fluorescent lights were controlled by a dimmer, permitting a wide range of intensity control.

Above all this array of lights was a large sheet of ⅛" opal Plexiglas. This plastic surface was supported by a large array of ¼" steel dowels. These dowels could be extended singly or in groups to form hills and valleys and when all were of the same height they provided an absolutely flat terrain. In addition, the entire light table could be hinged off the front edge so the city could be tipped, making the farthest portion of the city higher than the front portion by any angle up to 10 degrees. The runway portion was independently controlled and could remain flat while the city was on a slope.

On top of the Plexiglas were four large Kodalith negatives having a maximum contrast of five log steps. The individual points of light were small, clear circular areas of such a size that they would all represent point sources of light when viewed from at least 28 inches. Each of these clear portions was pressed into the soft wood with a special variation of a centering tool. The result was a raised series of small bumps like Braille. Each clear portion was raised above the surface .4 to .6 of a millimeter. This raising of the clear surfaces made it possible to control the luminances so they appeared equal from all viewing angles. If the surface had been perfectly flat, the luminances would be attenuated as a function of the viewing angle. To add the color of ground lights the individual cleared portions were hand-painted with food coloring to give the appearance of mercury vapor, sodium arc, tungsten, and neon lights. The model was not designed to represent a particular city but rather to have

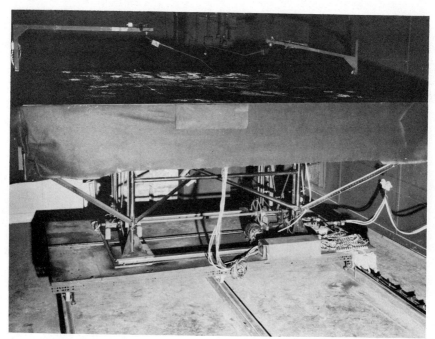

Figure 5. Simulated city, other aircraft traffic, and control-tower system.

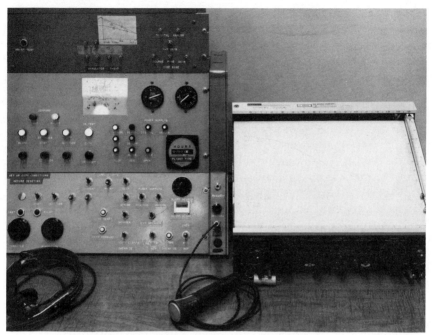

Figure 6. Experimenter's console and X–Y plotter readout.

some features typical of many cities. The principal architect of the simulated city, a psychologist named Bill Williams, had grown up in Pittsburgh and rivers passing through the city were reminiscent of Pittsburgh. "Nightertown," as the city was named, appeared to be so much like many cities, however, that we often overheard debates between passersby as to what city was represented. Pittsburgh, St. Louis, Washington, D.C., Seattle, and Miami were all candidates. Pilots involved in the actual experimentation confirmed that we were successful in making it look like a city from the air. The 12 pilots in the first experiment all thought the simulator was moving toward the city and were surprised to find that the city really moved toward the simulated aircraft cockpit (Figure 5).

The dependent measures in this quantitative research were selected to reflect pilot performance for the task of approach and descent. The readouts were: The position of the platform and the extension of the legs, which were fed through a computer and controlled an X-Y plotter that drew a graph representing the approach path of the aircraft in terms of altitude and distance. Experimenters outside the cab could also read the indicated airspeed in different phases of the approach from a duplicate airspeed indicator. At periodic intervals a tape recorder acted as the tower operator calling the pilot to request his estimated altitude. These techniques produced the dependent measures of generated altitude, estimated altitude, and airspeed (Figure 6).

In some experiments the work loads for the pilots were varied by introducing other aircraft flying above the city which had to be reported as to their location, heading, and relative altitude from the 727. These aircraft were physical models with lights provided by fiber optics representing the rotating beacon, wing-tip lights, and taillights of an aircraft about the size of a 747. They were programmed to appear and disappear as if clouds prevented the pilots from seeing them at all times. The accuracy with which pilots could report the position of the other traffic was also used as a dependent measure.

After building the simulator, the next step in the investigation was to quantitatively evaluate each of the various factors and their interaction as they affected pilot performance on night visual approaches. One of the 16 experiments is described as an example of these quantitative assessments. The reader will recall that in our development of the problem, we stated a hypothesis that the visual angle cue might be the major source of information as to height and distance available from the visual scene. If this were modified by changes in the terrain it would materially affect the height the pilot would fly at for any given distance during a descent approach.

REPRESENTATIVE EXPERIMENTS

In experiment 12, we used as one of the major independent variables the topography of the city. The 20-mile-wide, 16-mile-deep city light pattern could be displayed as sloping upward so the lights furthest from the aircraft were 4,500 feet above the runway threshold. The runway threshold was depicted as being on the near side of the city. When a 3-degree, 2-minute slope was depicted, it formed one level of this variable. The second level was the depiction of a flat city where all lights were on the same horizontal plane. The second independent variable was the starting altitude. The problem began with the aircraft 20 miles from the city at either 15,840 feet or 10,000 feet altitude. These two altitudes were chosen since 10,000 feet represented the maximum altitude the FAA recommended for a jet aircraft 20 miles from the airport. The use of 15,840 feet at the same distance would make a flat city subtend the same visual angle at the beginning of the problem as a 3-degree-sloping city would subtend from 10,000 feet.

The third independent variable was the distribution of city lights. The first level included the runway edge, threshold, runway end, and sequence lights depicted for the landing area. The taxiways and support-building lights were also included in this airport complex, but no city lights were visible beyond the airport. The second level was similar to a

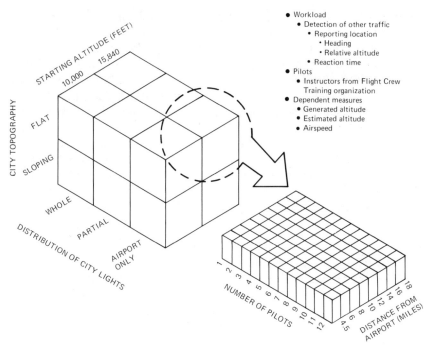

Figure 7. Night visual approach research study 12.

new city where the airport was built some 6 miles from the city limits with a band of darkness between the airport and the city light pattern. The third level was analogous to an older city where the city had been built out to and around the airport presenting a complete blanket of lights 20 miles wide and 16 miles deep. These three independent variables, and the levels that were included, formed the two 2×2×3 factorial designs illustrated in Figure 7.

In each of these cells, 12 pilots made one approach apiece. Measurements of altitude were recorded at eight different distances. The pilots in this study were all Boeing flight crew instructor pilots. At the time of the investigation their mean age was 46 and they averaged more than 10,000 hours of flying time. Most were qualified in from three to five types of aircraft. Their work was to train experienced pilots to transition to new jet aircraft and all were qualified in the 727. We added to their workload by requiring them to report the location, heading, and relative altitude of 16 other aircraft. Instructions were given in a typed booklet that included Standard Approach Charts. After they had read these instructions, any questions were answered by the experimenters and a preliminary familiarization trial flight was made. After becoming familiar with the simulator, they were asked if they had any further questions before starting any experimental runs. If they had none, they began their 12 approaches, 1 under each of the conditions of the experiments.

There were two unusual requirements leveled on the pilots. They were asked to make entirely visual approaches without the aid of altimetry or the elecronic glide slope they normally have available. The basis for this procedure was to measure the amount of information provided by the forward visual scene. It was explained to the pilots that they were the measuring "tool" through which we could obtain a quantification of the amount of information provided by the visual scene and that this was available only from experienced pilots. The pilots themselves had some doubts as to how well they could perform this task. However, the results of the control conditions indicate that they demonstrated exceptional skill in judging and flying to a horizontal plane of lights.

RESULTS

The results of experiment 12 are representative of most of the investigations conducted in this series. We will begin with the results when the "airport only" was available in the visual scene.

When the pilots were flying to the flat terrain, they described a descent approach represented by the solid line and the filled circles of

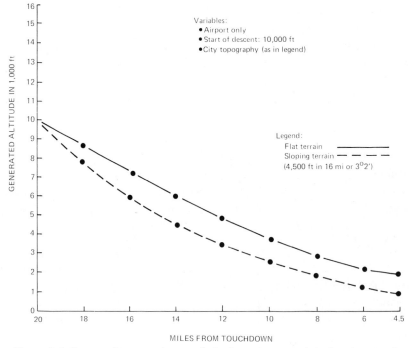

Figure 8. Influence of topography on pilot's descent–approach to the airport only.

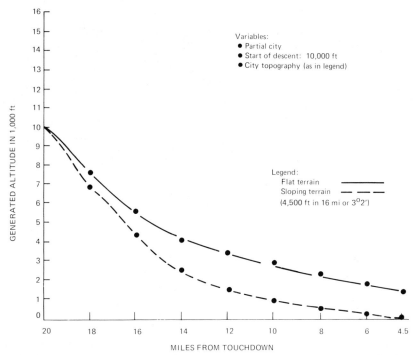

Figure 9. Influence of topography on pilot's descent–approach to new city not yet built out to airport.

Figure 8. In this illustration the descent began at 10,000 feet. It is not necessary to represent the two different altitudes or beginning altitudes in this experiment as they were not significantly different in their influence on pilot performance. Note that the "straight-in approach" was not a straight line but a slightly curved path. Also, the final altitude at 4½ miles out was 2,000 feet. This would have corresponded to a visual angle of 1 degree 29 minutes. In comparison, the approach made to the same airport when it was on a sloping terrain departs from 10,000 feet at a higher descent rate, and the final altitude at a distance of 4½ miles is 800 feet. The visual angle in this instance is 1 degree 31 minutes. These results are very supportive of the visual angle hypothesis since they differed by only 2 arc minutes. The pilots flew to two very different altitudes representing the same visual angle.

It was expected that when the city lights were available, the greater amount of information inherent in the lights would result in more precise flying by the pilots. In the next figure (Figure 9), note that when the partial city was represented, the airport and its immediate environment were separated from the major part of the city by a band of darkness 6 miles deep. The descent path to the flat city is again not a straight line but

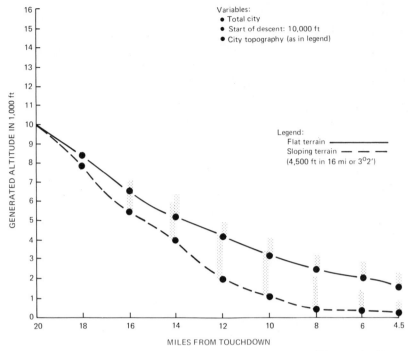

Figure 10. Influence of topography on pilot's descent–approach to older city built out to airport.

represented by the arc of a circle. The final altitude reached at 4½ miles is 1,400 feet. This is a much better approximation of the final altitude that the pilots were hoping to attain—e.g., 1,240 feet—and it is the equivalent of a 3-degree glide slope at 4½ miles. The additional lights represented by the city appear to have improved the pilot's performance. However, when the city lights are on an upward-sloping terrain, and not a valid representation of a flat plain, the pilots fly to a dangerously low altitude. In this particular instance the final altitude at 4½ miles of distance was zero! Actually 11 of the 12 pilots passed through zero altitude in making their approach to the partial city when it was on a sloping terrain.

During the approaches to the total city where there was a plateau of lights all the way from the beginning of the runway to 16 miles inland, the pilot's performance was similar to the partial city with the exception that they did not fly quite as low to the sloping city. The final altitude for the sloping city was 200 feet. This represented a visual angle of 2 degrees 43 minutes, which was very similar to the 2 degrees 45 minutes represented by the same city on a flat ground when the pilot's final altitude was 1,300 feet. These data for all the conditions of the older city, the partial city, and the airport by itself all support the visual angle theory.

Figure 10 presents some very interesting data generated by the recording of the pilot's estimate of his altitude as requested by "tower operator." The height of the bars above each of the data points gives the average estimated altitude while flying toward the city. Notice that when flying toward the sloping center it is only at 6 and 4½ miles of distance that these estimates began to significantly differ from the altitude generated while flying toward the flat surface. These data support the visual angle hypothesis in that the pilots believe they were flying higher than they actually were when they were approaching the sloping city. Their estimates indicate the scenes were very similar, as they thought they were flying the same altitude above the terrain.

In Figure 11 notice that the approach to the partial and complete cities has become very low at 8 miles' distance from touchdown. If the flight path remains low, the parallax of the lights is below the threshold for perceived motion for all speeds up to 240 miles per hour. Therefore, the relative motion cue appears so late in the descent approach that it does not serve as a warning to the pilot that he has flown excessively low until it is too late to recover from a dangerously low altitude.

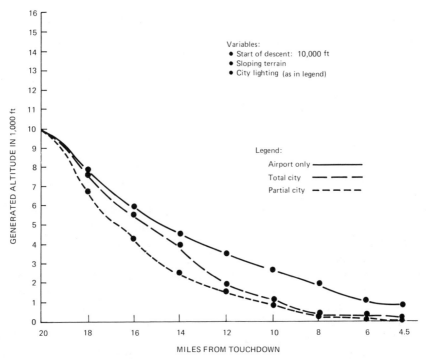

Figure 11. Comparative influence of topography on pilot's approach–descent toward three scenes.

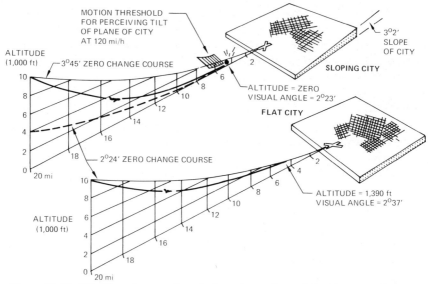

Figure 12. Modification of approach paths by topography and distribution of lights.

Figure 12 represents a summary of these results as well as an explanation of what may have been happening in many of the accidents. In the foreground figure, from 10,000 feet of altitude and 20 miles out, if a plane flies along the black curve and continues to follow this zero change course, the visual angle would be 2 degrees 24 minutes and would bring the airplane at the proper height to the threshold of the runway. However, the average performance by the pilots indicates that they depart with too rapid a descent, initially forming an arc of a circle and finally ending up 4½ miles out at 1,390 feet of altitude. This represents a visual angle of 2 degrees 37 minutes. The upper drawing is a representation of when the terrain is up-sloping and could be said to provide a misleading visual angle. If the aircraft were to depart from 10,000 feet and 20 miles of distance, the true zero change course would be 3 degrees 45 minutes. Again, if the pilot had maintained this he would have arrived at the runway at the proper height. The average performance from the experimental data indicates that, in this instance, the departure from 10,000 feet was followed by a much more rapid descent until the plane's position approximated the 2-degree-24-minute visual angle course that is conventional for the flat terrain situation. At 10 miles the rate of descent was decreased to approximate the 2-degree-24-minute course, the more practiced condition in normal operations. However, since the visual angle is invalid, the visual angle of 2 degrees 23 minutes leads the pilot to zero altitude at 4½ miles out!

We would certainly not consider this "pilot error" in the usual sense. The pilot is actually performing a very good approximation to the familiar visual angle he uses day in and day out in making approaches to flat terrain. The tragedy occurs when he makes this same approximation to up-sloping terrain where the proper visual angle will lead him to a fatally low altitude at some distance from the runway. The perceptual errors occur when the pattern of lights on the ground is irregular and does not outline a terrain variation, and the information about the terrain is not available to the pilot. However, if streets or other regular alignment of lights provide a perspective that will indicate the up-sloping terrain, he will disregard a familiar visual angle, recognizing that he is not approaching flat terrain. If the lights are few enough, or random enough, so that no terrain information is available, then the visual angle he customarily uses can be invalid as well as valid. He must determine which applies in this particular approach by depending on some other means of judging altitude and distance.

CONFIRMING DATA

The experimenters were aware of the danger from their review of the accident literature of some 27 major airports in which the conditions of irregular light patterns and topographic slopes have been pointed out by the occurrence of landing short accidents. Air safety considerations suggested sending inquiries to pilots around the world for information about other airports and cities that might cause this type of accident but which, at the time of their initial report, had not been identified through an aircraft accident. In response to these inquiries the experimenters received an interesting letter from Flight Lieutenant A. I. Aitken, an RAF pilot, then stationed at El Adem, Libya. He was one of the most experienced night flyers (Hunter aircraft) stationed at this RAF field. He began his letter by quoting the title of an Air Force article (Kraft and Elworth, 1968) describing this research. "How High Is Up"—Lt. Aitken wrote— "for him about 130 feet." While making a night approach to the runway at El Adem, with the aid of radio and radar, he overshot and was advised to go around and come in again. Since a C-130 was landing ahead of him, he made a longer straight-in approach than is normal for his fighter plane. While making this approach, he hit a hill some 3 miles from the end of the runway. His description of the accident is illustrated in Figure 13. The box in the upper left depicts how he saw the runway, the approach lights, and the C-130 out ahead at the same moment he impacted with the 130-foot-high hill. Fortunately, the impact was not hard enough to severely damage the aircraft and Lieutenant Aitken went around and came in for a successful landing.

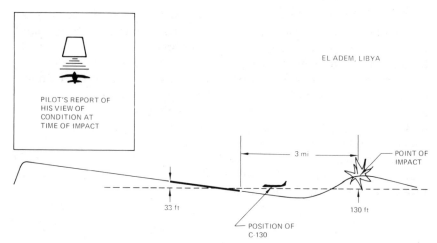

Figure 13. Accident report of N.V.A.R. Type; *Interceptor* Reader's Report, Fl. Lt. A. I. Aitken, R.A.F.

The explanation comes from the experimental data described above. The 10,000-foot runway had an upward slope such that the far end was 33 feet higher than the threshold. This would correspond to a visual angle of 19 minutes for the runway's length when viewed from 3 miles at 130 feet of altitude. Had Lieutenant Aitken been approaching a flat runway, 200 feet of altitude would have provided the same visual angle and a clearance of the hill by a comfortable 70 feet.

SUMMARY

The results of our analysis and the series of experiments can be summarized as follows:

1. It must be assumed that the pilots were not monitoring their altimeters with sufficient frequency, and that they were confident of their ability to judge altitude on the basis of the information available from the visual scene.

2. In making a visually guided approach at night, the pilots rely on the relatively unchanging visual angle provided by the distant light pattern to judge altitude. If the terrain is flat, such cues are adequate and the estimated altitude is accurate.

3. However, when the terrain is sloping, the pilots nevertheless respond as if they were approaching flat terrain, with the result that they systematically overestimate their actual altitude. (In these examples, the terrain was always up-sloping. Down-sloping terrain causes the pilot to assume the plane is lower than is actually the case.) This misleading cue is potent enough to induce experienced pilots to descend to dangerously

low altitudes. Such data are consistent with the conditions under which many of the night approach accidents actually occurred.

SUBSEQUENT ACTION

After the publication of these data, steps were immediately taken by a number of major airlines to avoid a repetition of these tragic accidents. A simple and obvious remedial measure is to make the pilots aware of this "height" illusion and encourage them to monitor their altimeters during night visual approaches. By changing standard cockpit procedures—for example, by requiring the copilot to verbally call out altitude—the problem has apparently been eliminated at least for a number of major airlines. Unfortunately, as of this writing, night visual approach accidents in which this illusion may be a contributing factor are still reported. One of these involved a small charter airline and another a commuter carrier. More recently, the Federal Aeronautics Administration has introduced measures to inform all pilots of these dangers. Dissemination of this information will, it is hoped, further reduce if not eliminate the problem.

EXPERIMENTAL RESEARCH

Experimental confirmation of the results described here have been reported by a number of independent investigators. Palmer (1972) of NASA Ames used a stroke writer, a computer-generated image in which he could generate a depiction of San Jose Airport, which is on flat terrain, and for comparison a special data base, which had no lights between the aircraft and the city, with the city on an upward-sloping terrain. He tested experienced airline pilots flying a 747 simulator with and without a "heads-up display." This display optically superimposes altitude information on the visual scene so that it is not necessary to look at the cockpit display in order to monitor altitude. Whenever the heads-up display was not available, he obtained a significant increase in pilot variability when approaching the city with no forward lights and sloping terrain. This increased variability confirms the influence of the terrain variable.

More recently Stout and Stephens (1975), using a Vital II computer-generated image in a DC-10 simulator, studied a large number of variables such as windshear and instrument variability. Included in the series was the effect of flying over darkness, i.e., "the black hole," on approach to the runway. They report that this variable produced the largest variance of all the variables studied. The median altitude at each successively nearer distance in the approach describes a flight path similar to that found in the 1968–1969 night visual approach research.

The experimental results are not a product of the particular simulator nor the particular experimental design. Wulfeck, Queen, and Kitz (1974), in their investigation of visual estimates of the pitch angle of naval flattops equipped with two kinds of edge lighting, parallel and tow-in, found that from distance of 1½, 1, and ½ mile, observers could differentiate visual angles representing pitch of 3 arc minutes. This is a close correspondence to the differences found by the initial experimenters between two sets of approaches to the runway and provides a reassuring confirmation of the original results.

These subsequent studies indicate that these data are reliable. However, confirming information on validity comes from the success of instructor pilots in demonstrating to their students that unusually low approaches may occur when the forward visual scene is used as the sole reference on approaches over darkness. Frank Jones, a skillful instructor pilot, had found, as other instructors also report, that it is difficult to instill awareness of this dangerous illusion through verbal instruction. While training South American pilots, he found that approaches made toward Rio de Janeiro over the dark Amazon forest were an excellent training ground. He would cover the altimeter of the student pilot and ask him to make a straight-in approach while he maintained a careful watch on his altimeter. After a portion of the descent–approach was complete, he would ask the student pilot to estimate his altitude and compliance with the glide slope. Then he would uncover the altimeter on the student's side. The students were invariably shocked at how much lower they were than their expectation, further confirmation that measures to increase awareness of the dangers of the "black hole effect" were indeed necessary.

ACKNOWLEDGMENT

The author wishes to express his deep gratitude to Dr. C. L. Elworth for his effective contributions to this research program.

REFERENCES

Kraft, C. L. Measurement of height and distance information provided pilots by the extra-cockpit visual scene. *Visual Factors in Transportation Systems.* National Academy of Sciences–National Research Council, Washington, D.C., 1969, December, 84–101.

Kraft, C. L., and Elworth, C. L. How high is up? *Interceptor,* 1968 (October), *10*(10), 4. Hqs., ADC, Ent AFB, Colorado.

Kraft, C. L., and Elworth, C. L. Night visual approaches. *Boeing Airliner,* 1969a, March–April, 2.

Kraft, C. L., and Elworth, C. L. Flight deck work load and night visual approach performance. AGARD CP No. 56, December, 1969b. Advisory Group for Aerospace Research and Development of the North Atlantic Treaty Organization.

Palmer, E. A. Night visual approaches—pilot performance with and without a head-up display for standard and noise abatement approaches. NASA, TM X-62, 1972, 187.

Stout, C. L., and Stephens, W. A. Results of simulation experimentation for approach and landing safety. 20th Technical Conference, International Air Transportation Association, November 10–15, 1975.

Wulfeck, J. W., Queen, J. E., and Kitz, W. M. The effect of lighted deck shape on night carrier landing. Dunlap and Associates, Inc., for Engineering Psychology Programs, Office of Naval Research, Department of the Navy, Arlington, Virginia. NR 196-115, October 1974.

JOURNALS AND SAFETY MAGAZINES THAT PUBLISHED NIGHT VISUAL APPROACH RESEARCH DATA AS AN ACTION TO ALERT PILOTS

Aviation (French); Safety Corner, *AOPA Pilot; Flight Safety Foundation's Pilot's Safety Exchange Bulletin;* M.I.T. *Education in Creative Engineering Seminar; The MAC Flyer,* U.S.A.F.; *Airline Management and Marketing;* Hazard Prevention; *System Safety Society;* Flight Safety Focus, *The Flight Safety Committee,* London; *Aerospace Safety,* AFRP; Airline Pilot, *Airline Pilots Assn.;* Flight Safety Quarterly, *Air West;* Air Safety, *Pakistan Internation Airlines;* Professional Pilot, *Data Publications;* The South African Pilot, *South African Airways Pilots Assn.;* Blind Spots IV, *FAA Aviation News;* Safety Check, *Flying; Aeroclub,* Venezuela. The Bulletin, *American Psychological Assn.*

Index

Rich and others (Eds)

(s) Psychology